Historical Dictionary
of the
1 9 5 0s

Historical Dictionary
of the
1 9 5 0s

JAMES S. OLSON

GREENWOOD PRESS
Westport, Connecticut • London

Library of Congress Cataloging-in-Publication Data

Olson, James Stuart, 1946–
    Historical dictionary of the 1950s / James S. Olson.
      p. cm.
    Includes bibliographical references and index.
    ISBN 0–313–30619–2 (alk. paper)
      1. United States—Civilization—1945-   —Dictionaries. 2. Nineteen fifties—
Dictionaries. I. Title.
    E169.12.O44   2000
    973.92–dc21   99–049694

British Library Cataloguing in Publication Data is available.

Library of Congress Catalog Card Number: 99–049694
ISBN: 0–313–30619–2

First published in 2000

Greenwood Press, 88 Post Road West, Westport, CT 06881
An imprint of Greenwood Publishing Group, Inc.
www.greenwood.com

Printed in the United States of America

∞™

The paper used in this book complies with the
Permanent Paper Standard issued by the National
Information Standards Organization (Z39.48–1984).

10 9 8 7 6 5 4 3 2 1

Contents

Preface

It should come as no surprise that Americans in the 1990s look back nostalgically on the 1950s. The "baby boom" generation sat as children in front of new television sets watching *The Mickey Mouse Club*, *I Love Lucy*, *Leave It to Beaver*, *Father Knows Best*, *Make Room for Daddy*, and *Gunsmoke*, and today they can watch reruns of those old programs on cable. Television and rock-and-roll revolutionized pop culture in the 1950s, while Vietnam, race riots, widespread drug abuse, and protest movements were still in the future. Tens of millions of Americans headed for new homes in the suburbs and traveled on weekends in new automobiles. The lastest electrical appliances adorned their new homes, and they believed that they were the most prosperous and powerful people on earth.

But they were not necessarily the happiest people in the world. The possibility of global thermonuclear war with the Soviet Union troubled many, and deepening racial tensions gave rise to shrill debates over the meaning of freedom, democracy, and equality. Millions of women felt strait-jacketed by rigid role expectations, and millions of men chaffed under the demands of corporate conformity. Television programs and their advertisers, from news broadcasts to situation comedies, told Americans how to think and how to live, but a sense of rebellion began to brew behind the facade of contentment. It manifested itself in rock-and-roll, the budding civil rights movement, and the appearance of a youth culture, and it would eventually explode during the 1960s.

The *Historical Dictionary of the 1950s* includes hundreds of essays about the prominent people, issues, scandals, fads, events, ideas, films, radio and television programs, and court cases of the decade. All unsigned entries are my own. Asterisks in the text indicate a cross-reference to another entry.

I wish to express my appreciation to the professional librarians at the Newton Gresham Library of Sam Houston State University for their assistance, and to Cynthia Harris, my editor, at Greenwood Publishing Group.

A

THE ABBOTT AND COSTELLO SHOW. During the 1930s and 1940s, Bud Abbott and Lou Costello built a successful comedy act that played on vaudeville and then on radio. Abbott played the straight man and Costello the comic, although Costello was the heart and soul of the act, a gifted performer capable of impromptu humor and wacky improvisation. The story line revolved around Abbott and Costello, two unemployed actors who live in a rooming house managed by a Mr. Fields, who constantly pesters the two for their back rent. In the fall of 1952, *The Abbott and Costello Show* premiered on syndicated television. Critics assailed the program as stupid and juvenile, but audiences loved it, at least as long as Abbott and Costello used their tried and true material. After fifty-two episodes, however, they had exhausted the sight gags, practical jokes, and physical comedy routines, and the show began losing steam. The last new show aired in 1953.

The Abbott and Costello Show proved to be extraordinarily popular, however, in the television rerun markets. For years during the 1950s, it was a staple of Saturday morning television, and viewers never seemed to tire of the episodes. The reruns also kept Abbott and Costello in the public eye, which strengthened their stand-up comedy careers on the night club circuit. All that stopped in 1957 when the two broke up and went their separate ways.

SUGGESTED READINGS: Tim Brooks and Earle Marsh, *The Complete Directory to Prime Time Network and Cable TV Shows, 1946–Present*, 1995; Stephen Cox and John Lofflin, *The Abbott and Costello Story*, 1997.

ABBOTT, BURTON. *See* BURTON ABBOTT TRIAL.

ACHESON, DEAN. Dean Gooderham Acheson was born to a prosperous, old-line New England family in Middletown, Connecticut, on April 11, 1893. A brilliant child, he was able to read and write before first grade. Certain that pedigreed credentials were the key to a life of power and prosperity, and equally certain that their family had a destiny to play in world affairs, the Achesons sent their son to Yale, where he graduated in 1915. He then went on to Harvard Law School, where he received his degree in 1918. Acheson's performance at Harvard put him at the top of his class, and he won the most prized clerkship of all—serving as private secretary to Supreme Court Justice Louis Brandeis. When he left Brandeis in 1921, Dean Acheson was already a Washington insider—at the tender age of twenty-eight. He was also wired into the Democratic party's political network.

The 1920s was a bad time for Democrats in Washington, D.C. A succession of Republican presidents—Warren G. Harding, Calvin Coolidge, and Herbert Hoover—controlled the White House, and Congress was firmly in Republican hands. Acheson practiced law privately, although he still yearned for a career in public service.

The Great Depression gave him his opportunity. In the congressional elections of 1930, voters put Democrats in control of Congress, and in the presidential election of 1932, Franklin D. Roosevelt swept Herbert Hoover from office. With Democrats in power again for the first time since Woodrow Wilson had been president, Acheson returned to public service, this time as undersecretary of state. His stay there was short lived, however. Late in 1933, when Roosevelt and his New Dealers decided to inflate the money supply with the gold purchasing program, Acheson protested. In his mind, the scheme was foolhardy, based on flawed economic logic. He spoke out against it, and President Roosevelt fired him.

Acheson nevertheless earned himself a place in Roosevelt's heart. At the swearing-in ceremony of his successor at the State Department, Acheson showed up in good spirits, full of best wishes and congratulations. He was neither petulant nor bitter, and his behavior impressed Roosevelt. Acheson returned to private legal practice, and in 1941 Roosevelt named him assistant secretary of state. Acheson became undersecretary of state in August 1945, and in July 1946 President Harry Truman* appointed him to his cabinet as secretary of state.

At the State Department, Acheson presided over the early stages of the Cold War* with the Soviet Union. Convinced of the reality of an international Communist conspiracy based in and presided over by the Kremlin, Acheson wholeheartedly embraced the containment policy* in which U.S. foreign policy became dedicated to preventing any more nations from being swept into the Soviet orbit. The Truman Doctrine, the Marshall Plan, and the Berlin Airlift were all examples of the containment policy at work during the late 1940s.

Acheson was also in power when communism made its most spectacular gains around the world. The Soviets dropped the Iron Curtain around Europe, making Estonia, Latvia, Lithuania, Poland, Hungary, Czechoslovakia, Romania, Yugoslavia, and Bulgaria little more than Soviet satellites. In 1949 China fell to Mao Zedong* and the Chinese Communists. That same year, the Soviet Union detonated an atomic bomb* of its own, ending the U.S. monopoly on nuclear weapons, and Acheson and Truman found themselves the objects of bitter political criticism from Americans who believed that they had mismanaged the Cold War.

Life got worse after the outbreak of the Korean War.* The surprise North Korean attack on South Korea caught the United States off guard, and when the Chinese entered the war, it turned into a bloody stalemate that continued into 1953. By that time, American voters had tired of Democratic leadership, and they voted Dwight D. Eisenhower* into the White House. In January 1953, Dean Acheson's tenure as secretary of state came to an end. He returned to his law practice. Acheson never again held an official government post, although he did serve as an informal foreign policy consultant to Presidents John F. Kennedy* and Lyndon B. Johnson.* Dean Acheson died on October 12, 1971.

SUGGESTED READINGS: Dean Acheson, *Present at the Creation*, 1969; Walter Isaacson and Evan Thomas, *The Wise Old Men: Six Friends and the World They Made*, 1986; *New York Times*, October 13, 1971.

THE ADVENTURES OF ELLERY QUEEN. During the 1930s, mystery writers Frederic Dannay and Manfred Bennington Lee created the character of Ellery Queen, a private detective and mystery writer who, in spite of his absentmindedness, managed to get to the bottom of every conceivable type of crime. In 1939 *The Adventures of Ellery Queen* became a popular detective program on CBS radio. In 1950 the new ABC network trumped CBS and aired *The Adventures of Ellery Queen* on television.* The television program starred Richard Hart as Ellery Queen, but Lee Bowman assumed the role in 1952. The show went off the air in 1952, but NBC television resurrected it in 1958 and 1959. It was again canceled and remained off the air until 1975, when NBC tried the show for the last time.

SUGGESTED READING: Tim Brooks and Earle Marsh, *The Complete Directory to Prime Time Network and Cable TV Shows, 1946–Present*, 1995.

THE ADVENTURES OF KIT CARSON. *The Adventures of Kit Carson*, a popular syndicated television* show of the early 1950s, revolved loosely around the career of Kit Carson, the famous explorer and scout of the Old West. Veteran Western actor Bill Williams played the role of Kit Carson, and Don Diamond played the part of his sidekick "El Toro." The show, first released in the fall of 1951, targeted adolescent boys with an interest in cowboys and Indians. Before its cancellation in 1954, a total of 104 episodes had been produced. *The Adventures of Kit Carson* managed to remain popular in the rerun television schedule throughout the 1950s.

SUGGESTED READING: Tim Brooks and Earle Marsh, *The Complete Directory to Prime Time Network and Cable TV Shows, 1946–Present*, 1995.

THE ADVENTURES OF OZZIE AND HARRIET. Oswald "Ozzie" George Nelson was a native of Iowa who formed his own band when he was just fourteen years old. By the time he graduated from Rutgers University Law School in 1930, he had become one of the country's most well-known big band leaders. In 1938 he married Peggy Lou "Harriet" Snyder. They had two sons. David was born in 1936 and Eric (*see* Nelson, Rick) in 1941. In October 1944, *The Adventures of Ozzie and Harriet*, a situation comedy, premiered on CBS radio. The on-air Nelson family lived in middle-class comfort, with Ozzie at the center of a series of hilarious, well-meaning, but disaster-prone schemes; Harriet provided reason and stability. The two boys wisecracked at their father's antics, providing another level of comedy. The show remained on CBS into the 1948 season, when it switched briefly to NBC radio before coming back to CBS. With the onset of the 1949 season, *The Adventures of Ozzie and Harriet* was a weekly staple on ABC radio.

During the early 1950s, with David and Ricky in their early teens, *The Adventures of Ozzie and Harriet* was one of the most popular radio programs in the country. Nelson wrote and produced the show, and he knew instinctively that the advent of television* would doom radio programming. In 1952 he took *Ozzie and Harriet* to television, where the program thrived on ABC for the next fourteen years. The radio version of the situation comedy was canceled in 1954.

Television historians argue that the situation comedies of the 1950s reflect the growing American obsession with conformity and consumerism, and *The Adventures of Ozzie and Harriet*, one of the most popular programs in television history, certainly did so. Ostensibly, the program was a real-life portrayal of the Nelson family: Ozzie and Harriet played themselves as father and mother, and sons David and Ricky did the same. They lived in a large, comfortable, two-story house somewhere in suburbia,* where they enjoyed all the perquisites of the post–World War II American dream—the house, automobiles, and the latest electrical appliances.

Ozzie was a stay-at-home father, and Harriet was a stay-at-home mother. The parents were kind and understanding, and the boys, at worst, were innocently rebellious. Viewers noticed the irony, of course. Ozzie did not seem to have a job; he was always at home, and he never talked about work. He was a bit of a bumbler, unable to fix things around the house but always in a good mood; Harriet was the responsible one. *The Adventures of Ozzie and Harriet* aired from 1952 until 1966, and millions of Americans watched the Nelsons raise their boys from adolescents to married young men. The idealized portrait of the American family suited viewers in the 1950s, but it became increasingly dated and irrelevant during the 1960s. Viewers watched the last episode on September 3, 1966.

SUGGESTED READINGS: Philip Bashe, *Teenage Idol, Travelin' Man: The Complete Biography of Rick Nelson*, 1992; John Dunning, *On the Air: The Encyclopedia of Old-Time Radio*, 1998; Charles Garrod, *Ozzie Nelson and His Orchestra*, 1991; Ozzie Nelson, *Ozzie*, 1973.

THE ADVENTURES OF RIN TIN TIN. *The Adventures of Rin Tin Tin* was a popular Western television* series of the 1950s. During the 1920s and 1930s,

Hollywood had produced a host of "Rin Tin Tin" films, all featuring a German Shepherd dog who battled Indians, bandidos, and criminals in the Old West. The television series, which premiered on ABC on October 15, 1954, featured Lee Aaker as the boy Rusty and James Brown as Lt. Rip Masters, a cavalry officer posted at Fort Apache in Arizona Territory. In the story line, Rusty had been orphaned in an Indian raid, and the soldiers adopted him. Lt. Masters, Rusty, and Rin Tin Tin, for thirty minutes every Friday evening, protected the nearby community of Mesa Grande from Indians and desperadoes. *The Adventures of Rin Tin Tin* remained in prime time until its last telecast on August 28, 1959. For the next four years, it could be seen in rerun broadcasts on ABC and then on CBS.

SUGGESTED READING: Tim Brooks and Earle Marsh, *The Complete Directory to Prime Time Network and Cable TV Shows, 1946–Present,* 1995.

THE ADVENTURES OF ROBIN HOOD. *The Adventures of Robin Hood* premiered on CBS television on September 26, 1955, and remained on the air until its last broadcast on September 22, 1958. It starred Richard Greene as Robin Hood, Bernadette O'Farrell as Maid Marian, Ian Hunter as Sir Richard, and Alexander Gauge as Friar Tuck. Filmed on location in England, it revolved around the adventures of Robin Hood and his gang, who robbed the rich and fed the poor from their hideout in Sherwood Forest and foiled all attempts at punishment from the sheriff of Nottingham (Alan Wheatley) and the evil Prince John (Donald Pleasence). After its last broadcast in September 1958, *The Adventures of Robin Hood* continued to appear in reruns on CBS for the next two years where it became part of the Saturday morning lineup.

SUGGESTED READING: Tim Brooks and Earle Marsh, *The Complete Directory to Prime Time Network and Cable TV Shows, 1946–Present,* 1995.

THE ADVENTURES OF SUPERMAN. *The Adventures of Superman* was one of the most popular television* series of the 1950s. In the 1930s, Jerry Siegel and Joe Shuster created the comic book character Superman, and the "Adventures of Superman" became an instant hit when it reached syndicated newspapers in 1938. The comic strip, which had a run of twenty-eight years, did not disappear from newspapers until 1967. The comic strip also spawned a popular radio show from 1940 to 1951, as well as seventeen animated Paramount cartoons and a movie.

In the Superman story line, the infant boy Kal-el is sent via rocket ship to Earth by his parents just before their own planet, Krypton, is destroyed. The rocket crash-lands in Smallville, an obscure town in the Midwest, where the boy is raised by Eben and Sarah Kent. They name him Clark. Clark possesses superhuman powers, and the Kents teach him to use those powers only to protect the weak, to battle evil, and to implement justice. At the age of twenty-five, Clark Kent moves to the city of Metropolis and takes a job as a reporter for the *Daily Planet,* a newspaper presided over by crusty editor Perry White. There Kent becomes close to reporter Lois Lane and cub reporter and photographer

Jimmy Olson. Lane and Olson constantly find themselves in harm's way, the victims of criminals and conspirators, and Superman always manages to rescue them using his super strength, his ability to fly, and his imperviousness to bullets and bombs.

The Adventures of Superman, first released in television syndication in the fall of 1952, starred George Reeves as Clark Kent and Superman, Phyllis Coates as Lois Lane, Jack Larson as Jimmy Olson, and John Hamilton as Perry White. A total of 104 episodes were produced between 1952 and 1957. George Reeves became typecast as Superman and was never able to find other any acting work, and he committed suicide in 1959. Throughout the late 1950s and 1960s, The Adventures of Superman appeared in rerun format, and its opening lines became a mantra to the baby boom* generation: "Faster than a speeding bullet! More powerful than a locomotive! Able to leap tall buildings at a single bound . . . Superman . . . strange visitor from another planet who came to Earth with powers and abilities far beyond those of mortal men! Superman, who can change the course of mighty rivers, bend steel with his bare hands, and who, disguised as Clark Kent, mild-mannered reporter for a great metropolitan newspaper, fights a never-ending battle for truth, justice, and the American way."

SUGGESTED READING: Sam Kashner, Hollywood Kryptonite: The Bulldog, the Ladies, and the Death of Superman, 1996.

THE ADVENTURES OF WILD BILL HICKOK. The Adventures of Wild Bill Hickok, a popular television* Western of the 1950s, was loosely based on the life of Wild Bill Hickok—a real-life Pony Express rider and Union military scout in the Old West. The series, which told the story of U.S. Marshal James Butler "Wild Bill" Hickok, premiered in syndication in April 1951, starring handsome Guy Madison as Hickok and 300-pound, raspy, squeaky-voiced Andy Devine as his sidekick Jingles. On his horse Buckshot, Hickok killed or captured bad guys and rescued damsels in distress, while Jingles helped as much as a 300-pound deputy could. A total of 113 episodes of The Adventures of Wild Bill Hickok were produced, and they were aired from 1951 to 1958. They could later be seen in Saturday morning and weekday afternoon reruns.

SUGGESTED READING: Tim Brooks and Earle Marsh, The Complete Directory to Prime Time and Cable TV Shows, 1946–Present, 1995.

THE AFFLUENT SOCIETY. The Affluent Society is the title of John Kenneth Galbraith's 1958 best-selling book about the American economy. Galbraith graduated from the University of Toronto in 1931 and went to graduate school at the University of California at Berkeley, where he earned a Ph.D. in economics in 1934. Except for a year at Princeton (1939–1940), four years in Washington D.C., during World War II, and during a tour as ambassador to India (1961–1963), Galbraith spent virtually his entire professional career in the economics department at Harvard University. A leading liberal economist trained in Keynesian values, Galbraith gained public popularity in 1958 with his book *The Affluent Society*, which looks at America through the lens of the consumer culture.*

Galbraith trusted the federal government and its ability through macroeconomic techniques—spending and taxation—to manage a modern industrial economy so as to prevent serious unemployment and serious inflation. Galbraith argued that for the first time in the history of the world, a society had developed in which prosperity, not poverty, was the norm for most people. Ironically, Galbraith offered a critique of the process by which such an accomplishment had been achieved. Huge productivity gains had actually brought about an overabundance of consumer goods, which had then produced an economy in which advertisers tried to convince affluent people to buy things they did not really need.

What had then appeared in the economy was a vast gap between private wealth and public squalor. Although large numbers of Americans were very prosperous, a minority suffered from poverty, unemployment, and homelessness. The only way to address that concern, Galbraith believed, was government investment in the public sector. He lambasted "trickle-down" economics, in which market forces were left to determine public outcomes. The federal government should engage in more direct management of the private economy. Galbraith lambasted the conventional wisdom that long-term economic growth could be based on increases in the production of consumer goods. The result, Galbraith claimed, was a "social imbalance" of prosperity on the one hand but dilapidated infrastructure and poverty on the other.

Conservatives, of course, were aghast at Galbraith's suggestions, but *The Affluent Society* resonated with millions of people. The book remained atop the best-seller list for nearly a year. Conservative critics ridiculed some of Galbraith's contentions, especially the fact that he was so critical of an economy that had managed to replace poverty with prosperity as its norm.

SUGGESTED READINGS: John Kenneth Galbraith, *A Life in Our Times*, 1981, and *The Affluent Society*, 1958; David Halberstam, *The Fifties*, 1993.

AFL-CIO. The American Federation of Labor-Congress of Industrial Organizations is the largest labor union in the United States. In 1882 Samuel Gompers formed the American Federation of Labor (AFL), a national labor union which organized workers only in the skilled trades. Skilled workers enjoyed leverage in labor disputes, and when Gompers called a strike, management often had difficulty finding the workers necessary to continue operations. Because of Gompers's philosophy, the American Federation of Labor became the first successful national labor union in U.S. history.

During the 1930s, labor leaders, including John L. Lewis of the United Mine Workers and Sidney Hillman of the Amalgamated Clothing Workers, decided to organize workers in mass production industries, which employed large numbers of unskilled and semiskilled labor. The times were propitious for success because of the Great Depression and President Franklin D. Roosevelt's New

Deal, which was quite friendly to organized labor. The National Industrial Recovery Act of 1933 and the National Labor Relations Act of 1935 protected the right of labor unions to bargain collectively. With the protection of the federal government, the Committee of Industrial Organization, renamed the Congress of Industrial Organizations (CIO) in 1936, successfully organized workers in the automobile, steel, rubber, mining, and clothing industries.

For the next nineteen years, the AFL and the CIO competed for the hearts of American workers. When the election of Dwight D. Eisenhower* in 1952 ended twenty years of Democratic control of the White House, labor leaders worried that their political influence might be on the wane. In 1953 the AFL and the CIO found a joint unity committee to explore the possibilities of a merger, and the committee spent two years drafting a charter. They agreed to end the practice of raiding members from one another's unions, and they guaranteed the continuation of the policy of individual union autonomy. In 1955 George Meany,* head of the plumbers' union, organized the merger of the two unions, bringing 14.6 million workers under a single union umbrella. The new AFL-CIO represented more than 90 percent of all American labor union members.

At the first convention of the new AFL-CIO, George Meany was elected president and Walter Reuther,* vice president. Meany was a cigar-chewing, old-school union organizer who had succeeded in the day when goons, organized crime, and bosses dominated the labor movement. Reuther, the hard-nosed head of the CIO, had come up through the ranks of the United Automobile Workers. The new AFL-CIO exerted extraordinary political clout, particularly in favor of Democratic party candidates. The leaders of the AFL-CIO were bitter anticommunists.

The merger created consternation in Republican circles, where union racketeering was considered a serious national problem. To protect itself from government intervention, the AFL-CIO purged its ranks of corrupt officers, including David Beck, president of the Teamsters.* In fact, AFL-CIO leaders decided that the ranks of the Teamsters were so corrupt that the entire union had to be purged. In 1957 the AFL-CIO expelled the Teamsters' Union and its two million members.

With the appearance of the AFL-CIO, Republicans began to condemn the power exercised by the labor movement in American politics. Of course, Democratic candidates countered that Republicans were suffering from a case of "sour grapes," since they had long enjoyed the backing of large corporations and the interest groups supporting them. In 1960 the AFL-CIO marshaled all of its resources to elect Democrat John F. Kennedy* as president of the United States.

SUGGESTED READINGS: Arthur J. Goldberg, *AFL-CIO: Labor United*, 1956; Archie Robinson, *George Meany and His Times: A Biography*, 1981.

AIRLINE INDUSTRY. During the 1950s, the American airline industry grew geometrically, while railway travel fell dramatically. After World War II, the commercial airline industry adopted a number of military technologies that made passenger travel faster and more efficient. Aircraft also became larger, allowing them to carry more passengers per trip and reduce ticket prices. Between 1950 and 1958, the number of annual airline passengers jumped from 17.3 million to 38 million. In 1955 airline travel eclipsed railway travel as the commercial vehicle of choice.

The most significant technological innovation was the advent of commercial passenger jet service. In October 1958, the British Overseas Airways Corporation started the first transatlantic passenger jet service. Its Havilland Comet IV jet flew from London to New York City. The flight took six hours and twelve minutes, compared to the more than twelve-hour flight of propeller aircraft. Three weeks later, Pan American Airways began similar service. In 1958 Douglas Aircraft began marketing its new DC-8 passenger jet. Boeing's 707 was soon carrying passengers cross country and across the Atlantic as well.

Passenger jet service had a dramatic impact on American life. Some well-to-do Americans became known as "jet-setters" because they could fly anywhere, even for just a day or two. Businessmen were able to travel, in a matter of hours, distances that used to take days, making them infinitely more efficient. Professional sports franchises, which formerly had been confined to the East Coast and Midwest, proliferated and spread across the country, led by the decisions in 1957 by the Brooklyn Dodgers* to relocate to Los Angeles and the New York Giants to San Francisco.

Serious problems, especially involving airport infrastructure, acccompanied the rapid growth of the industry. Few airports were equipped for the rapid growth in the number of passengers. Roads to and from airports became highly congested, baggage handling was a nightmare, and terminal facilities were extremely crowded. The runways of many airports were not long enough to handle passenger jets, and the skies became too crowded. Few commercial aircraft were equipped with radar, and pilots flew "by the seat of their pants," a method suitable to earlier days when fewer planes were in the skies. Air traffic control problems now became severe. After a collision between a TWA and a United Airlines jet over the Grand Canyon on June 30, 1956, which killed 128 people, the federal government ordered the installation of radar on all commercial airliners. In 1958 Congress established the Federal Aviation Administration to oversee air traffic safety.

Throughout the 1950s and 1960s, a construction boom took place in and around American airports, much of it financed by federal, state, and local governments. Terminal facilities were expanded, runways lengthened, and roads improved. Five airlines dominated the domestic industry—United, Eastern, Trans World Airways, and American—and Pan American controlled the bulk of the overseas routes.

SUGGESTED READING: Carl Solberg, *Conquest of the Skies: A History of Commercial Aviation in America*, 1979.

THE ALDRICH FAMILY. *The Aldrich Family* was one of television's* first successful situation comedies. It premiered on NBC on October 2, 1949, and remained on the air until its last broadcast on May 29, 1953. It starred a succession of actors as Henry Aldrich—Robert Casey, Richard Tyler, Henry Girard, Kenneth Nelson, and Bobby Ellis. The television series, based on the successful radio series of the same name, revolved around the life of a typical American teenager, Harry Aldrich, whose antics, practical jokes, puppy loves, and problems resonated with a generation of young Americans. A popular phrase of the show had Henry's mother yelling, "Henry! Henry! Henry!," and Henry replied, "Coming, Mother!" Millions of Americans were soon repeating it.

SUGGESTED READING: Tim Brooks and Earle Marsh, *The Complete Directory to Prime Time Network and Cable TV Shows, 1946–Present*, 1995.

ALFRED HITCHCOCK PRESENTS. In 1955 Hollywood's most legendary film director turned his hand to television.* *Alfred Hitchcock Presents* premiered on CBS on Sunday evening, October 2, 1955, and although the series switched back and forth between CBS and NBC, it remained on the air until its cancellation in September 1965. Hitchcock offered up weekly doses of suspense, intrigue, horror, mystery, and the macabre, all within the context of his own genius. Alfred Hitchcock* welcomed viewers at the beginning of each episode, and he was not above letting evil triumph, a quite uncommon phenomenon for 1950s television. Replete with surprise endings, black humor, and startling twists, *Alfred Hitchcock Presents* was one of the most creative programs on television during the 1950s.

SUGGESTED READINGS: Tim Brooks and Earle Marsh, *The Complete Directory to Prime Time Network and Cable TV Shows, 1946–Present*, 1995; Donald Spoto, *The Dark Side of Genius: The Life of Alfred Hitchcock*, 1983.

ALGERIA. In 1958 Ferhat Abbas, the leader of the Provisional Government of the Algerian Republic, remarked, "For more than a century, Algeria has been like a mouse in a French laboratory, fastened down while the French make experiments on it." In saying so, Abbas set the tone for the crumbling of one more pillar in the French Empire. Located in the Maghrib of North Africa, Algeria had adopted Arab culture and Islamic religious beliefs in the seventh century, and in the sixteenth century it became the westernmost extension of the Ottoman Empire. The Ottomans had barely established control over Algeria, however, before their own political dominion began to shrink, and until 1800 Algeria was semiautonomous. In 1830 France blockaded Algiers and a French army invaded. Under the leadership of Abd al-Qadir, Algerians mounted a bloody resistance struggle that lasted until 1847, when Qadir was captured.

The French Empire remained intact in North Africa until after World War II, when French-educated Algerian nationalists began to demand independence. Ahmed ben Bella emerged as the leader of the nationalist forces, and his National

Liberation Front (FLN) launched an insurrection against France on November 1, 1954. Rebels bombed French sections of towns and cities and conducted random acts of violence against French settlers. Eventually, France deployed 500,000 troops to battle ben Bella's 6,000 guerrillas. Within four years, 21,000 French soldiers were dead, as were more than 300,000 Algerians. The Algerian war became so unpopular in France that it toppled the government on May 13, 1958, and brought General Charles de Gaulle back into power. Political negotiations with the rebels, along with more fighting, continued until March 1962 when a cease-fire was announced. On July 3, 1962, Algeria received its independence. Along with France's defeat in 1954 at Dien Bien Phu in Indochina (*see* Dien Bien Phu, Battle of), Algeria made it abundantly clear to the world that the French Empire, in particular, and empires in general, were doomed.

SUGGESTED READINGS: Raphael Danziger, *Abd al-Qadir and the Algerians: Resistance to the French and Internal Consolidation*, 1977; Alf A. Heggoy, *Insurgency and Counterinsurgency in Algeria*, 1972.

ALLEN V. MERRILL (1957). The case of *Allen v. Merrill* revolved around whether reservation Indians had the right to vote in state elections. The state of Utah had decided that since reservation Indians paid no state taxes and were not subject to state criminal jurisdiction, they did not meet residency requirements for voting in state elections. In essence, so the argument went, Indians on reservations were insulated from state legal citizenship by their trust relationship with the federal government. The U.S. Supreme Court heard *Allen v. Merrill* and overturned the ruling. By that time, the state legislature had already repealed the restriction. As a result, Utah today is remembered as the last state in the Union to grant voting rights to Native Americans.

SUGGESTED READINGS: Stephen L. Pevar, *The Rights of Indians and Tribes: The Basic ACLU Guide to Indian and Tribal Rights*, 1992; Charles F. Wilkinson, *American Indians, Time and the Law*, 1987; John R. Wunder, *"Retained by The People": A History of American Indians and the Bill of Rights*, 1994.

AMERICAN BANDSTAND. One of the longest running programs in the history of television* had its start in 1953 as a local music and dance program in Philadelphia, Pennsylvania, and Dick Clark took it national in 1957 when ABC agreed to a daily after-school broadcast. Clark was convinced that rock-and-roll* music would become a permanent fixture in American popular culture, and teenagers proved him correct. They flocked home from school every day by the millions, turned on television sets, and tuned into *American Bandstand.*

American Bandstand featured local teenagers dancing to rock-and-roll records. Clark also invited rock-and-roll artists to perform live, and the show became a regular stop in the record promotion circuit. The power of televison made instant celebrities of the performers appearing on the show. *American Bandstand*, which enjoyed high ratings among teenagers, also helped destigmatize rock-and-roll music. Dick Clark was a wholesome, squeaky-clean host who dressed in a conservative business suit, white shirt, and tie and reassured an older generation that rock-and-roll was not sinister and dangerous but actually good clean fun and that it could fit comfortably into American middle-class culture. In one format or another, *American Bandstand* remained on ABC television for the next thirty years. *American Bandstand* remained a part of ABC's weekday television lineup until August 1963 when it became a once-a-week program broadcast on Saturday afternoons until 1987.

SUGGESTED READING: Michael Shore and Dick Clark, *The History of American Bandstand*, 1985.

AMERICAN COMMUNICATIONS ASSOCIATION V. DOUDS (1950). In the years immediately following World War II, Americans became quite paranoid about the problem of domestic revolutionaries and radicals, especially members of the Communist party. America soon found itself in the midst of the Red Scare,* and Communist party members were harassed and often imprisoned. In 1949 the National Labor Relations Board (NLRB) began requiring union officers to swear that they were not Communist party members before they would be allowed to testify before the NLRB. Union officers who were members of the Communist party considered the ruling a violation of their First Amendment rights and sued. The case of *American Communications Association v. Douds* reached the U.S. Supreme Court in 1950. In its decision, the Court sided with the NLRB, upholding the right of a government agency to require such testimony. Civil libertarians condemned the decision as a setback for First Amendment rights.

SUGGESTED READING: 339 U.S. 382 (1950).

AMERICAN FRIENDS OF VIETNAM. The American Friends of Vietnam, a political advocacy group, was formed in Washington, D.C., in 1955. Also known as the "Vietnam Lobby," the group included Francis Joseph Cardinal Spellman,* Senators John F. Kennedy* and Mike Mansfield, and Supreme Court Justice William O. Douglas.* They supported the government of President Ngo Dinh Diem of South Vietnam as a political alternative in Southeast Asia to Ho Chi Minh's* Communist nationalism. Diem had never been tainted by association with the French Empire, and he was a bitter anticommunist. Lobby members convinced Dwight D. Eisenhower's* administration to throw American support behind Diem in his battle to keep South Vietnam from falling to Ho Chi Minh. Eisenhower went along, although he had his suspicions about Diem. Eisenhower was right. The Vietnam Lobby portrayed Diem as a believer in democracy and individual rights, but he was actually a petty autocrat. Historians looking back on the Vietnam War* hold the Vietnam Lobby responsible for launching the United States on the road to escalation.

SUGGESTED READINGS: Hillaire Du Berrier, *Background to Betrayal: The Tragedy of Vietnam*, 1965; Frances FitzGerald, *Fire in the Lake: The Vietnamese and the*

Americans in Vietnam, 1972; Robert Sheer and Warren Hinckle, "The Vietnam Lobby," *Ramparts*, January 25, 1969, 31–36; Denis Warner, *The Last Confucian*, 1963.

AMOS 'N' ANDY. In one version or another, *Amos 'n' Andy* was a popular radio comedy program from 1926. It was titled *Sam 'n' Henry* until 1955, when the television situation comedy *Amos 'n' Andy* eclipsed it. Historians now identify *Amos 'n' Andy* as the most popular radio program in American history. For many years during the 1930s, movie theaters would interrupt films and pipe *Amos 'n' Andy* into the theater, resuming the film only after the radio program had finished. Otherwise, moviegoers would have stayed home in droves on the evenings of the *Amos 'n' Andy* broadcasts. During the early 1950s, *Amos 'n' Andy* broadcast every Sunday evening at 7:30 P.M. on CBS radio.

The program featured Freeman Gosden and Charles Correll, two white men, who portrayed two African American men in Harlem. *Amos 'n' Andy* trafficked in the most egregious racial stereotypes. The main characters fulfilled white expectations of black behavior. Amos Jones, a hardworking family man, owned the fledgling Flesh Air Taxi Company, drove a taxicab, and dispensed counsel and wisdom to his friends. Andrew H. Brown, who was considerably less reliable, was a good-hearted fellow vulnerable to the schemes of shysters and con men. Lightnin' was the dim-witted, slow-talking janitor at the Mystic Knights of the Sea lodge. George "The Kingfish" Stevens was the conniving, sleazy foil cooking up get-rich schemes. His wife, Sapphire, was the strong, loud black woman who had no tolerance for her husband's schemes. Gosden and Correll faked black dialect and filled it with malapropisms.

Beginning in the 1930s, the National Association for the Advancement of Colored People (NAACP) leveled intense criticism against the show, claiming that it portrayed black people as stupid, lazy, and dishonest. The NAACP sued CBS, demanding that the network pull the show from the air, but CBS refused. *Amos 'n' Andy* was the network's most popular, and most profitable, program. The radio version of *Amos 'n' Andy* was canceled in 1955, but only because the televison situation comedy *Amos 'n' Andy* had become a hit. In place of the radio program, CBS aired *The Amos 'n' Andy Music Hall*, in which Amos, Andy, Lightnin', "The Kingfish," and Sapphire introduced musical and comedy acts and engaged in comic banter. It was canceled in 1960.

In 1951 CBS brought *Amos 'n' Andy* to the television screen, with Alvin Childress starring as Amos Jones, Spencer Williams, Jr., as "Andy" Brown, Tim More as George "The Kingfish" Stevens, Ernestine Wade as Sapphire Stevens, and Lillian Randolph as Madame Queen. The show premiered on CBS on June 28, 1951, and remained on the air until its cancellation on June 11, 1953. The show then became a real moneymaker for CBS Films because it went into wide distribution as a rerun.

It was also a source of embarrassment to the network. The NAACP had continued its long protests because of the show's negative stereotyping of black people. CBS did not respond well until the civil rights movement* gained momentum in the late 1950s and early 1960s. The NAACP staged protest demonstrations at stations broadcasting the reruns, and CBS decided that the negative publicity was not worth the profits. In 1964 it stopped syndicating *Amos 'n' Andy* reruns.

SUGGESTED READING: Bart Andrews and Argus Juilliard, *Holy Mackerel! The Amos 'n' Andy Story*, 1986.

AND GOD CREATED WOMAN. *And God Created Woman*, one of the most controversial films of the 1950s, starred French actress Brigitte Bardot and was directed by her husband, Roger Vadim. The movie was unabashedly erotic, complete with nudity and Bardot's sultry, unbridled, on-screen abandon. The plot was predictable. Bardot played a young, beautiful nymphomaniac married to a stodgy older man. She has an affair with his brother. Offscreen, Bardot's hijinks gave the film an air of reality. Her affair with the film's star, Jean-Louis Trintignant, ended her marriage to Vadim. Although religious critics condemned the film as pornographic, it was a box office success and gave European "art" films a new cache in the United States.

SUGGESTED READINGS: Glenys Roberts, *Bardot*, 1985; Jeffrey Robinson, *Bardot: An Intimate Portrait*, 1994.

ANDREA DORIA. The *Andrea Doria*, an Italian luxury liner, was sailing from Genoa to New York City when, late in the evening of July 25, 1956, a Swedish passenger ship, the *Stockholm*, collided with the *Andrea Doria*, opening an enormous gash in its side. A huge rescue effort ensued, and journalists around the world followed the events closely, wondering whether they were witnessing another *Titanic*-like incident. After all, engineers had declared the *Andrea Doria* unsinkable because of its state-of-the-art technology and a hull divided into eleven watertight, separate compartments. By 10:00 the next morning, nearly 1,700 people had been rescued, but 52 were dead.

A subsequent investigation only increased the controversy surrounding the collision. Both the *Andrea Doria* and the *Stockholm* had been equipped with the latest radar technology. How could a collision have happened? No definitive conclusions were ever reached. Captain Piero Calamai of the *Andrea Doria* and third officer Johan-Ernst Carstens-Johannsen, who had been the officer in charge of the *Stockholm* at the time of the collision, disagreed about everything, from weather conditions and visibility to directional orientation. In the end, both shipping companies decided to give up any attempt to assess blame and instead established a joint fund to handle all legal claims, which eventually exceeded $40 million.

SUGGESTED READINGS: William Hoffer, *Saved!: The Story of the Andrea Doria*, 1979; Alvin Moscow, *Collision Course*, 1988; *New York Times*, July 26–30, 1956.

ANKA, PAUL. Paul Anka was born in Ottawa, Canada, on July 30, 1941. His parents were Lebanese immigrants who ran a restaurant in the city. A talented musician, Anka was writing music and entertaining adult audiences by the time he was ten years old. In September 1956, his father bought him a trip to Hollywood, where Anka recorded a song—"I Confess"—with Modern Records. One year later, after winning a trip to New York City by saving soup can labels, he went to ABC and auditioned by singing "Diana," a song he had written. ABC promoted the record, and by 1958 it was at the top of the popular music charts. He quickly became a teen idol and proved not to be a one-hit wonder. In 1958 Anka's "You Are My Destiny" reached number seven, and his "Crazy Love" hit number fifteen. In 1959 "Lonely Boy" made it up to number one on the charts, and "Put Your Head on My Shoulder" was number two. Anka had become one of the most successful songwriters and performers in the country. He also starred in the films *Girls Town* in 1959 and *Look in Any Window* in 1960.

During the 1960s, Anka fell out of the pop limelight, but he continued to write songs and perform in German, French, and Italian, and he remained very successful on the concert circuit. Anka did not have another number one hit until 1974, when his "(You're) Having My Baby" went platinum. Over the course of his career, Anka has seen more than four hundred of his compositions recorded. Among the more famous of those songs was "My Way," recorded by Frank Sinatra,* and "She's A Lady," which Tom Jones made into a hit.

SUGGESTED READING: Patricia Romanowski and Holly George-Warren, *The Encyclopedia of Rock & Roll*, 1995.

ANNIE OAKLEY. *Annie Oakley*, which premiered in syndication in January 1954, was loosely based on the life of Annie Oakley, a woman who lived between 1859 and 1926 and came to be known for her skills as a sharpshooter in the Buffalo Bill Wild West traveling show. The television series converted her into a law enforcer living in the town of Diablo, where she took care of her little brother Tagg and finished off desperadoes. Gail Davis starred as Annie Oakley, and Jimmy Hawkins played the role of Tagg. Eighty-one episodes of *Annie Oakley* were produced. The last episode was broadcast in December 1956.

SUGGESTED READING: Tim Brooks and Earle Marsh, *The Complete Directory to Prime Time Network and Cable TV Shows, 1946–Present*, 1995.

ANTARCTIC TREATY OF 1959. With imperialism on the wane around the world, a more cooperative attitude had come to prevail among the world powers over the exploitation of the last frontier—Antarctica. On December 1, 1959, leaders from twelve nations—the United States, Argentina, Australia, Belgium, Chile, France, Great Britain, Japan, New Zealand, Norway, South Africa, and the Soviet Union—met in Washington, D.C., and signed the treaty. The treaty proclaimed Antarctica a military-free zone, banned weapons testing there, and prohibited radioactive waste disposal there.

SUGGESTED READINGS: *New York Times*, December 1–4, 1959.

ARDEN, EVE. Eve Arden was born Eunice Quedens in Mill Valley, California, in 1912. She became fascinated with the theater as a child, and as soon as she finished school she began touring the country with theatrical groups. In 1934 Quedens secured a role in a revival of Ziegfeld's *Follies*. A producer suggested a name change to Eve Arden, and the new stage name stuck. In 1937 she won small parts in the films *Oh, Doctor!*, *Stage Door*, *Slightly Honorable*, *She Couldn't Say No*, and *She Knew All the Answers*.

Arden's radio career began in 1945 when she won a small part in *The Danny Kaye Show*. In 1946 she won a starring role in *Sealtest Village Store*. After a chance meeting with CBS boss William Paley,* Paley suggested her for the role of Miss Brooks. The situation comedy premiered on CBS radio on July 19, 1948, and was an instant hit. It remained on the air until July 7, 1957. In 1952 CBS took the cast of *Our Miss Brooks* and created a television* situation comedy of the same name. The television and radio shows played simultaneously and were both huge hits. The television show lasted in prime time until September 21, 1956. Eve Arden remained a steady presence in American entertainment and became a beloved figure in the popular culture. She died on November 12, 1990.

SUGGESTED READINGS: Eve Arden, *Three Faces of Eve: An Autobiography*, 1988; Tim Brooks and Earle Marsh, *The Complete Directory to Prime Time Network and Cable TV Shows, 1946–Present*, 1995; John Dunning, *On the Air: The Encyclopedia of Old-Time Radio*, 1998.

ARMY-McCARTHY HEARINGS. *See* RED SCARE.

ARTHUR GODFREY AND HIS FRIENDS. See GODFREY, ARTHUR.

ARTHUR GODFREY'S TALENT SCOUTS. See GODFREY, ARTHUR.

THE ARTHUR MURRAY PARTY. Arthur and Kathryn Murray built a string of successful dance studios in the 1940s and 1950s, and *The Arthur Murray Party* was little more than a commercial for the dance studios. It was a variety show that premiered on ABC television on July 20, 1950, and during the course of the decade, the show switched around among CBS, ABC, and NBC. The program also featured dance instruction, performances by guest stars, and chatty conversation between hostess Kathryn Murray and her guests. Its last broadcast aired on September 6, 1960.

SUGGESTED READING: Tim Brooks and Earle Marsh, *The Complete Directory to Prime Time Network and Cable TV Shows, 1946–Present*, 1995.

ASIAN FLU. The Asian flu was the world's primary killer epidemic disease in the twentieth century. It first erupted on a mass scale in 1918, and during the course of the next eighteen months, it killed more than 21 million people around the world. The disease has existed for centuries, originating when a virus typically associated with swine jumped species and infected human beings. Victims typically became sick with severe flu-like symptoms, and many died within twenty-four hours. The Asian flu was the world's most feared plague, rivaled only by polio in the United States during the 1950s.

Panic struck in 1955–1956 when a mutant form of the disease, known as Type-A influenza, appeared in China and killed thousands of people. It was only a matter of time, epidemiologists warned, before influenza would cross the ocean and infect Americans. The World Health Organization warned of a deadly global epidemic, one that would exceed that of 1918–1919. In the United States, a crash program to develop a vaccine began in earnest. Early in 1957, in the United States, an experimental vaccine was tested successfully on volunteer inmates at the Maryland State Correctional Institute in Patuxent. When it proved to be 70 percent effective, a number of pharmaceutical companies began mass-producing the vaccine. By the end of 1957, the companies had produced 85 million doses of the vaccine.

The Asian flu reached San Francisco late in the summer of 1957, but widespread inoculations had already taken place. By the winter of 1957–1958, the Asian flu had struck approximately 20 million Americans, but because of the vaccine, most suffered only mild symptoms. Deaths from the epidemic numbered in the thousands, not in the millions as many epidemiologists had feared.

SUGGESTED READING: "Asian Flu: The Outlook," *Time*, August 12, 1957, 74.

ATOMIC BOMB. The atomic bomb played a key role in the evolution of the Cold War* during the late 1940s and early 1950s. Development of the atomic bomb had its initial beginnings when World War II broke out in Europe and physicist Albert Einstein warned President Franklin D. Roosevelt that Adolf Hitler and the Germans had made development of enormously destructive nuclear weapons a high priority. The president eventually launched a crash program—known as the Manhattan Project—to produce the world's first atomic weapon, based on the principle of nuclear fission, and in July 1945 American scientists detonated the first device. Early in August 1945, United States pilots dropped atomic bombs on Hiroshima and Nagasaki, Japan, bringing the war to a rapid conclusion.

After the war, the United States government accelerated its program to develop more destructive atomic bombs. In July 1946 two atomic bombs were detonated on Bikini Atoll in the Pacific, and between April and May 1948, three more were detonated at Eniwetok Atoll. But on September 24, 1949, Americans learned that they did not have a monopoly on nuclear weapons. On that day, the Soviet Union detonated its own nuclear weapon. In the atmosphere of the evolving Cold War, with the United States and the Soviet Union growing more hostile toward one another, a nuclear arms race ensued that gave Americans apocalyptic fears. When it was learned that the Soviets had developed their own atomic bomb not through independent research but through espionage aided by American spies, the public grew even more cynical.

The era of the atomic bomb came to an end, however, on November 1, 1952, when American scientists exploded the first hydrogen bomb. Based on the principle of nuclear fusion rather than nuclear fission, hydrogen bombs were infinitely more powerful than atomic bombs and escalated fears about the possibility of an arms race that could eventually destroy the entire world in a nuclear conflagration.

SUGGESTED READING: Richard Rhodes, *The Making of the Atomic Bomb*, 1986.

AUNTIE MAME. *Auntie Mame*, a two-act Broadway comedy, opened at the Broadhurst Theater on October 31, 1956. Based on the novel written by Patrick Dennis, the play, written by Jerome Lawrence and Robert E. Lee, revolved around a dizzy, scatterbrained Auntie Mame, played by Rosalind Russell, who discovers that she must take in and raise her orphaned nephew, Patrick Dennis (played by Jan Handzlik). A liberal and free thinker who gives a full rein to Patrick's desires, Mame encounters criticism from friends, neighbors, and even the authorities, who urge her to be more strict with Patrick. Mame trusts her instincts, however, and Patrick grows up to be a successful, well-balanced adult. In the last act, the grown-up Patrick returns with his own son to visit Mame, and she promptly spirits the boy off to Europe to work her magic on him. *Auntie Mame* had a run of 639 performances on Broadway, and then touring companies took it throughout the United States in the late 1950s and early 1960s.

SUGGESTED READINGS: Gerald Bordman, *The Oxford Companion to American Theater*, 1992; *New York Times*, November 1, 1956.

AUTOMOBILE INDUSTRY. By the end of World War II, Americans' pent-up demand for automobiles had reached unprecedented proportions. Because of wartime production demands, Detroit had stopped producing automobiles, and the number of cars on the road dropped by more than four million. There were 25.8 million registered cars in 1945, but half of them were more than ten years old and millions were worth little more than their scrap value. Between 1945 and 1950, Detroit converted back to automobile production, and in 1950 Americans purchased more than eight million vehicles. By 1955 the number of registered automobiles exceeded 52 million.

During the 1950s, it became quite clear that the American love affair with the automobile had become a pop culture obsession and the backbone of the economy. In many ways, the car underwrote the American passion for individual freedom. Throughout U.S. history, Americans had worshiped at the altar of individual freedom. During the eighteenth and nineteenth centuries, freedom tended to be interpreted in political terms—the right to vote and hold public office. During the late nineteenth and twentieth centuries, Americans added an economic dimension to their definition of freedom—the right to work and make a living, to get ahead, and to enjoy the good life. The automobile was the epitome of personal freedom—the right to go wherever one wanted to go, whenever one wanted to do it.

The typical automobile in the 1950s was high on style but low on fuel efficiency and safety. The cars were bedecked with tail fins resembling those on jet aircraft, lots of chrome, ostentatious grills, and fancy paint jobs. Most of them featured large, eight-cylinder, gas-guzzling engines. Company advertising worked to convince Americans that happiness could come into their lives because of the type of automobile they owned. Also, to sustain demand for new cars, Detroit developed the idea of "planned obsolescence"—changing external model styles every few years in order to make older cars quickly become undesirable.

The economy reflected the dominance of the automobile. In 1950 American automobile manufacturers produced 6.7 million cars. General Motors, Ford, and Chrysler, which dominated the industry, became known as the "Big Three." The other auto manufacturers, including such as Kaiser-Frazier, Nash, Packard, Hudson, Studebaker, and Willys-Overland, were weak and vulnerable. In 1954 Nash and Hudson merged, only to be taken over by Chrysler a short time later. Kaiser-Frazier merged with Willys-Overland, but the new company soon declared bankruptcy. Packard went out of business in 1958, and Studebaker closed down in 1963.

The downside of the automobile was obvious. Air pollution increased geometrically during the 1950s, as did traffic congestion and parking space shortages in major cities. To escape the congestion and pollution, many businesses began relocating to suburbs, which led to even more housing construction and the rise of shopping malls. Fast-food restaurants and motels sprouted like weeds across the American landscape. To make highway travel even easier, Congress passed the Federal Interstate Highway Act of 1956, also known as the National Highway Act* of 1956, which authorized the construction of 41,000 miles of modern, limited-access freeways. The legislation led to the world's finest highway system and a genuine national marketplace for goods and services.

The automobile nevertheless had its critics. Some argued that the automobile was leading to the destruction of downtown business districts, since so many well-educated, professional workers had relocated to the suburbs. Others complained about the environmental problems associated with automobiles—oil consumption, air pollution, traffic congestion, and the disposal of used rubber tires. Others charged that the automobile had all but stifled the development of mass transit systems in the United States, and that it had destroyed the railroad as a passenger transportation system, leaving the United States the only major country in the world without a system of rail transit.

During the 1950s, the heyday of the American automobile, the hard times that the automobile industry would experience in the 1960s had already appeared on the economic horizon. In 1949 foreign manufacturers sold only 12,000 cars in the United States, while American companies sold more than five million. During the 1950s, the Germans began to sell the Volkswagen in the low-price segment of the market—a car that appealed to buyers who could not afford to buy a new American car. By the end of the decade, imports had gained a market share of 10 percent—more than 600,000 units in the United States.

Japanese manufacturers began to enter the market in the 1960s, providing lower-cost, more fuel-efficient trucks and automobiles to cost-conscious American buyers. By 1970 imports accounted for 1,230,000 unit sales in the United States, or 15.3 percent of the market. With the jump in oil prices in the 1970s, fuel-efficient foreign cars became even more popular, and in 1975 imports captured 18 percent of the market. By the late 1980s, that percentage had increased to more than 25 percent and to nearly 30 percent in the late 1990s.

SUGGESTED READINGS: James J. Fink, *The Car Culture*, 1975 and *The Automobile Age*, 1988; David Halberstam, *The Reckoning*, 1986; John Keats, *The Insolent Chariots*, 1958; Douglas T. Miller and Marion Nowak, *The Fifties: The Way We Really Were*, 1977; John B. Rae, *The American Automobile: A Brief History*, 1965; Marco Ruiz, *100 Years of the Automobile, 1886–1996*, 1985.

AVALON, FRANKIE. Frankie Avalon was born Francis Avallone on September 18, 1939, in Philadelphia, Pennsylvania. A trumpeter at first, Avalon began making singles appearances when he was just sixteen, and in 1958 he recorded "DeDe Dinah," which hit number seven on the pop charts. He soon became one of several prominent teen idols in American popular music. During the next two years he had six top-ten hits: "Ginger Bread," "Bobby Sox to Stockings," "A Boy Without a Girl," "Just Ask Your Heart," "Venus," and "Why," the last two of which hit number one on the pop music charts. Avalon also appeared regularly on Dick Clark's *American Bandstand*,* and he starred in several movies, including *Disc Jockey Jamboree* (1957), *Guns of the Timberland* (1960), *The Alamo* (1960), *The Carpetbaggers* (1962), and *Beach Blanket Bingo* (1965).

During the late 1960s and early 1970s, Avalon's career went into a holding pattern, but he became a hit again in 1979 in the film *Grease*, in which he sang "Beauty School Dropout." The appearance jump-started his career. Since then, Avalon has continued to perform on the resort club circuit with Bobby Rydell* and Fabian* as one of the "Golden Voices."

SUGGESTED READING: Patricia Romanowski and Holly George-Warren, *The Encyclopedia of Rock & Roll*, 1995.

B

BABY BOOM. The term "baby boom" was coined by journalists to describe the post–World War II increase in American fertility. During the Great Depression, birthrates had fallen, and World War II took so many men away from home that the decline continued. When the war ended and the GIs were mustered out of the military, marriage rates skyrocketed, and so did the birthrates. In 1945 the country recorded 1.6 million marriages; in 1946, 2.3 million. In 1947 more than 3.8 million babies were born in the United States, and between 1948 and 1953, more babies were born in the United States than in the previous thirty-year period. Predictably, the American population boomed too, from 150 million people in 1950 to 179 million people in 1960.

The baby boom had a dramatic impact on American economic and social life. Demand for toys, diapers, baby food, children's clothes, and larger cars exploded. Home construction and then public school construction enjoyed unprecedented gains. Demands on government for education, health care, and other social services increased dramatically. By the early 1960s, the so-called baby-boom generation was ready to enter college, and they formed the backbone of the youth rebellion, the civil rights movement,* and the antiwar movement of the 1960s.

SUGGESTED READINGS: Landon V. Jones, *Great Expectations: America and the Baby Boom Generation*, 1980; Elaine Tyler May, *Homeward Bound: American Families in the Cold War Era*, 1988.

BACHELOR FATHER. *Bachelor Father*, a highly successful television situation comedy of the late 1950s and early 1960s, premiered on CBS on September 15, 1957, starring John Forsythe as Bentley Gregg, a wealthy Hollywood attorney raising his niece Kelley, who was played by Noreen Corcoran. More comic relief was provided by Sammee Tong, who played houseboy Peter Tong. The comic situations revolved around the problems of a middle-aged bachelor trying to raise a rambunctious teenager. Bentley, a ladies' man, was anxious to wine and dine beautiful women, and his niece frequently tried to work as a matchmaker. The last episode of *Bachelor Father* was broadcast on September 25, 1962.

SUGGESTED READING: Tim Brooks and Earle Marsh, *The Complete Directory to Prime Time Network and Cable TV Shows, 1946–Present*, 1995.

BAGHDAD PACT. Early in 1955, Iraq and Turkey signed the Baghdad Pact, a mutual security treaty in which both signatories promised to assist one another in the event of a Soviet attack. Anxious to construct a series of anti-Soviet security arrangements around the world, the United States helped promote the Baghdad Pact. Great Britain, Pakistan, and Iran* signed the Baghdad Pact later in the year. In November 1955, with assistance but not the formal cooperation of the United States, the signatories to the Baghdad Pact formed the Middle East Treaty Organization (METO). In 1958, however, Iraq withdrew from the Baghdad Pact after undergoing a coup d'état, and the United States then signed bilateral security treaties with Pakistan, Turkey, and Iran. Those three countries then established the Central Treaty Organization to replace METO.

SUGGESTED READINGS: Thomas A. Bryson, *American Diplomatic Relations with the Middle East, 1784–1975*, 1977; Paul V. Hammond, *Cold War and Detente*, 1975.

BALDWIN, JAMES. James Baldwin was born in New York City on August 22, 1924. He was raised in Harlem by a very religious African-American family, and by the time he was ten years old he was working as a boy preacher in several storefront Harlem churches. Even as a child, he displayed a gift for writing. He came to the attention of a gifted black writer, Richard Wright, who helped Baldwin apply for several scholarships. In 1945, armed with a Eugene Saxton Scholarship and a Rosenwald Scholarship, Baldwin left the United States and took up permanent residence in France, where his writing career flourished. His first novel, *Go Tell It on the Mountain*, was published in 1953. The novel— heavily autobiographical and concerned with the tortured issues of racial and sexual identity—won critical acclaim and put Baldwin on the American literary map. He followed that novel with an anthology of his own essays, *Notes of a Native Son*, in 1955. Baldwin's second novel, *Giovanni's Room*, which appeared in 1956, deals with the homosexual relationship between an American and a Frenchman. Another collection of his essays, entitled *Nobody Knows My Name* (1960), brought him critical acclaim in the United States.

With the outbreak of the civil rights movement,* Baldwin left his self-imposed exile in France and returned to the United States, where he became the preeminent literary voice in the struggle for black equality. His third novel, *Another Country*, was a critical and commercial success in 1962, and *The Fire Next Time* was a best-seller in 1964. It is considered by many to be the most telling, brilliant essay in the history of African-American protest. After his 1968 novel *Tell Me How Long the Train's Been Gone*, Baldwin entered a long period of literary dormancy. In the mid-1970s, however, he returned to print with *If Beal Street Could Talk* (1974), *The Devil Finds Work* (1976), *Little Man, Little Man: A Story of Childhood* (1977), and *Just Above My Head* (1979). He was just as prolific in the 1980s, writing *Remember This House* (1980), *The Evidence of Things Not Seen* (1985), and *The Price of the Ticket* (1985). The onset of the gay rights movement in the 1970s and 1980s further established Baldwin's reputation as a literary freedom fighter.

SUGGESTED READING: James Campbell, *Talking at the Gates: The Life of James Baldwin*, 1991.

BEAT THE CLOCK. Produced by Mark Goodman and Bill Todman, *Beat the Clock*, an audience participation show and quiz show, premiered on CBS on March 23, 1950. Bud Collyer served as the emcee. Guests selected from the studio audience were asked to answer questions. If they missed the answers they had to perform outlandish stunts—like balancing eggs on one's head or walking an obstacle course wearing scuba gear—within fixed time limits, usually 60 seconds. The humor was physical and slapstick, but enough people tuned in to keep *Beat the Clock* on the air until its last broadcast on February 16, 1958.

SUGGESTED READING: Tim Brooks and Earle Marsh, *The Complete Directory to Prime Time Network and Cable TV Shows, 1946–Present*, 1995.

BEATS. During the 1950s, the rise of suburbia,* the consumer culture,* and television* and films created a culture of conformity in the United States. Although tens of millions of Americans, buoyed up by the decade's economic prosperity, enthusiastically participated in the prevailing culture, critics did emerge, and none were more acerbic than the so-called Beats. The movement began at Columbia University in the late 1940s, where a contingent of students led by Allen Ginsberg,* Jack Kerouac,* and William Burroughs rejected the conventions of middle-class society—consumerism, suburbia, bureaucracy, social convention, and authority. Ginsberg openly avowed his homosexuality and refused to view it as wrong or immoral. The students protested the insistence of modern society that happiness could be found only in monogamous heterosexuality, conformity, and consumption.

In 1954 Ginsberg moved to Berkeley, California, where he soon emerged as the poet laureate of the Beat Generation. Beats experimented with drugs as a means of exploring sensory experience and inner feelings, worked to protect the underdogs in American society, promoted individual faithfulness to sexual identity—whether homosexual or heterosexual—and called for a rejection of all individual-limiting social conventions. They also adopted a bohemian lifestyle that disdained cleanliness, modern appliances, clothing fads, close-cropped hair, and suits and ties. *Howl and Other Poems*, Ginsberg's first book, published in 1956, became the focus of a huge censorship controversy when San Francisco authorities tried to outlaw sale of the work. The U.S. Supreme Court eventually declared unconstitutional the ordinance allowing the suppression of the book.

The other leading light of the Beat movement was Jack Kerouac. In 1957 Kerouac published his second novel, *On the Road*, which features Sal Paradise and Dean Moriarty, two hipsters who drive back and forth across America, eschewing the values of a society whose only goal is the consumption of more goods. Although Kerouac had labored for years on the novel, Beat promoters hailed it as an icon to spontaneity, claiming that Kerouac had written it in one sitting during an amphetamine-induced creative blitz. *On the Road* quickly became the Bible for the Beat generation. Historians look back to the Beats as the forerunners of the counterculture that emerged in the 1960s when many young Americans took to the streets to protest discrimination, war, pollution, and middle-class values.

SUGGESTED READINGS: Ann Charter, *Kerouac: A Biography*, 1973; Jake H. Ehrlich, ed., *Howl of the Censor*, 1956; Dennis McNally, *Desolate Angel: Jack Kerouac, the Beat Generation, and America*, 1979; Barry Miles, *Ginsberg: A Biography*, 1989; Michael Schumacher, *Dharma Lion: A Critical Biography of Allen Ginsberg*, 1992; Michael White, ed., *Safe in Heaven Dead: Interviews with Jack Kerouac*, 1990.

BELLOW, SAUL. Saul Bellow was born on July 10, 1915, in Lachine, Quebec, Canada, to Russian Jewish emigré parents. He was raised in a poor neighborhood in Montreal, where French, Russian, English, and Yiddish were all spoken. That experience gave him a rich sense of language and its texture, which later enriched his fiction. He spent two years (1933–1935) as an undergraduate at the University of Chicago before transferring to Northwestern University, where he earned a degree in anthropology. Bellow started graduate school at the University of Wisconsin but dropped out after a semester in order to pursue his writing interests.

His first novel, *Dangling Man*, which appeared in 1944, won him critical acclaim but not commercial success. Nine years later, his novel *The Adventures of Augie March* won a National Book Award and placed Bellow permanently on the map of American literature. In this picaresque commentary on American life, Augie March is a sort of Jewish Huck Finn, stuck in the modern world of the north side of Chicago. Its first-person narrative, idiomatic and richly textured, struck readers as an American original. In 1956 Bellow wrote his novella *Seize the Day*, in which he describes the problems of a troubled individual who lives on the upper west side of New York. *Henderson the Rain King*, a comic novel set in mythical Africa and published in 1959, further cemented Bellow's reputation among the American literati. In 1964 Bellow wrote his greatest novel, *Herzog*, which revolves around Moses Herzog, a middle-class Jewish intellectual living in the United States. *Humboldt's Gift* (1975) won a Pulitzer Prize, and in 1976 Bellow was awarded the Nobel Prize for Literature. Historians today identify Bellow as a creative genius, a Jewish-American writer whose voice transcends the ethnic and religious community of his birth. Among his other works are *Mr. Sammler's Planet* (1970), *To Jerusalem and Back* (1976), *The Dean's*

December (1982), and *More Die of Heartbreak* (1987). Today Bellow teaches at the University of Chicago.

SUGGESTED READINGS: Daniel Fuchs, *Saul Bellow: Vision and Revision*, 1984; Gilbert M. Porter, *Whence the Power? The Artistry and Humanity of Saul Bellow*, 1974.

BENEDETTO, ANTHONY DOMINICK (TONY BENNETT). Tony Bennett was born in Queens, New York, on August 13, 1926. Gifted with a rich singing voice, he worked as a singing waiter in Italian restaurants in New York City, where he developed a style characterized by good articulation, a bemused attitude, and the ability to put classical jazz themes to song. An appearance on the *Arthur Godfrey Show* in 1949 got him a spot touring with Pearl Bailey, and Bob Hope picked him up to open his shows at the Paramount Theater in New York. He changed his name to Tony Bennett in 1950 and signed a contract with Columbia Records. His song "Because of You" became a number-one hit in 1951, and he then had a number of subsequent hits recording with the Percy Faith Orchestra. Among those hits were "Rags to Riches" and "Stranger in Paradise" in 1953, "There'll Be No Teardrops Tonight" in 1954, and "I Left My Heart in San Francisco" in 1962. Critics hailed such albums as *The Beat of My Heart* (1957), *When Lights Are Low* (1964), and *The Movie Song Album* (1966). Bennett's career declined during the late 1960s and 1970s, but during the late 1980s and 1990s, he had a revival when young people went crazy for the so-called retro movement that resurrected jazz and swing.

SUGGESTED READINGS: Tony Bennett, *Tony Bennett: What My Heart Has Seen*, 1996; Matthew Hoffman, *Tony Bennett*, 1996.

BEN-HUR. First released in November 1959 as a remake of the 1926 silent movie of the same name, *Ben-Hur* was an epic Bible film based on Lew Wallace's novel *Ben-Hur*, first published in 1880. During the 1950s, to compete with television,* Hollywood made a number of so-called spectacle films, and *Ben-Hur* was by far the best and the most popular of these. Americans in 1959 were still trying to come to terms with the Holocaust, and *Ben-Hur* was part of a genre of films, including *Exodus* and *Spartacus*, that depicted Jewish courage and the values of liberty.

Produced by Metro-Goldwyn-Mayer and directed by William Wyler, *Ben-Hur* starred Charlton Heston as Judah Ben-Hur, a prince of Judea at the time of the Roman occupation. Because of unfounded accusations of sedition, Ben-Hur is sentenced to life as a galley slave, but he manages to win his freedom by saving a Roman consul during a shipwreck. The consul adopts him and takes him into his prosperous, politically powerful family. Ben-Hur eventually returns to Jerusalem to defeat his Roman nemesis, Massala (played by Stephen Boyd), and rescue his family from a leper colony. In the process, he converts to Christianity. *Ben-Hur*, a box-office hit in 1959, continues to be a staple of Easter Sunday television.

SUGGESTED READING: *New York Times*, November 22, 1959.

BENNETT, TONY. *See* BENEDETTO, ANTHONY DOMINICK.

BENNY HOOPER INCIDENT. One of the major causes célèbres of the 1950s was the so-called Benny Hooper incident. In May 1957, seven-year-old Benny Hooper fell down a 21-foot-deep well shaft that was only 10 inches wide. The Hoopers lived in Manorville, Long Island, and Hooper's father was digging an irrigation well. The press descended on Manorville, as did hundreds of rescuers. The entire world tuned into the event, and after 24 hours, Benny was pulled alive from the shaft. Dr. Joseph Kris, a Manhattan physician, attended to Benny when he was rescued and for several days of hospitalization after the rescue.

A huge controversy erupted, however, when Kris sent a $1,500 bill for his services to the Hooper family. Benny's father made only $62 a week as a truck driver, and his mother, a telephone operator, made $43 a week. Dr. Kris soon found himself the subject of withering criticism, especially when the Hoopers publicly expressed their fears that other volunteers involved in the rescue effort might also bill them for their services. Kris tried to explain himself, but few people wanted to listen to his point of view. Even the American Medical Association (AMA) took Kris to task, issuing a press release saying that Kris "was rendering a public service and acting in the noblest tradition of medicine when he stood by while the boy's life hung in the balance. . . . The AMA feels however, that not one doctor in a thousand would have charged a fee. We strongly disagree with the action of the doctor in this case." Although Kris withdrew the bill, the incident led to severe criticism of the medical establishment.

SUGGESTED READINGS: Richard Carter, *The Doctor Business*, 1958; E. J. Kahn, Jr., "Billy and Benny," *New Yorker*, June 8, 1957, 117, 119–23.

BERGEN, EDGAR. Edgar Bergen was born on February 16, 1903, in Chicago, Illinois, to Swedish immigrant parents. The family later moved to Iowa to run a dairy farm. A natural-born entertainer, the young Bergen, at age eleven, ordered through the mail a book entitled *The Wizard's Manual*, from which he learned the art of ventriloquism. He also developed magic tricks, sang and danced, and told funny stories. He made his own dummy and began performing for family members and friends. While in high school, he paid a wood-carver to create a more realistic dummy for him, and then he performed skits in which he satirized teachers, friends, and public figures. Since the voice of the dummy seemed to be making the comments, he became quite popular.

After high school, Bergen attended Northwestern University as a pre-medical student, but he dropped out to hit the road with his act—"Edgar Bergen, the Voice Illusionist." Bergen saw the world, performing throughout Europe, South America, the United States, and Canada, and he finally did vaudeville in New York City. In 1936 Bergen made an appearance on the Rudy Vallee's *Royal Gelatin Hour* on NBC radio, and he was an immediate hit. NBC gave him his own show in 1937.

Bergen remained on the air for the next twenty years, with *The Edgar Ber-*

gen/Charlie McCarthy Show, which was sometimes known as *The Charlie McCarthy Show*. The show brought the biggest stars of radio, vaudeville, Broadway, and film to visit with Bergen and his sarcastic dummy, Charlie McCarthy. McCarthy flirted with the women guests and insulted the men. Bergen's daughter Candice, who became a film and television star in her own right in the 1980s and 1990s, began appearing on the show when she was six years old. During the 1950s, Americans revered Bergen as the godfather of comedy-variety shows. After a performance at Caesar's Palace in Las Vegas, Bergen died quietly on October 1, 1978.

SUGGESTED READINGS: *New York Times*, October 2, 1978; Skip Press, *Candice and Edgar Bergen*, 1995.

BERNSTEIN, LEONARD. Leonard Bernstein, perhaps the greatest virtuoso in modern American music, was born on August 25, 1918, in Lawrence, Massachusetts. His parents were immigrant Russian Jews. Bernstein's musical gifts were abundantly apparent even when he was a small child. Before he was twelve years old, he had decided to become a composer and orchestral conductor. He was accepted into Boston's prestigious Latin School, where he graduated in 1935. He then matriculated to Harvard and in 1939 earned a degree. From Cambridge, Massachusetts, Bernstein moved to Philadelphia, where he studied conducting at the Curtis Institute. It did not take him long to make his mark on the world of classical music. In 1942, at the age of twenty-three, he wrote his Symphony No. 1 ("Jeremiah"), and its reception earned him his first real job as assistant conductor of the New York Philharmonic. Bernstein then had a stroke of luck. When Bruno Walter, the New York Philharmonic's conductor, fell ill on November 14, 1943, Bernstein had to fill the breach that evening, and he conducted the orchestra to rave critical reviews. At the tender age of twenty-three, Leonard Bernstein had won a place of honor and respect for himself in the rarified atmosphere of orchestral music.

Bernstein did not confine himself to the world of classical music. One year after his debut with the New York Philharmonic, he wrote the score for the hit Broadway musical *On the Town*. Demonstrating an eclectic brilliance that had no peer, he wrote Symphony No. 2 ("The Age of Anxiety") in 1949 and then the score to the musical *Peter Pan* in 1950. His other compositions during the 1950s included *Wonderful Town*, *Candide*, and *West Side Story*, and he wrote the ballet music for *Fancy Free* and *Facsimile*. When Bernstein was named conductor of the New York Philharmonic in 1958, the *New York Times* dubbed him the "Renaissance man of American music." His 1959 book *The Joy of Music* was a best-seller, and his Symphony No. 3 ("Kaddish") cemented his reputation as America's greatest living composer.

Bernstein remained at the podium of the New York Philharmonic until 1969, when he retired to pursue other musical and political interests. He had long been active in the civil rights movement* for African Americans, and in the late 1960s and early 1970s, he added opposition to the Vietnam War* to his list of liberal political credentials. During the rest of the 1970s and throughout the 1980s, Bernstein was an advocate for gay rights and a crusader in raising money for AIDS research. He died on October 14, 1990.

SUGGESTED READINGS: *New York Times*, October 15, 1990; Joan Peyser, *Bernstein: A Biography*, 1987.

BERRY, CHUCK. Charles Edward Anderson (Chuck) Berry was born October 18, 1926, in San Jose, California. In spite of a rough adolescence, Berry was an excellent guitarist. Between 1944 and 1947, Berry served a prison sentence for attempted robbery, and after being paroled, he worked on a General Motors assembly line. At nights, he studied cosmotology. After graduating, Berry worked as a beautician and formed a band, which became well known in the St. Louis area. In 1955, with an endorsement from Muddy Waters, Berry sent a demo tape of his song "Maybelline" to Alan Freed* in New York. Freed agreed to give the song radio time if he could be listed as cowriter of the song. "Maybelline" became Berry's first top-ten hit. During the next three years, Berry's other rock-and-roll* hits included "School Day," "Rock & Roll Music," "Sweet Little Sixteen," and "Johnny B. Goode." Berry was extremely popular on the rock music concert tours, and his "duckwalk" on stage while playing the guitar became legendary.

Berry's career crashed in 1959 when he was accused of violating the Mann Act by hiring a 14-year-old part-Hispanic part-Apache girl to leave Texas and move to St. Louis. She did, and Berry put her to work in his St. Louis club. An antiprostitution measure, the Mann Act forbade the transporting of women across state lines for immoral purposes. Berry fought the case in court, and a judge threw out his first trial because of the racist behavior of the federal prosecutor. Berry was convicted in a second trial and spent two years in a federal prison. When he was paroled in 1964, the Beatles had taken over the rock-and-roll world. His career never recovered, but Berry remained extremely popular on the concert tour, and in 1972 he had another number one hit, "My Ding-a-Ling." Berry, who lives in Wentzville, Missouri, continues to have legal problems, including accusations of tax evasion, marijuana possession, and child abuse.

SUGGESTED READING: Chuck Berry, *Chuck Berry: The Autobiography*, 1986.

BETSY McCALL DOLL. In September 1952, *McCall's* magazine, a monthly publication targeted at middle-class woman, included a paper doll, named Betsy McCall, with the magazine. In subsequent issues, clothing and hairstyle cutouts were included to dress up the paper doll. McCall's also marketed a plastic Betsy McCall doll, and advertisers sold dresses, shoes, and hats patterned after the doll's clothes. With each issue, a Betsy McCall cartoon strip chronicled Betsy's adventures with her businessman father, stay-at-home mother, pet dog "Nosy," and a variety of friends. For millions of middle-class adolescent girls, Betsy

McCall constituted an idealized alter ego and provided an image for the American family during the 1950s.

SUGGESTED READING: *McCall's*, 1952–1960.

BEULAH. The situation comedy *Beulah*, a spinoff from the black maid on the *Fibber McGee and Molly** radio program, premiered on ABC television on October 3, 1950. It starred Ethel Waters as Beulah, a sassy but wise maid to the Hendersons, a middle-class white family. In 1952 Louise Beavers assumed the role of Beulah. Butterfly McQueen starred as Beulah's scatterbrained friend Oriole. The Hendersons moved from minor crisis to minor crisis, with Beulah dispensing wisdom and providing stability. The last episode was broadcast on September 22, 1953.

SUGGESTED READING: Tim Brooks and Earle Marsh, *The Complete Directory to Prime Time Network and Cable TV Shows, 1946–Present*, 1995.

THE BIG BOPPER. *See* RICHARDSON, JILES PERRY.

THE BIG SHOW. *The Big Show* was a popular radio variety program that aired on Sunday evenings on NBC radio from November 1950 to April 1952. Tallulah Bankhead served as the mistress of ceremonies, and guests included such performers as Fred Allen, Jimmy Durante, Ethel Merman, Frankie Laine, Danny Thomas, and Groucho Marx. The program was expensive—up to $100,000 a show—and represented a last-ditch effort by NBC to retain, in the wave of intense competition from television,* a weekly radio variety show. The effort was doomed to failure. NBC and ABC were offering up Sunday night television variety programs, and audiences preferred video images to audio sound. NBC canceled *The Big Show* in 1952 and worked to develop a Sunday night variety show, which became *The Ed Sullivan Show*.*

SUGGESTED READING: John Dunning, *On the Air: The Encyclopedia of Old-Time Radio*, 1998.

THE BIG STORY. Sponsored by Pall Mall and the Lucky Strike cigarettes, *The Big Story* was a popular crime series broadcast on NBC radio from 1947 until 1955. The stories in the series were based on true crime stories, although the writers heavily dramatized them. Its only continuing character was Bob Sloane, who narrated the program. Murder mysteries provided *The Big Story*'s staple themes, and for several years the program rivaled Bing Crosby's *Philco Radio Time* as radio's top-rated weekly show. It remained on radio until March 1955. On September 16, 1949, NBC brought *The Big Story* to television,* where it remained until its last broadcast on June 28, 1957.

SUGGESTED READINGS: Tim Brooks and Earle Marsh, *The Complete Directory to Prime Time Network and Cable TV Shows, 1946–Present*, 1995; John Dunning, *On the Air: The Encyclopedia of Old-Time Radio*, 1998.

BIG TOWN. *Big Town*, a popular dramatic series of the 1950s, premiered on CBS television on October 5, 1950, and remained at CBS until October 1954, when NBC picked it up. It starred Patrick McVey as Steve Wilson, the editor of a crusading newspaper, the *Illustrated Press*, in a mythical city called Big Town. The paper's star reporter, Lorelei Kilbourne, was played by four actresses during the show's life: Mary K. Wells, Julie Stevens, Jane Nigh, and Beverly Tyler. Steve Wilson worked hard to root out corruption, expose organized crime, and crusade for political reforms. *Big Town* was last broadcast on October 2, 1956.

SUGGESTED READING: Tim Brooks and Earle Marsh, *The Complete Directory to Prime Time Network and Cable TV Shows, 1946–Present,* 1995.

THE BLACKBOARD JUNGLE. During the 1950s, Americans were preoccupied with the problem of juvenile delinquency,* and such films as *The Blackboard Jungle* and *Rebel Without a Cause* exacerbated the concern. Released in March 1955, *The Blackboard Jungle* starred Glenn Ford as Richard Dadier, a teacher in a crime-ridden inner-city high school, and Vic Morrow and Sidney Poitier as students Artie West and Gregory Miller, respectively. The film was based on a novel by Evan Hunter. Most of the students are unruly hoodlums who have no respect for authority and no desire to learn, and the teachers put their lives on the line every day in class. In the climactic scene, Mr. Dadier has to defend himself against the knife-wielding West. The film was an exaggeration, to be sure, but most Americans were worried that it was close enough to reality to be cause for great alarm about the future of the country.

SUGGESTED READING: *New York Times*, March 21, 1955.

THE BLOB. *The Blob* was one of the classics of the 1950s genre of horror-monster films. Released in November 1958, the film starred Steve McQueen in one of the actor's earliest leading roles. The 1950s was a time when Americans worried about domestic communism, outer space, and nuclear weapons, and *The Blob* played on two of those themes. A shooting star surreptitiously deposits a small amount of mysterious gelatin in a small American town. Against a bucolic backdrop of a Main Street complete with church spire, drugstore, soda fountain, dry goods store, and movie theater, the slow-moving gelatin eats unsuspecting citizens, growing in size after each meal. Critics panned the special effects and wondered why more people did not manage to simply outrun, or even outwalk, the monster. Eventually, town leaders call in the U.S. Army and Air Force, which freeze the blob into a solid chunk and fly it to the Arctic, where it is unceremoniously dumped, leaving only Eskimos to worry about becoming its new staple. Film historians classify *The Blob* as typical Cold War popular culture. An alien force had invaded small-town America and, except for quick-thinking federal and military officials, had almost destroyed it.

SUGGESTED READING: *New York Times*, November 2, 1958.

BOB AND RAY. Bob Elliott and Ray Goulding developed a successful radio and night club comedy act in the 1930s and 1940s, which relied primarily on satire, puns, double entendres, and other verbal gags. They were especially adept at satirizing radio soap operas, and NBC picked up the act and premiered Bob and Ray on television* on November 26, 1951. Audrey Meadows played the part of Linda Lovely in their spoof "Mary Backstage, Noble Wife." They made fun of cowboy shows, quiz shows, and anything else television offered up to viewers. NBC canceled the series on September 28, 1953.

SUGGESTED READING: Tim Brooks and Earle Marsh, *The Complete Directory to Prime Time Network and Cable TV Shows, 1946–Present*, 1995.

THE BOB CUMMINGS SHOW. *The Bob Cummings Show*, one of the more popular television situation comedies of the 1950s, premiered on NBC on January 2, 1955, switched to CBS in July 1955, and then returned to NBC in September 1957. It starred Robert Cummings as Bob Collins, a bachelor and photographer who spent his days taking pictures of beautiful models. Rosemary DeCamp starred as Margaret MacDonald, the photographer's wise-cracking widowed sister. Ann B. Davis played Schultzy, Collins's assistant. *The Bob Cummings Show* left prime time with its last episode on September 15, 1959, but NBC changed the title to *Love That Bob* and converted it to a daytime series, which played until 1961.

SUGGESTED READING: Tim Brooks and Earle Marsh, *The Complete Directory to Prime Time Network and Cable TV Shows, 1946–Present*, 1995.

BOGART, HUMPHREY. Humphrey Bogart was born in New York City on December 25, 1899. His mother was a noted artist and illustrator and his father was a successful surgeon. He joined the U.S. Navy during World War I and then worked at a number of jobs—clerk for an investment company, tugboat inspector, and theatrical company manager. He enjoyed the theater and during the 1920s secured a string of small roles on Broadway. Bogart signed a contract with the Fox studio in 1931 and appeared in several Westerns, but he did not have the good looks of a cowboy hero. His career lagged until 1934 when he appeared as a gangster in *The Petrified Forest*. Surly, snarling, and menacing in the role, Bogart won critical acclaim and launched his career.

He eventually went on to make fifty films, the most memorable of which are *High Sierra* (1941), *Casablanca* (1942), *The Treasure of Sierra Madre* (1948), *The African Queen* (1951), *The Caine Mutiny* (1954), and *The Desperate Hours* (1955). He won an academy award for his portrayal of the crusty, gin-swilling Mr. Ornott in *The African Queen*, and film historians especially remember his performance as the cowardly Captain Queeg in *The Caine Mutiny*. Bogart was an outspoken opponent of the House Un-American Activities Committee and went to Washington, D.C., in 1947 to protest its Red Scare* tactics. He was not blacklisted, however, because his stature in the industry was simply too great. He fell ill with cancer in 1956 and died on January 14, 1957.

SUGGESTED READINGS: Jeffrey Myers, *Bogart: A Life in Hollywood*, 1997; *New York Times*, January 15, 1957.

BOMB SHELTERS. During the late 1950s and early 1960s, a bomb shelter craze, or fad, swept through the United States. The great fear of nuclear weapons, first ignited in 1949 when the Soviet Union detonated its first atomic bomb,* assumed huge proportions in 1957, when the Soviets launched *Sputnik*,* an artificial satellite, into orbit around the earth, proving that they had the technology to deliver nuclear bombs anywhere. More than anything else, *Sputnik* destroyed the sense of geographical security Americans had enjoyed for so many years. Talk of nuclear annihilation infected the popular culture like an epidemic disease.

Alarmed about the potential devastation of nuclear warfare, many Americans began to construct bomb shelters. Such wide circulation magazines as *Popular Mechanics*, *Time*, and *Life* ran do-it-yourself articles on how to construct backyard bomb shelters. The Cadillac of bomb shelters, which cost up to $10,000 to construct, included electric generators, air-filtration systems, Geiger counters, food, water, clothing, and all the other necessities for a long stay underground.

Critics pointed out that backyard bomb shelters would be of little use in the event of a thermonuclear war. Widespread devastation, elimination of all the nation's infrastructure, and long-term radioactive contamination would destroy civilization and render life all but unlivable. Nevertheless, hundreds of thousands of families tried to protect themselves anyway. By the mid-1960s, the bomb shelter craze had largely run its course.

SUGGESTED READING: "Atomic Hideouts," *Popular Mechanics*, November 1958, 146–48.

BONANZA. During the 1950s, the Western melodrama reigned supreme in American popular culture, and nowhere was its presence more dominant than on television.* The frontier had played a central role in U.S. history, and most Americans still had strong attachments to their own, or their country's, rural roots. The television Western *Bonanza* premiered on NBC on September 12, 1959, and rocketed to the top of the Nielsen's ratings list. *Bonanza* was set on the post–Civil War Ponderosa, a huge ranch located near Virginia City, Nevada. Lorne Green starred as Ben Cartwright, the wise patriarch of the Ponderosa spread. A widower, he presided over a family consisting of three sons: Adam (Pernell Roberts), "Hoss" (Dan Blocker), and "Little Joe" (Michael Landon). The Cartwrights had to deal with desperadoes, Indians, and a host of other challenges as they attempted to maintain and build their own cattle and timber empire. *Bonanza* remained a staple of American television until the last episode aired on January 16, 1973.

SUGGESTED READINGS: Tim Brooks and Earle Marsh, *The Complete Directory to Prime Time Network and Cable TV Shows, 1946–Present*, 1995; Stephen Calder, *The Ponderosa Empire*, 1995.

BOND, JAMES. James Bond, or Agent 007, is the lead character in a series of internationally popular, best-selling novels by Ian Fleming, a British writer. Fleming spent World War II in the employ of British naval intelligence, where he developed some basic ideas about espionage. *Casino Royale*, the first of the James Bond novels, was published in 1953. Bond epitomizes good, and his foils—a series of dictators and international conspirators out to secure control of the world—are universally evil. Fleming laced his stories with sexual encounters: Bond was suave, handsome, and sophisticated, a real ladies' man, and his female conquests were all beautiful, exotic foreign women. Early in the 1960s, the character of James Bond made it to the big screen in a series of films starring Sean Connery.

SUGGESTED READINGS: Raymond Benson, *The James Bond Bedside Companion*, 1988; Bruce A. Rosenberg, *Ian Fleming*, 1989.

BOONE, PAT. Pat Boone was born Charles Eugene Boone in Jacksonville, Florida, on June 1, 1934. Just after high school, he married Shirley Foley, the daughter of country western star Red Foley. As a student at North Texas State College, he won a local talent contest and secured appearances on Ted Mack's and Arthur Godfrey's* amateur shows. He did so well that Godfrey invited him back for several more appearances. Boone signed with Republic Records in Nashville, and his 1955 remake of Fats Domino's* "Ain't That a Shame" was a number-one hit. During the next seven years, Boone was one of rock-and-roll's* most successful performers. Among his hits were four number-one singles: "Don't Forbid Me" (1957), "Love Letters in the Sand" (1957), "April Love" (1957), and "Moody River" (1961). In 1957 Boone starred in two films, *Bernardine* and *April Love*. In 1957 he also launched his own television show, *The Pat Boone-Chevy Showroom*, which remained on the air for three years. Boone's career peaked in 1962. Since then, he has continued to perform on the resort circuit and with wife and four daughters. He has also been a spokesman for a variety of Christian causes.

SUGGESTED READINGS: Pat Boone, *Together: 25 years with the Boone Family*, 1979; Patricia Romanowski and Holly George-Warren, *The Encyclopedia of Rock & Roll*, 1995.

BOSTON BLACKIE. During the early 1900s, George Randolph Chester wrote stories about Blackie Daw, a con artist, and *Cosmopolitan* and *Redbook* magazines picked up the character and turned him into Boston Blackie, a reformed criminal and private detective. The character resonated with American readers, and Boston Blackie was subsequently featured in a number of B-movies and pulp magazine stories. In September 1951 the *Boston Blackie* television show premiered in syndication, starring Kent Taylor as Boston Blackie and Lois Collier as his girlfriend, Mary Wesley. Dapper, shrewd, and impeccably well-dressed, Boston Blackie always managed to keep a few steps ahead of the police and solve crimes for them. Fifty-eight episodes of *Boston Blackie* were produced before it was cancelled in 1953.

SUGGESTED READING: Tim Brooks and Earle Marsh, *The Complete Directory to Prime Time Network and Cable TV Shows, 1946–Present*, 1995.

BOSTON CELTICS. The Boston Celtics were the premier professional sports franchise during the 1950s. When the decade began, professional basketball was popular at the local and regional levels, but it did not possess a national identity. Far more Americans followed college basketball, especially its two season-ending tournaments, the National Invitational Tournament (NIT) and the National Collegiate Athletic Association (NCAA) Tournament. In fact, professional basketball had come on hard times. The National Basketball League (NBL) and the Basketball Association of America (BAA) both folded in 1949. In 1950, with seventeen teams, the National Basketball Association (NBA) was formed. By the end of 1951, only eleven teams survived. Three years later, the NBA had dwindled to eight teams: Syracuse, New York, Boston, Philadelphia, Fort Wayne, Minneapolis, Rochester, and Milwaukee. By 1959 the Fort Wayne franchise had relocated to Detroit, and the Rochester and Milwaukee franchises had disappeared, with new teams appearing in Saint Louis and Cincinnati.

What changed the NBA and turned it into a runaway success was the league's decision to integrate, which began when the Boston Celtics signed Chuck Cooper of Duquesne University, as well as the advent of a faster paced game. The Boston Celtics pioneered the fast break, the behind-the-back pass, and the no-look pass, all of which generated huge fan interest. Bob Cousy, the Boston point guard, pioneered the techniques—at least at the professional level.

The Boston Celtics dynasty began when the team drafted center William (Bill) Russell* of the University of San Francisco. Russell had led San Francisco to two back-to-back NCAA titles, and he had an immediate impact in Boston. Russell played aggressive defense and was an especially good rebounder, who quickly outbounded the ball to Cousy, setting up the team's legendary fast breaks. Coached by Red Auerbach, the Celtics won their first NBA championship in 1957, and between 1957 and 1969 they accumulated 10 more championships, including 8 successive championships between 1959 and 1966.

SUGGESTED READINGS: Bob Cousy, *The Killer Instinct*, 1975; Dan Shaughnessy, *Seeing Red: The Red Auerbach Story*, 1995; George Sullivan, *The Boston Celtics: Fifty Years*, 1996.

BRANDO, MARLON. Marlon Brando was born in Omaha, Nebraska, on April 3, 1924. A free spirit—undisciplined according to his father—he was expelled from a military academy. He wanted to act and after digging ditches for several years, he moved to New York City, where he studied at Lee Strasberg's Actors' Studio. There he converted to what was known at the time as "the Method"—in which an actor played a role after attempting to understand the psyche, emotions, and motivations of characters. Brando developed an image of smoldering power, which came through during the 1940s, when he became a Broadway star. He debuted on Broadway in *I Remember Mama* (1944) and won a New York theater critics award for his performance in *Truckline Cafe* (1946). His performance as Stanley Kowalski in Tennessee Williams's *A Streetcar Named Desire* (1947) earned him a reputation as America's leading young actor.

He made the transition to film in 1950, when he played the part of a paralyzed World War II veteran in *The Men* (1950). Brando reprised his Kowalski role in the 1951 film *A Streetcar Named Desire.* In 1952 he portrayed Mexican revolutionary Emiliano Zapata in *Viva Zapata!* After a critically acclaimed part in *Julius Ceasar* (1954), Brando firmly established his screen persona as an independent, internally directed rebel in two films: *The Wild One* (1954) and *On the Waterfront* (1954). In *The Wild One*, Brando played the leather-jacketed leader of a motorcycle gang that terrorizes a small town somewhere in Middle America. As such, he was on the cutting edge of the youth rebellion that would soon sweep through America. In *On the Waterfront*, for which he won an Academy Award, he portrayed a blue-collar longshoreman who is unwilling to submit to bureaucrats, lawyers, and racketeers.

Throughout the 1950s—in such other films as *Desiree* (1954), *Guys and Dolls* (1954), and *The Young Lions* (1958)—Brando continued to impress audiences, critics, and theater owners, who consistently voted him to the top-ten list of box-office draws. During a decade in which pressures to conform dominated American life, Brando carved out a persona of narcissistic freedom and individual expression.

His career came on hard times in the 1960s, especially after the film *Mutiny on the Bounty* (1962), in which he played Fletcher Christian, bombed at the box office. His career, however, bounded back in the 1970s. He won an Academy Award for his portrayal of Don Corleone in *The Godfather* (1972), but he refused to accept the award. In fact, he sent Sacheem Littlefeather to the Academy Awards ceremony to refuse the award and to denounce Hollywood's portrayal of Indian people on film. He also starred in *Last Tango in Paris* (1973), a critically acclaimed but controversial, X-rated film, and he made a great deal of money with small parts in *Superman* (1978) and *Apocalypse Now* (1979). In 1989 Brando received an Oscar nomination for *A Dry White Season*, a film about apartheid in South Africa.

SUGGESTED READINGS: Gary Cary, *The Only Contender*, 1985; Richard Schickel, *Brando: A Life in Our Times*, 1991.

BREAK THE BANK. Bert Parks pioneered the *Break the Bank* radio quiz show in the 1940s, and it premiered on ABC television on October 22, 1948, with Parks as the host and Bud Collyer as cohost. Contestants, selected from the studio audience, chose a category from which they were asked a series of increasingly difficult questions. The rewards for correct answers were increasingly lucrative. For 1950s quiz shows, *Break the Bank* was a "big-money show," with prizes sometimes reaching $10,000 or more. The show aired at various times on ABC, NBC, and CBS. In October 1956, NBC renamed it *Break the $250,000 Bank*. The show was finally canceled. Its last episode was broadcast on January 15, 1957.

SUGGESTED READING: Tim Brooks and Earle Marsh, *The Complete Directory to Prime Time Network and Cable TV Shows, 1946–Present*, 1995.

BREAKFAST WITH DOROTHY AND DICK. *Breakfast with Dorothy and Dick* was a popular morning radio talk show that was broadcast from 1945 to 1963. Although it was a local series broadcast from WOR radio in New York City, the station's 50,000-watt power allowed the program to be heard by more than twenty million people. It featured Dorothy Kilgallen, a popular theater critic, and her husband, Richard Kollmar, a veteran radio actor. The show was heard live at 8:15 A.M. every morning except Sunday, when a prerecorded broadcast was aired. The show's format was the breakfast table, where Dorothy and Dick discussed the latest films and plays, gossiped about celebrities, and exchanged advice and comments with their two children, Dickie and Jill. The family canary—Robin—regularly chirped in.

SUGGESTED READING: John Dunning, *On the Air: The Encyclopedia of Old-Time Radio*, 1998.

BRENNAN, WILLIAM. William Joseph Brennan, Jr., was born on April 25, 1906, in Newark, New Jersey. He was the second of eight children in an immigrant Irish Catholic family. His father shoveled coal in a local brewery for a living, was busily engaged in local Democratic party politics, and possessed an activist social philosophy. The younger Brennan graduated from the Wharton School of the University of Pennsylvania and took a law degree at Harvard. He then went into private practice in Newark, specializing in labor law. He joined the U.S. Army during World War II and spent much of the war troubleshooting labor problems for Undersecretary of War Robert Patterson.

After the war, Brennan returned to private practice, and in 1949 he accepted an appointment as a judge in the New Jersey Superior Court system. He was an outspoken advocate of the rights of criminal defendants, and he also spoke out against the excesses of the Red Scare,* comparing the antics of Senator Joseph McCarthy* of Wisconsin to the Salem witchcraft hysteria of the 1690s. Brennan became a judge in the appellate division in 1950 and a justice on the New Jersey Supreme Court in 1952. He was still serving in that position when President Dwight D. Eisenhower* named him to the U.S. Supreme Court in 1956. Senator McCarthy cast the only dissenting vote in the Senate against the confirmation of Brennan. Brennan later wrote, "I count his negative vote as the most impressive accomplishment of my career."

As an associate justice on the Supreme Court, Brennan became part of the liberal majority of Earl Warren* that revolutionized American jurisprudence. Many judicial historians consider Brennan, a gentle liberal who always pushed the envelope of individual rights, to have been the architect of the Warren Court.

Brennan became Warren's closest colleague on the Court. Brennan was the leader in fashioning the "one man, one vote" logic in *Baker v. Carr* (1962) and the supremacy of the federal government over state decisions in *Cooper v. Aaron** (1958), which undermined the massive resistance doctrine of Southern segregationists. Brennan wrote prominent opinions about restricting loyalty oaths and government regulation of pornography, recognized a broad freedom of association, and was a consistent proponent of individual civil rights. During the 1970s and 1980s, Brennan often found himself in dissent, disagreeing with many of the conservative decisions of the Supreme Court under Warren Burger and William Rehnquist. Brennan retired from the court in 1990.

SUGGESTED READINGS: Hunter Clark, *Justice Brennan: The Great Conciliator*, 1995; Roger L. Goldman, *Justice William J. Brennan, Jr.: Freedom First*, 1994.

BRIDGE ON THE RIVER KWAI. In 1958 David Lean's film *Bridge on the River Kwai* premiered around the world. The movie established Lean as the film industry's greatest epic film director. Starring Alec Guinness and William Holden, the film told the story of a Japanese prisoner-of-war (POW) camp in Burma during World War II. The Japanese commander of the camp is a sadistic autocrat who despises the POWs, most of whom are British soldiers who surrendered at Singapore in 1942. The POWs are being forced to build a railway bridge over the River Kwai. In order to maintain the discipline of his troops, the British commander decides to build the bridge efficiently and on schedule, and in the process the bridge begins to consume his life. When British commandos make their way into the jungle to destroy the bridge, the commander actually helps the Japanese defend it. In the end, he loses his life and the bridge is destroyed. The film succeeded in portraying the numbing brutality of war as well as its fundamental irrationality. Alec Guinness won a best actor Academy Award for his performance as the British commander.

SUGGESTED READING: Kevin Brownlow, *David Lean: A Biography*, 1996.

BRINK'S ROBBERY. On January 17, 1950, armed robbers staged a daring crime at the Boston headquarters of Brink's Company, the nation's premier armored car delivery service. It was masterminded by Tony "The Pig" Pino, a safecracker and small-time hoodlum who had spent four years planning the heist. At gunpoint, seven bandits bedecked in pea coats and masks stole $2.8 million in cash, checks, and money orders, the biggest robbery in U.S. history. They then escaped, seemingly, into thin air.

The Brink's job soon assumed an exaggerated place in American popular culture. Because the country was in the throes of the Red Scare,* some concluded it was a Communist job, and J. Edgar Hoover,* head of the FBI, vowed to get to the bottom of the conspiracy. The Soviets, of course, had nothing to do with the robbery; it was the work of several small-time Boston criminals who had masterminded the heist of a lifetime. They managed to elude capture until 1956, when one gang member, "Specs" O'Keefe, confessed. Fortunately for the FBI, his confession came just eleven days before the statute of limitations ran out on the crime. O'Keefe plea-bargained with the federal government and informed on his ten comrades. All of them were arrested, but only $50,000 of the money was ever recovered. Millions of Americans expressed disappointment when the FBI closed the case, since the Brink's robbers had all but become icons in the popular culture.

SUGGESTED READINGS: *New York Times*, January 18–20, 1950; Noel Vehn, *Big Stick-Up at Brinks!*, 1977.

BROKEN ARROW. *Broken Arrow*, a television Western of the late 1950s, premiered on ABC television on September 25, 1956, starring John Lupton as Tom Jeffords, an Arizona Indian agent, and Michael Ansara as Cochise, chief of the Chiricahua Apaches. Unlike other Westerns, in which the whites and Indians always killed each other, the premise of *Broken Arrow* was cooperation between Jeffords and Cochise to battle renegade Indians and the whites who exploited Indians. *Broken Arrow* remained on the air until its last broadcast on September 18, 1960.

SUGGESTED READING: Tim Brooks and Earle Marsh, *The Complete Directory to Prime Time Network and Cable TV Shows, 1946–Present*, 1995.

BROOKLYN DODGERS. During the 1950s, the Brooklyn Dodgers, along with the New York Yankees, was a professional baseball franchise whose reputation and following transcended its own city. The Dodgers, nicknamed "The Bums," had earned a reputation over the years for scrappy determination, and because team owner Branch Rickey had integrated professional baseball by signing Jackie Robinson,* the Dodgers enjoyed real notoriety. The names of Dodger players, including Robinson, Roy Campanella, Duke Snyder, Gil Hodges, Johnny Padres, and Junior Gilliam, became household words. Appearances against the New York Yankees in the 1955 and 1956 World Series cemented Dodger popularity.

In 1957, however, the Dodgers broke the hearts of Brooklyn fans when they announced the relocation of the franchise to Los Angeles. The advent of commercial passenger jet* service now made it possible for a professional sports team to traverse the country in a matter of hours, and the huge market of Los Angeles beckoned. Out in Los Angeles, they would not have to compete in the New York media market, which also contained the New York Yankees and the New York Giants baseball teams. Ebbets Field in Brooklyn seated less than 35,000 people, and the city of Los Angeles promised to help them finance a new, state-of-the art stadium. The Dodgers first played in Los Angeles in 1958, using the Los Angeles Coliseum as a temporary stadium. The Dodgers won the National League pennant in 1959, and in three home games against the Chicago White Sox, they drew crowds of 92,394, 92,560, and 92,706—the highest total for a three-game series in baseball history. Brooklyn fans have never forgiven the Dodgers for making the move.

SUGGESTED READINGS: Doris Kearns Goodwin, *Wait Till Next Year*, 1998; Roger Kahn, *The Boys of Summer*, 1998; Marvin Miller, *A Whole Different Ball Game: The Sport and Business of Baseball*, 1992.

BROWN V. BOARD OF EDUCATION OF TOPEKA, KANSAS (1954). In 1954 the U.S. Supreme Court heard a series of five cases dealing with the legality of forced racial segregation in public schools. Lower courts had rejected all of the lawsuits, but attorneys for the National Association for the Advancement of Colored People appealed all five. Thurgood Marshall,* later to become the first African-American justice on the U.S. Supreme Court, argued all five cases. The *Brown* decision, the first one the Court heard, involved Linda Brown, an eleven-year-old girl who had to cross a railroad yard to attend a segregated school for blacks, even though another public school was located across the street. Her father filed the lawsuit, claiming that such school rules and the laws behind them were inherently discriminatory and violations of the Fifth and Fourteenth Amendments to the U.S. Constitution.

In 1896, in *Plessy v. Ferguson*, the Supreme Court had decided that "separate but equal" public accommodations were not inherently discriminatory; ever since, the "Jim Crow" system of segregation had enjoyed the backing of the law. Marshall argued that "separate but equal" was discriminatory for two reasons. First, the supplies and buildings provided black students were almost always inferior to those offered to white students. Second, public school segregation ostracized black children and stigmatized them for being black, which deprived them of self-esteem and often made them ashamed of their heritage.

At the time, the Supreme Court was presided over by Chief Justice Earl Warren,* whom President Dwight D. Eisenhower* had appointed to the Court because he was a conservative. Once on the Court, however, Warren's true political colors came out, and he created the most liberal Court in U.S. history. Warren agreed with Marshall's contentions, and he worked with the other justices until he had their full support. In a unanimous decision, the court decided that separate but equal public accommodations and schools were inherently unequal.

The South rose up in rebellion and promised to resist the court order. Governor Herman Talmadge of Georgia called the *Brown* decision "a mere scrap of paper." In many ways he was right. The U.S. Supreme Court had declared segregation unconstitutional, but it took another twenty years before desegregation actually began to take place on a large scale in the South.

SUGGESTED READINGS: Richard Kluger, *Simple Justice: The History of Brown v. Board of Education and Black America's Struggle for Equality*, 1977; Arnold S. Rice, *The Warren Court, 1953–1969*, 1987; Carl Rowan, *Dream Makers, Dream Breakers: The World of Thurgood Marshall*, 1993.

BUCKLEY, WILLIAM F., JR. William Frank Buckley, Jr., was born in New York City on November 24, 1925, to a wealthy family that had made its fortune in the Texas oil business. A precocious child, in 1931 the six-year-old William Buckley wrote a letter to the king of England demanding that Great Britain repay its World War I debt to the United States. After graduating from the Millbrook Academy in 1943, Buckley attended the University of Mexico before enlisting in the U.S. Army.

After mustering out of the army in 1946, Buckley enrolled at Yale, where he edited the *Yale Daily News*. He graduated in 1950 and then came to national attention with his book *God and Man at Yale* (1950), which excoriated Yale for the liberal bias in its curriculum and in its faculty. He then bought hundreds of copies and had them distributed at Yale's commencement ceremonies in 1951, enraging the administration in New Haven. He accused the Yale faculty of being overwhelmingly left wing. He also said that he would "rather be governed by the first 500 names in the Boston phone directory than the faculty of Harvard." Buckley worked for the Central Intelligence Agency in 1951 and 1952, and in 1954 he published *McCarthy and His Enemies*, a book that praised the Wisconsin senator's crusade against domestic communism. Buckley saw nothing wrong with a society defending itself from alien ideas.

In 1955 Buckley launched *National Review*, a weekly magazine of news and opinion to rival what he considered to be the liberal bias in such magazines as *Newsweek* and *Time*. In doing so, he became the most prominent conservative intellectual in the country. He warned of the evils of communism and criticized the New Deal bureaucracy that had taken over the federal government. In 1959 Buckley published his book *Up from Liberalism*, in which he reiterated his fundamental political philosophy and demanded an uncompromising, tough foreign policy toward the Soviet Union, which he considered to be the twentieth century's most evil force. Since then, via the *National Review*, a syndicated newspaper column, and his television show *Firing Line*, Buckley has carved out his position as America's leading conservative, a position he still holds today.

SUGGESTED READINGS: Jeffrey Hart, *The American Dissent: A Decade of Modern Conservatism*, 1966; John B. Judis, *William F. Buckley, Jr.: Patron Saint of the Conservatives*, 1988.

BURTON ABBOTT TRIAL. The Burton Abbott case revolved around the 1955 kidnaping, rape, and murder of fourteen-year-old Stephanie Bryan in Oakland, California. The teenager failed to return home after school on April 28, 1955, and a large-scale search failed to locate her. On July 15, 1955, however, Georgia Abbott found in the basement of her home a purse, ID card, textbooks, glasses, and brassiere belonging to Stephanie. Both she and her husband denied any knowledge of how the items found their way into the basement. Their son, Burton Abbott, a twenty-seven-year-old accounting student, told police that at the time of the crime he had been at the family's vacation cabin in the Trinity County mountains, nearly 300 miles away. Five days later, police found Stephanie's body in a shallow grave near the cabin. Burton Abbott's trial began in November 1955, and although the case against him was purely circumstantial,

he displayed an arrogant, amused attitude in court, alienating jurors and journalists alike. He insisted the police case was a frame-up, but jurors did not
believe him. Abbott was convicted and sentenced to death. He died in California's gas chamber on March 15, 1957.

SUGGESTED READINGS: *Newsweek*, February 6, 1956, 29; *Time*, March 25, 1957,
25.

C

CALYPSO. Calypso, a musical form that developed in the Caribbean islands of Trinidad and Tobago, took the United States by storm in the 1950s. Part-African, part-Caribbean, calypso became popular in the United States in 1956 when Harry Belafonte, a Jamaican born in Harlem, released his album *Calypso*, which included such hit songs as "Jamaica Farewell" and "The Banana Boat Song (Day-O)." The album spent 31 weeks at the top of the American pop music charts, and by 1959 it had become the first million-selling LP (long playing) album in American history.

SUGGESTED READING: Keith Warner, *Kaiso! The Trinidad Calypso*, 1997.

CAMBODIA. Ever since the 1850s, Cambodia had been, along with Tonkin, Annam, Cochin China, and Laos, one of the five colonies in French Indochina. Cambodia, known anciently as Kampuchea, was inhabited largely by ethnic Khmer people. In 1941, after Germany had conquered France and Japan had occupied much of French Indochina, the French government proclaimed Norodom Sihanouk, who claimed descent from Cambodia's royal family, king of the country.

Sihanouk, a nationalist, yearned for Cambodia's full independence from France. He bided his time, watching as Ho Chi Minh* and his Vietminh army united Cochin China, Tonkin, and Annam into Vietnam and fought for independence themselves. France deemed Vietnam much more valuable to the empire than Cambodia, and decided not to resist in 1953 when Sihanouk proclaimed martial law, dissolved the Cambodian parliament, and declared the country's independence. At the time of his announcement, Sihanouk was on a world tour, which he personally had dubbed the Royal Campaign. In November 1953, France agreed to withdraw its political and military forces and recognize Cambodian independence. Sihanouk had taken the first step toward the annihilation of the French empire in Indochina. France turned its attention to preserving Vietnam's colonial status, but it would be a futile quest. The age of empire was over.

SUGGESTED READINGS: David Chandler, *A History of Cambodia*, 1983; George Coedes, *The Making of Southeast Asia*, 1966.

CAN-CAN. A two-act musical comedy, *Can-Can* premiered at the Shubert Theater in New York City on May 7, 1953. It was based on a book of the same name written by Abe Burrows; Cole Porter wrote the music and the lyrics. *Can-Can* centers around a Montmartre café in Paris, where the scandalous "can-can" dance is raising the eyebrows of moral critics. Judge Aristide Forestier, played by Peter Cookson, is charged with investigating the café, and he brings a straight-laced, moral self-righteousness to the task. He soon falls victim to the can-can's magic, however, and to La Mome Pistache, the beautiful owner of the café. Such Cole Porter songs as "Allez-vous-en," "Can-Can," "C'est Magnifique," and "I Love Paris" made their way into the popular culture. *Can-Can* enjoyed a run of 892 performances before leaving Broadway for road tours.

SUGGESTED READINGS: Gerald Bordman, *The Oxford Companion to American Theater*, 1992; *New York Times*, May 8, 1953.

CANTOR, EDDIE. Edward (Eddie) Cantor was born as either Isadore Itzkowitz or Edward Israel Iskowitz on January 31, 1892, to Russian immigrant parents on the Lower East Side of Manhattan in New York City. Later in life he often claimed both names as his given names. He was orphaned as a child and raised by his grandmother in tenement-house poverty. She enrolled him in school as Edward Kantrowitz, which was her surname, and he later anglicized it to Cantor. He was a petty criminal as an adolescent, but he discovered that he could make money singing and telling jokes in bars and saloons. A job as a singing waiter at Coney Island brought him to the attention of Jimmy Durante, who was playing piano at the restaurant. Cantor won parts in the Ziegfeld Follies of 1917, 1918, and 1919, and during the 1920s he enjoyed an impressive career on Broadway and in vaudeville. He became a national figure in January 1931 when he appeared on crooner Rudy Vallee's radio show. The appearance led to his own radio program—the *Chase and Sanborn Hour*—which became a major ratings success.

Cantor pioneered the idea of live audience participation, telling jokes, interacting with the studio audience, interviewing celebrities, and offering up a top-notch variety show, all at the same time. He remained on the air in one form or another into the early 1950s, by which time his reputation for wit, sharp dialogue, and strong opinions had become legendary. Cantor went into television* in September 1950, hosting the *Colgate Comedy Hour*; however, in the conformist atmosphere of the 1950s, Cantor was too independent and possessed too much of an edge. Most Americans wanted to be entertained, not intellectually and politically challenged. His program was canceled in October 1953.

Cantor continued to appear in a variety of entertainment venues throughout the decade. He died on October 10, 1964.

SUGGESTED READINGS: Eddie Cantor, *My Life Is in Your Hands*, 1932, and *Take My Life*, 1957; *New York Times*, October 11, 1964.

CASTRO (RUZ), FIDEL. Fidel Castro was born on August 13, 1927, in Mayari, Cuba. He attended the University of Havana in the late 1940s and acquired a law degree there in 1950 as well as a radical political philosophy. He became an inveterate opponent of the regime of Fulgencio Batista, and early in the 1950s he became involved in an armed struggle against the regime. Castro led an attack on the Moncada military barracks in Santiago, Cuba, on July 26, 1953, which he had hoped would spawn a more generalized uprising among the Cuban people. It did not happen, and Castro was arrested, convicted, and sentenced to a fifteen-year prison term. In 1955, when Batista extended a general amnesty to political prisoners, Castro was released and went into exile in Mexico. There he developed a political following among other Cuban exiles and planned another rebellion. Castro returned to Cuba in 1957 and launched the armed struggle. By that time, Batista's political corruption, elitism, and oppressive tactics had alienated the Cuban masses. Castro's revolution rapidly gained support, and on December 31, 1958, the Batista government collapsed. Fidel Castro now ruled Cuba with an iron hand of his own.

A confirmed nationalist who resented the long reach of the United States and American corporations in Cuban affairs, Castro yearned to make a statement about the reality of Cuban independence and pull his country out of its orbit around the United States. He was also a socialist who believed that government could ameliorate the vast economic gap between the rich and the poor. Soon after his political triumph, he began nationalizing American-owned property on the island. The Dwight D. Eisenhower* administration in the United States demanded a return of the property or full compensation for it, but Castro defiantly refused to comply. In 1961 he formally proclaimed Cuba a socialist society. The United States then cut its diplomatic ties to Cuba and imposed an economic embargo on all Cuban-produced products. Since then, relations between the two countries have steadily deteriorated. Despite predictions of his imminent demise, Fidel Castro was still firmly in control of Cuba in 2000.

SUGGESTED READINGS: Lee Lockwood, *Castro's Cuba, Cuba's Fidel*, 1969; James S. Olson and Judith E. Olson, *The Cuban-Americans: From Triumph to Tragedy*, 1995; Thomas Paterson, *Contesting Castro: The United States and the Triumph of the Cuban Revolution*, 1994; Richard E. Welch, *Response to Revolution: The United States and Cuba, 1959–1961*, 1985.

THE CAT IN THE HAT. *The Cat in the Hat* (1957), a best-selling book that revolutionized children's literature, was written and illustrated by Theodor Seuss Geisel, known as Dr. Seuss. Seuss was convinced that the existing primers of the day, such as the Dick and Jane series, were hopelessly boring and made no real sense to children. Learning to read, he believed, ought to be fun, not a phonetical bore. *The Cat in the Hat* is a breezy story put to almost musical rhyme. The cat is a mischievous hero playing out a funny story line. Children loved the book, and parents loved reading it to them. *The Cat in the Hat* launched Seuss on a writing career that made him a multimillionaire.

SUGGESTED READING: Ruth K. McDonald, *Dr. Seuss*, 1988.

CAT ON A HOT TIN ROOF. *Cat on a Hot Tin Roof*, a two-act play by Tennessee Williams, opened in New York City at the Morosco Theater on March 24, 1955. Fascinated with the decadence and dysfunctions of Southern life, Tennessee Williams focused on a family in the process of unraveling. Margaret Pollitt, played by Barbara Bel Geddes, is a strong matriarch married to Brick (Ben Gazzara), an alcoholic still living the glory days of his high school football career. He is the son of Mississippi's richest cotton planter, "Big Daddy," played by Burl Ives. At a family reunion, all hell beaks loose. Margaret tells Brick that she has had an affair with his best friend, Skipper, who happens also to be a homosexual. Big Daddy accuses Brick of being a homosexual himself, so Brick in turn reveals to everyone that Big Daddy is dying of cancer. Afraid of being cut out of Big Daddy's will, Margaret then lies, telling everyone that she is pregnant. *Cat on a Hot Tin Roof* had a run of 694 performances on Broadway. It stood in sharp contrast to the idyllic family values programs appearing nightly on television* in the 1950s.

SUGGESTED READING: *New York Times*, March 25, 1955.

CATCHER IN THE RYE. *Catcher in the Rye* (1951) is J. D. Salinger's famous and controversial novel about the odyssey of teenage misfit and prep-school dropout Holden Caulfield, a curious, self-critical, and compassionate moral idealist whose attitudes are controlled by a rigid hatred of hypocrisy. *Catcher in the Rye* is hilariously irreverent, a sarcastic critique of every established institution imaginable. During the late 1950s and throughout the 1960s, *Catcher in the Rye* became required reading in thousands of high school and college American literature courses, and the book influenced the thinking of millions of young American readers. Holden Caulfield became an antihero, a symbolic icon for a decade in which rejection of parents, church, military, and country became the rite of passage for an entire generation of educated young people. The organization, humor, and theme in *Catcher in the Rye* all make it one of the most influential novels in American literary history. It created a pop culture icon that outlasted the age in which it was written, a fan club that forced Salinger into seclusion, and a generation with a new and unprecedented affinity for rebellion.

SUGGESTED READINGS: Frederick Gwynne, *The Fiction of J. D. Salinger*, 1979; Ian Hamilton, *In Search of J. D. Salinger*, 1988.

CENSORSHIP. During the 1950s, the federal courts grappled with the problem of censorship. The First Amendment to the U.S. Constitution specifically prohibits Congress from passing any law abridging freedom of speech and of the press, and the Fourteenth Amendment to the Constitution applies those same restrictions to state and local governments. On the other hand, many constitutional scholars insisted that the Founding Fathers had never intended to protect obscene materials. Defining just what constitutes obscenity became the crucial challenge, as it continues to be today.

The advent of television* in the 1950s escalated the controversy. As Americans watched more television, they attended fewer movies, and film producers began searching for ways to attract consumers back into movie theaters. Cinemascope* and 3-D* were two gimmicks, but offering material on screen that could not be broadcast on television was another way to lure customers to the theater. As film producers offered more salacious material and images, some critics became convinced that moral degradation was overwhelming American values.

In 1952 the U.S. Supreme Court heard *Burstyn v. Wilson*, the decade's first major censorship case. The New York State Board of Regents, which enjoyed legal power to review films and to determine whether they were obscene, had banned the showing of the film *The Miracle* because it was "sacrilegious." In the film, a young peasant girl confuses a local hobo for Saint Joseph and allows him to have sexual intercourse with her. She becomes pregnant. The young girl goes insane, insisting that she is the Virgin Mary and that the infant she carries is the baby Jesus. The film's producer filed a lawsuit, arguing that his First and Fourteenth Amendment rights had been violated. The Court sided with the producer and overturned the powers of the New York State Board of Regents, claiming that "under the First and Fourteenth Amendments a state may not ban a film on the basis of a censor's conclusion that it is 'sacrilegious'."

In 1953, when Earl Warren* became chief justice of the U.S. Supreme Court, the trend toward more liberal obscenity standards continued. Two cases in particular demonstrated the Court's evolving position. In California, David Alberts, a bookseller, had been convicted for advertising and selling "lewd materials." Claiming that his rights to due process had been violated, Alberts filed a lawsuit, and the case of *Alberts v. California* began winding its way through the federal court system. In the second case, the federal government had prosecuted Samuel Roth, who owned a pornographic bookstore. Roth claimed that his Fifth and Fourteenth Amendment rights to due process had been violated, and that his First Amendment right to freedom of expression had also been denied. He filed the *Roth v. United States* lawsuit.

The Supreme Court used both cases to establish new standards on obscenity and censorship. Justice William Brennan* wrote the majority opinion, which upheld the right of government to outlaw obscene materials. He wrote, "All ideas having even the slightest redeeming social importance . . . have the full protection of the guarantees of the First Amendment . . . but implicit in the history of the First Amendment is the rejection of obscenity as utterly without redeeming social importance." That was the easy part. Brennan then had to define obscenity. In doing do, he generated the following statement, which continues to drive federal law today: "Whether to the average person, applying contemporary community standards, the dominant theme of the material taken as a whole appeals to prurient interests." The definition, of course, satisfied few people, since it was so open to interpretation.

In 1959 the Supreme Court had the opportunity to put Brennan's definition to a legal test. In 1958 the New York State Board of Regents had declared the film *Lady Chatterley's Lover** obscene on the grounds that it portrayed adultery as a proper form of behavior. The film's producer, Kingsley International Corporation, sued, and the case reached the Supreme Court in 1959. In *Kingsley International Corporation v. Board of Regents*, the court unanimously overturned the Board of Regents' ban as unconstitutional. Although the film contained controversial material that might offend public morality, its purpose was not to arouse lust.

SUGGESTED READING: Morris Leopold Ernst, *Censorship: The Search for the Obscene*, 1964.

CENTRAL TREATY ORGANIZATION. *See* BAGHDAD PACT.

CHAMBERS, WHITTAKER. David Whittaker Chambers was born Jay Vivian Chambers in Philadelphia, Pennsylvania, on April 7, 1901. His father was a newspaper artist and his mother was a retired actress. He endured an unhappy childhood, primarily because of the deterioration of his parents' marriage. He grew up in Lynbrook, New York, and when his parents separated, he changed his name to David Whittaker Chambers. While he was a student at Columbia University during the 1920s, Chambers joined the Communist party, and in 1925 he went to work for the *Daily Worker* as a translator and linguist. Disillusioned with Stalinism, Chambers quit the party in 1929 and proclaimed himself a socialist instead. His disaffection was short-lived. He rejoined the Communist party in 1931 and became very active in party activities, even engaging in espionage activities on behalf of the Soviet Union. He became very well-connected in the Communist Party of America.

In 1938 Chambers again broke with the party and became a fanatical anticommunist. Henry Luce* hired him to work for *Time* magazine, and he eventually rose to become an editor. In 1948 Chambers appeared before the House Un-American Activities Committee (HUAC), where he testified that the federal government was riddled with communists and former communists. Chambers's allegations resonated during the Red Scare* atmosphere of the late 1940s, but nothing compared to his charges that Alger Hiss,* president of the Carnegie Endowment for World Peace, had spied for the Soviet Union during the 1930s. During the 1930s and World War II, Hiss had been a trusted adviser to the Franklin D. Roosevelt administration.

Hiss vehemently denied the charges, but Chambers stuck by his claims and even produced a series of microfilmed documents, which he had hidden in a carved-out pumpkin, that implicated Hiss. Liberals accused Chambers and Congressman Richard M. Nixon,* who headed the HUAC, of being on a witch-hunt, and in Hiss's first trial for treason, a hung jury could not convict. In a subsequent trial, however, Hiss was convicted of perjury and sentenced to five years in prison. In the meantime, Chambers became a hero to American conservatives. William F. Buckley, Jr.* hired him as an editor and writer for the *National Review*. Throughout the 1950s, Chambers continued to write and speak out about the evils of communism. Chambers died on July 9, 1961.

SUGGESTED READINGS: Whittaker Chambers, *Witness*, 1952; Allen Weinstein, *Perjury: The Hiss-Chambers Case*, 1978.

THE CHANTELS. The Chantels constituted one of the earliest of the so-called girl groups of early rock-and-roll.* Formed in New York City in 1956, the group included Arlene Smith as lead vocalist, Lois Harris, Sonia Goring, Jackie Landry, and Rene Minus. All of them were students at the same parochial high school in the Bronx—Saint Francis de Chantelle School. Their first big hit came in 1958 when they released "Maybe," which reached number two on the rhythm-and-blues charts and number fifteen on the pop charts. Subsequent hits included "Look in My Eyes" (1961) and "Well, I Told You" (1961). The Chantels disbanded in 1970.

SUGGESTED READING: Patricia Romanowski and Holly George-Warren, *The Encyclopedia of Rock & Roll*, 1995.

CHARLES, RAY. Ray Charles was born Charles Ray Robinson in Albany, Georgia, on September 23, 1930, and he was raised in Greenville, Florida. A case of untreated glaucoma began taking away his sight in 1937 and left him blind by the time he was twelve years old. A gifted pianist, he invested his energies in music. From 1937 to 1945, he attended the Saint Augustine School for the Deaf and the Blind, where he learned to play the clarinet, saxophone, trumpet, and organ as well. After the death of his parents, he hit the road playing with dance bands, and so as not to be confused with middleweight boxing champion Sugar Ray Robinson,* he changed his name to Ray Charles.

In 1951, after recording for several independent record companies, he had his first rhythm-and-blues hit—"Baby Let Me Hold Your Hand." He joined the Guitar Slim Band in 1953 and did the arrangement for "The Things That I Used to Do," which sold more than a million copies. Atlantic Records signed Charles in 1954, and there he began to develop what eventually came to be known as "soul" music—a blend of gospel, blues, country, and jazz. Charles's next big hit was "I've Got a Woman," which reached number two on the rhythm-and-blues charts in 1955. His "What'd I Say" in 1959 was a number-one hit on the rhythm-and-blues charts and a number six on the pop charts. He then signed with ABC-Paramount Records and had two more number-one hits in 1960— "Georgia On My Mind" and "Hit the Road, Jack." By the end of the decade, Ray Charles was widely recognized among soul, rock-and-roll,* and country and western performers as "The Genius."

During the 1960s, Charles experienced problems with a heroin addiction. He overcame the habit and returned to his music, adding show tunes, country and western, and jazz standards. In 1986 he was inducted into the Rock and Roll Hall of Fame. He continues to perform today, but he is best known to younger audiences because of his commercials for Pepsi-Cola.

SUGGESTED READINGS: Ray Charles, *Brother Ray: Ray Charles's Own Story*, 1992; Ruth Truk, *Ray Charles: Soul Man*, 1992.

CHERYL CRANE INQUEST. Late on the evening of April 4, 1958, Los Angeles police were summoned to the Beverly Hills home of legendary movie actress Lana Turner. In an upstairs bedroom, they found the body of Johnny Stompanato, Turner's lover and bodyguard of Mickey Cohen, a well-known gambler. Stompanato had been stabbed to death. The media descended on the scene and within hours the whole country knew about the incident. Turner told police that her fourteen-year-old daughter, Cheryl Crane, had committed the murder. Turner and Stompanato had had a stormy and often violent relationship, and on the evening of April 4, during a heated argument, Stompanato had threatened to kill Turner. Cheryl ran to the kitchen, got an eight-inch butcher knife, returned to the bedroom, and plunged it into Stompanato's abdomen, severing his aorta. The inquest held on April 11, 1958, to determine whether Cheryl should stand trial for murder was attended by television* crews from all the major networks and photographers from around the world. After several hours of testimony, a coroner's jury ruled that the murder was justifiable homicide and that Cheryl Crane would not be charged with murder.

SUGGESTED READINGS: Cheryl Crane and Cliff Jahr, *Detour*, 1988; Lana Turner, *Lana: The Lady, the Legend, the Truth*, 1982.

CHESSMAN, CARYL. Caryl Chessman, the so-called Red Light Bandit, was one of the most notorious criminals of the 1950s. Throughout the 1940s in Southern California, the Red Light Bandit, as the press dubbed the criminal, attacked couples parked in cars in secluded places. He mounted a red searchlight on his car so that it would resemble a police car in the dark. He robbed the couples at gunpoint and often took the women back to his car where he raped them. He did not murder them, but many were traumatized badly enough to require long-term psychiatric hospitalization. Chessman had a record as a petty criminal, and on January 23, 1948, police arrested him because his automobile matched a description given by several victims. In the glove compartment of the car, police found a handgun and a small flashlight that resembled the one used by the Red Light Bandit. During his initial custody, Chessman confessed to the crimes.

The police case against Chessman had problems. He retracted his confession, and while several victims positively identified him, other victims just as positively said he was not their attacker. At the trial, Chessman decided to act as his own attorney, and the presiding judge was openly hostile to him. He was convicted under California's "Little Lindbergh" law, which stated that any kidnaping with robbery as a motive was punishable by the death penalty. Actually, the law had been written with kidnaping for ransom in mind, and Chessman's case did not fit that profile. Nevertheless, he was sentenced to death. The court reporter who had taken notes at the trial died before making a verbatim transcript. All of these issues became grist for Chessman's appeal of his death sentence.

Chessman managed to keep his appeal in the judicial system for twelve years, avoiding eight scheduled execution dates. While he was on death row, he wrote *Cell 2455, Death Row* (1954), which became a best-seller, making Chessman a celebrity of sorts. Opponents of capital punishment rallied to his cause, and millions of people signed petitions asking for commutation of his sentence to life. Among those pleading Chessman's cause were Billy Graham* and Eleanor Roosevelt. Conservatives just as passionately argued that Chessman deserved the death penalty for his crimes. On May 2, 1960, Chessman ran out of options, and he was executed in California's gas chamber.

SUGGESTED READINGS: Caryl Chessman, *Cell 2455, Death Row*, 1954; *New York Times*, May 2–4, 1960.

CHEYENNE. *Cheyenne*, one of early television's* most successful Western dramatic series, premiered on ABC on September 20, 1955, starring Clint Walker as Cheyenne Bodie, a tall, strong, Western drifter who every week could be found in another venue in another part of the Old West, destroying villains, romancing pretty women, laboring as a wagon train trail scout, or working as a lawman. At 6 feet, 6 inches in height and 260 pounds, Clint Walker was an imposing figure, and *Cheyenne* exploited his sheer size. The last episode of *Cheyenne* was broadcast on September 13, 1963.

SUGGESTED READING: Tim Brooks and Earle Marsh, *The Complete Directory to Prime Time Network and Cable TV Shows, 1946–Present*, 1995.

THE CHIPMUNKS. The Chipmunks are one of the most unique groups in rock-and-roll* history. David Seville produced the "Chipmunk" sound at first by speeding up a tape. In March 1958 his song "Witch Doctor" reached number one on the pop music charts. He then developed a studio technique revolving around synchronized tracks of music recorded at different speeds, giving the songs their characteristic squeaky, high-pitched sound. Late in 1958, he created three voice characters—Alvin, Theodore, and Simon—and dubbed the trio "The Chipmunks." Their first record, "The Chipmunk Song," was released in December 1958 and rocketed to the top of the music charts, selling 3.5 million copies in just five weeks. They followed that up with several subsequent hits, including "Alvin's Harmonica," "Alvin's Orchestra," "Rudolph the Red-Nosed Reindeer," and "The Alvin Twist." In 1961 CBS gave them a weekly television show, *The Alvin Show*, which music historians remember as the first music video. The show stayed on the air for one season. By 1962 the Chipmunks had been eclipsed by other rock-and-roll groups.

SUGGESTED READING: Patricia Romanowski and Holly George-Warren, *The Encyclopedia of Rock & Roll*, 1995.

CINEMASCOPE. The advent of television* early in the 1950s had confronted Hollywood with a real challenge. Weekly movie attendance fell dramatically in 1950 and 1951 as millions of families chose to stay at home huddled around a television set rather than venture out to a movie theater. Another problem facing the film industry was the fact that most movie houses were located downtown in urban centers, but large numbers of middle-class moviegoers were relocating to the suburbs. Many Americans simply did not want to get in the car and drive downtown at night, particularly since the downtown areas of many cities had acquired a gritty, rundown appearance.

Hollywood producers became desperate for any gimmick or fad that might attract people back to theaters, and Cinemascope, like 3-D,* was one of them. Cinemascope was based on a simple principle: enlarge the screen in movie theaters to make moviegoing seem even more different from television. The conventional ratio of a movie screen was 1.33 times as wide as it was high; in Cinemascope, the screen was 2.5 times as wide as it was high. In 1953 Twentieth Century-Fox released *The Robe*, the first film to be projected in Cinemascope. Unlike 3-D, Cinemascope was highly popular with movie audiences and soon became a staple of the industry.

SUGGESTED READING: Pauline Kael, *5001 Nights at the Movies*, 1982; David Shipman, *The Great Movie Stars: The International Years*, 1972.

THE CISCO KID. *The Cisco Kid*, which premiered in syndication late in 1950, starred Duncan Renaldo as the Cisco Kid and Leo Carrillo as his sidekick, Pancho. Ziv Television eventually produced 156 episodes of *The Cisco Kid*. The character of Cisco had its origins in O. Henry's short story "The Caballero's Way." O. Henry's Cisco was a Robin Hood–type character who robbed the rich to give to the poor. The character was featured in a variety of films and radio series during the 1920s, 1930s, and 1940s. In the television show, Cisco, impeccably dressed in a tailored black suit, drips Latin charm. Atop his horse Diablo, Cisco fights for truth, justice, and romance. Pancho, his sidekick, is everything Cisco is not—fat, dumb, and an expert with a whip. *The Cisco Kid* became one of the most popular children's Western series in television* history. Its last episode was broadcast in 1956, but the show continued to appear in reruns for years.

SUGGESTED READING: Tim Brooks and Earle Marsh, *The Complete Directory to Prime Time Network and Cable TV Shows, 1946–Present*, 1995.

CIVIL RIGHTS ACT OF 1957. The civil rights movement* was in its infancy in the 1950s, highlighted by the U.S. Supreme Court's decision in the *Brown* *v. Board of Education of Topeka, Kansas** case of 1954, which ordered the desegregation* of public schools. Opposition to desegregation assumed enormous proportions in the South, and because Southern Democrats enjoyed so much seniority in Congress, it was extremely difficult to implement civil rights legislation. At the same time, however, African Americans were exerting more and more power in the Democratic party in the North, and their demands for equality generated increasing levels of support. The Civil Rights Act of 1957 was the first civil rights legislation passed at the federal level since Reconstruction. It was a modest measure that established a civil rights commission and a civil rights division in the Department of Justice to investigate cases of individuals being prevented from voting because of their race. The law had few teeth to it and lacked enforcement machinery, but it was a symbolic victory for the fledgling civil rights movement.

SUGGESTED READING: Hugh Davis Graham, *Civil Rights and the Presidency: Race and Gender in American Politics, 1960–1972*, 1992.

CIVIL RIGHTS MOVEMENT. During the 1950s, the civil rights movement, long confined to the federal courts, broke out into a larger political arena in the United States. In 1896 the U.S. Supreme Court had decided in *Plessy v. Ferguson* that racial segregation was constitutional if public facilities were equal for both races. With that decision, the Court gave "separate but equal" a constitutional rationale. For decades, the National Association for the Advancement of Colored People (NAACP) had conducted a legal battle to outlaw de jure discrimination and segregation, or segregation and discrimination by virtue of state and local law. They wanted to overturn *Plessy v. Ferguson*. The NAACP argued that the law should be "color blind" and that every citizen should be treated equally. "Jim Crow," or the legal segregation of black people, should be destroyed according to NAACP lawyers, who were led by Thurgood Marshall.*

In the 1940s, the NAACP began to experience real success in the federal courts. In its 1941 decision in *Mitchell v. United States*, the Supreme Court declared that denying a Pullman sleeping berth on a passenger railroad to a black traveler violated the Interstate Commerce Act. Five years later, in *Morgan v. Virginia*, the court overturned a state law requiring segregation in interstate bus seating. White primary elections were declared unconstitutional in *Smith v. Allwright* (1944), as were literacy tests in *Schnell v. Davis* (1949). Two decisions in 1948—*Shelley v. Kraemer* and *Hard v. Hodge*—declared unconstitutional the so-called restrictive covenants that excluded blacks from certain housing developments.

Three subsequent decisions drove the final nail into the coffin of *Plessy v. Ferguson*. In 1950 the Supreme Court rendered its decision in *Sweatt v. Painter*,* outlawing a Texas statute creating a separate public law school for blacks. During the same session, the court decided *McLaurin v. Oklahoma*,* overturning a University of Oklahoma requirement for segregated seating for black students in its law school. Finally, in *Brown v. Board of Education of*

*Topeka, Kansas** (1954), the Supreme Court specifically overturned *Plessy v. Ferguson* and outlawed racial segregation in public schools.

Most white Southerners resented the court order and staged what they called "massive resistance" to prevent the desegregation of their schools. They fought back in the courts, closed down public schools, and even resorted to violence, as in the 1957 fight over the integration of Central High School in Little Rock, Arkansas.* In face of such blatant refusal to obey the law of the land on the part of Southern whites, black activists resorted to "civil disobedience" of their own. Groups such as the Congress of Racial Equality (CORE), founded by James Farmer in Chicago in 1942, set their sights on ending the segregation of all public facilities in America. CORE first used the tactic of sit-ins to bring about the desegregation of restaurants in Chicago, and CORE chapters soon appeared in other major cities of the Midwest and Northeast. By the late 1950s, CORE was advocating the use of mass protest and passive resistance to achieve its goals.

The modern civil rights movement began on a commuter bus in Montgomery, Alabama. One day in 1955 Rosa Parks, tired after a long day of work, sat down on a city bus and refused to move to a back seat at the request of the driver. He forced her off the bus. The decision set off a chain reaction in which African Americans boycotted Montgomery city buses and pushed the system toward bankruptcy, demanding integration and more black bus drivers. The leader of the boycott, a young minister named Martin Luther King, Jr.,* rocketed to national prominence as the boycotts spread to other Southern cities. Facing bankruptcy, the Montgomery transit system agreed to integrate. King used the bus boycott in Montgomery as a political springboard to launch his nonviolent protest movement against de jure segregation and discrimination.

SUGGESTED READINGS: Numan V. Bartley, *The Rise of Massive Resistance: Race and Politics in the South During the 1950s*, 1969; James Duram, *Moderate Among Extremists: Dwight D. Eisenhower and the School Desegregation Crisis*, 1981; Jennifer L. Hichschild, *The New American Dilemma: Liberal Democracy and School Desegregation*, 1984; Lewis B. Mayhee, ed., *Higher Education in the Revolutionary Decade*, 1967.

CLARK, TOM C(AMPBELL). Tom Campbell Clark was born September 23, 1899, in Dallas, Texas. After graduating from high school, he did a stint in the U.S. Army during World War I. After the war, Clark attended the University of Texas, where he earned an undergraduate degree in 1921 and a law degree in 1922. The Clark family had a long history of activity and influence in Texas Democratic party politics, and Tom Clark joined the family law firm. He practiced there until 1927, when he became the civil district attorney in Dallas. Clark stepped down from that post in 1932 and returned to the family law firm. In 1937, when President Franklin D. Roosevelt appointed him special assistant in the Department of Justice, Clark relocated to Washington, D.C. He specialized in antitrust cases against big business.

During World War II, Clark came to the attention of Senator Harry Truman* of Missouri, who was investigating business fraud. In the antitrust division of the Justice Department, Clark had focused on companies making fraudulent claims on the federal government. In 1943 Roosevelt named Clark assistant attorney general of the United States, and when Roosevelt died in 1945 and Truman became president, Clark was appointed to the cabinet as attorney general of the United States. In that position, Clark proved to be a zealous anticommunist who enforced existing laws against radicalism to the fullest extent. In 1949 Truman nominated Clark as an associate justice of the U.S. Supreme Court and the Senate confirmed him.

Clark took the oath of office as a conservative, but his exposure to the Supreme Court of Chief Justice Earl Warren* soon moderated his judicial and political philosophy. In *Mapp v. Ohio* (1961), for example, Clark wrote the Court's opinion banning the use of illegally seized evidence in state criminal trials. He also wrote the majority opinion in *Abington School District v. Schempp* (1963), which banned the recitation of the Lord's Prayer and Bible readings in public schools. Clark also proved to be an independent justice. In 1952, in *Youngstown Sheet and Tube v. Sawyer,* he voted against President Truman and struck down his seizure of the nation's steel mills. In doing so, he earned the president's wrath.

Clark resigned from the Supreme Court in 1967 when President Lyndon B. Johnson* appointed his son, William Ramsey Clark, as attorney general of the United States. The elder Clark felt that his resignation was necessary to avoid any appearance of conflict of interest. Tom Clark died on June 13, 1977.

SUGGESTED READINGS: Don Larrimer, *Biobibliography of Justice Tom Clark*, 1985; *New York Times*, June 14, 1977; Alvin T. Warnock, *Associate Justice Tom C. Clark: Advocate of Judicial Reform*, 1972.

CLIBURN, VAN. Van Cliburn was born in Fort Worth, Texas, on July 12, 1934. A musical prodigy, he studied piano and attended the Juilliard School in New York City, where he became friends with Rosina Lhevinne, who had graduated from the Kiev Conservatory in the Soviet Union. She helped imbue Cliburn with an appreciation for Russian culture and the Russian musical tradition. In fact, the young Texan became a certifiable Russophile. In 1954 he won the Levintritt Competition, which led to bookings with major orchestras throughout North America.

In 1958 Cliburn's career rocketed into the musical stratosphere. He entered the first Tchaikovsky International Competition, held that year in Moscow, and took the contest by storm. He played Tchaikovsky's First Piano Concerto and Rachmaninoff's Third so brilliantly that jurors decided immediately that he should win the first prize; however, 1958 was at the height of the Cold War,* just six months after the launch of *Sputnik** and *Sputnik II.** The competition's organizers sought permission from Soviet Premier Nikita Khrushchev* to award Cliburn first place. Many die-hard Communist ideologues would not want to admit that capitalism could have produced such genius, but Khrushchev concurred and Cliburn won the prize.

He returned to the United States as a national hero, someone who had beat the Soviets at their own game in their own backyard. President Dwight D. Eisenhower* hosted a special White House reception for Cliburn, and New York City gave him a ticker tape parade, an event usually reserved for war heroes, athletes, and politicians. He signed a contract with RCA, and his recording of a Tchaikovsky concerto became the first classical album in history to sell more than one million copies. Van Cliburn became a household name in the United States. He concertized widely throughout the United States during the next two decades, but critics eventually charged that he had fallen into a creative rut, performing the same pieces in the same way over and over again, never taking risks with his interpretations. Cliburn retired in 1978. A decade later he came out of retirement, but in the United States at least, he never regained the popularity he enjoyed during the late 1950s and early 1960s.

SUGGESTED READINGS: Abram Chasins, *The Van Cliburn Legend*, 1959; Howard Reich, *Van Cliburn*, 1993.

THE COASTERS. The Coasters were one of the most popular rock-and-roll* groups of the late 1950s and early 1960s. Although its membership changed over the years, the group first formed in 1955 around Carl Gardner, Bobby Nunn, Billy Guy, and Leon Hughes. They sang for Atlantic Records, and their first rhythm-and-blues hit came in 1956 with the release of "Down in Mexico." The next year, "Searchin'" hit number three on the pop music charts, adding millions of white fans to their originally black audience. They then moved to New York City. During the next three years, the Coasters had four more top-ten hits—"Yakety Yak," "Charlie Brown," "Along Came Jones," and "Poison Ivy"—and became the most popular black rock-and-roll group in the country. Although they remained popular on the concert tour, their hit records declined in the 1960s, and their last record to make the top forty came in 1971 with "Love Potion No. 9."

SUGGESTED READING: Patricia Romanowski and Holly George-Warren, *The New Encyclopedia of Rock & Roll*, 1995.

COLD WAR. The term "Cold War" has been used for two generations, and recently by historians, to describe the political, economic, and military rivalry between the United States and the Soviet Union and the People's Republic of China from 1945 to 1991. Actually, the Cold War's roots stretch back to the era of World War I. The Bolshevik Revolution in 1917 and the rise of the Communists to power in Russia frightened many Americans, who worried that the new Soviet Union would try to foist revolution on the entire world. Those fears escalated during the 1920s when Soviet authorities launched a concerted attack on Jews and Christian churches, and when news concerning Premier Joseph Stalin's* purges against millions of his own people become known. In 1939 and 1940, when war broke out in Europe and Soviet troops invaded Finland, Estonia, Latvia, Lithuania, and Poland, most Americans became convinced that communism's march across the globe had started.

The United States, of course, was hardly innocent in contributing to the early development of Soviet-American hostility. In 1918–1920, President Woodrow Wilson deployed American troops to Russia to fight against the Bolsheviks during Russia's bloody civil war, and when the Bolsheviks triumphed, the United States had been badly discredited. Also, from 1918 to 1933, the United States refused to extend diplomatic recognition to the Soviet Union on the grounds that it was an illegitimate communist state, and the Soviet authorities resented such ideological persecution. U.S. diplomatic recognition of the Soviet Union did not occur until 1933, when the Great Depression's economic demands made international trade, and hence diplomatic relations, seem imperative.

During World War II, even though the United States and the Soviet Union were allies in the war against Germany and Japan, tensions mounted between the two countries. Because the Soviet Union took such a beating early in the war from the invasion of Germany, Stalin begged President Franklin D. Roosevelt to open a second front in Europe, which would force the Germans to divide their army in two. Roosevelt delayed the invasion until June 1944 to make sure that the U.S. military was fully prepared for such an offensive. The Soviets accused Roosevelt of intentionally delaying the invasion so that the Germans and Soviets would keep killing one another. At the same time, the United States resented the fact that the Soviet Union did not declare war on Japan until August 1945, *after* atomic bombs had been dropped on Hiroshima and Nagasaki. By the time peace came to the world in August 1945, the United States and the Soviet Union had developed mutual resentments and a rivalry that quickly evolved into the Cold War.

The event that precipitated the Cold War was the Soviet Union's refusal after the end of World War II to withdraw its troops from Eastern Europe. Americans intensely debated the decision and the Soviets' unwillingness to allow free elections in Eastern Europe. Many historians of Russia and Eastern Europe claimed that the Soviet presence there was only the latest episode in a centuries-old expansionist imperative among Russian Slavs to unify other Slavic peoples under their authority. Russian Slavs vastly outnumbered other Slavic peoples—Belorussians, Ukrainians, Poles, Czechs, Slovaks, Slovenians, Croatians, Serbs, and Bulgars—and had long dreamed of bringing them into their own political and cultural orbit. Soviet communism reflected only the most recent manifestation of Russian Slavic expansionism.

Liberals in the United States argued that the Soviets were only responding to the disastrous events of the twentieth century. In 1914, with the outbreak of World War I, they had gone to war with Germany and had suffered enormous casualties. And less than a quarter of a century later, Germany had invaded again, this time killing tens of millions of Soviet citizens. Determined to prevent such costly invasions from the West in the future, the Soviets had occupied

Eastern Europe to create a buffer zone there. The next invader of Russia from the West would have to fight its way through several million Soviet troops before ever reaching the Motherland. Such an invasion would be so costly that nobody would ever undertake it.

Political conservatives saw Marxism-Leninism at work. They viewed the Soviet Union's refusal to withdraw from Eastern Europe after the war as positive proof that communism was on a quest to take over the world and that Eastern Europe was only a first step. They warned that Western Europe would be next and then Asia, Africa, the Middle East, and Latin America. To prevent that, the United States had to erect a series of military, diplomatic, economic, and political barriers to Soviet expansion. U.S. foreign policy eventually evolved according to the third view.

In 1947, in an article published in *Foreign Affairs*, former U.S. Ambassador to the Soviet Union George Kennan* called for the "containment" of the Soviet Union. This containment policy* became a new American foreign policy. The United States became committed to containing the Soviet Union behind its 1945 military frontiers. At first, Kennan envisioned containment in political and economic rather than military terms. In 1946 the United States had announced the Truman Doctrine to provide economic assistance to Greece and Turkey in their battles to put down Communist insurgencies, and in the Marshall Plan of 1947–1948, the United States supplied $10 billion to reconstruct the economies of Western and Central Europe. Such assistance was based on the sound logic that stable economies were not fertile breeding grounds for Communist insurgents.

But containment soon assumed a military dimension. In 1947 the Soviet Union cut off highway access to West Berlin. The city of Berlin had been divided at the end of World War II into West Berlin and East Berlin, with the western portion of the city tied to the West and based on democratic elections and capitalism, while East Berlin was completely a Communist entity. The economy of West Berlin thrived, while that of East Berlin deteriorated, and the Soviet Union became embarrassed about the number of East Berliners defecting to West Berlin. Since both West Berlin and East Berlin sat deep inside East Germany, the Soviet Union decided to try to starve West Berlin by prohibiting imports of food, clothing, and fuel.

If West Berlin fell within the Soviet Union's orbit, the containment policy would be undermined, but President Harry Truman* did not want war with the Soviet Union either. Instead of trying to open the highways to West Berlin with ground troops, Truman organized a massive airlift to keep the city in food, clothing, and fuel. Under existing treaty arrangements, the United States had the right to use airspace over East Germany and to fly aircraft into West Berlin. For more than a year, in tens of thousands of sorties, U.S. cargo planes flew in and out of West Berlin. At the end of the year, the Soviet Union backed down and reopened the highways.

The Cold War became even more complex in 1949 when Mao Zedong* and the Chinese Communists succeeded in taking control of China. They renamed the country the People's Republic of China and called for revolution throughout Asia. With the fall of China, the world's most populous country had entered the Communist orbit along with the Soviet Union, the world's geographically largest country. When the Soviet Union detonated its own atomic bomb in 1949, Americans found themselves in a global struggle for survival.

When North Korea invaded South Korea in 1950, the Cold War heated up, and U.S. policy makers began applying the containment doctrine to Asia. When Communist Chinese troops joined the fight late in 1950, the Korean War* threatened to escalate into the dreaded nuclear world war. War raged on the Korean peninsula until an armistice was signed in 1953, but conflict there continued, leaving Korea a potential hot spot in the Cold War during the 1960s, 1970s, and 1980s. Within weeks of the signing of the armistice in Korea in 1953, the Soviet Union detonated its first hydrogen bomb,* elevating American paranoia another notch.

The Korean experience inevitably pulled the United States into the conflict in Indochina, even though the political situation there was vastly different. In both Eastern Europe and Korea, the containment policy had been applied to settings where external Communist military aggression, in the form of Soviet or Communist Chinese troops, had invaded noncommunist states. In Vietnam, nationalists led by Ho Chi Minh* had rebelled against the French empire in Indochina. Ho Chi Minh was certainly a Communist, but he was also a genuine nationalist committed to liberating his country from European imperial domination. In Vietnam, communism was an internal phenomenon tied inextricably with nationalism, not a foreign, oppressive ideology. In 1950 the United States began supplying hundreds of millions of dollars in military and economic assistance to help France keep its colony and defeat Ho Chi Minh. It was all in vain. In 1954, at the Battle of Dien Bien Phu,* France was defeated, and the United States, confusing communism with nationalism, became more deeply involved in Southeast Asia. That involvement would lead to the disastrous Vietnam War* of the 1960s and 1970s.

By the mid-1950s, the Cold War had become a global phenomenon as the United States and the Soviet Union tried to line up client states around the world. To prevent Soviet and Chinese aggression, the United States encouraged the establishment of regional security alliances. The North Atlantic Treaty Organization (NATO), the Southeast Asian Treaty Organization (SEATO), the Central Treaty Organization, the Organization of American States (OAS), and ANZUS (Australia, New Zealand, and the United States) linked the United States with dozens of nations around the world in a mutual endeavor to prevent future Communist aggression.

The Cold War peaked during the 1950s when the Soviet Union launched *Sputnik*,* an artificial satellite, into orbit around the earth. *Sputnik* demonstrated to the entire world that Soviet technology, in many ways, had surpassed that of the United States, and that America's traditional geographical security behind the protection of two oceans was at an end. If the Soviets could put a satellite in orbit, they could deliver nuclear weapons to the United States. By the end of the decade, the United States and the Soviet Union were engaged in a bitter, dangerous struggle for control of the world, with the rivalry played out against a backdrop of possible thermonuclear war.

SUGGESTED READINGS: Douglas S. Blaufarb, *The Counterinsurgency Era: U.S. Doctrine and Performance 1950 to the Present*, 1977; Alexander L. George and Richard Smoke, *Deterrence in American Foreign Policy*, 1974; John Newhouse, *War and Peace in the Nuclear Age*, 1989.

COLE, NAT KING. Nat King Cole was born Nathaniel Adams Cole on March 17, 1919, in Montgomery, Alabama. He was raised in Chicago, where his father was a preacher. By the time he was twelve years old, Nat was playing the piano and organ at church. He then began touring with a band named the Rogues of Rhythm and eventually settled in Los Angeles. In 1937 he formed the King Cole Trio; in 1943, Capitol Records signed them to a recording contract. Their first song, "Straighten Up and Fly Right," was a hit. "The Christmas Song" in 1946 was another huge hit. Cole also earned the respect of jazz purists for his skills at the piano, but it was his smooth, two-octave-range voice that eventually gave him a national reputation and a $10,000 a week income. His deep, rich voice resonated with audiences, who appreciated his delivery, which exhibited his years of playing a jazz piano. In 1950 Cole's song "Mona Lisa" rocketed to the top of the pop charts, selling more than three million single copies.

Cole was a member of the National Association for the Advancement of Colored People and an outspoken advocate of civil rights and equality for black people. During a 1956 concert in Birmingham, Alabama, a white mob attacked him on stage during his performance, and he often experienced racial discrimination at other venues. In spite of it, however, Cole managed to attain a national image because of such hits as "Route 66," "Too Young," "I Love You for Sentimental Reasons," "Walking My Baby Back Home," "Somewhere Along the Way," "Smile," and "Unforgettable." Cole became the first black entertainer to attain the national stature of such legendary white artists as Frank Sinatra* and Tony Bennett.* Cole died of lung cancer on February 15, 1965.

SUGGESTED READINGS: Daniel Mark Epstein, *Nat King Cole*, 1999; *New York Times*, February 15, 1965.

COLLEGE BASKETBALL SCANDALS. In 1951 a huge scandal erupted in the ranks of college basketball. During the previous eighteen years, Coach Clair Bee had made Long Island University (LIU) the premier powerhouse in college basketball. The LIU Blackbirds played in Madison Square Garden before large crowds and a vast radio audience, and winning games assumed a priority over all other things. Bee engaged in shady recruiting tactics and engendered a win-at-all-costs culture on the team, and by the late 1940s more than a few people noted that LIU won games but never covered the point spread set by gamblers. They would win by six points in games they were picked to win by ten, or three points when the odds predicted a five-point win. Suspicions that some LIU players were shaving points, or intentionally winning by less than the point spread in return for cash payments, became widespread. Those rumors were confirmed early in 1951 when a number of LIU players were arrested. The police then arrested players at the City College of New York, New York University, and Manhattan College, casting a shadow of scandal over basketball throughout the Northeast. The scandal then spread west, and players were arrested at such basketball powerhouses as the University of Kentucky, Bradley University, and the University of Toledo.

The college basketball scandals caught the nation off guard. At the height of the Red Scare,* some blamed communism for corrupting the minds of American youth; others saw a decline in moral standards at work. Combined with the West Point scandal* the same year, the college basketball crimes convinced many Americans early in the 1950s that a serious malaise blanketed the country and that it boded ill for the future of America.

SUGGESTED READING: Randy Roberts and James Olson, *Winning Is the Only Thing: Sports in America Since 1945*, 1989.

COLOR TELEVISION. *See* TELEVISION.

COMMON MARKET. After World War II, faced with the overwhelming economic power of the United States, European leaders began discussing ways of rebuilding their own economies. Economic theory predicted that if trade barriers between the countries of Europe could be removed, economic growth would accelerate. In 1950 French foreign minister Robert Schuman called for a common market in which tariffs over the shipment of coal and steel would be eliminated. In 1952 the so-called Schuman Plan received the endorsement of France, West Germany, Italy, Belgium, Luxembourg, and the Netherlands; and the European Coal and Steel Community (ECSC) was founded. The steel industry boomed in Europe.

In 1957 Belgium, West Germany, Italy, France, the Netherlands, and Luxembourg signed the Treaty of Rome, which established the European Economic Community (EEC), nicknamed the Common Market. It expanded the ECSC principles to other industries, exempting agriculture. The signatories also formed the European Atomic Energy Community (EURATOM). In 1960 Austria, Great Britain, Denmark, Norway, Portugal, Sweden, and Switzerland formed a similar pact known as the European Free Trade Association (EFTA). Finally, in 1967, the EEC, ECSC, and EURATOM fused into the European Community (EC). Ireland, Denmark, and Great Britain have subsequently joined the EC.

SUGGESTED READING: Paul Armitage, *The Common Market*, 1978.

CONANT, JAMES BRYANT. James Bryant Conant was born in Dorchester, Massachusetts, on March 26, 1893. He was educated at the Roxbury Latin School and entered Harvard in 1910. A brilliant chemist, Conant earned a bachelor's degree at Harvard in 1914 and his Ph.D. in 1916. During World War I, he worked for the federal government developing poison gas weapons systems, and in 1919 he took an assistant professorship in the chemistry department at Harvard. He performed brilliant work on the chemical composition of chlorophyll, and in 1929 he became Sheldon Emery Professor of Organic Chemistry. Two years later, he was named chair of the chemistry department. In 1933 he was named president of Harvard, a post he filled for the next twenty years. During World War II, he served as a scientific and political advisor on the Manhattan Project, which developed the atomic bomb.

As president of Harvard, Conant became a strong advocate of the merits of a liberal education, which he defined as scientific and mathematical literacy and a strong founding in the history and values of Western civilization. Students with such a liberal education, he believed, could think critically and adjust to the inevitable changes that would come to business and society. In 1953, at the age of sixty, Conant stepped down as president of Harvard to become U.S. ambassador to West Germany.

During the rest of his career, Conant focused his attention on what he called the "crisis in American public school education." The Soviet Union's success in launching *Sputnik*,* an artificial satellite, into orbit convinced tens of millions of Americans that the technological gap between the Communists and the West could be addressed only through education. Conant's solution was to create in public schools specific educational "tracks" for "gifted," "average," and "slow" students. Through the liberal use of intelligence tests, school administrators would group students into tracks and design separate curricula for their abilities. The tracks would be followed throughout a high school student's career. Gifted students would be prepared for higher education by classes rich in science, mathematics, technology, and foreign languages; slower students would be prepared for vocational careers. In the future, Conant argued, American public high schools would have to develop a comprehensive curriculum to serve a wide variety of students. Only in good public schools would democracy survive. Conant also urged more direct parental involvement in the public schools. Conant's ideas had a dramatic impact on public school policy throughout the 1950s and 1960s. James Conant died on February 12, 1978.

SUGGESTED READINGS: James B. Conant, *The American High School Today*, 1959, and *My Several Lives: Memoirs of a Social Inventor*, 1970; *New York Times*, February 12, 1978.

CONSUMER CULTURE. During the 1950s, consumerism became the dominant force in American popular culture. When World War II ended, so did the shortages in consumer goods that had characterized the American economy since the bombing of Pearl Harbor. Most Americans had accumulated substantial savings during the war—largely because of high wages, overtime pay, and a lack of consumer goods—and they were ready to buy. The advent of television,* financed by mass advertising campaigns from Madison Avenue, made consumerism a new American religion. Happiness could be found, so the prevailing mantra went, in the purchase of ever increasing volumes of consumer goods: cars, homes, furniture, appliances, clothing, vacations, and so on. The consumer culture boosted the American economy, making it the most powerful and prosperous in the world.

The consumer culture, however, invited intense criticism from intellectuals and moralists, most of whom tried to call attention to the emptiness of the consumer culture, and to its opportunity costs. A host of books appeared that criticized the impact of consumerism and conformity in American culture. The first assault on the consumer came in 1950 with the publication of *The Lonely Crowd** by David Riesman, Nathan Glazer, and Reuel Denney. *The Lonely Crowd* was an indictment of middle-class consumerism and the pressures for conformity that so characterized the 1950s. The book claimed that most Americans were "other-directed" rather than "inner-directed"—dominated by the expectations of consumer-obsessed peers, as expressed by advertisers in the mass media, rather than by "inner-directed" individualistic needs. One might think that other-directed people would fit into groups better and that society would be more cooperative, but in actuality, it led to alienation because people did not cooperate out of personal conviction but only out of an empty need to belong.

In 1955 Sloan Wilson's novel *The Man in the Gray Flannel Suit** picked up some of those themes and became a best-seller. The book concerns a fictional family obsessed with "keeping up with the Joneses." They try to find happiness in the conformist world of post–World War II America, where consumer values frown on dissent and individuality. The husband works for a large company where middle managers are expected to wear gray flannel suits, long-sleeved white dress shirts, conservative ties, and polished black shoes. Eventually, they tire of the emptiness of it all and conclude that the values of corporate and suburban America are hollow and, in the long run, very unsatisfying.

In his 1957 book *The Hidden Persuaders*,* Vance Packard argues that the modern economy has produced a great variety of businesses competing to sell essentially similar products. The differences between varieties of a soft drink, peanut butter, or beer are minimal, so companies hire psychologists to determine consumer tastes and biases and marketing experts to link those tastes to certain products. They use colors, celebrities, and sexuality to make products seem more inherently attractive. Between 1950 and 1960, advertising expenditures jumped from $5.7 billion annually to $12 billion. Packard lamented the rise of a consumer society, where the purchase of an endless series of products seemed to become an end in itself. Americans had come to link happiness and success in life with the acquisition of more and more and bigger and bigger goods, and Vance Packard described just how advertisers had brought about this consumer culture.

Harvard economist John Kenneth Galbraith approached the problem from a similar perspective. In his 1958 book *The Affluent Society*,* Galbraith argues that consumerism has produced a vast gap between private wealth and public squalor. Although large numbers of Americans were very prosperous, a large minority suffered from poverty, unemployment, and homelessness. Galbraith lambasted the conventional wisdom that long-term economic growth could be based on increases in the production of consumer goods. The result, Galbraith claimed, was a "social imbalance" of prosperity on the one hand but decaying infrastructure and poverty on the other.

The Organization Man* is the title of William Whyte's scathing attack on modern American society. Published in 1956, the book claims that because of corporate values, bureaucracy, and the consumer culture, America had lost touch with its Puritan roots and the ethic of hard work, self-reliance, and innovation. Modern society, Whyte argued, destroyed individual initiative in the name of group cooperation, which inevitably led to rigid, highly structured institutions whose primary goal was self-perpetuation. Although Whyte acknowledged that cooperation was necessary in society, he also feared that the demands of corporations and bureaucracies stifled initiative, creativity, and the expression of individual values.

In 1959 Vance Packard came out with *The Status Seekers*, a book that assails consumer culture. In it, Packard claims that Americans have become obsessed with the acquisition of consumer goods, not because they need them but because the ownership of them conveys status in a society that has forgotten its core values. Happiness, too many Americans believed, came not from religion, strong families, and healthy marriages but from the possession of fancy cars, the latest fashions, and modern electrical conveniences, all of which increased one's status in the society.

SUGGESTED READINGS: Erik Barnouw, *Tube of Plenty*, 1990; John Kenneth Galbraith, *The Affluent Society*, 1958; Vance Packard, *The Hidden Persuaders*, 1957, and *The Status Seekers*, 1959; David Riesman, Nathan Glazer, and Reuel Denney, *The Lonely Crowd*, 1950; William H. Whyte, *The Organization Man*, 1956 ; Sloan Wilson, *The Man in the Gray Flannel Suit*, 1955.

CONTAINMENT POLICY. The doctrine of "containment" was the key U.S. foreign policy of the post–World War II era. First pronounced by George Kennan,* former U.S. ambassador to the Soviet Union, in a 1947 article published in *Foreign Affairs*, "containment" was committed to keeping the Soviet Union confined behind its 1945 military boundaries. In other words, the United States was essentially willing to let Eastern Europe slip into the Soviet orbit, since Soviet troops had occupied the region since 1944. For all intents and purposes, the United States would acquiesce in the Soviet domination of Estonia, Latvia, Lithuania, East Germany, Poland, Czechoslovakia, Hungary, Yugoslavia, and Bulgaria. At the same time, the United States would work diligently to prevent Soviet expansion to points farther west.

In the beginning, containment was primarily nonmilitary, focusing on economic and technical assistance, and it was embodied in such programs as the Marshall Plan in 1948 to rebuild the European economies and the Truman Doctrine in 1947 to provide the funds needed by Greece and Turkey to fight Communist guerrillas. As the Cold War* escalated in the late 1940s, however, containment took on new global, military dimensions. Its first real test came in 1948 when the Soviet Union sealed off West Berlin in hope of starving the city into submission and incorporation into the Eastern Bloc. President Harry Truman* mounted the Berlin airlift to keep the city fed and supplied until the Soviet Union backed down.

After the fall of China in 1949, containment came to imply the encirclement of the People's Republic of China and the Soviet Union with a network of military alliances: the North Atlantic Treaty Organization, the Baghdad Pact,* the Southeast Asia Treaty Organization, and the enormous military buildup of the 1950s and 1960s. When the North Koreans invaded South Korea in 1950, the United States intervened in the conflict in the name of containment. Containment reached its peak during the Dwight D. Eisenhower* years and the tenure of Secretary of State John Foster Dulles* (1953 to 1959).

When the French were expelled from Indochina after the Battle of Dien Bien Phu* in 1954, the United States began increasing its commitment to prevent a Communist takeover. American policy makers were applying the containment doctrine to Vietnam, assuming that Soviet and Chinese aggression were behind the North Vietnamese crusade to reunite the country. The domino theory* and the containment policy fit nicely together in the 1950s and early 1960s. Not until the mid-1960s, when American policy makers began to see that communism was not a single, monolithic movement orchestrated from Moscow, did the application of containment to Vietnam begin to seem counterproductive. Ho Chi Minh,* the leading Communist in Vietnam, was not an external, foreign invader of the country but a nationalist committed to liberating Vietnam of French imperial authority. In applying the containment doctrine to Indochina, the United States made a fundamental miscalculation that led to the disastrous Vietnam War.* By the late 1960s and early 1970s, American policy makers accepted the importance of colonialism and nationalism in the history of the anti-French and anti-American movements in Vietnam. By that time as well, American policy makers realized that communism was a polycentric movement requiring creative, individual responses.

Still, containment remained at the core of U.S. foreign policy. When the Soviet Union invaded Afghanistan in 1979, American policy makers worried that the Soviets were making a run for control of the Persian Gulf. Throughout the 1980s, the United States provided technical an economic assistance to the Afghan guerrillas fighting against the Soviet army. As an expression of U.S. foreign policy, containment survived until the disintegration of the Soviet Union in 1991. Even today, it continues to exert an impact on many American policy makers, who keep a wary eye on Russia.

SUGGESTED READINGS: Douglas S. Blaufarb, *The Counterinsurgency Era: U.S. Doctrine and Performance 1950 to the Present*, 1977; John L. Gaddis, "Containment: A

Reassessment," *Foreign Affairs* 55 (July 1977), 873–87; Alexander L. George and Richard Smoke, *Deterrence in American Foreign Policy*, 1974.

COOK, SAM. Sam Cook was born in Chicago, Illinois, on January 22, 1935. A gifted songwriter and performer, he became an icon among "soul" music crooners because of his suave, smooth, and sophisticated style. By 1951 he was widely recognized on the gospel music circuit, where he was lead vocalist for the Soul Stirrers, and in 1957 he became a pop sensation when his song "You Send Me" sold 1.7 million records and reached number one on the pop music charts. In quick succession, he produced a string of top pop hits, including "Only Sixteen" (1959), "Everybody Loves to Cha Cha" (1959), "Chain Gang" (1960), "Wonderful World" (1960) "Sad Mood" (1961), "Twistin' the Night Away" (1962), "Bring It On Home to Me" (1962), "Another Saturday Night" (1963), and "Shake" (1965). On December 11, 1964, Cook was killed under suspicious and still unresolved circumstances. The night manager of a Los Angeles hotel said that she shot Cook after he raped another guest and then tried to assault her. The authorities ruled the death justifiable homicide, but unanswered questions still raise doubts about the nature of Cook's death.

SUGGESTED READINGS: *New York Times*, December 12–13, 1964; Patricia Romanowski and Holly George-Warren, *The New Encyclopedia of Rock & Roll*, 1995.

COOPER, GARY. Gary Cooper was born Frank James Cooper in Helena, Montana, on May 7, 1901. He attended Grinnell College in Iowa for two years but then moved to Los Angeles in 1924. He worked as a door-to-door salesman until Warner Brothers hired him to work for $10 a day as a rider in Western films. Upon hearing that Tom Mix was making $15,000 a week as a movie cowboy, Cooper changed his name to Gary and got some bit parts. His first major role came in 1926 in the film *The Winning of Barbara Worth*. He soon hit pay dirt in Hollywood, and in 1929 and 1930, Cooper starred in ten films, including *Virginian* and *Morocco*. In the process, he became a pop culture icon as an All-American hero. Tall, handsome, and laconic, Cooper became America's leading man. He won an academy award for his 1940 role in *Sergeant York*.

During the late 1940s and early 1950s, when the Red Scare* swept through Hollywood, Cooper's conservative Republican political philosophy made him suspect among liberals. But he was less outspoken than people like John Wayne,* and he did not make as many enemies. His performance in the controversial film *High Noon** (1953) won him his second academy award. By that time Cooper's health was slipping, and he was old for a fifty-two-year-old man. He made his last film, *The Naked Edge*, in 1960 and died of cancer on May 13, 1961.

SUGGESTED READINGS: Jeffrey Myers, *Gary Cooper: American Hero*, 1998; *New York Times*, May 14, 1961.

COOPER V. AARON **(1958).** In the *Cooper v. Aaron* case of 1958, the U.S. Supreme Court finally settled the controversy surrounding the desegregation of Central High School in Little Rock, Arkansas.* Lawyers for the Little Rock school district claimed that because white hostility over integration was so intense, the safety of black children could not be guaranteed in the public schools and that, therefore, school segregation needed to be continued. The National Association for the Advancement of Colored People insisted that the police powers had to be employed to protect individual rights, and that the hostility of some people in the society was not reason enough to deny rights to others. The Supreme Court agreed and ordered school officials to find a way to guarantee the safety of schoolchildren and to integrate the schools. They did. In 1959 Central High School in Little Rock, Arkansas, opened without serious incident to black or white students.

SUGGESTED READINGS: Elizabeth Huckaby, *Crisis at Central High: Little Rock, 1957–1958*, 1980; Robert Sherrill, *Gothic Politics in the Deep South: Stars of the New Confederacy*, 1968; 358 U.S. 1 (1958).

CRANE, CHERYL. *See* CHERYL CRANE INQUEST.

CREDIT CARD. Credit cards have been a fixture of American retailing since the late 1800s, when department stores, and later oil companies, allowed customers to make purchases and pay their bills at the end of the month. The idea of a general third-party credit card that could be used at a variety of establishments had to wait until 1950. After World War II, with the boom in consumer purchases, the market was ripe for a revolution in the consumer credit industry, and Frank X. McNamara came up with the Diner's Club* card. A New York City attorney, McNamara one evening in 1950 found himself without cash at a Manhattan restaurant. He decided it would be a real convenience to customers and a good marketing idea for restaurants to develop a credit card that could be used to buy meals at restaurants. McNamara's company would reimburse restaurants for their bills, and then he would bill the customers. Restaurants would pay McNamara a small fee per transaction, and he would charge interest to cardholders each month. Essentially, McNamara was extending unsecured loans to cardholders. Along with Alfred Bloomingdale and Ralph Snyder, McNamara established the Diner's Club and signed up 27 upscale Manhattan restaurants. By early 1951, the Diner's Club was collecting more than $1 million a year.

McNamara, Bloomingdale, and Snyder decided to expand the Diner's Club purchasing power beyond restaurants to other consumer goods. The Diner's Club card could be used to purchase goods and services at a variety of places around the country. Diner's Club became the third party to the transaction, extending credit to the customer, providing customers to the seller, and charging them both for the service. The Diner's Club saw credit as the product they were selling, not any particular commodity, service, or brand name. It was an uphill struggle. The airline, retail, and oil companies fought the idea because it competed with them, and many merchants resented the fee they were charged. Nevertheless, Diner's Club stayed the course and pioneered a new industry.

Other entrepreneurs soon thought of expanding the card idea beyond the world of restaurants and cafes. In 1958 American Express marketed a card for travel expenses, and within three months they had issued 250,000 cards. The idea of a general-use credit card that could be employed at all kinds of retail establishments would be the next step, and in 1959 the Bank of America in California issued the BankAmericard, which eventually evolved into the Visa card. It was the birth of a new industry that would revolutionize banking, finance, and consumerism.

SUGGESTED READING: Lewis Mandell, *The Credit Card Industry: A History*, 1990.

THE CRUCIBLE. *The Crucible*, written by Arthur Miller, premiered at the Martin Beck Theater in New York City on January 22, 1953. Deeply concerned about violations of civil liberties taking place during the Red Scare* in the late 1940s and early 1950s, playwright Arthur Miller decided to write a play about bigotry, fear, and dictatorship. He set the play, starring Madeleine Sherwood, Fred Stewart, Arthur Kennedy, and Beatrice Straight, late in seventeenth-century Massachusetts at the peak of the Salem witch trial paranoia. The politically charged atmosphere allows innuendo to be accepted as fact and leads to the executions of innocent people. The play is preachy and didactic, more a product of Miller's outrage than his writing skills, but it did serve as a statement against Senator Joseph McCarthy* and others who railroaded innocent people because of their political beliefs. *The Crucible* had a run of 197 performances.

SUGGESTED READINGS: Gerald Bordman, *The Oxford Companion to American Theater*, 1992; *New York Times*, January 23, 1953.

CUBA. During the 1950s, the island nation of Cuba came to symbolize the complex issues involved in the Cold War.* In 1952 Fulgencio Batista staged a military coup d'etat and established dictatorial control over the island. His political despotism caught Latin American observers off guard. Between 1933 and 1944, Batista had presided over Cuba as president and had earned a reputation for good government, at least in the context of what that meant in Latin America. He did line his pockets and those of his close associates, but he also championed good government, ran a relatively efficient bureaucracy, and developed a stable economy. When he voluntarily retired in 1944, the country was in good condition, politically stable and more prosperous than ever before.

No sooner did he retire than the country collapsed into a sea of corruption, economic decline, and political exploitation. Cubans all but begged Batista to return to power, and in 1952 he did so, staging a military coup and taking an iron grip on the country. This time, however, Batista did not have a reform bone left in his body. He suspended all political liberties, went into league with the wealthiest landowners who owned the largest sugar plantations, and presided over an enormous widening in the gap between the rich and the poor. He negotiated lucrative relationships with the American mafia, which controlled the drug, gambling, and prostitution rackets in Havana, and with large, multinational American corporations that had invested huge amounts of money in Cuba. The U.S. government essentially became a coconspirator in the arrangement, because of Batista's bitter anticommunism. In the rhetoric of the Cold War, he hated communism and seemed to maintain political stability and a pro-U.S. posture at home. The U.S. government had no difficulty in dealing with Fulgencio Batista, even if he was a hopeless despot.

Poverty, suffering, and seething discontent soon spawned revolutionary dissidents, none of them more charismatic than Fidel Castro,* a young attorney. On July 26, 1953, Castro launched an insurrection against Batista, but it failed miserably. The attempted rebellion was premature and poorly planned. Castro was sentenced to fifteen years in prison, and his rebellion was soon known among Cuban revolutionaries as the "26th of July Movement." He was paroled in 1955 and went to live in Mexico, where he continued to plot Batista's overthrow. In 1957 Castro returned to Cuba, hiding out in mountainous jungles and adopting "Cuba for Cubans" as his rallying cry.

Most of Cuba's six million citizens were willing to listen, especially the landless peasants, poor urban workers, and middle-class businessmen who felt that the United States had a stranglehold on the Cuban economy and were underwriting the Batista regime. Many of Castro's claims were valid. American companies owned 40 percent of the Cuban sugar industry, 10 percent of the mines, 80 percent of public utilities, and controlling interests in banking, tourism, and oil refining. Batista had personally siphoned off $40 million of Cuban assets for his personal accounts and had imprisoned or killed most of his political opponents.

Fidel Castro and his Fidelistas steadily recruited more and more support from the Cuban masses, and Batista's political base became increasingly confined to an elite few. On January 1, 1959, the Fidelistas overran Havana. Batista fled into exile, taking his millions with him, and Cubans poured into the streets in celebration. Anti-Batista rhetoric mixed closely with anti-American pronouncements, and Fidel Castro assumed virtually dictatorial powers.

Castro then worked to fulfill his revolutionary promises. For landless peasants, he expropriated millions of acres of American-owned property—more than $1 billion worth—and distributed it to peasants. In the process, Castro became the most popular man in the history of Cuba. "Cuba is no longer dedicated to the service of her millionaires," he proudly announced.

The Dwight D. Eisenhower* administration, at the behest of American corporations angry that their assets in Cuba were going up in revolutionary smoke, demanded the return of the property, but Castro refused. Castro then turned on the gambling, drug, and prostitution industries in Cuba, most of which were controlled by organized crime elements in the United States. They, in turn, organized assassination attempts on Castro, all of which failed. Finally, in February 1960, Castro signed a contract in which the Soviet Union agreed to purchase five million tons of Cuban sugar. When U.S.-owned oil refineries refused to purchase Soviet oil, Castro seized the refineries. By the end of 1960, the United States had imposed a trade embargo on Cuba and cut diplomatic ties. In defiance of the Monroe Doctrine, a Soviet-satellite state now existed in the Caribbean.

SUGGESTED READINGS: Thomas Paterson, *Contesting Castro: The United States and the Triumph of the Cuban Revolution*, 1994; Richard E. Welch, *Response to Revolution: The United States and Cuba, 1959–1961*, 1985.

CUBAN AMERICANS. During the 1950s, the United States served as a beacon for political refugees from Communist countries, but by far the most spectacular and enduring immigration came from Cuba.* On January 1, 1959, Fidel Castro* seized power in Cuba from the corrupt regime of Fulgencio Batista and quickly implemented a series of reforms that launched the so-called Golden Exile. The Castro government's left-wing philosophy became abundantly clear when it began expropriating property and engaging in socialist rhetoric. Between January 1 and June 30, 1959, a total of 26,527 Cubans immigrated to the United States. By the end of the year, that number exceeded 56,000 people. Most of them were well-to-do Cubans who had been closely associated with the Batista government or with American-owned companies. South Florida in general, and Miami in particular, became their destination of choice.

They arrived in the United States dedicated to overthrowing Castro and regaining their former lives. The refugees were certain that Castro could not hold on for long, that the revolutionaries would self-destruct or that the United States, as it had so often done in the past, would restore the upper class to power and protect its own investments on the island. But the exodus of Cuba's highly educated, upper-class elite, while badly damaging the country's economy, actually made another revolution less likely, allowing Castro to consolidate his political authority. He redistributed land to the country's most desperately poor peasants, implemented universal health care, vastly improved Cuba's public education system, and engaged in a steady stream of anti-American rhetoric, blaming the United States for allowing organized crime to penetrate Cuba and drown the country in a sea of gambling, prostitution, pornography, and drugs. In 1999, forty-one years after the revolution, Cuban Americans were still waiting for the demise of the Castro regime.

SUGGESTED READINGS: James S. Olson and Judith E. Olson, *The Cuban-Americans: From Triumph to Tragedy*, 1995; Thomas Paterson, *Contesting Castro: The United States and the Triumph of the Cuban Revolution*, 1994; Richard E. Welch, *Response to Revolution: The United States and Cuba, 1959–1961*, 1985.

CUSHING, RICHARD CARDINAL. Richard James Cushing, a native of Boston, Massachusetts, was born on August 24, 1895. His family consisted of devout Irish Catholics, and he was destined for the clergy. Cushing first attended

Boston College and then in 1921 graduated from Saint John's Seminary. Upon his graduation, he took his vows as a Roman Catholic priest. Gregarious and political in the best sense of the word, Cushing labored for two years as a parish priest in Roxbury and Somerville, Massachusetts, and he came to the attention of his superiors because of his abilities to put parish finances in order. In 1922 he was appointed assistant director of the Society for the Propagation of the Faith in Boston, where he quickly established a reputation as a fund-raiser without peer. He became director of the society in 1925. The archbishopric of Boston was one of the premier institutions of the American Church, and as Cushing's reputation there grew, so did his profile in Rome. In 1939 he was appointed auxiliary bishop of Boston, and five years later, he became bishop. Cushing remained at the head of the archbishopric for the rest of his life.

Cushing also developed a strong political profile during the 1950s. He was an inveterate anticommunist and sympathized with the Red Scare* tactics of Senator Joseph McCarthy* of Wisconsin. For Cushing, communism was atheistic, amoral, and aggressive, the equivalent of the anti-Christ, and he wanted to see it destroyed. In 1958 the Vatican raised him to cardinal. Cushing was closely associated with the Democratic party in Boston, and he counted the family of Joseph Kennedy among his closest friends. When John F. Kennedy* was elected president of the United States in 1961, Cushing's reputation grew even more, and he became the most influential Roman Catholic prelate of his era. He was also a strong supporter of the reforms implemented by Vatican II. Richard Cardinal Cushing died on November 2, 1970.

SUGGESTED READINGS: John H. Cutler, *Cardinal Cushing of Boston*, 1970; *New York Times*, November 3, 1970.

D

DAMN YANKEES. *Damn Yankees*, a two-act musical comedy, opened at the 46th Street Theater in New York City on May 5, 1955. The play was based on a book by George Abbott and Douglass Wallop, and Jerry Ross and Richard Adler supplied the music and lyrics. *Damn Yankees* tells the story of Joe Boyd (Robert Shafer), an aging, frustrated outfielder for the lowly Washington Senators who wants more than anything else to dethrone the New York Yankees* and lead the Senators to the World Series. When he screams out that he would surrender his soul for that opportunity, the devil magically appears as a Mr. Applegate, played by Ray Walston. Applegate instantly transforms Boyd into a young, gifted athlete named Joe Hardy, played by Stephen Douglass. Eventually, Hardy tires of it all, even though he is successful, because he misses his wife. Applegate produces the lovely Lola (Gwen Verdon) to comfort him, but Hardy spurns her and eventually returns home, renouncing the deal with the devil and sending the Senators into a tailspin. The most memorable songs from *Damn Yankees* include "You Gotta Have Heart," "Shoeless Joe from Hannibal, Mo.," "Whatever Lola Wants," "Near to You," and "Two Lost Souls." *Damn Yankees* had a run of 1,019 performances.

SUGGESTED READINGS: Gerald Bordman, *The Oxford Companion to American Theater*, 1992; *New York Times*, May 6, 1955.

THE DANNY THOMAS SHOW. *The Danny Thomas Show*, one of television's most successful situation comedies, premiered as *Make Room for Daddy* on ABC on September 29, 1953, starring comedian Danny Thomas as Danny Williams, a night club entertainer, and Jean Hagen as his wife, Margaret. Rusty Hamer played his six-year-old son, Rusty, and Sherry Jackson, his eleven-year-old daughter, Terry. Louise Beavers and then Amanda Randolph played Louise, the sardonic maid in the Williams household. The show was renamed *The Danny Thomas Show* beginning with the 1957 season. Jean Hagen had quit the show that year, and after a year in which Danny Williams courted several women, he married Kathy O'Hara, played by Marjorie Lord. The premise of the show had the loud-mouthed but soft-hearted Danny Williams trying to cope with the antics of his rambunctious children. Actor Hans Conreid appeared frequently as Uncle Tonoose, the wisecracking patriarch of the family. *The Danny Thomas Show* remained on the air until its last broadcast on September 2, 1971.

SUGGESTED READING: Tim Brooks and Earle Marsh, *The Complete Directory to Prime Time Network and Cable TV Shows, 1946–Present*, 1995.

DAVIS, MILES. Miles Davis was born in Alton, Illinois, on May 25, 1926. His father was a dentist. A gifted musician on the trumpet, he worshiped Dizzy Gillespie and Charlie Parker, and in 1949 he recorded *Birth of the Cool*, a highly introspective album that garnered him enormous respect among jazz musicians. Davis was well known as a musical genius among jazz aficionados, but after his 1955 appearance at the Newport Jazz Festival,* he rocketed to the top of the profession. He then assembled what many consider the best jazz quintet in history—Davis on trumpet, John Coltrane on the saxophone, Red Garland on piano, Paul Chambers on bass, and Philly Jo Jones on piano. Until Davis came along, jazz had been wedded to bebop music with its busy, cascading sounds, but the jazz that Davis played was plaintive and even mournful, smooth and extraordinarily introspective. Creative and innovative, Davis remained at the top of the world of jazz into the 1970s, by which time he had blended jazz and rock into a new musical form known as fusion. Miles Davis died on September 28, 1991.

SUGGESTED READINGS: George Crisp, *Miles Davis*, 1997; *New York Times*, September 29, 1991.

DAVY CROCKETT. One of the great fads of the 1950s was engendered by Walt Disney's television series *Davy Crockett*, broadcast in three episodes over ABC television in 1955. Loosely, indeed very loosely, based on the life of America's nineteenth-century frontier hero Davy Crockett, the series garnered a television audience in the tens of millions and spawned a cottage industry of related paraphernalia. "The Ballad of Davy Crockett," the program's theme song, sold more than four million copies when it was released later that year. Books on Davy Crockett's life were published and republished, and more than fourteen million copies were sold in 1955 and 1956. Disney also licensed more than 3,000 Davy Crockett merchandise items, including coonskin hats, lunch boxes, T-shirts, toy and real guns, towels, ukeleles, fishing gear, comic books, underwear, tooth brushes, and dolls.

SUGGESTED READINGS: Richard Schickel, *The Disney Version*, 1968; Steven Watts, *The Magic Kingdom: Walt Disney and the American Way of Life*, 1997.

DEAN, JAMES. James Dean, the quintessential icon of the 1950s, was born on February 8, 1931, in Marion, Indiana. Orphaned as a child, he was raised by relatives and found an outlet for his confused identity on stage. After high school, he went to the University of California at Los Angeles (UCLA) and studied acting under James Whitmore. While at UCLA he won roles as an extra in *Sailor Beware* (1951), *Fixed Bayonets* (1951), and *Has Anybody Seen My Gal?* (1952). Whitmore recognized his talent and sent him to New York to hone his skills. Dean studied at the Actor's Studio under Lee Strasberg, where he became a devotee of "the Method," in which actors attempted to understand the psyche, emotions, and motivations of the characters they played. He also secured parts in two Broadway plays, *See the Jaguar* (1952) and *The Immortalist* (1954). Elia Kazan caught a performance of *The Immortalist* and was impressed. At the time Kazan was casting his film *East of Eden*, and he offered Dean the role of Cal. The film, based on John Steinbeck's novel of the same name, was a hit, and Dean received critical praise.

That success earned him the part that cemented his place in pop culture history. In the 1955 film *Rebel Without a Cause*,* Dean played Jim Stark, a teen-aged boy ridden with angst and tormented by a sense of alienation that he cannot understand. He rebels against parents, teachers, police, and the world at large, but not for any purpose except rebellion as an end in itself. His costume for the film—an open leather jacket over a white T-shirt with blue jeans and boots—caught the fancy of millions of American teenagers, who saw in Jim Stark an alter ego for their own growing restlessness with the conformity of the 1950s.

In his third major film role, Dean was once again a rebel, but this time with a cause—making money. In *Giant*, he played Jet Rink, the Texas oil wildcatter who strikes it rich. One day after finishing the shooting on *Giant*, on September 30, 1955, Dean got into his new Porsche, revved it up to 115 miles per hour, and collided with another car. Dean was killed instantly. Three weeks later, *Rebel Without a Cause* was released. Dean's death, of course, guaranteed huge moviegoing audiences, and he all but became a saint in American pop culture, worshiped in death by millions of teenagers.

SUGGESTED READINGS: David Dalton, *James Dean: The Mutant King*, 1983; Joe Hyams, *James Dean: Little Boy Lost*, 1992.

"DEAR ANN," "DEAR ABBY." "Ann Landers" was the title of a daily advice column that appeared in the Chicago *Sun-Times*. Esther Friedman was a 37-year-old housewife in 1955 when she was offered the opportunity to write the column. Her first column appeared on October 16, 1955, and her wit, honesty, and willingness to refer people to medical, financial, and psychological counselors quickly earned her a wider audience. Soon other papers began picking up the column. Friedman's success with "Dear Ann" inspired her twin sister, Pauline, to work out a similar arrangement with the *San Francisco Chronicle*. Soon, the "Dear Abby" column was appearing in nationwide syndication.

The two sisters quickly became barometers of middle-class expectations as well as shapers of middle-class culture in the United States. In their columns, Americans addressed such issues as divorce, gender, sexuality, childhood, illness, poverty, and family relations. Both women took a no-nonsense approach to the advice columns, and in doing so they helped destigmatize a wide variety of cultural issues in the United States. Both columns still appeared regularly in the late 1990s.

SUGGESTED READING: Janice Pottker, *Dear Ann, Dear Abby: The Unauthorized Biography of Ann Landers and Abigail Van Buren,* 1987.

DEATH OF A SALESMAN. *Death of a Salesman* is the title of a two-act play written by Arthur Miller, which opened at the Morosco Theater in New York City on February 10, 1949. In sharp contrast to the prevailing values of the 1950s, which idealized the consumer culture and the pursuit of income, *Death of a Salesman* offered up a critique of American society. Willy Loman, played by Lee J. Cobb, is an aging traveling salesman who can no longer produce the volume his employers demand. Willie's life has been his work, and, as a result, his family has become distant. His son, Biff (Arthur Kennedy), has never forgiven Willie for having had an affair with a woman he picked up on the road. In the end, Willie is fired, and his life is ruined. He finally commits suicide in a car crash in order to ensure that his family will receive his $20,000 life insurance policy. *Death of a Salesman* had a run of 742 performances.

SUGGESTED READING: *New York Times,* February 10, 1949.

DEATH VALLEY DAYS. *Death Valley Days,* one of the longest running programs in television history, was always produced in syndication. It premiered in 1952 and remained on the air until 1975. Those years were the heyday of the television Western, and the show's setting was the harsh desert of California in the nineteenth century, where hard-bitten settlers tried to eke out an existence. In an unforgiving environment, resolute pioneers built new lives for themselves. *Death Valley Days* was narrated by Stanley Andrews from 1952 to 1965, by Ronald Reagan in 1965 and 1966, by Robert Taylor from 1966 to 1968, by Dale Robertson from 1968 to 1972, and by Merle Haggard in 1975.

SUGGESTED READING: Tim Brooks and Earle Marsh, *The Complete Directory to Prime Time Network and Cable TV Shows, 1946–Present,* 1995.

DENNIS V. UNITED STATES (1951). In 1950, at the height of the Red Scare,* Congress passed the Smith Act, which made it a federal offense to advocate the overthrow of the U.S. government or to establish an organization dedicated to the overthrow of the U.S. government. Civil libertarians criticized the legislation as a gross violation of an individual's First Amendment rights to freedom of speech and freedom of the press.

In 1951 the case of *Dennis v. United States* put the Smith Act to its constitutional test. In New York, eleven members of the American Communist party had been convicted of violating the Smith Act. They sued, and the case reached the U.S. Supreme Court in 1951. The defendants claimed that they had met only to discuss the merits of overthrowing the U.S. government, not actually to plan

such an event. The Court nevertheless upheld the convictions, arguing that the government had the right to stop revolutions before they got under way.
SUGGESTED READING: 341 U.S. 494 (1951).

DESEGREGATION. By the end of the 1940s, pressure was mounting throughout much of the United States for desegregation of the public schools. Between 1914 and 1945, millions of African Americans had left the South to work in factories of the North and West, and they gradually moved into the Democratic party, where they became an important constituency. Northern Democrats interested in winning primaries and general elections sought votes in the black community, and one way of appealing to them was to condemn racism and segregation. Also, more than a million black men had served in the U.S. military during World War I. They came home convinced that if they had risked their lives for their country, they were entitled to equality. Also, they had lived overseas in communities far less racist than those in the United States, and they had become accustomed to being treated with a measure of respect.

For years, the National Association for the Advancement of Colored People (NAACP) had filed lawsuits against segregated public schools, and the suits began to bear fruit in the 1950s. After World War II, G. W. McLaurin, an African-American student, began working on a doctoral degree in education at the University of Oklahoma. McLaurin was admitted to graduate school, but university officials then segregated him in school classrooms, the cafeteria, and the library. He filed a civil rights lawsuit, claiming that racial segregation in a public school violated his Fourteenth Amendment rights. In June 1950, the U.S. Supreme Court agreed. *McLaurin v. Oklahoma State Regents** was a milestone in the desegregation of public education in the United States.

The Supreme Court rendered a similar verdict in *Sweatt v. Painter** in 1950. In 1946 Herman Sweatt, an African American, applied for admission at the University of Texas (UT) Law School. UT rejected his application because he was black, and Sweatt sued, arguing that racial discrimination denied him his Fourteenth Amendment rights. In response, UT established a separate law school for blacks, staffed by part-time faculty. Sweatt was not satisfied, refused to attend, and continued to pursue the lawsuit. In June 1950, the U.S. Supreme Court sided with Sweatt and found UT guilty of racial discrimination. There was resistance, even in the face of Supreme Court orders. Both the University of Virginia and the University of Georgia publically remained defiant and refused to admit black students. Still, *McLaurin v. Oklahoma* and *Sweatt v. Painter* led to the desegregation of professional programs—medicine, dentistry, and law—throughout the country.

Desegregation of public elementary and secondary schools was close behind. By 1953 five separate but similar NAACP lawsuits had reached the Supreme Court from Clarendon County, South Carolina; Prince Edward County, Virginia; Topeka, Kansas; Wilmington, Delaware; and Washington, D.C. Each revolved around a public school district practice of racially segregating African-American students into separate schools. The NAACP argued that such segregation in a tax-supported public school violated the Fourteenth Amendment to the Constitution, which forbade state and local governments to abridge the constitutional rights of its citizens. The NAACP also argued that the schools did not even meet the standard of *Plessy v. Ferguson* (1896), which had claimed that separate but equal facilities were constitutional. The NAACP argued that segregated schools had become decidedly unequal in facilities, equipment, and resources. The NAACP also claimed that even if the separate facilities were equal, they would still be unconstitutional, since segregation imposed a devastating psychological stigma on black children.

The Supreme Court decided to hear the *Brown v. Board of Education of Topeka, Kansas** case and allow that verdict to decide the other four cases. Chief Justice Earl Warren* acted as a jurist and as a politician in getting a unanimous decision from the other justices. The decision declared public school segregation unconstitutional. In his written decision, Warren stated, "In the field of public education, the doctrine of 'separate but equal' has no place. Separate educational facilities are inherently unequal. Therefore, we hold that the plaintiffs and others similarly situated . . . are . . . deprived of the equal protection of laws guaranteed by the Fourteenth Amendment." The Supreme Court then ordered that desegregation take place with "all deliberate speed." Legally, at least, public school segregation was dead.

In reality, however, it continued to thrive. State law mandated segregation in Alabama, Arkansas, Delaware, Florida, Georgia, Kentucky, Louisiana, Maryland, Mississippi, Missouri, North Carolina, Oklahoma, South Carolina, Tennessee, Texas, Virginia, West Virginia, and the District of Columbia. Only five states—Delaware, Maryland, Missouri, West Virginia, and the District of Columbia—began immediately to implement desegregation. The others refused. Throughout the rest of the South, defiance and "massive resistance" ensued. Several states even threatened to close public schools if integration became inevitable.

The flashpoint of the resistance movement took place in Little Rock, Arkansas.* On September 2, 1957, the day before the school year began, Governor Orval Faubus* of Arkansas announced that he would not offer police protection to black children entering the public schools. The black children, now dubbed the "Little Rock Nine" by journalists, would face possible threats to their lives. The children nevertheless showed up to attend classes at Central High School on September 4, 1957. The Arkansas National Guard surrounded the school and would not let them enter.

President Dwight D. Eisenhower,* who was trying to avoid a constitutional crisis, met with Faubus and convinced him to remove the national guard troops. On September 23, when the nine black students again tried to attend school, an angry mob gathered outside the school and threatened the students. When the mob refused to disperse the next day, Eisenhower nationalized the Arkansas National Guard, which put the troops under his command, and sent in troops from the 101st Airborne Division to protect the black students. The Little Rock Nine finally began their first day of school on September 25. Faubus, however, was not finished. Masses of white students left Central High School, which effectively closed down the school in 1958–1959. Faubus tried to start a system of private schools for white students, but the movement petered out. In 1959 Central High School opened as an integrated high school.

Similar resistance occurred in other Southern states. State governments closed some public schools, offered funding for private schools, and implemented a host of other schemes. By the end of the 1950s, the public schools of Alabama, Georgia, Louisiana, Mississippi, and South Carolina remained fully segregated.

SUGGESTED READINGS: James Duram, *Moderate Among Extremists: Dwight D. Eisenhower and the School Desegregation Crisis*, 1981; Jennifer L. Hichschild, *The New American Dilemma: Liberal Democracy and School Desegregation*, 1984; Lewis B. Mayhew, ed., *Higher Education in the Revolutionary Decades*, 1967.

THE DIARY OF ANNE FRANK. Based on Anne Frank's *Anne Frank: The Diary of a Young Girl*, the best-selling, true story of a Jewish girl who eventually died in a Nazi death camp, *The Diary of Anne Frank*, a two-act play, opened at the Cort Theater in New York City on October 5, 1955. The play begins when Otto Frank (Joseph Schildkraut), patriarch of the Frank family, returns to the apartment in Amsterdam where Mr. Kraler (Clinton Sundberg) had concealed the Franks in an attic for years from the Gestapo. While looking around the attic, Frank discovers the diary of his daughter Anne (Susan Strasberg), and he recalls those years of fear and happiness. Otto was the only one of the family to survive after the Gestapo found them and shipped them all to a concentration camp. Anne's diary ends with an extraordinary statement: "In spite of everything, I still believe people are really good at heart." *The Diary of Anne Frank* had a run of 717 consecutive performances.

SUGGESTED READING: *New York Times*, October 6, 1955.

DIEN BIEN PHU, BATTLE OF. Between 1945 and 1953, Ho Chi Minh* and his guerrilla Vietminh army, who demanded full Vietnamese independence from France, steadily gained ground against French imperial forces in Indochina. France was desperate to maintain its imperial foothold in Asia, and Vietnam was the key. French military commanders in Indochina had grown frustrated with a guerrilla war of ambushes, booby traps, assassinations, and hit-and-run tactics; the Vietnamese proved to be a surprisingly elusive enemy. The French yearned for a conventional war where infantry, artillery, and airpower—all of which the French had in abundance—could deliver a punishing blow to the Vietnamese.

In 1953 the French felt that such a battle was looming. General Henri Navarre, commander in chief of the French forces in Vietnam, decided to build a military outpost at the village of Dien Bien Phu in far northwestern Vietnam, near the border with Laos. Navarre believed that French troops stationed there would make the movement of Vietminh troops back and forth between Laos and Vietnam more difficult and would cut the Vietminh off from their Laotian opium sources. The Vietminh marketed opium in order to generate cash for their war effort. Navarre also hoped that the Vietminh would decide to attack the base.

He prepared for such an offensive. Navarre placed the French outpost in the middle of a valley that was surrounded by rugged mountains. He thought that the Vietminh would not be able to deploy artillery into the mountains, and that French artillery would cut the Vietminh to pieces as they attacked across the broad, flat valley floor. But Navarre badly miscalculated. General Vo Nguyen Giap, the Vietminh commander, had 200,000 porters at his disposal, and they dismantled artillery pieces, carried them into the mountains, and reassembled them there. The Vietminh then cut off the roads leading into Dien Bien Phu to make it difficult for France to resupply its troops there. When the Vietminh artillery laid siege to the air base at Dien Bien Phu, it was impossible to get supplies to the troops.

While the French ran out of food and ammunition, Giap had his troops dig trenches, with hand shovels, closer and closer to the French lines. There would no human-wave infantry assaults across open fields, where the French could subject the troops to withering fire. The Vietminh tunnels inched closer and closer to French lines during the spring of 1954.

As the fall of Dien Bien Phu became imminent, France appealed to the United States for intervention. President Dwight D. Eisenhower* pondered the request, and plans were drawn up for aircraft carrier–based air strikes against Vietminh positions, but the code-named Operation Vulture was never carried out. Eisenhower decided that U.S. intervention carried more risks than it was worth.

On May 7, 1954, the Vietminh launched a final assault on the French outpost. More than 10,000 French troops, hungry and poorly supplied, could not hold out, and the Vietminh overran the outpost. The French soldiers became prisoners of war, and the French empire in Indochina was doomed. At the Geneva Convention, which was in session while Dien Bien Phu fell, France eventually agreed to Vietnamese independence.

SUGGESTED READINGS: Bernard Fall, *Hell in a Very Small Place: The Siege of Dien Bien Phu*, 1966; Jules Roy, *The Battle of Dien Bien Phu*, 1965.

THE DINAH SHORE SHOW. *The Dinah Shore Show* was one of the few television variety shows hosted by a woman that succeeded commercially. The variety show, hosted by Dinah Shore, a successful vocalist from the 1940s and early 1950s, premiered on NBC television on October 5, 1956. Chevrolet sponsored the program, and its theme song, "See the USA in your Chevrolet," became the show's trademark. *The Dinah Shore Show* was a staple in NBC's Sunday evening lineup until 1961, when *The Dinah Shore Show* moved to Friday evenings and *Bonanza** took over the time slot. The show revolved around Dinah Shore songs and her chatty, breezy talk and featured performances by some of entertainment's biggest names. The show's last broadcast aired on May 12, 1963.

SUGGESTED READINGS: Tim Brooks and Earle Marsh, *The Complete Directory to Prime Time Network and Cable TV Shows, 1946–Present*, 1995; Bruce Cassidy, *Dinah! A Biography*, 1979.

DINER'S CLUB. In 1950 the first modern credit card*—Diner's Club—was introduced. Department store credit cards, in which consumers purchased goods and then paid for them over time, had existed since the late nineteenth century. The Diner's Club card took that traditional concept and added a unique twist: organizing a variety of vendors who would accept the card, and then directly sending one bill a month to purchasers who had used the card. The organizers of the Diner's Club—Alfred Bloomingdale, Frank McNamara, and Ralph Snyder—signed up restaurants across the country and charged them a small percentage fee for each transaction. The credit card company paid the restaurants and assumed responsibility for collecting from the customers. The credit company also made money by investing monthly payments in short-term bank deposit accounts and collecting interest. Although the Diner's Club credit card would, within the next twenty years, be upstaged by Master Card and Visa credit cards, which branched out into all types of consumer transactions, not just restaurant purchases, it nevertheless pioneered a financial practice destined to become the most popular in the world.

SUGGESTED READING: Lewis Mandell, *The Credit Card Industry: A History*, 1990.

DISNEYLAND. Before Disneyland, most amusement parks around the world were somewhat shabby, located in run-down urban areas, and known for the smell of stale popcorn, lowlife carnival barkers, and grime. Parents interested in a family outing often avoided amusement parks for fear of running into drunks, drug addicts, and grifters. Walt Disney, who headed a movie studio known for animation and family entertainment, decided that a market existed for a wholesome, family amusement park. Skeptics warned him against the endeavor, which they were certain would bankrupt the studio. In fact, he had trouble finding financing for the grandiose project. To many investors, amusement parks seemed like dinosaurs, relics of the entertainment past. Disney poured his own fortune into the project, and he received backing from ABC television, which broadcast his weekly television series.

Disney selected a 160-acre site in Orange County, California, just outside the sleepy town of Anaheim, and built a state-of-the-art facility. In fact, it was well beyond state-of-the-art. Disney had reinvented the amusement park. Disneyland featured Fantasyland, Frontierland, Adventureland, and Tomorrowland—four individual theme parks in one. Rides throughout Disneyland reflected previous

Disney cartoons and films. The park was clean and fresh, and the workers were unfailingly kind and gracious.

Skeptics who predicted a financial disaster for Disneyland could not have been more wrong. The park opened to great fanfare on July 17, 1955, and during the next six months, more than one million visitors bought tickets to Disneyland. During 1956, its first full year of operation, Disneyland earned $10 million, and by 1965 it had earned more than $200 million, turning Walt Disney's enterprises into the world's greatest entertainment venue.

SUGGESTED READINGS: Richard Schickel, *The Disney Version*, 1968; Steven Watts, *The Magic Kingdom: Walt Disney and the American Way of Life*, 1997.

DIVINE, FATHER. The name "Father Divine" was the pseudonym of George Baker, an African-American leader who established a unique ministry and civil rights constituency in the United States. Baker was born on Hutchinson Island, Georgia, in 1877, but joined the mass migration of Southern blacks to the North during World War I. He settled in Sayville, Long Island, New York, where he assumed the pastorate of a local black church. Baker was as interested in his parishioners' temporal welfare as he was in their spiritual needs, and he found ways of supplying food, clothing, and housing to the destitute. He relocated his ministry to Harlem in 1933 and founded the Father Divine Peace Mission Movement. From Harlem, he established branch missions in Chicago, Detroit, Buffalo, Boston, Philadelphia, and Baltimore. He also developed a cult of personality that soon convinced many of his followers that he was a divine figure, the earthly incarnation of God. Baker promoted a simple moral code, advising followers to avoid tobacco, movies, racism, and lust, and to avoid the use of the terms "white" or "Negro" to refer to other human beings, since all people were brothers and sisters. He preached no formal theology, only the importance of making sure that none of God's children was hungry or cold. Father Divine died on September 10, 1965.

SUGGESTED READINGS: Arthur H. Fauset, *Black Gods of the Metropolis*, 1971; *New York Times*, September 11, 1965.

DNA. DNA is an acronym for deoxyribonucleic acid, the molecule inside all living cells that carries an organism's genetic code. Biologists had known about DNA since 1869, but it was not until 1943 that microbiologist Oswald Avery postulated its role in heredity. Even though scientists knew that DNA had a key function in passing on genetic traits from one generation to another, they still had no idea just how the mechanism worked.

In 1953 two scientists at Cavendish Laboratories at Cambridge University in Great Britain made the key discovery. Biophysicist Francis Crick and biologist James D. Watson began working with X-ray diffraction photographs of British biophysicists Rosalind Franklin and Maurice Wilkins and determined that the structure of DNA was a double helix, or two intertwined strands of polymers that spiraled. When a cell divides, they concluded, its DNA separates into two individual strands, and each strand becomes the building block for another double helix in the new cell. Each strand of the DNA double helix contains an identical series of genes. In such a way, genetic traits are passed on.

Crick and Watson published their findings in the April 1953 issue of the British journal *Nature*. Their published findings revolutionized biology and created the new scientific disciplines of molecular biology and modern genetics. The discovery also had a dramatic, revolutionary impact on agriculture and medicine. The scientific community immediately understood the portent of their discovery, and in 1962 Crick and Watson were awarded the Nobel Prize for Medicine.

SUGGESTED READINGS: James Watson, *The Double Helix: A Personal Account of the Discovery of the Structure of DNA*, 1980; Trevor Illtyd Williams, *Science: A History of Discovery in the Twentieth Century*, 1990.

DOCTOR ZHIVAGO. *Doctor Zhivago* is the title of Boris Pasternak's monumental Russian novel. Russians love poetry, and ever since the 1920s they had recognized Pasternak as the country's greatest living poet. As a young man, Pasternak had held out great hope for the Bolshevik Revolution—that its sense of brotherhood, equality, and sharing might create history's first perfect society. As time went by, however, Bolshevism's paranoia, Josep Stalin's* megalomania, and the tens of millions of Russian deaths at the hands of Communist politicians converted Pasternak into an enemy of the state. In 1946 he began work on his novel *Doctor Zhivago*.

Doctor Zhivago tells the story of Yuri Zhivago, a physician and poet who finds himself caught up in the vortex of World War I and the civil war that engulfed Russia in the wake of the Bolshevik Revolution. While Russia is immersed in ideological battles that kill millions of people, Zhivago simply wants to maintain his personal life—to work, laugh, write, make love, and raise children. The book's sympathetic treatment of Christianity and Russian tradition enraged Communist ideologues, as did its implied criticism of Karl Marx, V. I. Lenin, and Stalin. Pasternak could not find a Russian publisher, and in 1957 he smuggled the manuscript out of the Soviet Union to Italy, where it soon appeared in dozens of languages.

Pasternak immediately felt the repercussions of publication. The Union of Soviet Writers expelled him, as did the Union of Translators. He lost his job, was put under house arrest, and became the target of official ridicule and harassment. The only thing that saved him from disappearing into a gulag prison camp was his international fame. In 1958 he received the Nobel Prize in Literature. Although he was forced to turn down the prize, it did guarantee his survival in the Soviet Union. Within the United States, Pasternak became a symbol of the oppressiveness of the Soviet state and an icon to freedom during the Cold War.* Pasternak died suddenly in 1960.

SUGGESTED READINGS: Peter Levi, *Boris Pasternak*, 1990; Larissa Rudova, *Understanding Boris Pasternak*, 1998.

DOMINO, FATS. Fats Domino was born Antoine Domino in New Orleans, Louisiana, on May 10, 1929. By the time he was ten years old, he was playing the piano for decent money in New Orleans clubs, where he acquired his distinctive boogie-woogie and classic rhythm-and-blues style, which was characterized by easy patterns with the left hand and right-handed arpeggios. His first solo rhythm-and-blues hit, "Goin' Home," came in 1952, and he followed that up with another hit, "Going to the River." In 1955 he had a crossover pop hit when "Ain't That a Shame" reached the top ten and sold nearly 1.5 million records. During the next five years, he was one of the most popular performers in rock music, with a string of top-ten hits that included "I'm in Love Again" (1956), "Blueberry Hill" (1956), "Blue Monday" (1956), "I'm Walkin'" (1957), "Whole Lotta Lovin'" (1958), and "Walkin' to New Orleans" (1960). During the 1960s, new rockers like the Beatles and the Rolling Stones eclipsed Domino, although most of them acknowledged the huge impact he had had on their music.

SUGGESTED READING: Patricia Romanowski and Holly George-Warren, *The Encyclopedia of Rock & Roll*, 1995.

DOMINO THEORY. The so-called domino theory was an important U.S. foreign policy principle during the 1950s. It was first announced by President Harry S. Truman* in 1946 when he proposed the Truman Doctrine. Unless the United States provided military aid assistance to Greece and Turkey, the president argued, both countries and much of the Middle East would fall, like a row of dominoes lined up against each other, to Communist aggression. In April 1954, during the Battle of Dien Bien Phu,* President Dwight D. Eisenhower* announced the same idea about Southeast Asia, arguing that if Vietnam fell to Communist guerrillas, the rest of the region, including Cambodia, Laos, Thailand, and Burma, would fall as well, and perhaps much of East Asia. Malaysia, Indonesia, New Zealand, Australia, and the Philippines would also be threatened. French policy makers reinforced the idea, since they wanted to induce the United States to rescue the besieged French army at Dien Bien Phu. Because of the domino theory, American policy makers in the 1950s developed the mindset that any Communist insurgency anywhere in the world posed a potential threat to the United States, since it could trigger a neighboring country to fall to communism as well. It was the domino theory at work that led the United States into its disastrous involvement in the Vietnam War.* Because of the domino theory, the United States assumed the role of global policeman during the 1950s.

SUGGESTED READINGS: Richard J. Barnet, *Roots of War: The Men and Institutions Behind U.S. Foreign Policy*, 1972; James S. Olson and Randy Roberts, *Where the Domino Fell: America and Vietnam, 1945–1995*, 1995.

THE DONNA REED SHOW. During the 1950s, television* presented an idealized version of the American family, and no situation comedy better fit this stereotype than *The Donna Reed Show*. A product of the ABC network, it premiered on September 24, 1958, starring Donna Reed as Donna Stone, a house-wife in an upper middle-class home. Carl Betz starred as her pediatrician husband, with Shelley Fabares as her daughter, Mary, and Paul Petersen as her son, Jeff. The Stones lived in a classic, two-story colonial home in the suburb of Hilldale. They were prosperous and successful. Donna Stone was a stay-at-home mother and her husband was a hardworking, sensitive, dedicated physician. The teenagers were rambunctious but innocent, and the family was fully functional. ABC broadcast the last episode of *The Donna Reed Show* on September 3, 1966.

SUGGESTED READING: Tim Brooks and Earle Marsh, *The Complete Directory to Prime Time Network and Cable TV Shows, 1946–Present,* 1995.

DOO-WOP. Late in the 1950s, rock-and-roll music became characterized by the so-called doo-wop sound, a form of rhythm-and-blues harmonic vocalizing. The roots of doo-wop could be found in urban black vocal groups during the early 1950s, and from there it spread to white bands. In intricate harmonic arrangements, performers would repeat phonetic and nonsense syllables, such as "doo-wop." Among the most representative of the doo-wop singles were "Sh-Boom" by the Chords, "Earth Angel" by the Penguins, "Book of Love" by the Monotones, and "Little Darlin'" by Maurice Williams.

SUGGESTED READING: Patricia Romanowski and Holly George-Warren, eds., *The New Rolling Stone Encyclopedia of Rock & Roll,* 1996.

DOUGLAS, WILLIAM O(RVILLE). William Orville Douglas was born on October 16, 1898, in Maine, Minnesota, to a poor farming family. That childhood poverty left him, for the rest of his life, acutely sensitive to the needs of the poor and downtrodden. A battle with polio rendered that sensitivity even more keen. Douglas was raised in Yakima, Washington, and for the rest of his life he had an appreciation for the environment and, as he called it, "the great outdoors." In 1920 Douglas graduated from Whitman College and then earned a law degree at Columbia University in New York City.

After graduation, Douglas joined a prestigious Wall Street law firm, and he was on the fast track to a very lucrative career, but he grew suspicious of his corporate clients, who were, he said, "[O]nly interested in making money, lots of money, no matter what the consequences to society. I felt dirty dealing with them." After two years on Wall Street, Douglas joined the law faculty at Columbia. The academic life appealed to him, and in 1929 he joined the faculty of the Yale Law School and soon became a premier figure in finance law. In 1936 President Franklin D. Roosevelt appointed Douglas to the Securities and Exchange Commission (SEC). Douglas became chairman of the SEC in 1937 and soon symbolized the "Second New Deal's" focus on corporate regulation, antitrust action, and progressive taxation. In 1939 Roosevelt appointed Douglas an associate justice of the U.S. Supreme Court to replace the retiring Louis Brandeis.

Douglas was destined to become a major force on the Supreme Court. An unabashed liberal, he believed that the federal government had the right to intervene in economic matters to make sure that big corporations and concentrated wealth did not abuse the rights of the poor and the weak. Corporate property rights, he was convinced, did not supercede the basic needs and rights of individual citizens. Not surprisingly, Douglas vigorously supported antitrust activities undertaken by the Department of Justice and pro-labor legislation at the state and national levels. He was also a civil libertarian who protected individual rights from corporate and government abuse. In 1951 he vigorously dissented in *Dennis v. United States** when the Court upheld convictions of American Communist party members for advocating the overthrow of the federal government. Douglas interpreted the Bill of Rights literally and, in doing so, became one of the most prominent civil libertarians in the history of the Supreme Court. He fit perfectly into Chief Justice Earl Warren's* court, anchoring the liberal wing in censorship, civil liberties, civil rights, and desegregation issues.

He was also a cantankerous justice who often intentionally inflamed political enemies, a trait which, when added to his lifestyle and liberal views, guaranteed him political difficulties. He was divorced three times between 1954 and 1966, and after each divorce he quickly married a much younger woman. In 1953 and 1970, special House judiciary subcommittees opened impeachment hearings on Douglas, but the hearings only generated headlines, not any real evidence. Douglas suffered a serious stroke in January 1975, and later in the year he resigned, having served longer on the Supreme Court than any other justice in American history. Douglas died on January 19, 1980.

SUGGESTED READINGS: Vernon Countryman, *The Judicial Record of Justice William O. Douglas*, 1974; William O. Douglas, *The Court Years, 1939–1975*, 1980.

DRAGNET. *Dragnet*, a realistic police drama, premiered on NBC radio on June 3, 1949. Starring Jack Webb as Sergeant Joe Friday of the Los Angeles Police Department (LAPD), *Dragnet* offered up true crime stories taken from the records of the LAPD. Included in the cast over the years were Barton Yarborough, Barney Phillips, and Ben Alexander as a succession of Friday's partners. Webb was a dedicated friend of the police, and the LAPD cooperated in the series, providing him access to records in return for his promise that confidentiality would not be compromised. Joe Friday was a tough, no-nonsense cop who was not afraid to wear his conservative views on his sleeve, but he was also compassionate, exactly what most people expected in an ideal police officer.

Each episode began with a tell-tale promise: "Ladies and gentlemen . . . the story you are about to hear is true. Only the names have been changed to protect the innocent." Unlike previous radio police dramas, *Dragnet* handled even nasty crimes, like sexual assaults and murders, and it followed the investigation of the crime through the trial and sentencing of those convicted. The program lasted until February 26, 1957, when NBC canceled it.

By that time, Jack Webb and NBC had made a successful weekly television series out of *Dragnet*. *Dragnet* was television's most popular and successful television police drama. The television version premiered on NBC on January 3, 1952. Based on true stories, its documentary quality was enhanced by the terse, narrative voice of Webb. *Dragnet* had a realistic quality, and its conservative values—good-guy cops and bad-guy criminals—resonated with the prevailing values of the 1950s. *Dragnet* remained on prime time television until its last broadcast on September 10, 1970. By then, audiences had come to find it too conservative, almost hokey in its values.

SUGGESTED READINGS: Tim Brooks and Earle Marsh, *The Complete Directory to Prime Time Network and Cable TV Shows, 1946–Present*, 1995; John Dunning, *On the Air: The Encyclopedia of Old-Time Radio*, 1998; Jack Webb, *The Badge*, 1958.

DRIVE-IN THEATER. The first drive-in theaters, in which moviegoers watched films from their cars in outdoor parking lot ampitheaters, appeared in the 1920s, but the business proliferated rapidly during World War II. By 1948 the United States possessed 820 drive-in theaters. Then the real boom occurred, and in 1952, the number of drive-ins had skyrocketed to more than 3,300. The typical drive-in theater had room for 500 to 600 cars, although some had as many as 3,000 parking places. Families could pile the kids into a car, without dressing up, and go to a movie without having to pay a babysitter. Ticket prices were cheaper than in regular theaters.

SUGGESTED READING: "The Colossal Drive-In,"*Newsweek* 50 (July 22, 1957).

DUFFY'S TAVERN. *Duffy's Tavern* premiered on CBS radio on July 29, 1940. Actor Ed Gardner played Archie, the manager of Duffy's Tavern, which was described as "the eyesore of the East Side where the elite meet to eat." Archie helped create the national stereotype of New Yorkers as outspoken and sometimes rude by insulting guests who came to the bar on Third Avenue. They tried to come back with their own one-liners, only to be put down by Miss Duffy's barbed wit. Shirley Booth played Miss Duffy, daughter of the absentee proprietor. Critics hailed *Duffy's Tavern* for its originality and willingness to push the limits of convention. The show shifted to the Blue Network from 1942 to 1944, and then NBC radio picked it up and kept it on the air until its last airing on January 18, 1952.

SUGGESTED READING: John Dunning, *On the Air: The Encyclopedia of Old-Time Radio*, 1998.

DULLES, JOHN FOSTER. John Foster Dulles was born on February 25, 1888, in Washington, D.C. His family moved to Watertown, New York, later in the year, and Dulles grew up there. He spent six months of his high school years in Lausanne, Switzerland, where he studied French and German. He attended Princeton University and gave some thought to a career in the ministry, but in 1911 he decided on a life in the foreign service. He spent a year at the Sorbonne in Paris and then another year studying law at Georgetown University.

Dulles then passed the bar examination without finishing a degree and joined the New York law firm of Sullivan and Cromwell. He soon developed an expertise in international law.

Dulles's formal diplomatic career began in 1917 when President Woodrow Wilson dispatched him to Central America to convince Panama, Nicaragua, and Costa Rica to declare war on Germany. His success cemented his growing reputation in the foreign policy establishment. Dulles finished World War I as a member of Bernard Baruch's War Trade Board.

During most of the decade of the 1920s, as well as several years in the early 1930s, Dulles was in Europe as counsel to the American Commission to Negotiate Peace, where he worked on reparations issues. He also served as special counsel to the bankers working on the Dawes Plan to reconstruct European debt arrangements. When Franklin D. Roosevelt and the Democrats came to power in Washington, D.C., in the 1930s, Dulles returned to private law practice, although he remained well known in Washington as an articulate Republican spokesman on foreign policy issues. In 1939 Dulles wrote his first book, *War, Peace, and Change*, which was a severe criticism of the Treaty of Versailles.

During the late 1940s and early 1950s, Dulles allied himself with the moderate wing of the Republican party, even though he remained critical of the containment policy,* hoping to liberate countries trapped behind the Iron Curtain, and advocated a tougher stance toward the Soviet Union. He nevertheless cooperated in the development of a bipartisan foreign policy. He was a strong supporter of the Marshall Plan and the Truman Doctrine. At President Harry Truman's* request in 1950, Dulles assumed responsibility for negotiating a peace treaty with Japan and regional security treaty arrangements with Australia, New Zealand, and the Phillippines.

In 1953 President Dwight D. Eisenhower* appointed Dulles to his cabinet as secretary of state. To appease the right wing of the Republican party, which was mired deeply in the Red Scare,* Dulles purged the State Department of its liberal and left-wing analysts and instituted more rigid, demanding security regulations for employment, promotion, and surveillance. Dulles realized that he could not afford to be accused of being "soft on communism."

Dulles's term as secretary of state was also characterized by the policy of "brinkmanship." As part of his New Look* defense policy, President Eisenhower had reduced conventional military forces, which forced Dulles to rely more on the threat of nuclear weapons in resolving disputes and in making the Soviets more cautious and conservative. Brinkmanship came to describe Dulles's repeated practice of threatening war, even nuclear war, to force the Soviet Union and the People's Republic of China to redesign their aggressive foreign policies. Dulles resorted to the threat, for example, in 1956 when the Soviet Union invaded Hungary and threatened to intervene in the Suez crisis.*

Critics charged that John Foster Dulles was too much of a moralist to be an effective diplomatic. His own convictions about right and wrong were so firm that he had a difficult time compromising and easily offended those who did not readily accept his view of the world. Dulles resigned as secretary of state in 1959 when he fell ill with stomach cancer. He died on May 14, 1959.

SUGGESTED READINGS: Eleanor Lansing Dulles, *John Foster Dulles*, 1963; Michael A. Guhin, *John Foster Dulles: A Statesman and His Times*, 1972; Ronald W. Pruessen, *John Foster Dulles: The Road to Power*, 1982.

E

THE ED SULLIVAN SHOW. *The Ed Sullivan Show* was the most popular and influential variety show in television* history. Ed Sullivan, a veteran New York City journalist without a charismatic bone in his body, conceived the idea for the show, and it premiered on CBS television as *Toast of the Town* on June 20, 1948. It became the linchpin of CBS's Sunday night lineup for the next twenty-three years. Sullivan was hardly destined for television success. He was awkward, delivered his lines in a deadpan voice, and exhibited body movements that became fodder for a generation of mimic comedians. The show had a vaudeville flavor to it, with comedians, circus acts, ventriloquists, and acrobats co-existing peacefully with rock stars, Broadway hits, and the ballet. Over the years, virtually every major performer in American entertainment appeared on *The Ed Sullivan Show*.

The Ed Sullivan Show was so influential that it became a hallmark for new entertainers. If they could get on *The Ed Sullivan Show*, as Elvis Presley* did in 1956 and the Beatles did in 1964, they had demonstrated their place in American popular culture. During the late 1960s, however, the show's ratings began to decline. Younger viewers had little interest in the awkward host, and *The Ed Sullivan Show*'s viewers became older and less valued by advertisers. CBS canceled the show, and its last broadcast came on June 6, 1971.

SUGGESTED READING: Jerry Bowles, *A Thousand Sundays: The Story of the Ed Sullivan Show*, 1980.

THE EDDIE CANTOR SHOW. See CANTOR, EDDIE.

THE EDGAR BERGEN/CHARLIE McCARTHY SHOW. *See* BERGEN, EDGAR.

EDSEL. The Edsel will no doubt go down as one of the greatest consumer product design disasters in U.S. history. During the 1950s, Ford Motor Company tried to develop a new automobile that would appeal to young, well-to-do families no longer interested in small roadsters but not ready yet for the station wagons or the largest Oldsmobiles, Buicks, Dodges, and Pontiacs. They hoped to appeal to families able to afford a car priced in excess of $5,000, a substantial sum in the 1950s.

Instead of conducting careful market research to determine the needs and tastes of that consumer constituency, Ford let engineers design not only the mechanics and technology of the car but also its style. The result was the Edsel, named after Edsel Ford, a son of company founder Henry Ford. With great fanfare and an advertising blitz, Ford released the Edsel in the fall of 1957, with 1958 as its model year. The car was shaped like a box, with square borders, and it sported an odd, oval-shaped grille. One critic described the grill as looking like "an Oldsmobile sucking a lemon." The word lemon stuck, because consumers wanted nothing to do with Edsel. Sales were abysmal, and the publicity surrounding the car was so intense and so negative that Ford decided to abandon the Edsel. Two years after its release, the model was discontinued.

SUGGESTED READINGS: Peter Collier, *The Fords: An American Epic*, 1988; Loren D. Estleman, *Edsel: A Novel of Detroit*, 1995.

EINSTEIN, ALBERT. Albert Einstein was born on March 14, 1879, in Ulm, Germany. His father was a mechanical engineer and a Jew, though a nonpracticing one. Einstein grew up in Munich. In school, he was only a mediocre student. Because of his unrivaled brilliance, he was constantly bored. The family moved to Milan, Italy, in 1895, and the next year he entered the Federal Polytechnic School in Zurich, Switzerland. During his years there, he made steady progress and graduated, without really impressing anybody. His failure to win a university teaching position in physics led him to employment at the Swiss Patent Office in Bern.

Even while laboring at the patent office, Einstein did brilliant work in theoretical physics, and in 1905 he published a series of articles in the *Annals of Physics* that established his special theory of relativity and proved to be the most seminal work in physics since the seventeenth-century work of Sir Isaac Newton. Einstein then submitted "A New Determination of Molecular Dimensions," for which the University of Zurich awarded him a Ph.D. With his work, which established the equivalence of mass and energy and the constant factor of the velocity of light, Einstein unlocked the mysteries of atomic energy. From 1913 to 1933, Einstein served as director of the Kaiser Wilhelm Institute of Physics in Berlin. By 1919 he had finished his work on the general theory of relativity and was awarded the Nobel Prize. In 1923 he published *The Principle of Relativity*. By that time, he was an avowed pacifist and Zionist.

When Adolf Hitler came to power in Germany in 1933, Einstein became a vocal opponent of Nazism and had to emigrate to the United States, where he became a professor at the Institute for Advanced Study at Princeton. In 1939, worried that Germany might construct an atomic bomb* first and use it to destroy innocent people around the world, Einstein wrote a letter to President Franklin D. Roosevelt urging him to see to it that the United States developed such a weapon first. In terms of his professional career, Einstein spent the rest of his life working on his unified field theory, trying to find the relationship between gravitation and electromagnetism.

During the late 1940s and early 1950s, Albert Einstein became an icon to the American people of the mysterious, powerful new world of science. His benign demeanor somehow reassured Americans that the new atomic age might not necessarily mean the destruction of mankind. When he died on April 18, 1955, Albert Einstein was mourned by a scientific establishment who knew that his brilliance would not be seen again and by a general public who had come to admire and even revere him.

SUGGESTED READINGS: Jeremy Bernstein, *Einstein*, 1973; Saloman Bochner, *Einstein Between Centuries*, 1971; Ronald W. Clark, *Einstein: The Life and Times*, 1971; Philip Frank, *Einstein: The Life and Times*, 1949.

EISENHOWER, DWIGHT D(AVID). Dwight David Eisenhower was born in Denison, Texas, on October 14, 1890. His parents, David Jacob Eisenhower and Ida Elizabeth Stover Eisenhower, actually named him David Dwight Eisenhower at birth, but the future president later reversed the order of his two given names, primarily out of respect for his father. He acquired the nickname "Ike" as a child, and the moniker stuck. The family moved to Abilene, Kansas, in 1891, where the elder Eisenhower worked as a mechanic at a local creamery. Ike was raised on a steady diet of hard work, academic studies, and household chores.

Although Eisenhower's mother was a pacifist, he dreamed of an appointment to the U.S. Military Academy at West Point, and he succeeded in 1911, over his mother's vehement objections. When he graduated four years later from West Point, he had an academic standing of 61st out of a class of 164 cadets, and a disciplinary standing of 125th. He was neither flamboyant nor assertive, but he inspired a quiet confidence in others. Although he never impressed anybody with intellectual brilliance, few ever doubted Eisenhower's ability to complete any task he had assumed as his own.

Upon his graduation, Ike was commissioned a second lieutenant and was posted to Fort Sam Houston in San Antonio, Texas, where he met Mamie Doud (*see* Eisenhower, Mamie Doud). They married in July 1916. Eisenhower so impressed his superiors with his ability to train troops after World War I erupted that he was denied repeated requests for a combat posting to Europe. The failure to get combat experience during the greatest conflict in the history of the world, Eisenhower was convinced, would doom him to a mediocre military career. When the war ended, Eisenhower had a task corps training command with the rank of lieutenant colonel. Peace brought a reduction in rank to captain, although he was soon promoted to major.

At that point, it appeared that his predictions of a mediocre career would prove correct. He remained in the rank of major for the next fifteen years. After service at Fort Dix and Fort Benning, he graduated from the Tank School at Camp Meade, Maryland, and then spent two years in the Panama Canal Zone. In 1925 Eisenhower graduated first in a class of 275 officers at the Command and General Staff School at Fort Leavenworth, and his performance impressed students and faculty alike. His next posting was not, on the surface, a very impressive one—the American Battle Monuments Commission—but General John "Black Jack" Pershing, who had headed up the American Expeditionary Force in Europe during the war—was in charge of the commission, and Eisenhower's service there linked him into the army's most powerful network of officers.

In 1928 Eisenhower graduated from the National War College, and the next year he was assigned as an executive assistant in the office of the deputy secretary of war. Between 1933 and 1939, Eisenhower served as an assistant to General Douglas MacArthur* and returned from the Philippines as a lieutenant colonel. He then became executive officer of the 15th Infantry Regiment at Fort Ord, and soon was promoted to brigadier general and given command of the 9th Army Corps.

When World II broke out in Europe, Eisenhower joined the staff of Chief of Staff George Marshall, where his logistical abilities soon became evident. Marshall was immediately impressed with Eisenhower's administrative abilities and organizational genius. In 1942 Marshall overlooked a number of senior general officers and appointed Eisenhower commanding general of U.S. forces training for European deployment. In August 1942, Marshall named Eisenhower commander of the Allied force set to invade North Africa, and his success there gave him command of the invasion of Sicily in 1943. In December 1943, he was named commander of Operation Overlord, and his success in defeating the German Army won him promotion to general of the army.

After the war, Eisenhower became chief of staff of the army, a post he held for more than two years. He served as president of Columbia University from 1948 to 1950, and from 1950 to 1952, he was commanding general of the military forces of the North Atlantic Treaty Organization (NATO). Eisenhower left NATO in July 1952 to begin his campaign for the presidency. He defeated Senator Robert Taft* of Ohio for the Republican presidential nomination, and in the general election, he beat Democratic nominee Adlai E. Stevenson,* the governor of Illinois.

During his presidential administration, Eisenhower charted a moderate course, distancing himself from the radical right, led by Senator Joseph McCarthy* of Wisconsin, and placing himself in the middle of the political road. Eisenhower had little sympathy for the Red Scare,* which he considered little more than gross excess and political posturing. Although careful not to be too publically critical of McCarthy, Eisenhower let insiders know that he felt McCarthy was little more than a second-rate political fraud willing to do or say anything in order to get reelected.

In terms of domestic policy, Eisenhower did not try to turn back the clock on the New Deal, understanding instinctively that most Americans had come to accept the necessity of a government safety net to protect people from extreme swings in the business cycle. Instead of slashing such programs, as Republican conservatives demanded, Eisenhower for the most part left them alone, even allowing modest increases. Although he was slow to move on civil rights issues, and was disturbed by Martin Luther King, Jr.'s* commitment to civil disobedience, Eisenhower did not hesitate to send federal troops to Little Rock, Arkansas,* in 1957, when Governor Oval Faubus* refused to implement court-ordered school desegregation.*

During a time of rapid social change—with the onset of the youth rebellion and the advent of rock-and-roll*— Eisenhower projected a grandfatherly image to a country in turmoil, reassuring everyone that times really were not that hard, that America was fundamentally sound, and that the future was bright. In doing so, Eisenhower, or "Ike" to the country and the world, became an icon of confidence and stability.

In foreign affairs, Eisenhower charted the country through the Cold War's* dangerous waters. He minced few words in letting the People's Republic of China know in 1952 and 1953 that he was willing to use greater force in order to bring the Korean War* to a conclusion, but in 1954, when Vice President Richard M. Nixon* and Admiral Arthur Radford, chairman of the joint chiefs of staff, urged Eisenhower to intervene to prevent the defeat of French forces in Indochina, he demurred, refusing to get involved in another land war in Asia. When the Soviet Union put *Sputnik** into orbit in 1957, Eisenhower reassured Americans that it was not the end of the world—the American economy and American technology were up to challenging the Soviets. Although Secretary of State John Foster Dulles* threatened massive retaliation*—the use of nuclear weapons in world affairs—Eisenhower was more circumspect, conveying to the Soviets the assuredness that he would not behave capriciously and threaten world survival. When Eisenhower left office in 1961, he was highly respected by most Americans, and that respect only increased during his post-presidential years. During the 1960s, he frequently advised Presidents John F. Kennedy* and Lyndon B. Johnson.* Eisenhower died of a heart attack on March 28, 1969.

SUGGESTED READINGS: Stephen Ambrose, *Eisenhower: Soldier, General of the Army, President-Elect, 1890–1952*, 1983, and *Eisenhower: The President*, 1984; Merle Miller, *Ike the Soldier: As They Knew Him*, 1987; Richard Rovere, *Affairs of State: The Eisenhower Years*, 1956.

EISENHOWER, MAMIE DOUD. Mamie Doud was born on November 14, 1896, in Boone, Iowa. She came from an extremely close, socially prominent family. In 1915, while her family was wintering in San Antonio, Texas, she met Dwight D. Eisenhower,* a young army officer stationed there. "Ike," as she called him, also worked as a local high school football coach. They married in 1916, and she began the laborious, politically demanding job of being the wife of an army officer on the make. He rose steadily through the ranks and became a worldwide hero in 1944–1945 when he commanded Allied forces during the D-Day invasion of Europe and the final assault on Germany. She lived in New York City with him after the war during his stint as president of Columbia University, and when he won election in 1952 as president of the United States, Mamie Eisenhower became the First Lady. She presided over the White House with grace and dignity, exuding hospitality, and became a symbol, for better and for worse, of what American culture expected of women in the 1950s. Behind the scenes, she was a trusted adviser to the president; in public she was a dutiful, devoted wife. Mamie Eisenhower died in 1979.

SUGGESTED READINGS: Dorothy Brandson, *Mamie Doud Eisenhower*, 1954; Steve Neal, *The Eisenhowers: Reluctant Dynasty*, 1978.

ELECTION OF 1950. The political atmosphere in the fall of 1950 was highly charged in America. The domestic Red Scare* was assuming proportions that could only be called paranoid, and the Korean War* seemed to be spinning out of control. An inflationary spiral had a death grip on the economy, and President Harry Truman's* Fair Deal had little appeal to most voters. The fall of China to Mao Zedong* and the Communists, and the Soviet Union's success in detonating an atomic bomb convinced many Americans that President Harry Truman and the Democrats were either grossly incompetent or part of some treasonous conspiracy to accelerate communism's march around the world. Republicans began pushing the campaign theme "Liberty Against Socialism," which resonated with large numbers of people.

More compelling was the Republican claim that Truman and the Democrats had "lost China" to the communists. Democrats countered that the United States never had China to lose, that China had fallen to communism because its own government had been hopelessly corrupt and exploitive of hundreds of millions of Chinese. But most Americans were not listening. They were unhappy and frustrated with the state of the country, and they registered that discontent in record numbers. More than 41 million people voted in the congressional elections of 1950, and Republicans came out the winners. Democrats lost five seats in the U.S. Senate and two seats in the House of Representatives. They still controlled Congress, but their margin in the Senate had dropped from 7 seats to 2 and in the House from 88 seats to 36. The elections of 1950 helped persuade President Harry Truman not to run for reelection in 1952.

SUGGESTED READINGS: *New York Times*, November 4–8, 1950.

ELECTION OF 1952. In 1952 the political climate was even more charged than it had been in 1950. The military stalemate in Korea (*see* Korean War) satisfied nobody, and critics accused the Truman administration of incompetence. The Cold War* with the Soviet Union was escalating, and American fears of the Soviet nuclear theat were rapidly turning into paranoia. Republicans kept up a vitriolic, ongoing attack against the New Deal and the Fair Deal and called for reductions in the role and scope of the federal government. Finally, the right wing of the Republican party continued to orchestrate the Red Scare,* led by the rabid histrionics of Senator Joseph McCarthy* of Wisconsin.

President Harry Truman* was eligible to run for reelection. He had entered the White House in April 1945 after the sudden death of Franklin D. Roosevelt, and in 1948 he had stunned the world with his upset victory over Governor Thomas Dewey of New York. In 1949, however, Truman's political fortunes plummeted. The Soviets detonated an atomic bomb,* China fell to Mao Zedong* and the Communists, and the Red Scare convinced many Americans that Democrats were either guilty of conspiracy or gross incompetence in allowing communism, at home and abroad, to enjoy such stunning victories. Convinced that his chances for reelection were doomed, President Truman decided not to run.

Several Democratic candidates for the nomination emerged. Senator Estes Kefauver* of Tennessee, a conservative, actually defeated Truman in the New Hampshire primary, which helped the president decide not to run again. Kefauver, however, had enemies in the party. As a crusader against organized crime, he had exposed corrupt links between organized crime and several big city Democratic political party machines, and the bosses were determined to keep him from the nomination.

Governor Adlai Stevenson* of Illinois then emerged as a front-runner for the nomination. A well-known reformer, Stevenson was also known for his party loyalty, and he had earned a reputation as a friend of the labor movement, one of the Democratic party's most powerful constituencies. While Kefauver had openly criticized political corruption in the Truman administration, Stevenson had faithfully backed the president.

Finally, Vice President Alben Barkley toyed with the nomination. He had been popular in office, and Americans who loved Truman looked favorably on Barkley. But at seventy-four, Barkley had an age problem, and he had long been perceived as a foe of organized labor.

The Democrats held their convention in Chicago, and maneuvering for the nomination became intense. Kefauver quickly lost control over his delegates, and Barkley's candidacy never really got started. On the third ballot, Stevenson won the nomination. For his vice-presidential running mate, Stevenson selected Senator John Sparkman of Alabama, balancing the ticket between the Northern and Southern wings of the party.

In the Republican party, a battle for the nomination raged between Senator Robert Taft* of Ohio, who was known as "Mr. Conservative," and former General Dwight D. Eisenhower,* who took a more moderate position on most issues. Former California Governor Earl Warren* was a favorite-son candidate, and since California had so many delegates, he became a power broker between Eisenhower and Taft. Warren even had an outside chance, if Taft and Eisenhower deadlocked at the Republican National Convention, to emerge as a compromise candidate. Senator Richard M. Nixon* of California, angling for a vice-presidential candidacy himself, enraged Warren's supporters by throwing his support behind Eisenhower.

Taft was an outspoken opponent of a large federal government and openly called for dismantling the Fair Deal and the New Deal. He also had a reputation as a foreign policy isolationist. The two men fought it out in the primaries, but Republican voters eventually preferred Eisenhower's middle-of-the-road prag-matism to Taft's strident rhetoric. Most Americans were basically comfortable with the achievements of the New Deal and did not trust Taft's promises to pare back government programs. The Republican party also held its convention in Chicago. Eisenhower got the nomination, and to balance the ticket, the party selected Senator Richard M. Nixon of California for vice president. Nixon's credentials as an anticommunist were designed to appease the McCarthyites in the party's right wing. The Republican convention was the first in American history to be televised, and more than 75 million Americans tuned in, giving Eisenhower and Nixon even more recognition than they already had.

The Republican party's campaign was almost over before it began. Journalists revealed that a group of California businessmen had established an $18,000 slush fund to help Nixon with campaign expenses. Democrats tried to make a scandal out of the slush fund, and Eisenhower gave serious thought to dumping Nixon from the ticket.

In a last-ditch attempt to save his political career, Nixon went on television* to plead his case. An audience of sixty million people tuned in. Nixon's wife, Pat, joined him for the speech, and he denied using any of the money for personal needs. The only gift he had ever accepted, Nixon insisted, was the family dog "Checkers." In what is certainly one of the most maudlin perform-ances of his political career, Nixon cited his humble, working-class roots, his struggles to pay for college and law school, and his war record. More than 28 million Americans watched the nationally televised speech, which resonated well with voters. Eisenhower decided to keep Nixon on the ticket.

Nixon's "Checkers" speech revealed the significance of television, which was only beginning to come into its own as a vehicle for political campaigning. While Stevenson bought airtime to broadcast highly intellectualized, erudite half-hour analyses of the issues, the Republicans invented the "sound bite." They purchased time for short commercials featuring marching bands chanting "We like Ike! We like Ike!" Columnist Stewart Alsop nicknamed Stevenson "the Egghead," and the moniker stuck. In the end, Stevenson could not compete with Eisenhower's war record and the shrewd Republican campaign. Eisenhower won 33.9 million popular votes to Stevenson's 27.3 million, and Eisenhower had a landslide in the electoral college—442 to 89. The Republicans gained six seats in the U.S. Senate and nineteen seats in the House of Representatives, which gave them control of Congress.

SUGGESTED READINGS: "Bitter Beginnning," *Life* 33 (July 14, 1952); Paul T. David, Ralph M. Goodman, and Richard C. Bain, *The Politics of the National Conven-tion*, 1960; Porter McKeever, *Adlai Stevenson: His Life and Legacy*, 1989; "National Affairs," *Time* 60 (July 14, 1952) and (July 21, 1952).

ELECTION OF 1954. When the congressional elections rolled around in 1954, Republicans hoped to defy conventional logic and do well. Traditionally, the party out of power makes gains in the congressional elections, but President Dwight D. Eisenhower,* only two years into his presidency, enjoyed substantial popularity. He had brought the unpopular Korean War* to a conclusion, and the inflation surrounding the war was disappearing. Also, the tide had turned on the Red Scare,* and the issue seemed to be running out of steam. Democrats tried to criticize the Eisenhower administration for being too friendly to big business, and Vice President Richard M. Nixon* accused Democrats of being unfit to govern America because their ranks were littered with Communists. His charges raised a great deal of controversy, and it caused a minor backlash against Republicans. When the votes were finally counted, the Democrats had regained control of Congress, with a 29-seat margin in the House and a 1-seat margin in the Senate.

SUGGESTED READING: *Time*, 60 (October 6, 1952).

ELECTION OF 1956. As the election of 1956 approached, Democrats nursed hopes that President Dwight D. Eisenhower's* health might give them a chance to win the White House. In September 1955, the president had suffered a heart attack, and although his recovery had been uneventful, some Americans still had concerns. The president was extremely popular with the public, but Vice President Richard M. Nixon* was not, and Democrats made a great deal of the fact that Nixon was a "heartbeat away" from the White House. When Eisenhower suffered an attack of ileitis and had to undergo intestinal bypass surgery in June 1956, concerns about his health escalated. That, however, was the Democrats' only real issue. The economy was in excellent shape, and although the Cold War* with the Soviet Union was intensifying, most Americans considered Eisenhower the perfect man to lead the nation during a foreign policy or military crisis. Some worried Republicans tried to launch a "Dump Nixon" movement, and Eisenhower tried to get Nixon off the ticket to take a cabinet post, but Nixon refused. The president did not exactly like Nixon, or respect him for that matter, but Eisenhower was a military man, and Nixon had been a loyal vice president. The Eisenhower-Nixon team sought reelection.

The Democratic nomination was intensely contested. Adlai Stevenson,* the Democratic candidate in 1952, had the inside track for the nomination, but many Democrats had reservations about him. He had lost to Eisenhower in 1952, and many doubted whether he could defeat the president, who was even more popular now. Also, Stevenson's campaign style worried many Democrats. Stevenson was what a later generation would call a "policy wonk," a man who was extremely familiar with major public policy issues and enjoyed discussing and debating them. He was also uncomfortable on the campaign trail, at least in terms of the traditional backslapping, baby-kissing activities.

Senator Estes Kefauver* of Tennessee, who had contested the 1952 Democratic nomination with Stevenson, entered the race again, and he stunned Stevenson from the outset, winning the Democratic presidential primaries in New Hampshire and Minnesota. Stevenson criticized Kefauver for ignoring the issues, but the Tennessean continued his down-home barnstorming. Kefauver's problems, however, eventually stalled his campaign. He had never been popular with the major labor unions, a primary Democratic constituency, and the big city Democratic bosses loathed him because of his campaign to expose graft and corruption among them. At the Democratic National Convention held in Chicago, Stevenson enraged Southerners when he called for support of the U.S. Supreme Court's decision in *Brown v. Board of Education of Topeka, Kansas** (1954), which had ordered the desegregation of America's public schools. Some Southerners tried to convince Senator Lyndon B. Johnson* of Texas to seek the nomination, but it was too late. Stevenson had the delegate votes and won the nomination.

After Stevenson's nomination, however, another battle loomed at the convention. Senator John F. Kennedy* of Massachusetts made a concerted effort to secure the vice-presidential nomination, even though party managers wanted to give it to Kefauver, whose roots in Tennessee would balance the ticket between the North and the South. In the end, Kefauver won the vice-presidential nomination, but only by a razor-thin margin of 38 votes.

The campaign itself proved to be anticlimactic. President Eisenhower hit the campaign trail to prove that he had the health and physical strength to serve, and Stevenson continued to deliver his boring, if intellectually sophisticated, speeches. In the end, it was a landslide victory for Eisenhower, who beat Stevenson by 35.6 million popular votes to 26 million. The electoral college margin was 457 for Eisenhower to 73 for Stevenson. Oddly enough, however, the president's coattails were remarkably short. The Democrats actually gained 2 seats in the Senate and 17 seats in the House of Representatives.

SUGGESTED READINGS: Paul T. David, Ralph M. Goodman, and Richard C. Bain, *The Politics of the National Convention*, 1960; Porter McKeever, *Adlai Stevenson: His Life and Legacy*, 1989.

ELECTION OF 1958. As the congressional elections of 1958 approached, the Republicans realized that they were in political trouble. The economy had entered a recession, and unemployment had spiked up. Even worse, the Soviet Union had launched *Sputnik*,* an artificial satellite, into orbit in 1957, and tens of millions of American were scared, worried that the Russians might now have a way of putting nuclear bombs aboard rockets and targeting the mainland United States. It appeared to many Americans that the United States had fallen technologically behind the Soviet Union. Furthermore, Southern Democrats blamed Dwight D. Eisenhower* for the burgeoning civil rights movement.* Eisenhower had appointed Earl Warren* as chief justice of the U.S. Supreme Court, and the Court was proving to be the most liberal in American history. Its 1954 decision in *Brown v. Board of Education of Topeka, Kansas** to desegregate public schools had enraged Southerners and triggered the so-called massive resistance* movement. Eisenhower's decision to send U.S. Army troops to guarantee the integration of Central High School in Little Rock, Arkansas,*

had further alienated southerners. The elections proved to be a political disaster for Republicans. They lost 13 seats in the Senate and 48 seats in the House of Representatives. Democrats also secured six state governorships.

SUGGESTED READINGS: *New York Times*, November 5–8, 1958.

EMMETT TILL CASE. In the summer of 1955, Emmett Till, a 14-year-old resident of Chicago, Illinois, was spending his vacation with relatives in Mississippi. On the afternoon of August 24, Till went to a local grocery store with his cousins. What happened next is still uncertain. Till whistled habitually to control a speech defect, but the store owner's wife, a white woman, claimed that Till whistled at her and then groped her and made lewd remarks. Till's cousins insisted that he had done nothing of the kind.

Several days later, Roy Bryant, the store owner, conspired with his half brother, J. W. Milam, to kidnap Till. They beat and tortured Till, and when they found a photograph of a white woman in Till's wallet, they shot the boy and dumped his body in a local river. When the boy was found several days later, both men were arrested for murder. In the subsequent trial, however, an all-white male jury acquitted the two men after deliberating for only one hour. White Southerners insisted that justice had been done, but the Northern and world press roundly condemned white racism in the South.

SUGGESTED READING: Stephen J. Whitfield, *A Death in the Delta: The Story of Emmett Till*, 1989.

THE EVERLY BROTHERS. The Everly Brothers were a highly successful rock duo in the late 1950s and early 1960s. Don Everly was born in Brownie, Kentucky, on February 1, 1937, and his brother Phil, on January 17, 1939. Their parents, Margaret and Ike Everly, had been minor country and western stars in the 1930s and 1940s, and the boys often went on tour with them. In 1956 Roy Acuff brought the two boys to Nashville and hired them to write songs. They recorded unsuccessfully that year for Columbia Records and then signed with Cadence Records. They had a huge hit in 1957 with "Bye Bye Love," which reached number two on the pop music charts. Its rock-and-roll* beat combined with harmonized, country vocals became an Everly Brothers trademark. During the next five years, while they toured around the world, the Everly Brothers sold more than $35 million in records and had dozens of hits, including four number-one records: "Wake Up Little Susie," "All I Have to Do Is Dream," "Cathy's Clown," and "Bird Dog." Other hits included "Till I Kissed You" and "When Will I Be Loved." Their last hit came in 1962 when "That's Old Fashioned" reached number nine. They were then eclipsed by the revolution brought to rock-and-roll by the Beatles and the Rolling Stones. Since then they have remained a popular touring group.

SUGGESTED READINGS: Phyllis Karpp, *Ike's Boys: The Story of the Everly Brothers*, 1980; Roger White, *Walk Right Back: The Story of the Everly Brothers*, 1984.

F

FABIAN. "Fabian" was born Fabiano Forte in Philadelphia, Pennsylvania, on February 6, 1943. One of the first "manufactured" teen idols, his fame was based more on good looks and record company promotion than on talent. In 1959 and 1960, he burst on the pop scene with three top-ten hits: "Turn Me Loose," "Tiger," and "Hound Dog Man," and he appeared in John Wayne's* film *North to Alaska* (1960). But Fabian then disappeared almost as quickly as he had appeared. He occasionally appeared on situation comedies, and on limited concert tour engagements, he was billed as one of the so-called Golden Voices.

SUGGESTED READING: Patricia Romanowski and Holly George-Warren, *The Encyclopedia of Rock & Roll*, 1995.

"THE FAMILY OF MAN." "The Family of Man," a photographic exhibition, was staged by American photographer Edward Steichen at the Museum of Modern Art in New York City in 1955. With the objective of showing the diversity and yet the universality of human beings, Steichen invited photographers from around the world to submit prints. From the two million submissions, Steichen put 503 on display. "The Family of Man," eventually viewed by more than nine million people, remains today one of the most popular museum exhibitions in history.

SUGGESTED READING: Edward Steichen, *The Family of Man*, 1955.

FATHER KNOWS BEST. *Father Knows Best*, one of radio's more successful situation comedies, premiered on NBC radio on August 25, 1949, with Robert Young starring as Jim Anderson, patriarch of the upper middle-class Anderson family. Anderson made a living as an insurance agent, and the program's plots revolved around the antics and troubles of his three teenaged children: Betty (Rhoda Williams), Bud (Ted Donaldson), and Kathy (Norma Jean Nilsson). Jim's wife, Margaret, was played by Jean Vander Pyl. They lived in the town of Springfield somewhere in the Midwest. Anderson dispensed sage advice to his children, helping them survive the pitfalls of adolescence. The series lasted into the 1953 season, by which time plans were in the works for a television* series of the same name. *Father Knows Best* eventually became one of the most popular and beloved situation comedies in television history.

The television version of *Father Knows Best* premiered on CBS on October 3, 1954, starring Robert Young as Jim Anderson, Jane Wyatt as his wife, Margaret, Elinor Donahue as daughter Betty, Billy Gray as son Bud, and Lauren Chapin as daughter Kathy. NBC signed the series in 1955, but it returned to CBS in 1958, remaining there until 1962, when ABC picked it up. Tens of millions of Americans tuned in each week and watched the Andersons grow up and grow older. They became the quintessential 1950s middle-class family— hardworking, stable, conservative, and functional. The show was still at its peak in 1962 when Robert Young, tired of the role, decided not to continue. The last episode of *Father Knows Best* was broadcast on April 5, 1963.

SUGGESTED READINGS: Tim Brooks and Earle Marsh, *The Complete Directory to Prime Time Network and Cable TV Shows, 1946–Present*, 1995; John Dunning, *On the Air: The Encyclopedia of Old-Time Radio*, 1998.

FAUBUS, ORVAL. Orval Eugene Faubus was born on January 7, 1910, in the poverty-stricken Greasy Creek region of northwestern Arkansas. His father, a poor farmer, was an avowed socialist who passed populist values on to his son. In 1928, with only an eighth-grade education, the younger Faubus passed the state teacher examination and went to work as a teacher in the town of Pinnacle. During the summer months, he picked crops in Michigan. Faubus joined the U.S. Army during World War II and rose to the rank of major in army intelligence. When he returned to Arkansas after the war, he became state highway commissioner.

Faubus was elected governor of Arkansas in 1953 and took office in 1954, the same year that the U.S. Supreme Court reached its decision in *Brown v. Board of Education of Topeka, Kansas.** At the time he was actually considered a liberal on racial matters. He appointed blacks to important posts in the state Democratic party, fought for teacher pay raises, built better roads in rural areas, and even allowed some early school integration to occur.

But, as opposition to *Brown v. Board of Education* mounted in America, Faubus had to face reelection, and he opted to turn the race in his favor. He knew that the key to political success in Arkansas had long been race, and he seized on the Supreme Court's decision to desegregate public schools as a means of generating political capital. In the first state legislative session after *Brown*, Faubus pushed and eventually signed measures establishing an anti-integration investigation in state government, allowing parents to refuse to allow their children to attend integrated schools, requiring the National Association for the Advancement of Colored People (NAACP) to hand over its membership lists to state investigators, authorizing state funds to finance segregated private schools, and permitting state public school funds for legal expenses in fighting deseg-regation court orders. In 1956 Faubus was elected to a second term as governor.

Faubus became a national figure in 1957 with the attempted integration of Central High School in Little Rock, Arkansas.* On September 2, 1957, the day before the school year began, Faubus announced that he would not offer police protection to black children entering the public schools. The black children, now dubbed the "Little Rock Nine" by journalists, would face possible threats to their lives. The children showed up for school at Central High School on September 4, 1957, but the Arkansas National Guard surrounded the school and would not let them enter.

President Dwight D. Eisenhower,* trying to avoid a constitutional crisis, met with Governor Faubus and convinced him to remove the national guard troops. On September 23, however, when the nine black students tried to attend school, an angry mob gathered outside the school and threatened the students. When the mob refused to disperse the next day, Eisenhower nationalized the Arkansas National Guard, which put the troops under his command, and sent in troops from the 101st Airborne Division to protect the black students. The "Little Rock Nine" began their first day of school on September 25. Faubus was not finished though. Masses of white students left Central High School, which resulted in the closing of the school in 1958–1959. Faubus tried to start a system of private schools for white students, but the movement petered out. In 1959 Central High School opened as an integrated high school.

To everybody and anybody who would listen in Arkansas, Faubus complained that the president had exceeded his authority and violated states' rights. To most Americans, he had become a symbol of racism and a bygone era, but to most white people in Arkansas, he had become a hero. He was reelected three more times. Faubus then left office and had a dismal post-gubernatorial career. He worked as a bank teller in Huntsville, Arkansas, and ran unsuccessfully for governor in 1970, 1974, and 1986. Faubus died on December 14, 1994.

SUGGESTED READINGS: Elizabeth Huckaby, *Crisis at Central High School*, 1980; *New York Times*, December 15, 1994; Robert Sherrill, *Gothic Politics in the Deep South: Stars of the New Confederacy*, 1968.

FEDERAL BUREAU OF INVESTIGATION. In the years immediately following World War I, J. Edgar Hoover* made a name for himself in Washington, D.C. An employee of the Justice Department, he helped Attorney General A. Mitchell Palmer direct his Red Scare crusade against suspected radicals and revolutionaries. When the Federal Bureau of Investigation (FBI) was formally established in 1922, J. Edgar Hoover was appointed to head the new law enforcement agency.

It was not until the 1930s, however, that the FBI began to become popular with the American public. During the Great Depression, Hoover's FBI agents, who had become known as "G-men," foiled the most notorious criminals of the age, including John Dillinger, George "Machine Gun" Kelly, Charles "Pretty

Boy" Floyd, and "Ma" Barker and her boys. When the United States entered World War II, Hoover changed the FBI's focus to espionage to ferret out Nazi and Japanese sympathizers in American society.

By the late 1940s and throughout the 1950s, however, as the Cold War* assumed larger and larger dimensions, Hoover targeted Communists and Communist sympathizers as the greatest threat to the republic, and once again he became an enthusiastic participant in another Red Scare.* Hoover considered his mission so important that he worked to place the FBI beyond the scrutiny of Congress and the rest of the executive branch. His agents assembled detailed dossiers on tens of thousands of Americans, including politicians and bureaucrats, and Hoover was not above blackmailing influential people in order to protect and promote the FBI. He leaked information to people like Senator Joseph McCarthy* and other fellow-travelers in his war on communism. The FBI remained quite popular with most Americans. Books like Don Whitehead's *The FBI Story* (1956), which was made into a film featuring actor Jimmy Stewart, and Hoover's own *Masters of Deceit* (1958) treated FBI agents as heroes.

When the civil rights movement* emerged in the late 1950s, Hoover was certain that it was riddled with Communists, and he tried to saddle Martin Luther King, Jr.,* with that label. He was especially concerned about the direction Chief Justice Earl Warren* was taking the Supreme Court, especially when the Court, in the name of civil liberties, put some brakes on the Red Scare's excesses. The Court's so-called Red Monday* decisions in 1957 irritated Hoover, because he felt the FBI's authority had been circumscribed.

During the 1960s, the FBI's popularity in general and Hoover's in particular nose-dived. The civil rights movement steadily gained in popularity, and as it did so, Hoover's single-mindedness seemed increasingly heavy-handed and anachronistic. When opposition to the Vietnam War* escalated, Hoover tried to use the FBI to ferret out suspected Communists and spies, but the antiwar movement, like the civil rights movement, gained in popularity in the 1960s, and J. Edgar Hoover's image was inversely related to it. He ceased being a celebrity and increasingly became seen as a reactionary. The FBI lost its heroic status.

SUGGESTED READINGS: Richard Gird Powers, *Secrecy and Power: The Life of J. Edgar Hoover*, 1987; Athan Theohharis, *Spying on Americans: Political Surveillance from Hoover to the Huston Plan*, 1978.

FEDERAL INTERSTATE DEFENSE HIGHWAY ACT OF 1958. *See* NATIONAL HIGHWAY ACT OF 1958.

FIBBER McGEE AND MOLLY. *Fibber McGee and Molly*, one of the most popular and enduring radio programs in American history, premiered on the Blue Network on April 16, 1935. It soon shifted to NBC radio, where it remained until its last broadcast on September 6, 1959. It starred Jim Jordan as Fibber McGee, a hopelessly unrealistic but gentle blowhard who dreams implausible dreams, tells tall tales, and frustrates his long-suffering wife, Molly, played by Marian Jordan. Fibber's high-pitched squeaky voice fit a whining character perfectly, and the shows revolved around life in the McGee home. The Jordans were veterans of vaudeville who had scratched their way up the entertainment ladder, and *Fibber McGee and Molly* made them household names. By the early 1940s, *Fibber McGee and Molly* regularly held a ratings position in the top five, and such signature comments as Molly's "heavenly days" became phrases in the language of American popular culture.

SUGGESTED READING: John Dunning, *On the Air: The Encyclopedia of Old-Time Radio*, 1998.

THE FLY. *The Fly* was a popular horror film of the 1950s. Released in August 1958, *The Fly* trafficked in America's love-hate relationship with modern science, which had produced a cure for polio and many other infectious diseases but had also developed nuclear weapons. An altruistic scientist, working in his home laboratory in Montreal, Canada, discovers how to disintegrate objects electromagnetically. When he foolishly decides to experiment on himself, a housefly inadvertently buzzes into the lab, and the two creatures exchange heads—the scientist now possesses a fly's head, and the fly now has his head. Audiences found the film exactly what director Kurt Neumann wanted it to be— horrifying and a testament to the dangers of tampering with nature and the unknown.

SUGGESTED READING: *New York Times*, August 30, 1958.

FONDA, HENRY. Henry Fonda was born in Grand Island, Nebraska, on May 16, 1905. After a brief stint at the University of Minnesota, he dropped out to pursue his real dream of an acting career. Fonda toured with a number of small theatrical troupes in the late 1920s and early 1930s and then moved to New York City. His first major Broadway role was in *The Farmer Takes a Wife* (1934), in which several Hollywood producers noticed him. The next year he reprised the role in his first film. Beginning with his 1938 performance in *Blockade*, Fonda had string of remarkable film performances, including *Young Mr. Lincoln* (1939), *Drums Along the Mohawk* (1939), *The Grapes of Wrath* (1940), *The Lady Eve* (1941), *The Male Animal* (1942), and *The Ox-Bow Incident* (1943). Because of his military service during World War II, Fonda did not make another film until 1947, when he appeared in *The Fugitive*. During the 1950s, Fonda's most memorable roles came in the tragic comedy *Mr. Roberts* (1955), in which he played an indefatigable naval officer, and in *Twelve Angry Men* (1957), in which he played a juror foreman in a controversial case. Fonda developed on stage a persona as an honest, simple man who could be trusted. He died on August 12, 1982.

SUGGESTED READINGS: Peter Collier, *The Fondas: A Hollywood Dynasty*, 1991; Henry Fonda, *Fonda: My Life*, 1981.

FOUR-MINUTE MILE. By the early 1950s, it had become a maxim of sports science that human beings were incapable of running a mile in less than four minutes. So convinced were they that no human body could process oxygen fast enough to break the four-minute barrier that they predicted the sudden death of any runner who got close to the record. Late in 1953, Roger Bannister, a medical student at Oxford University in Great Britain, set out to break the record. He rejected the sudden death concern, even though he was, in his own words, "prepared to die." On May 6, 1954, at a meet between the Oxford University track team and the British Amateur Athletic Union, Bannister ran for the record and broke it, completing the mile in 3:59.4. He fainted at the finish line and subsequently suffered a temporary color blindness, but he recovered fully. Six weeks later, John Landy of Australia ran the mile in 3:58, and within a year more than a dozen other runners had breached the four-minute mile, which no longer deserved to be called a "barrier."

SUGGESTED READINGS: *New York Times*, May 7–8, 1954.

FRANCIS, CONNIE. Connie Francis was born Concetta Maria Franconero in Newark, New Jersey, on December 12, 1938. A talented child, she could play the accordian when she was four years old, and she began to perform locally. In 1950 she appeared on Arthur Godfrey's* television talent show, and he suggested that she change her name to Connie Francis. She signed a contract with MGM records in 1955 but had several flops. Her father then suggested that she do an upbeat version of "Who's Sorry Now," a 1920s hit. His instincts proved correct. "Who's Sorry Now" reached number four on the pop charts in 1958. Francis quickly became one of rock-and-roll's* most popular stars. She recorded 36 top-25 hits, including "Stupid Cupid" (1958), "My Happiness" (1959), "Lipstick on Your Collar" (1958), and "Where the Boys Are" (1961). She also appeared in such hit films as *Where the Boys Are* (1960), *Follow the Boys* (1963), *Looking for Love* (1964), and *When the Boys Meet the Girls* (1965). Connie Francis dropped out of the rock limelight, especially after the so-called British invasion of such groups as the Beatles, the Rolling Stones, and the Dave Clark Five.

SUGGESTED READING: Connie Francis, *Who's Sorry Now*, 1984.

FRANKFURTER, FELIX. Felix Frankfurter was born on November 15, 1882, to a prominent Jewish family in Vienna, Austria. The family immigrated to New York City in 1894. A precocious and very ambitious young man, he had impressed adults, even as a child, with the power of his intellect. Frankfurter graduated from the City College of New York in 1901, graduated at the top of his class at Harvard Law School, and went to work in New York for Hornblower, Byrne, Miller, and Potter. After two years, Frankfurter signed on with Henry L. Stimson, the U.S. attorney for the southern district of New York. He followed Stimson to the War Department in 1909 and remained there for five years.

In 1914 Frankfurter returned to Harvard as a member of the law school faculty, and he soon became mentor to some of the most brilliant minds in America.

Committed to the belief that the law was rooted in a social context, Frankfurter insisted that his students study history, political science, sociology, and economics, as well as the law, and he urged them to try to look beyond tradition to make sure that the law remained rooted in social, political, and economic reality. Frankfurter soon earned a reputation for directing many of his most brilliant students into government service. During World War I, he worked for the President's Mediation Commission and for the War Labor Policies Board.

The decade of the 1920s proved critical in shaping Frankfurter's legal and political philosophy. He profoundly disagreed with the direction that Chief Justice Charles Evans Hughes was taking the U.S. Supreme Court, especially when it assumed an activist, centralized role in overturning social legislation at the state level. It was, Frankfurter believed, an unjust judicial assumption of legislative power and a violation of the principle of federalism. Frankfurter became an inveterate opponent of judicial activism at the federal level.

He also earned a liberal reputation for his defense of Nicola Sacco and Bartolomeo Vanzetti and such groups as the National Association for the Advancement of Colored People and the American Civil Liberties Union. During the New Deal years of the 1930s, Frankfurter acted as a legal advisor to the Franklin D. Roosevelt administration and sent dozens of his best students to work in New Deal agencies. In 1933 he spent a year at Oxford University, where he met macro-economist John Maynard Keynes and became a convert to his economic views. Upon returning to the United States in 1934, Frankfurter strongly encouraged Roosevelt to use government spending and tax policies as a means of stimulating the economy. By the end of the decade, Felix Frankfurter was one of the most influential men in the country, primarily because so many powerful government agencies were staffed by his former students.

In 1939 Roosevelt appointed him to the Supreme Court. As a liberal, Frankfurter wanted the Court to be less likely than its predecessor to overturn legislative decisions at the federal and local levels, where he considered democracy to be working in its purest form. Gradually, Frankfurter became a proponent of strict judicial self-restraint. He did not want to see a return to the 1920s and early 1930s when the Supreme Court had regularly overturned the regulatory decisions of state legislatures.

But that very commitment to judicial self-restraint caused problems for Frankfurter during the 1950s, when the Earl Warren* Court had become highly activist in overturning state laws limiting civil rights and civil liberties. Frankfurter generally believed that the first eight amendments to the Constitution applied to Congress, and he was inclined to protect individual rights when the offending party was the federal government. He was not convinced that the Fourteenth Amendment to the Constitution required application of those same eight amendments to the activities of state government, so he was inclined not to have the Court intervene when offending activities took place at the state and local levels. He did not believe that the federal courts should be in the business of overturning the work of popularly elected legislatures. At times, many liberals became quite critical of Frankfurter's judicial philosophy. Frankfurter retired from the court in 1962 and died on February 22, 1965.

SUGGESTED READINGS: Max Freedman, *Roosevelt and Frankfurter*, 1967; H. N. Hirsch, *The Enigma of Felix Frankfurter*, 1981; Michael E. Parrish, *Felix Frankfurter and His Times*, 1982.

FREED, ALAN. Alan Freed was born in Salem, Ohio, in 1922 to a middle-class family. His father was a clerk in a local clothing store. Alan attended Ohio State University for several years but did not graduate with a degree. His real interests were music, especially rhythm and blues. Freed played the trombone in an Ohio State band named the Sultans of Swing. After a two-year stint in the U.S. Army, Freed began his radio career at a small station in New Castle, Pennsylvania.

As a radio announcer, Freed coined the term "rock-and-roll"* to describe the rhythm-and-blues music that during the 1950s was beginning to appeal to a broader audience of white listeners. Freed played a key role in expanding its appeal and in doing so earned the nickname "Father of Rock and Roll." In 1954 he joined WINS in New York City and, calling himself the "King of the Moon Doggies," became one of the most popular radio personalities in the country. He also regularly appeared on the concert circuit announcing acts, always in his trademark brightly colored, checkered sport coat. Critics of rock-and-roll generally held Freed responsible for playing a central role in "corrupting the morals of American youth." In 1958 Freed left WINS for WABC and later WNEW-TV.

In 1960, however, his career nose-dived. The scandals associated with *The $64,000 Question* and *Twenty-One* on television opened the way for investigations into the music business, and Freed was soon charged with taking $30,650 in kickbacks from six record companies to play new releases on his radio programs. He initially denied the accusations, but in 1962 he plea-bargained his way out of the scandal and admitted guilt to some of the charges. The papers widely reported participation in what they labeled the payola* scandal. Freed received a six-month suspended sentence and a $300 fine. He left the radio business and moved to California. Two years later, his name surfaced again in the news when the Internal Revenue Service charged him with failing to pay taxes on $37,920 in payola income between 1957 and 1959. Freed's legal problems did not surprise those who felt rock-and-roll was bad for America. Freed died of uremic poisoning on January 20, 1965.

SUGGESTED READINGS: John A. Jackson, *Big Beat Heat: Alan Freed and the Early Years of Rock and Roll*, 1991; *New York Times*, January 21, 1965.

FRISBEE. The "frisbee," a flat, aerodynamically sound plastic saucer, was invented by the Wham-O Company of California in 1957, and within a decade it had become a fad among young people around the country. In 1967 the International Frisbee Association was formed, signifying the arrival of the toy as a national craze. In parks, beaches, school playgrounds, and university commons, throwing the frisbee became a ubiquitous activity among American young people.

SUGGESTED READING: Jane Stern and Michael Stern, *Encyclopedia of Pop Culture*, 1992.

FROM HERE TO ETERNITY. Published in 1951, *From Here to Eternity* was James Jones's first novel, and it received critical acclaim, including a National Book Award. Jones was stationed in Hawaii with the U.S. Army on December 7, 1941, when Japan launched its sneak attack on Pearl Harbor. He later remarked, "I remember thinking with a sense of the profoundest awe that none of our lives would ever be the same." For a number of years, most American readers wanted nothing more than patriotic propaganda in their literature, but by 1951, millions of people were finally ready to take a careful look at the meaning of the war. *From Here to Eternity* provided them that opportunity.

An epic novel of 861 pages, *From Here to Eternity* possesses a dark side, a new way of looking at World War II, one not previously encountered by Americans. The novel is set in Hawaii on the eve of the Japanese attack, and its realistic portrait of military life—sexual escapades, brutality, alcoholism, and profanity—shocked many readers, although most soldiers and sailors who read the book knew that it rang true. *From Here to Eternity* also offered a scathing look at bureaucratic inertia and political infighting in the U.S. military and suggested that at the heart of American unpreparedness in 1941 was a military mired in arrogance, cronyism, and naiveté. In 1953 Hollywood put the novel on the silver screen. The film starred Burt Lancaster, Donna Reed, Deborah Kerr, Montgomery Clift, and Frank Sinatra. Like the novel, the film pushed the edge of the moral envelope; Burt Lancaster's love-making scene on the beach with Deborah Kerr was considered highly risque. Frank Sinatra won an Oscar for his portrayal of Angelo Maggio.

SUGGESTED READING: James Jones, *From Here to Eternity*, 1951.

G

GABLE, CLARK. William Clark Gable was born in Cadiz, Ohio, on February 1, 1901. He was raised there and on a farm outside Ravenna, Ohio. Fascinated with the theater, he signed with a touring troupe in 1917. He left the troupe in Oregon and then worked as a lumberjack and telephone lineman. In 1924 he joined a theater company in Portland. Several minor roles on Broadway and Los Angeles caught the attention of movie scouts, and Gable made his screen debut in 1927 in *The Painted Desert*. He then signed with the MGM Studio and made a dozen pictures over the course of the next several years. For his performance with Claudette Colbert in *It Happened One Night* (1934), he won an academy award as best actor. During the next seven years, until the outbreak of World War II, Gable was one of Hollywood's most bankable male leads, and appeared in *Mutiny on the Bounty* (1935), *China Seas* (1935), *San Francisco* (1936), *Saratoga* (1937), *Test Pilot* (1938), and *Idiot's Delight* (1939). His reputation as the world's most popular actor was cemented by his performance as Rhett Butler in *Gone With the Wind* (1941).

After the Japanese bombed Pearl Harbor, Gable enlisted in the army air corps, even though he was forty-one years old. He served with distinction in combat and won the distinguished flying cross. Gable then returned to Hollywood and resumed his career in *Adventure* (1946), *The Hucksters* (1947), *To Please a Lady* (1950), *The Wide Missouri* (1951), *Lone Star* (1952), *Mogambo* (1953), and *Soldier of Fortune* (1955). That year he was Hollywood's leading man in terms of ticket sales, and the nickname "King of Hollywood" was often used to describe him. Later in the decade he made *Run Silent, Run Deep* (1958), and in 1960 he starred with Sophia Loren in *It Started in Naples*. After filming *The Misfits* with Marilyn Monroe, Gable died suddenly of a heart attack on November 16, 1960.

SUGGESTED READINGS: *New York Times*, November 17, 1960; Jane Ellen Wayne, *Clark Gable: Portrait of a Misfit*, 1993.

GANGBUSTERS. *Gangbusters*, a radio crime series, survived on the air for more than twenty-two years. Using an interview format, the show featured real cases garnered from state and FBI files. Taking advantage of the public's fascination with such criminals as John Dillinger, Ma Barker, and Bonnie and Clyde, as well as the FBI G-men who went after them, *Gangbusters* premiered on NBC radio on July 12, 1935. Hollywood made such films as *Little Ceasar* (1930) and *The Public Enemy* (1931) as part of that pop culture obsession. Each week the show would give out details of wanted criminals, including their physical characteristics, aliases, and habits. Each year, the FBI managed to arrest more than 100 accused criminals on the basis of tips from radio listeners. Although the program was canceled in 1957, it provided inspiration for subsequent television series of the same genre, including *Unsolved Mysteries* of the 1990s.

SUGGESTED READING: John Dunning, *On the Air: The Encyclopedia of Old-Time Radio*, 1998.

GATHINGS COMMITTEE. Deeply concerned about what he perceived as a dramatic increase in obscene publications and films, Congressman Ezekiel Gathings (D–AK) decided to hold a congressional investigation. While walking to work each day, Gathings had become very disturbed by the magazines he saw displayed openly in drugstore and street newsstands. "I thought, what is this country coming to if we are distributing this type of thing to the youth of the land? Then, to follow it through, these kids seem to have the idea that one must go out and commit rape." Gathings chaired the House Select Committee on Current Pornographic Materials. The hearings began on June 16, 1952. Gathings became so zealous in his crusade that he suffered public ridicule from some journalists.

The Gathings Report was issued in 1953. It condemned the paperback book industry for profiting from salacious material and advocated government censorship. The Gathings Report also claimed that the more than 100 million comic books sold each month contained obscene material. One critic told Gathings to worry "about real problems—like atomic bombs,* war, disease, and poverty—not the evils of comic books." Gathings charged that one in ten American men read "girlie magazines" each month. Publishers, of course, cited their First Amendment freedom and accused Gathings of exaggerating the issue. Ironically, the Gathings Report appeared at the same time as the first issue of Hugh Hefner's *Playboy** magazine. While the Gathings Report gathered dust, *Playboy* skyrocketed in circulation. Gathings became a laughingstock to many Americans. He retired from Congress in 1969.

SUGGESTED READING: "No Witch Hunt," *Newsweek*, July 7, 1952, 80.

THE GENE AUTRY SHOW. During the 1930s and 1940s, Gene Autry became a household figure in American entertainment as the "singing cowboy" who appeared in dozens of B films. CBS decided to give him his own television show, and *The Gene Autry Show* premiered on July 23, 1950. Backed by the theme song "Back in the Saddle Again," Autry and his sidekick Pat Burtram roamed the old Southwest dispensing justice and rescuing the innocent from danger and trouble. Autry always managed to sing a song in each episode, and he did tricks with his horse Champion, who became an icon in his own right to children of the baby boom* generation. The last episode of *The Gene Autry Show* was broadcast on August 7, 1956.

SUGGESTED READING: Tim Brooks and Earle Marsh, *The Complete Directory to Prime Time Network and Cable TV Shows, 1946–Present*, 1995.

THE GEORGE BURNS AND GRACIE ALLEN SHOW. The husband-and-wife team of George Burns and Gracie Allen became a headline vaudeville act in the 1920s, made the jump to radio in the 1930s and 1940s, and then starred in one of television's* most successful situation comedies during the 1950s. CBS first brought *The George Burns and Gracie Allen Show* to the air on October 12, 1950. The show revolved around their home, where the stable, unflappable George tried to cope with the zany, scatterbrained antics of his wife, Gracie. Gracie's conspirator in comedy was next-door neighbor Blanche Morton, played by Bea Benaderet, who tested the patience of her long-suffering accountant husband, Harry (played over the years by Hal March, John Brown, Fred Clark, and Larry Keating). For the first two years, the show was broadcast live, every other Thursday night, from New York, but in 1952 the show moved to Los Angeles where it was filmed before a studio audience and then broadcast weekly. The show came to an end in 1958 when Gracie Allen decided not to continue. The last episode was broadcast on September 22, 1958.

SUGGESTED READINGS: Tim Brooks and Earle Marsh, *The Complete Directory to Prime Time Network and Cable TV Shows, 1946–Present*, 1995; Cynthia Clements, *George Burns and Gracie Allen: A Biobibliography*, 1996.

GIANT. Released in 1956, *Giant*, an epic film, is set in Texas in the early twentieth century. The film starred Rock Hudson as Bick Benedict, a cattleman reluctantly forced into the oil age; Elizabeth Taylor as his wife, Leslie, the well-bred daughter of a prominent Kentucky family that raises thoroughbred horses; and James Dean* as Jett Rink, the upstart wildcatter who makes a fortune in oil. The film traffics such themes as old wealth versus new wealth and land versus money, as well as such questions as racism and discrimination, especially between Anglos and Mexican Americans. *Giant* was nominated for nine academy awards.

SUGGESTED READINGS: David Dalton, *James Dean: The Mutant King*, 1983; Joe Hyams, *James Dean: Little Boy Lost*, 1992.

GIBSON, ALTHEA. Althea Gibson was born in Silver, South Carolina, in 1927. During the 1930s, the Gibson family moved to New York City and rented an apartment in Harlem. She became active in the local Police Athletic League's programs. Because of Gibson's talent at paddleball, the Cosmopolitan Tennis Club gave her a scholarship to learn tennis. It changed Gibson's life.

At first, she competed in tournaments sponsored by the American Tennis Association (ATA), the black equivalent of the U.S. Lawn Tennis Association (USLTA). In 1944 and 1945, Gibson won back-to-back ATA national junior championships. African-American leaders soon targeted Althea Gibson to become the Jackie Robinson* of women's tennis and integrate the sport. White tennis champion Alice Marble began campaigning on Gibson's behalf, and in 1950, the USLTA allowed Gibson to compete in its national championship.

The increased level of competition improved Gibson's game, and she rose steadily in the USLTA's rankings. She was ranked ninth in the world in 1952 and seventh in 1953. In 1956, Gibson won both the singles and doubles championships at the French Open. Within two years, she was clearly the best woman tennis player in the world. In 1957 and 1958, Gibson won first place at Wimbledon and the U.S. Open.

SUGGESTED READINGS: Tom Biracree, *Althea Gibson*, 1989; Althea Gibson, *I Always Wanted to Be Somebody*, 1958.

GINSBERG, ALLEN. Allen Ginsberg was born on June 3, 1926, in New York City. He enrolled at Columbia University in 1943, but he was suspended from the university when the football coach found out that Jack Kerouac* was sharing Ginsberg's room. Ginsberg was at Columbia again in 1949 when he came to terms with his homosexuality and came out of the closet, an avowed homosexual at a time when homosexuality was illegal and socially unacceptable. He flaunted rules, rejected bureaucratic institutions, and disobeyed social conventions. Still unrepentant, Ginsberg allowed friends to store stolen goods in his apartment, and police eventually arrested him. Several prominent faculty members—including Lionel Trilling, Meyer Schapiro, and Herbert Weschler—rallied to his side, and on their advice, Ginsberg pleaded insanity. Instead of going to a penitentiary, he was taken to the mental ward of Columbia Presbyterian Hospital. After several months there, he promised to live a conventional life and was released.

Ginsberg tried to live a typical life of work, schedules, and heterosexuality, but he was frustrated and miserable. When asked by a psychiatrist what he wanted to do with his life, Ginsberg said, "I really would like to stop working forever—never work again . . . and do nothing but write poetry and have leisure to spend the day outdoors and go to museums and see friends." Not until he moved to Berkeley, California, in 1954 did Ginsberg begin to enjoy that type of life.

At Berkeley, Ginsberg emerged as a leading figure in the Beat* movement. To explore sensory experience and his inner feelings, he experimented with drugs, and he actively promoted the civil rights movement,* as well as gay rights. He labored to protect the underdogs in American society, and he openly advocated individual faithfulness to sexual identity—whether heterosexual or homosexual. All social conventions that limit individual potential or restrict individual sensory experiences should be rejected out of hand.

In California, Ginsberg also found himself in the center of an enormous legal and political controversy over the constitutionality of censorship. His first book, *Howl and Other Poems*, was published in 1956. *Howl* had been on sale at the City Lights Bookstore in San Francisco for eight months before police undercover officers purchased a copy and then arrested store owner Lawrence Ferlinghetti for selling obscene material. The subsequent trial became a major test case in the history of civil liberties in the United States. For the trial, Ferlinghetti secured the legal counsel of Jake Ehrlich, an attorney who had defended rapist Caryl Chessman* and stripper Sally Rand. The district attorney tried to convince the court that a book could be deemed obscene on the basis of the individual words contained in it, whether or not the words were read in context. Judge Clayton Horn disagreed and acquitted Ferlinghetti. Civil libertarians hailed the decision.

As a result of the trial, Allan Ginsberg became a celebrity, and *Howl*, a bestseller. Within a few years, however, Ginsberg became more politicized. He became an icon to the counterculture of the 1960s, but his own drug use tapered off as he committed himself to left-wing political causes. He even came to denounce recreational drug use. Ginsberg donated money to the civil rights and anti–Vietnam War movements, helped finance underground newspapers, and raised money for legal defense groups working on behalf of men and women Ginsberg considered to be political prisoners. After the Stonewall Inn riots of 1969, Ginsberg accelerated his efforts on behalf of gay rights, and during the 1980s he worked in a variety of AIDS causes. He aged well, maintaining his reputation as an artist of enormous talent and a man of great integrity. Allen Ginsberg died on April 5, 1997.

SUGGESTED READINGS: Jake H. Ehrlich, ed., *Howl of the Censor*, 1956; Barry Miles, *Ginsberg: A Biography*, 1989; *New York Times*, April 6–7, 1997; Michael Schumacher, *Dharma Lion: A Critical Biography of Allen Ginsberg*, 1992.

GO TELL IT ON THE MOUNTAIN. *Go Tell It on the Mountain* is the title of James Baldwin's* groundbreaking 1953 novel. A native of Harlem in New York City, Baldwin abandoned the United States in 1948 and moved to Paris, France, to write his novel. His mentor, black writer Richard Wright, had promised him that seeing his country from a distance would be highly enlightening. Paris in the 1950s enjoyed the world's most racially diverse intellectual community, and Baldwin thrived there, although he actually wrote much of the novel in Switzerland. *Go Tell It on the Mountain* is a richly detailed, sensitive tale of a young black man growing up in Harlem and trying to deal with racism, religion, family, and his homosexuality. Baldwin had intentionally not written a "protest novel," which had become almost formulaic in African-American literature. Instead, he created a novel about "people first, Negroes almost incidentally."

The novel made Baldwin one of the most famous blacks in the country. It received rave reviews and gave him a measure of financial security. He returned to the United States in 1957, where the budding young civil rights movement* inspired him and demanded his loyalty and support. Within a matter of months, Baldwin had emerged as the intellectual leader of the crusade for black equality in the United States.

SUGGESTED READING: James Baldwin, *Go Tell It on the Mountain*, 1953.

GODFREY, ARTHUR. Arthur Godfrey was born in New York City on August 31, 1903. After finishing high school, he worked at a number of odd jobs before joining the U.S. Navy, where he became a radio operator. After leaving the navy, he sold cemetery plots, traveled with a vaudeville group, and then joined the Coast Guard. In 1929, while in Baltimore, Godfrey acted on a dare from several friends and showed up at WFBR radio claiming that he could do a better job than their existing broadcasters. The station manager gave him a try, and Godfrey's wit, wisdom, honesty, and subdued sarcasm won him a permanent job. In 1930 he joined NBC radio doing the local news. He then went to work for WJSV radio in Washington, D.C., where he presided over an all-night talk and record-playing show. Godfrey came to national attention in 1945 when CBS assigned him to announce the funeral of President Franklin D. Roosevelt. The network then gave him his own morning series.

From April 30, 1945, to April 30, 1972, Godfrey presided over *Arthur Godfrey Time*, a daily morning radio broadcast of talk and live musical performances. Godfrey endeared himself to listeners because of his honesty and the fact that he could be risque without ever being dirty or salacious. At one point, *Arthur Godfrey Time* enjoyed a daily listening audience of 40 million people.

He was also very successful on television.* *Arthur Godfrey and His Friends*, a talk and musical variety show, premiered on CBS television on January 12, 1949, and remained on the air until April 28, 1959. His other television show, *Arthur Godfrey's Talent Scouts*, was also on the air from December 6, 1948, to July 21, 1958. Both shows attracted healthy audiences and succeeded in giving Arthur Godfrey an almost patriarchal status in American pop culture. Godfrey did not leave CBS radio until 1972. Arthur Godfrey died March 16, 1983.

SUGGESTED READINGS: Arthur Godfrey, *Stories I Like to Tell*, 1952; *New York Times*, March 17, 1983.

GRAHAM, BILLY. William Franklin (Billy) Graham was born on November 7, 1918, in Charlotte, North Carolina. He was the son of a dairy farmer, William Franklin Graham, and Morrow Coffey Graham, a homemaker. After graduating from high school he became a Fuller Brush salesman and was quite successful, winning several company awards for his sales volume. He attended Bob Jones University for several months before moving on to the Florida Bible Institute. He received a Th.B. degree there in 1940 and was ordained a Baptist minister. In 1943 he received a B.A. from Wheaton College. Graham was then hired as pastor of the First Baptist Church of Springfield, Illinois, where he remained until 1948. At that point, he became vice president of Youth for Christ, an evangelical organization that works with high school and college students.

In 1949 Graham organized the Los Angeles Crusade, where his charismatic preaching style brought him national attention. He was an innovator in using many forms of media to get the gospel message to the world. In 1950 he launched his national radio broadcast *Hour of Decision* and was invited to the White House to meet President Harry Truman.* That same year he founded World Wide pictures and World Wide publications, both of which promoted his message of salvation through Jesus Christ. His first book, *Peace of Mind*, was published in 1953. Graham then took his crusade worldwide and appeared before tens of thousands of people in Great Britain. His weekly syndicated newspaper column, "My Answer," first appeared in 1956, and in 1957 he founded the magazine *Christianity Today*. When the desegregation* controversy erupted in Little Rock, Arkansas,* in 1957, President Dwight D. Eisenhower* solicited Graham's advice, and subsequent presidents did the same. By the end of the decade, Billy Graham was America's premier evangelist, and that reputation survives today.

SUGGESTED READINGS: William Martin, *A Prophet with Honor: The Billy Graham Story*, 1991; John Pollock, *To All the Nations of the World: The Billy Graham Story*, 1985.

GRAND OLE OPRY. *Grand Ole Opry* premiered on WSM, a local Nashville, Tennessee, radio station, on November 28, 1925, and featured the best performers from country music. The show was the creation of George Dewey Hay, known as the "solemn ole judge," who, during a mule expedition into the Ozark Mountains, discovered a hillbilly culture that appeared to be cut out of the eighteenth century. He developed a passionate affection for mountain music. In 1924 Hay helped create *The National Barn Dance* at WLS radio in Chicago, and in 1925 he was hired by WSM in Nashville to produce a similar program. *Grand Ole Opry* was the result. At first, he gathered in mountain people and farmers who played unwritten songs with old stringed instruments. As the years passed and country music etched out its place in popular culture, the performers became professional musicians. NBC radio picked up *Grand Ole Opry* in 1939 and broadcast it to a national audience. *Grand Ole Opry* remained on the air until its last radio broadcast on December 28, 1957. By that time, a television* show of the same name eclipsed it in popularity, ratings, and revenues.

SUGGESTED READING: John Dunning, *On the Air: The Encyclopedia of Old-Time Radio*, 1998.

THE GREAT GILDERSLEEVE. *The Great Gildersleeve*, a spinoff from *Fibber McGee and Molly*,* premiered on NBC radio on August 31, 1941, and featured Harold Peary as Throckmorton P. Gildersleeve, a man who serves as water commissioner of the mythical town of Summerfield, somewhere in the

Midwest. Gildersleeve, owner of Gildersleeve Girdle Works, had been on a sales trip to Summerfield, and there he decided to stay. He gave up his girdle business and threw himself into the life of the town. He was a windbag but also an eligible bachelor; the show revolved around the windbag antics. Peary was an immigrant from Portugal who got into radio with station KZN in Oakland, California. He could sing, narrate, and tell jokes, and he soon moved to Chicago. In September 1939, he appeared on *Fibber McGee and Molly* as McGee's next-door neighbor. The two characters were perfect foils for one another, arguing constantly and taking advantage of each other at every opportunity. Audiences loved it, and in 1941 NBC gave Peary his own show, *The Great Gildersleeve*. Peary remained on the show until mid-1951, when he left over a salary dispute. Willard Waterman took over the role of Gildersleeve, but *The Great Gildersleeve* began losing ratings, and NBC broadcast the last episode on March 21, 1957.

SUGGESTED READING: John Dunning, *On the Air: The Encyclopedia of Old-Time Radio*, 1998.

"GREAT LEAP FORWARD." In 1958 Mao Zedong,* the Communist leader of the People's Republic of China, announced his "Great Leap Forward" program to effect an accelerated development of the agricultural and industrial sectors of the economy. It was the hare-brained scheme of a demented mind, and its consequences were catastrophic. Mao mobilized the entire Chinese workforce, armed them with hoes and rakes, and put them to work building roads, digging ditches and irrigation canals, and reclaiming land. He even had them construct backyard blast furnaces to fashion steel, which Mao believed would boost industrial production.

The Great Leap Forward ended up being a giant economic step backward. Agricultural production fell—partly because of the prevailing political chaos, partly because of poor weather, and partly because of diverting workers from the fields. To keep up with steel quotas, workers melted steel tools in their backyard blast furnaces and then handed over the metal to the government. The Chinese economy skidded to a halt amidst incredible political absurdities. When it was all over in 1962, more than 20 million Chinese peasants had starved to death in one of history's worst man-made famines.

SUGGESTED READING: Jack Dunster, *China and Mao Zedong*, 1983.

THE GREEN HORNET. *The Green Hornet*, radio's most popular juvenile adventure program, premiered on the Blue Network on January 31, 1936, at WXYZ radio in Detroit, Michigan, and in 1938 the Mutual network picked it up. Beginning in 1939, ABC radio broadcast it, usually twice a week in late afternoon time slots. It was modeled after *The Lone Ranger*,* with the character Britt Reid serving as the Green Hornet, a hero who rode around town not on a horse named Silver but in a modern silver automobile. Played by Al Hodge and then Bob Hall, Reid operated outside the law, but he always fought for justice and the protection of the innocent. Instead of Tonto as a sidekick, Britt Reid had Kato, a Filipino valet. Each show revolved around a difficult case. Journalist Ed Lowry of the *Sentinel* would supply details and patchy evidence to Reid, who would then break the case and see that justice was fulfilled. It remained on the air until 1952.

SUGGESTED READING: John Dunning, *On the Air: The Encyclopedia of Old-Time Radio*, 1998.

GUATEMALA. The Central American country of Guatemala became a Cold War* hot spot in 1954. Jacobo Arbenz Guzman, the president of Guatemala, had developed a socialist ideology, and early in 1954 he seized 234,000 acres from the United Fruit Company, a multinational U.S. business with huge amounts of property throughout the region. Guzman intended to distribute the land to Guatemalan peasants. He was also keeping company with known Communists. The United States expressed real concern that Guzman might turn Guatemala into a Soviet satellite in Central America. United Fruit demanded that the U.S. government intervene, but the Organization of American States (OAS) denounced and passed formal resolutions against U.S. military action.

Unwilling to defy the OAS overtly, President Dwight D. Eisenhower* ordered covert action to be taken by the Central Intelligence Agency (CIA). CIA operatives began training an insurgent Guatemalan army in the jungles of Nicaragua and Honduras. The CIA-trained army, which totaled only 400 men, also enjoyed air support in the form of seven fighter aircraft flown by CIA pilots. Early in June 1954, after the insurgent army attacked, key figures in the Guatemalan military decided to oppose Guzman, who resigned two weeks after the civil war started.

Colonel Carlos Castillo Armas seized control of Guatemala and imposed a military dictatorship. The fact that he abolished civil liberties mattered little to the United States, since he was a bitter anticommunist. The United Fruit Company soon got its land back, and Castillo Armas lined his own pockets and those of his close associates with public funds.

SUGGESTED READING: Nick Cullather, *Secret History: The CIA's Classified Account of Its Operations in Guatemala, 1952–1954*, 1999.

GUNSMOKE. Gunsmoke was radio's most popular Western dramatic series in the 1950s. It was developed by Norman Macdonnell and John Meston. Meston wrote the series, and Macdonnell produced and directed it. It premiered on CBS radio on April 26, 1952, with William Conrad playing the lead role of Matt Dillon, a U.S. marshal headquartered in Dodge City, Kansas, during the 1870s. Dillon, surrounded by the dim-witted but loyal Chester, the wise "Doc," and Kitty, owner of the Long Branch saloon, protects the citizens of Dodge City from desperadoes, drunken cowboys, marauding Indians, and con men. On June 18, 1961, CBS canceled the radio show because its *Gunsmoke* television show had become one of the most popular programs in America. William Conrad did not get the job of Matt Dillon on television because of his obesity.

CBS offered the role to John Wayne,* but Wayne at that time was Hollywood's most bankable actor, and Wayne suggested instead his friend James Arness. A relative unknown, Arness was, at six feet, seven inches, an imposing figure who could fill up the small screen. Arness accepted the role. Unlike other cowboy heroes of 1950s television, Arness was not a comic book figure who appealed to adolescents. Instead, *Gunsmoke* was billed as an adult Western, and the Nielsen ratings confirmed it. *Gunsmoke*, after it premiered on September 10, 1955, became staple fare for adults and young people on Saturday evenings. Arness played the role of U.S. Marshal Matt Dillon, with Milburn Stone as Doc Adams, Amanda Blake as Miss Kitty Russell, Dennis Weaver as Chester, and later Ken Curtis as Festus Hagen. Like the radio show, *Gunsmoke* was set in Dodge City, Kansas, in the 1870s.

From 1957 to 1961, *Gunsmoke* was television's top-rated program. It went into decline in the mid-1960s, when CBS gave it a one-hour format, but then recovered in 1967 when the network moved it from Saturday evenings to Monday nights. At one time, *Gunsmoke* competed with 30 other Westerns on television, and when it was broadcast for the last time on September 1, 1975, it was the only Western to have survived that long.

SUGGESTED READINGS: SuzAnne Barabas, *Gunsmoke: A Complete History and Analysis of the Legendary Broadcast Series*, 1990; Tim Brooks and Earle Marsh, *The Complete Directory to Prime Time Network and Cable TV Shows, 1946–Present*, 1995; John Dunning, *On the Air: The Encyclopedia of Old-Time Radio*, 1998.

GUYS AND DOLLS. *Guys and Dolls*, a musical based on stories by Damon Runyon, written primarily by Abe Burrows and directed by George Kaufman, with songs by Frank Loesser, premiered on Broadway at the 46th Street Theater on November 24, 1950. The characters—Nathan Detroit, Miss Adelaide, and Sarah Brown—are Times Square grifters, gamblers, and heart-of-gold do-gooders. A number of the play's songs entered American pop culture history, including "The Fugue for Tinhorns," "I've Never Been in Love Before," "Adelaide's Lament," "Sit Down, You're Rockin' the Boat," and "Luck Be a Lady." It had a run of 1,200 performances.

SUGGESTED READINGS: Gerald Bordman, *The Oxford Companion to American Theater*, 1995; *New York Times*, November 25, 1950.

H

HALEY, WILLIAM. William "Bill" Haley was born in Highland Park, Michigan, on July 6, 1925. A little known country and western singer, Haley cut his first record, "Candy Kisses," in 1943 and then toured widely throughout the South in small club bookings. In 1948 he became a disc jockey with WPWA radio in Chester, Pennsylvania, and he assembled a band, the Four Aces of Western Swing, to perform on the station. He soon formed another band known as the Saddlemen, and they signed a recording contract with Essex Records, but none of their records amounted to much on the charts. Haley then decided that there was a future if he could take high-energy black rhythm and blues and package it in a way that young white audiences would enjoy. Haley thus put himself on the cutting edge of rock-and-roll.*

In 1952 Haley changed the group's name to Bill Haley and the Comets and dumped the cowboy image. They recorded "Rock the Joint," which sold 76,000 copies, and their next song, which Haley wrote, was titled "Crazy Man Crazy." In 1953 it became the first rock-and-roll song to make its way onto the popular music charts. The Comets recorded Joe Turner's "Shake, Rattle, and Roll" in 1953, and it sold a million copies and became a top-ten hit in the United States and Great Britain. In 1955, with "Rock Around the Clock," Bill Haley and the Comets had a number-one hit. It was also on the sound track of a popular film about juvenile delinquency*—*Blackboard Jungle.** During the next two years, Bill Haley and the Comets were rock-and-roll's most popular artists, with twelve more top-forty hits, including "See You Later Alligator," "Burn That Candle," "Dim, Dim the Lights," "Razzle-Dazzle," and "R-O-C-K."

Haley's star then began to set. Slightly overweight and none too handsome, he did not generate much charisma for most teens, and he was eclipsed by Elvis Presley* and a host of other rock-and-roll stars. He remained quite popular in Europe, however, and toured there almost continually during the 1960s and

1970s. When he died of a heart attack on February 9, 1981, he had sold more than 60 million records.

SUGGESTED READINGS: *New York Times*, February 8, 1981; Patricia Romanowski and Holly George-Warren, *The New Encyclopedia of Rock & Roll*, 1995.

HAMMERSTEIN, OSCAR, II. Oscar Hammerstein II was born in New York City in 1895. A descendent of the illustrious Hammerstein theatrical family, he received his education at Columbia, where he teamed up with Richard Rodgers,* a student composer. Rodgers provided the music and Hammerstein the lyrics for a number of college theatrical productions. In 1918 Hammerstein went to work as a stage manager for his uncle, Arthur Hammerstein, who was producing *Sometime* on Broadway. Two years later, Hammerstein wrote a book and lyrics for the play *Always You*. That same year, he began working closely with Otto Harbach, and their teamwork soon produced the books and lyrics for *Wildflower* (1922), *Rose-Marie* (1924), *Sunny* (1925), *Song of the Flame* (1925), and *The Desert Song* (1926).

Hammerstein's reputation as America's greatest lyricist began to build in 1927, when he wrote, with Jerome Kern, the musical *Show Boat*. Musicologists today identify *Show Boat* as the first genuinely American musical with American themes. From *Show Boat* came such enduring hits as "Can't Help Lovin' Dat Man," "Make Believe," "Ol' Man River," and "Why Do I Love You?" Hammerstein followed *Show Boat* with *The New Moon* in 1928 and *Adeleine* in 1929. Except for *Music in the Air* (1932), the 1930s was a downtime for Hammerstein.

In 1943 he teamed up with Richard Rodgers, and together they became the most successful team of composers in theater history. They wrote nine shows, the first of which was *Oklahoma!* (1943). An extraordinary hit that had a run of 2,212 performances on Broadway, *Oklahoma!* included such popular hits as "Oh, What a Beautiful Morning," "People Will Say We're in Love," and "The Surrey with the Fringe on Top." Two years later, their *Carousel* opened on Broadway and had a run of 890 performances. Among its hit songs were "If I Loved You," "June Is Bustin' Out All Over," "Soliloquy," and "You'll Never Walk Alone." Their last collaboration during the 1940s was *South Pacific* (1949), which had a run of 1,925 consecutive performances. *South Pacific* produced a remarkable number of hit songs, including "Bali Ha'i," "I'm Gonna Wash That Man Right Outa My Hair," "Some Enchanted Evening," "There Is Nothin' Like a Dame," "A Wonderful Guy," and "Younger Than Springtime."

The decade of the 1950s was even more productive for Hammerstein and Rogers. In addition to *Me and Juliet* (1953), *Pipe Dream* (1955), and *Flower Drum Song* (1958), they wrote two of Broadway's greatest hits: *The King and I* (1951) and *The Sound of Music* (1959). The most memorable songs from *The King and I* are "Getting to Know You," "Hello, Young Lovers," and "I Whistle a Happy Tune." *The Sound of Music* included "Climb Every Mountain," "Do-

Re-Mi," "The Sound of Music," and "My Favorite Things." Oscar Hammerstein died in 1960.

SUGGESTED READING: Hugh Fordin, *Getting to Know Him*, 1977.

HARRIMAN, WILLIAM AVERELL. W. Averell Harriman was born in New York City on November 15, 1891. The Harrimans, one of America's richest families, had a fortune based in railroads, shipping, and investment banking. The younger Harriman received his education at Groton and Yale, and then he entered the family business, where he demonstrated a vision and acumen that exceeded even those of his father.

Harriman's interests in life, like those of many other men and women who inherit vast wealth, extended beyond making money, and in 1941 he accepted President Franklin D. Roosevelt's appointment to supervise the new Lend-Lease program, especially as it related to Great Britain. Harriman could see most of the world tumbling toward war, and he considered Lend-Lease the salvation of Great Britain. He exhibited effective diplomatic talents, and in 1943 Roosevelt appointed him U.S. ambassador to the Soviet Union, a job that fully acquainted him with Premier Joseph Stalin.* President Harry Truman* later named him ambassador to Great Britain and then U.S. administrator of the Marshall Plan. By the advent of the 1950s, Harriman had acquired a wealth of diplomatic experience and had earned the respect of most prominent world leaders.

Harriman then turned to politics and announced his candidacy for the 1952 Democratic presidential nomination. He lost to Governor Adlai E. Stevenson* of Illinois, but in 1954 Harriman was elected governor of New York. He used the governor's mansion in Albany to support the civil rights movement* and campaign for antipoverty programs. In 1958, however, his run for reelection stalled when New Yorkers selected Republican Nelson Rockefeller instead.

For the next several years, Harriman traveled widely and spoke out for what he called "competitive coexistence" with the Soviet Union. He was convinced that the Cold War* brinksmanship of the Dwight D. Eisenhower* administration might someday lead to a nuclear holocaust. In 1968, when President Lyndon B. Johnson* launched peace negotiations in Paris with North Vietnam and the Vietcong, Harriman was picked to head the U.S. delegation. He stepped down in 1969 when Richard M. Nixon* came to power. W. Averell Harriman died on July 26, 1986.

SUGGESTED READINGS: Rudy Abramson, *Spanning the Century: The Life of W. Averell Harriman*, 1992; *New York Times*, July 27, 1986.

HAUSER, GAYELORD. Gayelord Hauser was born in Germany in 1895 and immigrated to the United States in 1911. A bout with tuberculosis of the hip set him on a quest for nutritional health, and in 1920 he moved to Europe, where he made a study of nutritional ideas. Hauser returned to the United States in 1923 and began lecturing on proper nutrition and natural health. He also founded a health food business. In 1927 he settled in Hollywood, California, and soon became a guru of nutritional health. He wrote several popular health books, including *Harmonized Food Selection, with the Famous Hauser Body-Building System* (1930) and *Keener Vision Without Glasses* (1932). Hauser soon claimed such film stars as Greta Garbo, Marlene Dietrich, Paulette Goddard, and Gloria Swanson as his clients.

In 1950 Hauser secured national fame with the publication of his book *Look Younger, Live Longer*. The book hailed the virtues of Hauser's five "wonder foods": brewer's yeast, yogurt, powdered skim milk, wheat germ, and blackstrap molasses. Hauser's company sold all five products. After three years on bookshelves, *Look Younger, Live Longer* had sold more than 500,000 copies and had been translated into twelve languages. Hauser did radio talk shows, made television* appearances, and wrote a nationally syndicated newspaper column.

He also raised the ire of the Food and Drug Administration, which argued that Hauser's claims for the five wonder foods could not be substantiated. They insisted that Hauser stop employing the title "Doctor," since he had no such degree, medical or otherwise. But Hauser was beyond the FDA's reach, since the products he sold and urged people to use were not pharmaceutical in nature. In 1954 Hauser wrote another best-seller, *Be Happier, Be Healthier*, in which he preached the virtues of sunbaths and lying on slant boards. For all the controversy, however, Hauser obviously benefited from his own advice. He lived to be almost ninety years old, dying in 1984.

SUGGESTED READING: *Los Angeles Times*, July 28, 1984.

HAVE GUN, WILL TRAVEL. *Have Gun, Will Travel* is one of handful of radio programs that actually began on television.* Richard Boone's successful CBS television series *Have Gun, Will Travel* inspired a radio program of the same name. It premiered on CBS radio on November 28, 1958, and survived on the air until November 27, 1960. The television series remained on the air from 1957 until November 1963. In the radio version, John Dehner starred as Paladin, a soldier of fortune and well-meaning gunfighter. He had a conscience, sought to fulfill the demands of justice, and was ready to use violence to achieve it. He was headquartered at the Hotel Carlton in San Francisco but traveled throughout the West to make a living, charging by the level of difficulty of the job. Like most other Western heroes of the pulp press, radio, and television, Paladin was a loner, unattached to family or community, willing to go wherever necessary to complete the job. His only rule revolved around an unwillingness to work for corrupt, evil men. For the television series, CBS signed Richard Boone to play Paladin. The last television episode was broadcast on September 21, 1963.

SUGGESTED READINGS: Tim Brooks and Earle Marsh, *The Complete Directory to Prime Time Network and Cable TV Shows, 1946–Present*, 1995; John Dunning, *On the Air: The Encyclopedia of Old-Time Radio*, 1998.

H-BOMB. *See* HYDROGEN BOMB.

HEFNER, HUGH. See *PLAYBOY*.

HELSINKI OLYMPIC GAMES. The 1952 Olympic Games were held in Helsinki, Finland, but they became caught up in Cold War* politics. Tensions were running high in 1952. The United States was about to detonate a hydrogen bomb,* and the Korean War,* with U.S. troops battling North Korean and Communist Chinese troops, continued in spite of ongoing negotiations. When Soviet athletes arrived at Helsinki, they were housed in their own compound with the athletes of other "Iron Curtain" countries. The compound was fenced, with barbed wire, to keep athletes from defecting. News reporters and visitors were not allowed to enter.

In addition to the Soviet paranoia, the Republic of China in Taiwan claimed to be the only true representative of China. The People's Republic of China, of course, disagreed, and the International Olympic Committee (IOC) had to invite both countries to compete. When the Communist Chinese agreed to compete, the Taiwanese boycotted the games. The IOC then angered the Soviets by refusing to allow East Germany to send its own team. By the time the Helsinki Games closed, the Olympics had become thoroughly politicized. The Communist bloc countries and the West decided to let the Olympic Games stand as symbols of which way of life was superior. At Helsinki, the U.S. team won 41 gold medals to the Soviet team's 23 gold medals.

SUGGESTED READINGS: Christopher R. Hill, *Olympic Politics*, 1992; Martin Barry Vinokur, *More Than a Game: Sports and Politics*, 1988.

HEMINGWAY, ERNEST. Ernest Miller Hemingway was born July 21, 1899, in Oak Park, Illinois. His father was a prosperous physician who loved hunting, fishing, and the outdoors. The younger Hemingway never attended college. As soon as he graduated from Oak Park High School, he made his way to Europe, determined to be a part of World War I. He signed on as an ambulance driver for the Red Cross and was assigned to the Italian army. When the war ended, he returned to Chicago, but bouts of depression and insomnia left him miserable, and he returned to Europe and took up residence on the Left Bank in Paris. There he fell in with a budding young group of expatriates trying to make sense of what World War I had done to the world.

In 1926 Hemingway published his first major work of fiction, *The Sun Also Rises*, a novel about alienated Americans and Britons living in Spain and France during the 1920s. Hemingway returned to the United States in 1928 and spent the next decade in Florida, avoiding the New York literary community, which he loathed. His second novel, *A Farewell to Arms* (1929), even more autobiographical, is the story of a love affair between an American ambulance driver serving in the Italian army during the war and a nurse. He then turned to nonfiction. *Death in the Afternoon* (1932) is an anthology primarily about bullfighting, and *Green Hills of Africa* (1935) is a book about big game hunting. In 1940 he returned to fiction and wrote *For Whom the Bell Tolls*, a novel about the Spanish Civil War. During World War II, Hemingway served as a war correspondent and accompanied Allied troops on the D-Day invasion of France. His 1950 novel *Across the River and into the Trees* tells the story of an infantry colonel in Venice. His reputation achieved heroic proportions, literarily and personally. His novel *The Old Man and the Sea* (1953) remained on the best-seller lists for eighteen months and won a Pulitzer Prize. In November 1954, he became the sixth American to win the Nobel Prize for Literature.

What really captured the attention of Americans in the 1950s were Hemingway's harrowing adventures in Africa. In September 1953 he had embarked with his wife on a five-month African Safari, accompanied by a photographer from *Look* magazine. On January 23, 1954, their plane crashed in the Belgian Congo. They managed to crawl to safety, badly bruised, before the plane burst into flames. They made their way to a nearby river, where a river boat picked them up. A rescue team soon found the crash site and reported the Hemingways dead. The world began to mourn.

In the meantime, the river boat delivered them to another pilot, who agreed to fly them out of the Congo. That plane crashed too. Hemingway survived again, but this time he suffered a skull fracture, second-degree burns, and a ruptured kidney and spleen. News reports of his death confused friends and family members already in a state of mourning. When the world learned several weeks later that the Hemingways had survived, Ernest was hailed as a hero, but all of that good luck could not wash away the depression that tortured Hemingway's life. He died of a self-inflicted gunshot wound on July 2, 1961. Whether his death was an accident or suicide is still debated today.

SUGGESTED READINGS: Carlos Baker, *Ernest Hemingway: A Life Story*, 1969; Jeffrey Meyers, *Hemingway*, 1985.

HEPBURN, KATHARINE. Katharine Hepburn was born in Hartford, Connecticut, on May 12, 1907. She attended Bryn Mawr College and there acquired a passion for the theater. Hepburn made her debut on Broadway in 1932 with a part in *The Warior's Husband*. Her performance caught the eye of a Hollywood producer, and Hepburn left New York for Los Angeles. She first appeared on film in *A Bill of Divorcement* (1932), which garnered her critical acclaim and an instant reputation in Hollywood. Her 1933 performance in *Morning Glory* won Hepburn an academy award for best actress. Hepburn's other notable films in the 1930s included *Little Women* (1933) and *Alice Adams* (1935). In 1939, anxious to return to the theater, Hepburn performed on Broadway in *The Philadelphia Story*. Both on and off stage, Hepburn developed a reputation as a woman of strength and character. In an age when Hollywood starlets often resembled blonde bombshells like Jean Harlow, Hepburn could play romantic leads who had brains, spunk, and determination.

During the 1940s, her career and her life became entwined with that of legendary film star Spencer Tracy,* with whom she was deeply in love. Tracy, a devout Roman Catholic, never seriously considered divorcing his own wife, but he maintained a special relationship with Hepburn throughout the rest of his life. Many of their film comedies together, such as *Woman of the Year* (1942) and *Pat and Mike* (1952), became Hollywood classics.

Hepburn was not about to live under anybody else's shadow, even the long ones cast by people like Tracy. She periodically returned to Broadway to express her acting talents, and her most memorable stage performances came in *As You Like It* (1950) and *The Millionairess* (1952). In 1951, starring with Humphrey Bogart, she made one of Hollywood's classic films—*The African Queen*. She went on to win best acting Oscars in the following films: *Guess Who's Coming to Dinner* (1967), *The Lion in Winter* (1968), and *On Golden Pond* (1981). In recent years, health problems have confined Hepburn physically, but she remains Hollywood's most distinguished matriarch, a woman of confidence and an icon to feminism.

SUGGESTED READING: Katharine Hepburn, *Me*, 1991.

THE HIDDEN PERSUADERS. *The Hidden Persuaders* is the title of Vance Packard's best-selling 1957 book on the advertising industry. According to Packard, the modern economy had produced a great variety of businesses competing to sell essentially similar products. The differences between several varieties of a soft drink or peanut butter or beer were minimal, so companies hired psychologists to determine consumer tastes and biases and marketing experts to link those tastes to certain products. They used colors, celebrities, and sexuality to make products seem more inherently attractive. Between 1950 and 1960, advertising expenditures jumped from $5.7 billion annually to $12 billion. Packard said it best about the trend: "The cosmetic manufacturers are not selling lanolin, they are selling hope. . . . We no longer buy oranges, we buy vitality. We do not just buy an auto, we buy prestige."

The most important vehicle for conveying advertisements was television,* which came to dwarf radio and print publications By the end of the 1950s, the vast majority of American households had television sets, and tens of millions of Americans spent from fifteen to twenty hours per week watching programs and commercial advertisements. The combination of advertising and television played a key role in creating a national consumer culture* in America, in which an entire country came to purchase standardized products.

Critics lamented the rise of a consumer society, where the purchase of an endless series of products seemed to become an end in itself. Americans had come to link happiness and success in life with the acquisition of more and more and bigger and bigger goods, and Vance Packard described just how advertisers had brought about the consumer culture. At the same time, of course, the consumer culture was responsible for the steady growth in the economy that occurred during the 1950s.

SUGGESTED READINGS: Erik Barnouw, *Tube of Plenty*, 1990; Vance Packard, *The Hidden Persuaders*, 1957.

HIGGINS, MARGUERITE. Marguerite Higgins was born in Hong Kong, China, in 1920. She graduated from the University of California at Berkeley in 1941 and then earned a master's degree in journalism from Columbia in 1942. She went to work for the New York *Herald Tribune* and became one of a handful of women war correspondents covering the European theater. When Allied troops liberated the death camps at Buchenwald and Dachau, Higgins was with them. Higgins became chief of the *Tribune*'s Berlin office in 1947 and its Tokyo office in 1950. When North Korea invaded South Korea in 1950, Higgins covered the war, even though Homer Bigart, the *Tribune*'s official war correspondent, and the U.S. Army resented her presence there. In July 1950, Lieutenant General Walton Walker ordered her back to Japan, but Higgins appealed to General Douglas MacArthur* by telling him, "I'm not working in Korea as a woman. I am there as a war correspondent." MacArthur allowed her to return to the front, and the decision made her more popular than ever back home. In 1951 Higgins received the Pulitzer Prize for her reporting and was voted the Associated Press's "Woman of the Year."

After the Korean War* ended in 1953, Higgins returned to New York and continued writing. Among the books she subsequently wrote were *War in Korea: The Report of a Woman War Correspondent* (1951), *News Is a Singular Thing* (1955), *Overtime in Heaven: Adventures in the Foreign Service* (1964), and *Our Vietnam Nightmare* (1965). Maguerite Higgins died on January 3, 1966.

SUGGESTED READINGS: Marguerite Higgins, *War in Korea: The Report of a Woman War Correspondent*, 1951; Antoinette May, *Witness to War: A Biography of Marguerite Higgins*, 1991; *New York Times*, January 4, 1966.

HIGH NOON. A classic Western, *High Noon* was one of the most controversial films of the 1950s. Written by Carl Foreman and starring Gary Cooper as Marshall Will Kane of Hadleyville, a sleepy frontier town, *High Noon* was released in August 1952. On the day of his retirement and wedding, Kane must face a band of vicious, revenge-hungry armed criminals intent on seizing control of the town. Kane has a crisis of personal confidence, and the cowardly town folk abandon him, refusing to assist him. With the kind of courage few can muster to stand up to bullying, the sheriff battles the bad guys all alone.

While he was making the film, Foreman was called to Washington, D.C., to testify before the House Un-American Activities Committee (HUAC). Foreman took the Fifth Amendment and refused to name names on the grounds that it was nobody's business what his political affiliations were or had ever been. Foreman knew that he would be blacklisted in Hollywood as soon as *High Noon* was finished, so he intentionally rewrote scenes in the film to make sure that the world knew that he was protesting the HUAC and the Red Scare.* The people of Hadleyville possess no moral fiber and the sheriff must face evil all by himself. The film ends with a disgusted sheriff taking off his U.S. marshal's badge and crushing it under his boot. John Wayne later remarked that *High*

Noon was "the most un-American thing I've ever seen in my whole life." Foreman had no regrets, however, even though he was blacklisted. "I became the Cooper character in my own life," he later recalled.

SUGGESTED READINGS: Phillip Drummond, *High Noon*, 1992; *New York Times*, August 3, 1952; Russell Shain, "Hollywood's Cold War," *Journal of Popular Culture* Fall 1974, 335–50.

HIGHWAY PATROL. *Highway Patrol* was first released in syndication in September 1955. It starred veteran actor Broderick Crawford as Chief Dan Matthews, head of a highway patrol detective team in some Western state. Actually, the black-and-white cars and logo resembled those of California state troopers. With his gravelly voice and crusty exterior, Crawford gave off the impression of a fearless, no-nonsense cop who went after muggers, murderers, bank robbers, con men, and hijackers. *Highway Patrol* was one of the most successful syndicated programs in television.* Eventually 156 episodes were produced, and the show remained on prime time television into the 1959 season.

SUGGESTED READING: Tim Brooks and Earle Marsh, *The Complete Directory to Prime Time Network and Cable TV Shows, 1946–Present*, 1995.

HILLARY, EDMUND. *See* MT. EVEREST.

HISS, ALGER. Alger Hiss was born on November 11, 1904, in Baltimore, Maryland. His father ran an export-import business but committed suicide when Alger was just three. Alger graduated from the Johns Hopkins University in 1926 and went on to Harvard Law School, where he became a favorite student of Felix Frankfurter.* He clerked for U.S. Supreme Court Justice Oliver Wendell Holmes, Jr., in 1929, practiced law privately for several years, and when the Democrats took over the White House in 1933, Hiss went to work first for the Department of Agriculture and then for the Department of Justice. In 1936 he went to work for the State Department, where he remained until 1947.

During his career in the Franklin D. Roosevelt administration, Hiss enjoyed access to critically important national security information. He accompanied the president to Yalta, in the Soviet Union, in February 1945, when Roosevelt met with British Prime Minister Winston Churchill and Soviet Premier Joseph Stalin,* where plans were laid for the political contours of the post–World War II world. Hiss also attended the meetings in San Francisco several months later, where the United Nations was created. He served as the primary advisor to the U.S. delegation to the United Nations.

Until August 3, 1948, Hiss had worked in relative obscurity. On that day, Whitaker Chambers,* an editor at *Time* magazine and a man who had once been a Communist, testified before the House Un-American Activities Committee (HUAC) that, during the 1930s, he had been a member of a Communist cell in New York City. He told the HUAC that several current government officials had also been members of that cell. Included in that group was Alger Hiss. Hiss vehemently denied the charges and sued Chambers for libel. Chambers then charged Hiss, under oath, with having passed government documents to Soviet agents, which escalated the controversy from simple Communist party membership to treason and espionage.

Chambers also delivered to Congressman Richard M. Nixon,* who headed the HUAC hearings, five rolls of microfilm, dubbed the "pumpkin papers" because Chambers had concealed them inside a pumpkin on his upstate New York farm. Chambers claimed that Hiss had given him the microfilm. Because the statute of limitations had expired on the crime of treason, Hiss was indicted for perjury. Hiss went on trial in 1949, but the case ended up in a hung jury. Later in 1949, a second perjury trial resulted in Hiss's conviction. He was sentenced to five years in prison, and his incarceration began on March 22, 1951.

Liberals came to Hiss's defense, claiming that people like Nixon and Senator Joseph McCarthy* of Wisconsin had created a political atmosphere in America that guaranteed miscarriages of justice and that Hiss had been railroaded. Hiss eventually served three years and eight months of the sentence. Chambers became the darling of conservatives and wrote the best-selling book *Witness* in 1952. The case catapulted Nixon into the political limelight. He won a seat in the U.S. Senate in 1950, and in 1952 Dwight D. Eisenhower* selected him as his vice-presidential running mate. The Hiss case continues to generate scholarly debate today. Most liberals are still convinced that he was innocent; most conservatives that he was guilty. Hiss continued to insist on his innocence until his death on November 15, 1996.

SUGGESTED READINGS: Alger Hiss, *Recollections of a Life*, 1988; John Chabot Smith, *The Alger Hiss Story*, 1976; Allen Weinstein, *Perjury: The Hiss-Chambers Case*, 1978.

HITCHCOCK, ALFRED. Alfred Hitchcock was born on August 13, 1899, in London, England. He earned a degree in engineering at Saint Ignatius College in London and then went to art school. He worked as a designer for a London department store, but he was fascinated with films and determined to get into the business. In 1920 Hitchcock went to work illustrating and writing title cards for silent films, and he moved up quickly. He soon became a script writer and then an assistant director. He directed his first film, *The Pleasure Garden*, in 1926, and in 1929 his *Blackmail* became Britain's first financially successful talking picture. He followed that up with a series of financially successful spy thrillers, including *The Man Who Knew Too Much* (1934), *The 39 Steps* (1935), *Secret Agent* (1937), *Sabotage* (1937), and *The Lady Vanishes* (1938). David Selznick then brought him to Hollywood. Hitchcock's first American film was *Rebecca* (1940).

During the 1950s, Hitchcock earned a reputation for genius with his ability to mix the macabre, peril, and pursuit and to balance and juxtapose the commonplace and the bizarre. In a decade when Americans seemed obsessed with conformity, Hitchcock's artistic work was uniquely original, and moviegoers were drawn to it. He was unmatched at squeezing the most suspense out of a scene and a plot. Among his most memorable films during the decade were *Strangers on a Train* (1951), *Dial M for Murder* (1954), *Rear Window* (1954), *To Catch a Thief* (1955), *Vertigo* (1958), and *North by Northwest* (1959). His own signature in his films was a brief, personal cameo appearance in each film. Hitchcock also had a hit television* series, *Alfred Hitchcock Presents,** which remained on the air from 1955 to 1961. In subsequent years, Hitchcock's most memorable films included *Psycho* (1960), *The Birds* (1963), and *Torn Curtain* (1965). Alfred Hitchcock died on April 29, 1980.

SUGGESTED READINGS: Donald Spoto, *The Dark Side of Genius: The Life of Alfred Hitchcock*, 1983; David Sterritt, *The Films of Alfred Hitchcock*, 1993.

HO CHI MINH. Ho Chi Minh was born as Nguyen That Thanh in Nghe An Province of central Vietnam on May 19, 1890. Raised on a steady diet of anti-French, pro-Vietnamese ideas, Ho as a young man became a fervent Vietnamese nationalist committed to the destruction of French imperialism in Southeast Asia. After attending school in Hue, he traveled widely and eventually settled for several years in Paris, France, where he became politically active in the cause of Vietnamese independence. He also became a confirmed communist there. A founding member of the French Communist party in 1920, he moved to Moscow in 1924 and soon relocated to Canton, China, where he established the Indo-chinese Communist party. He returned to Vietnam in 1940 when World War II engulfed Asia. There, Ho allied himself with the United States in fighting Japanese occupation forces.

After the war, Ho Chi Minh proclaimed the independence of Vietnam, but the French soon returned to reassert their imperial control. Ho launched a guerrilla war against the French, but because of his communist credentials, the United States decided to back France. In 1954, after the French debacle at Dien Bien Phu and the subsequent Geneva Conference, Ho Chi Minh became president of the new Democratic Republic of Vietnam (North Vietnam). He expected to reunite North Vietnam with the Republic of Vietnam (South Vietnam) in 1956, when the Geneva Accords called for free elections. But the Dwight D. Eisenhower* administration, after determining that Ho Chi Minh would win those elections, canceled them, and Ho Chi Minh then directed his guerrilla campaign at the American-backed government of South Vietnam, headed by Ngo Dinh Diem.

Steadily during the next decade, Ho Chi Minh and his Vietcong guerrilla troops gained political and military ground in South Vietnam. The government of Ngo Dinh Diem was hopelessly corrupt and alienated from common people. To keep the government afloat, more and more U.S. economic and military assistance was required, and the American commitment there escalated. In 1965, the United States decided to fight a land war against Communist troops in South Vietnam. Ho Chi Minh had become a national hero to most Vietnamese in the north and the sourth. He died on September 2, 1969, but by that time the United

States had already committed itself to withdrawing from the war. In April 1975, Vietcong and North Vietnamese forces overwhelmed South Vietnam. The country was finally united under a Communist regime—the Socialist Republic of Vietnam. The city of Saigon was renamed "Ho Chi Minh City."

SUGGESTED READINGS: David Halberstam, *Ho*, 1971; Charles Fenn, *Ho Chi Minh: A Biographical Introduction*, 1973.

HOFFA, JAMES. James "Jimmy" Hoffa was born in Brazil, Indiana, on February 14, 1913. As a young man, he drove a truck for a living and joined the Teamsters* Union. Hoffa eventually decided to make the union his career, and he steadily moved up through the ranks, winning election as international vice president in 1952, where he served under President David Beck. By that time, the Teamsters was the largest, most powerful union in the country. It was also one of the most corrupt. In 1957 Senator John McClellan of Arkansas opened his investigation of labor union racketeering in the United States, and he targeted the Teamsters. Robert F. Kennedy, brother of Senator John F. Kennedy,* pursued the investigation with a vengeance. When Beck appeared before the McClellan Committee,* he took the Fifth Amendment more than 200 times, and most Americans concluded that he was probably guilty of all the crimes he had been accused of committing. A few weeks later, the AFL-CIO* expelled Beck from its membership.

In what the Department of Justice considered a corrupt election, Jimmy Hoffa was elected to replace Beck as head of the Teamsters, and in his testimony before the McClellan Committee, he too took the Fifth Amendment repeatedly. Beck was found guilty of embezzlement, tax evasion, and grand larceny. The AFL-CIO began to distance itself from Teamsters leadership, demanding that the union clean up its act. Hoffa escaped conviction because of a hung jury, and he assumed full control of the Teamsters in September 1958. In 1958 the AFL-CIO expelled the Teamsters and its two million members.

The federal government, however, was not done with Jimmy Hoffa and the Teamsters. John Kennedy won the presidential election of 1960, and he named his brother Robert attorney general. Robert Kennedy was indefatigable in his assault on Teamsters corruption, and in 1964, Hoffa was convicted of jury tampering. Hoffa eventually spent four years in a federal penitentiary. Although the federal government demanded that Hoffa resign from his position as president of the Teamsters, Hoffa refused, and he remained in the post during his years in prison. President Richard M. Nixon* pardoned him in 1971, hoping that Hoffa would be able to secure Teamster support for the Republican presidential ticket in the election of 1972.

After his release from prison, Hoffa remained active in Teamster politics, although inactivity had been a condition of his release. After a dinner with several Mafia figures in Bloomfield, Michigan, on July 30, 1975, Hoffa disappeared, never to be seen again. Rumors and speculation claimed that he had been killed because mobsters, who had millions tied up in Teamster Union pension funds, had decided that Hoffa had become a political liability. When he was declared legally dead in 1982, other rumors claimed that, after his murder, Hoffa had been buried in the cement foundation of the football stadium at the Meadowlands in New Jersey.

SUGGESTED READINGS: Steven Brill, *The Teamsters*, 1978; Walter Sheridan, *The Fall and Rise of Jimmy Hoffa*, 1972; Arthur A. Sloane, *Hoffa*, 1991.

HOGAN, BEN. Ben Hogan was born in August 13, 1912 in Dublin, Texas. After his father's death in 1923, Hogan moved with his mother to Fort Worth and began working as a caddy at a local golf club. Hogan turned professional when he was just seventeen, but his career was not marked by immediate success. He did not have what golfers call a "natural swing," but he did possess latent talent and an extraordinary work ethic. Hogan did not win a tournament for seven years and did not win a major championship for fifteen years. In 1946, however, Hogan's game into its own; he won thirteen events and became the dominant player on the professional golfers' tour. He won seven titles in 1947 and eleven in 1948. Hogan had the odds in every tournament he entered, and other professionals considered him to be the greatest golfer in the history of the game.

In 1949, while driving to Fort Worth from a tournament in Phoenix, Arizona, Hogan's car collided head-on with a bus. The accident crushed his pelvis, shattered the bones in both legs, and broke his ribs and collarbone. Physicians predicted he would never walk again, let alone play golf. Hogan, however, known as "the Hawk" because of his fierce determination, made a joke out of medical pessimism. Hogan surprised everyone eighteen months later when he won the U.S. Open, in spite of severe pain and having his legs wrapped in bandages. He became a symbol of courage and perseverance. The injuries, which left him in constant pain, however, limited the number of tournaments he could enter. In 1953 he entered only six tournaments, but he won five of them. More amazingly, three of the victories were majors—the Master's, the U.S. Open, and the British Open. No other golfer, before or since, has won three majors in a single year. Hogan eventually limped his way to sixty-three tournament victories, his last in 1959. It became increasingly difficult for him to complete a single round because of his legs, and he played his last tournament in 1971.

Hogan was also known for having the smoothest swing in the history of golf. He needed it. At 135 pounds, he was small for the professional golfing tour, and he had to make up for his lack of upper body strength with a scientifically tuned gold swing. He studied the mechanics of golf intensely, breaking the swing down into all of its component parts, and the results were extraordinary. Hogan won the U.S. Open in 1948, 1950, 1951, and 1953; the PGA in 1946 and 1948; the Master's in 1951 and 1953; and the British Open in 1953. After he retired from the PGA tour, Hogan spent his time playing in exhibition tournaments, teaching golf, and writing articles and books on golf. He also manufactured a highly successful line of golf clubs. Ben Hogan died on July 25, 1997.

SUGGESTED READINGS: Gene Gregston, *Hogan: The Man Who Played for Glory*, 1978; *New York Times*, July 26, 1997.

HOLDEN, WILLIAM. William Holden was born William Franklin Beedle, Jr., on April 17, 1918, in O'Fallon, Illinois. The family moved to California when Holden was an infant. He grew up in Monrovia and Pasadena. Holden was fascinated with acting, and in 1939, during a performance at the Playhouse Theater, a talent scout took note of him. Paramount Studios then signed him to a small role in the 1939 film *Million Dollar Legs*. The studio decided that he needed a better stage name, and he became known as William Holden.

Later in 1939, Holden got the title role in the movie *Golden Boy*, starring opposite Barbara Stanwick, and the film established him as a certifiable Hollywood star. He followed that up with *Our Town* in 1940. Holden served in the army air corps during World War II, and did not go back to work in Hollywood until 1946. He played a pathological gangster in *The Dark Past* (1948) and a suave writer in *Sunset Boulevard* (1950), for which he received an Oscar nomination. He won a best actor Oscar for his performance as a hard-bitten but courageous prisoner of war in *Stalag 17* (1953). Among Holden's other major films in the 1950s were *Apartment for Peggy* (1950), *Union Station* (1950), *Executive Suite* (1954), *Sabrina* (1954), *The Country Girl* (1954), *The Bridges at Toko-Ri* (1955), *Love Is a Many Splendored Thing* (1955), *Picnic* (1956), *The Key* (1958), and *The Bridge on the River Kwai*[*] (1958).

During the late 1950s and early 1960s, Holden abandoned Hollywood for a new life in Switzerland and Kenya, where he became very active in conservation. He returned to Hollywood in 1965, starred in *Alvarez Kelly*, and won critical acclaim for his 1971 performance in *The Wild Bunch*. Holden won another Oscar for his performance in *The Network* (1976). His last film was *The Earthling* in 1980. Holden died on November 16, 1981.

SUGGESTED READINGS: *New York Times*, November 17, 1981; Bob Thomas, *Golden Boy: The Untold Story of William Holden*, 1983.

HOLIDAY INN. The first Holiday Inn motel was constructed in Memphis, Tennessee, in 1954. Memphis architect and businessman Kemmons Wilson traveled frequently by automobile with his family, and his wife and children just as frequently complained about substandard conditions at roadside hotels. The rooms were too small, the bathrooms dirty and the inadequate, and the heating unreliable. Wilson became convinced that the ubiquitous presence of the automobile (*see* automobile industry) in American society would create a boom of vacation travel by car, and that Americans would be interested in overnight accommodations. At the time, their only choices were upscale hotels, usually in downtown urban areas, or low-level roadside motels in small towns and rural areas. Wilson hit on the idea of building motels that had all the quality and conveniences of high-class hotel rooms but were available in small towns and on roadsides throughout the country.

The idea proved to be a gold mine. Wilson had discerned exactly what would happen in the economy and exactly what American tastes would be. He constructed motels with good-sized rooms, bath and shower facilities, good heating and air-conditioning systems, television sets, and swimming pools. To make the Holiday Inns more family friendly, he made sure that children stayed for free in their parents' room. Between 1952 and 1962, Wilson built 280 Holiday Inns—a total of more than 31,000 rooms—in 35 states, and his green and gold corporate logo soon became one of the most recognizable corporate symbols in the United States. In the process, Wilson became a millionaire many times over.

SUGGESTED READING: Kemmons Wilson, *The Holiday Inn Story*, 1968.

HOLLY, BUDDY. Charles Hardin "Buddy" Holly was born in Lubbock, Texas, on September 7, 1936. He was an unlikely rock star, if physical appearance were the measure of success. Thin and bespeckled with horn-rimmed glasses, Holly looked more like a nerd than a rocker, at least until he turned on his electric guitar, which transformed him into an intense, assertive, and intelligent artist. Playing in garages, high schools, and then small clubs in Texas, Holly earned a reputation as the first white rock musician to employ a powerful rhythm-and-blues backbeat and overdubbing, in which a performer could then accompany himself. Buddy Holly songs like "Peggy Sue," "Oh Boy!," "Rave On," and "That'll Be the Day" became top-of-the chart hits in the United States and Great Britain.

Early in 1959, Holly decided to go on tour. Recently married and about to become a father, he needed extra cash, and he signed on with Winter Dance Party, a touring rock-and-roll* show that catered to rural audiences in the Midwest. Richie Valens* and J. P. Richardson* (the Big Bopper) were the tour's other attractions. Severe winter weather in February all but canceled the tour. On February 2, 1959, however, they chartered a private plane to fly them from Clear Lake, Iowa, to their next show in Moorhead, North Dakota. Soon after midnight, on February 3, the plane crashed in fog and heavy snow. The three rock stars were killed instantly.

SUGGESTED READINGS: *New York Times*, February 4, 1959; John Tobler, *The Buddy Holly Story*, 1979.

HOLLYWOOD TEN. The term "Hollywood Ten" was coined by journalists to describe a group of prominent film industry people who were cited in 1947 for contempt of Congress by the House Un-American Activities Committee (HUAC). At the time, the United States was in the grip of the Red Scare,* and fear of political radicals had reached extreme levels. In 1947 the HUAC had decided to conduct hearings into Communist infiltration of the film industry. Between October 28 and 30, 1947, the HUAC subpoenaed forty-one people.

Ten of them refused to answer the following question, "Are you now or have you ever been a member of the Communist party?" Those ten were Dalton Trumbo, Alvah Bessie, Herbert Biverman, Lester Cole, Edward Dmytryk, Ring Lardner, Jr., John Howard Lawson, Albert Maltz, Samuel Ornitz, and Adrian Scott. Each was cited for contempt of Congress, fined $1,000, and sentenced to jail terms of from six months to one year. They appealed the citations, but in 1950 they had to serve their prison terms.

Concerned about protecting the industry from intense public scrutiny and criticism, the heads of the major studios met at the Waldorf-Astoria Hotel in New York City late in 1947 and developed the blacklist, banning the Hollywood Ten and any other Communists and Communist sympathizers from working in the industry. On November 26, 1947, the Motion Picture Association of America released the following announcement: "We will forthwith discharge or suspend without compensation those in our employ and will not re-employ any of the ten until such time as he is acquitted or has purged himself of contempt and declares under oath that he is not a Communist. . . . We will not knowingly employ a Communist or a member of any party or group which advocates the overthrow of the Government of the United States by force, or by any illegal or unconstitutional methods." The blacklist survived throughout the 1950s, even though it was common knowledge that many blacklisted writers were working under pseudonyms. It was not formally breached until 1960, when producer Otto Preminger announced that he had hired Dalton Trumbo to write the screenplay for his film *Exodus*.

SUGGESTED READINGS: Bruce Cook, *Dalton Trumbo*, 1977; Bernard Dick, *Radical Innocence: A Critical Study of the Hollywood Ten*, 1989.

THE HONEYMOONERS. Although *The Honeymooners* is remembered as one of early television's* most beloved situation comedies, it nevertheless had a most unusual history in prime time. It first appeared in 1951 on *Cavalcade of Stars*, when Jackie Gleason created the role of Ralph Kramdon, the frustrated New York City bus driver always in search of, but never finding, a get-rich-quick money-making scheme. Art Carney appeared as Ed Norton, his plumber friend who lived in the next-door apartment. When Gleason launched his own variety show, *The Jackie Gleason Show*, on CBS in 1952, "The Honeymooners" was a frequent sketch. Audrey Meadows took the role as his long-suffering wife, Alice, and Joyce Randolph played the part of Trixie Norton, Alice's best friend and Ed's wife. On October 1, 1955, CBS premiered *The Honeymooners* as a weekly situation comedy. It remained on the air only until September 1956.

Compared to other situation comedies in the 1950s, *The Honeymooners* was unique. The Kramdens and Nortons lived in dingy urban apartments and barely squeaked by financially. They did not enjoy middle-class, suburban bliss, and they argued a great deal, often screaming at each other. Millions of American families could identify with the Kramdens and the Nortons, which explains the show's enduring appeal.

SUGGESTED READINGS: Tim Brooks and Earle Marsh, *The Complete Directory to Prime Time Network and Cable TV Shows, 1946–Present*, 1995; Audrey Meadows, *Love, Alice: My Life as a Honeymooner*, 1994.

HOOVER, J(OHN) EDGAR. J. Edgar Hoover was born in Washington, D.C., on January 1, 1895. He attended local public schools, and after receiving his high school diploma, he got a job as a clerk at the Library of Congress. He then attended night school at George Washington University and eventually earned his law degree. After passing the bar examination in 1918, Hoover went to work in the Alien Enemy Bureau of the Department of Justice, where he investigated political radicals. In 1919 he was appointed special assistant to Attorney General A. Mitchell Palmer and supervised the arrest and deportation of alien radicals. Palmer was then assigned to establish the Radical Division in the Department of Justice, and from that point on Hoover played a key role in the Red Scare* that Palmer unleashed on the country. In 1921, the Radical Division was renamed the Bureau of Investigation, which was the forerunner of the Federal Bureau of Investigation,* or FBI. Hoover became the director of that agency in 1924.

During the 1920s and early 1930s, Hoover professionalized the FBI, raising the caliber of its employees and improving their training. He also worked diligently on public relations, giving the FBI an extraordinarily high public profile. He nicknamed FBI agents "G-men," or "gangbusters," and the FBI pursued with a vengeance such popular criminals as Bonnie and Clyde, John Dillinger, "Pretty Boy" Floyd, "Ma" Barker," and others. By the end of the 1930s, Hoover had transformed the FBI into the nation's premier law enforcement agency.

With the outbreak of World War II, Hoover changed the agency's focus from gangbusting to surveillance for treason and espionage. He focused his attention on the Japanese-American, German-American, and Italian-American communities, trying to ferret out fascist sympathizers. His own hatred of communism also put him on the track of political radicals. President Franklin D. Roosevelt put Hoover in charge of organizing the national effort to coordinate the nation's antiespionage and antisabotage programs.

With the end of World War II and the almost immediate onset of the Cold War,* Hoover's focus shifted to antiradicalism and anticommunism. In essence, he had resurrected his paranoia of the early 1920s and shifted it to the late 1940s and 1950s. Hoover soon had a reputation as the country's number one "Redhunter," a reputation he treasured, since he felt that communism was the antithesis of democracy and free enterprise capitalism. Both Presidents Franklin D. Roosevelt and Harry S. Truman* gave Hoover specific authorization to use wiretapping to keep track of political radicals and subversives, and the FBI was also charged with conducting background checks on all potential federal employees.

Hoover's greatest concern in life was the reputation of the FBI, and he often walked a careful political tightrope to protect the agency. During the Red Scare of the late 1940s and early 1950s, Hoover kept his distance from Senator Joseph

McCarthy,* whom he considered to be politically dangerous. When McCarthy asked for access to FBI files, Hoover steadfastly denied the request. His caution proved well founded when McCarthy self-destructed.

By the 1950s, J. Edgar Hoover had become one of the most powerful men in the country. Over the years, the agency had collected information on tens of thousands of influential Americans—politicians, actors, sports figures, civil rights leaders, and radicals—and Hoover was not above judiciously using the information to get his way in Washington. Congressmen, U.S. senators, and presidents feared him because of what he knew about their private lives. When Hoover turned 70 in 1965, President Lyndon B. Johnson* waived the mandatory retirement law to allow Hoover to remain in office, and President Richard M. Nixon* did the same in 1969. J. Edgar Hoover died on May 2, 1972.

SUGGESTED READINGS: Richard G. Powers, *Secrecy and Power: The Life of J. Edgar Hoover*, 1987; Stanford J. Unger, *The FBI*, 1976.

HOUSE RESOLUTION 698. In the years after World War II, the retreat from the Indian New Deal of the Roosevelt administration accelerated, and the pressures to assimilate American Indians increased dramatically. Opposition to federal supervision of the Indian tribes and tribal resources increased as well, primarily because local economic interests wanted access to Indian land. Early in the 1950s, the termination* movement came to represent the desires of those non-Indians who wanted to end federal supervision of Indian tribes. Senator Arthur V. Watkins of Utah and Congressman E. Y. Berry of South Dakota sponsored the termination movement in Congress. In 1952 House Resolution 698 asked Dillon Myer, head of the Bureau of Indian Affairs (BIA), to report on the status of the Bureau of Indian Affairs and to prepare a termination program. The resolution also requested a list of BIA services that could be turned over to the states or terminated outright. House Resolution 698 became the opening salvo in what became the termination wars of the 1950s and 1960s.

SUGGESTED READING: Larry W. Burt, *Tribalism in Crisis: Federal Indian Policy, 1953–1961*, 1982.

HOXEY CANCER CURE. Quack cures for cancer have flourished in American history ever since the colonial era, and the 1950s was no exception. The most prominent concoction in that decade came from the fertile mind of Harry M. Hoxey, a former coal miner who began to market patent medicines in 1924. His grandfather first developed a so-called cancer cure from the blood of horses. It did not help him much. He died of cancer. The younger Hoxey added to the brew a secret mix of licorice, red clover, burdock root, stillingia root, poke root, cascara, ash bark, potassium iodide, and a host of other natural and not so natural ingredients. Hoxey claimed that he could cure cancer, at a price of $460 per treatment. He opened clinics in Dallas, Texas, and Portage, Pennsylvania.

The Food and Drug Administration argued that Hoxey's medicine had no effect on cancer, and in 1953 a federal court filed an injunction to shut down the Hoxey clinics. Hoxey fought back. He managed to win political support from Senator William Langer, and he won a $1.05 million libel suit against Dr. Morris Fishbein, editor of the *Journal of the American Medical Association.* Although the federal government continued to harass Hoxey, he managed to stay in business from a clinic in Mexico. In 1973 Hoxey died of pancreatic cancer.

SUGGESTED READING: James Cook, *Remedies and Rackets,* 1958.

HUBBARD, L. RON. *See* SCIENTOLOGY, CHURCH OF.

HULA HOOP. The hula hoop was the great toy fad of the 1950s. In 1958 Arthur Melin and Richard Knerr, who owned the Wham-O Manufacturing Company, marketed a plastic ring that was about 42 inches in diameter. They had picked up the idea from a form of Australian calisthenics that used a hoop. Each hula hoop cost $1.98. Users stepped inside the hoop, twirled it at waist level, and then did a "hula dance" with their hips in order to sustain the hoop's gyrations. The fad started in California in July and quickly spread eastward. Wham-O sold 25 million hula hoops in four months. In November 1958, the fad died as quickly as it had started. By that time, however, more than 100 million hula hoops had been sold worldwide.

SUGGESTED READING: Peter Skilnik, *Fads: America's Crazes, Fads, & Fancies,* 1978.

HUNGARIAN REBELLION. After World War II, Soviet troops did not withdraw from Eastern Europe as Joseph Stalin* had promised. Actually, Stalin had no intention of pulling Soviet troops back across the border. After two world wars, both of which had inflicted severe losses on Russia and the Soviet Union, Stalin wanted to maintain a buffer zone between his own country and Germany, France, and Great Britain. That buffer zone, which the West nicknamed the "Iron Curtain," brought Poland, Latvia, Lithuania, Estonia, Czechoslovakia, Hungary, Yugoslavia, and Bulgaria within the Soviet political orbit. More than one million Soviet troops occupied those countries, and Stalin set up puppet Communist regimes in all of them.

When Joseph Stalin died on March 5, 1953, hopes soared throughout Eastern Europe, and Nikita Khrushchev's* modest liberalization campaign in 1954 and 1955 fostered more hope. In October 1956, anti-Soviet protests in Poland encouraged Hungarian nationalists. On October 23, thousands of university students massed in downtown Budapest to show support for the Polish rebels. They called for the complete withdrawal of Soviet troops from Hungarian soil, freedom of speech, freedom of the press, and free elections. They also demanded that Imre Nagy, a prominent political reformer, become head of state. The students marched on the state radio station. As they closed in, police fired into the crowd and killed several demonstrators.

The deaths precipitated a broad-based rebellion. Khrushchev ordered Soviet troops, in tanks and armored personnel carriers, to occupy downtown Budapest and crush the rebellion. The Hungarian army quickly disintegrated, with many troops joining the rebelling students. The Hungarian government collapsed, and the Hungarian Communist party named Imre Nagy premier. Wasting no time, Nagy pulled Hungary out of its Warsaw Pact alliance with the Soviet Union and opened the government up to new political parties. Soviet troops withdrew from Budapest, and hundreds of thousands of people hit the streets to celebrate.

The celebration lasted one week. Khrushchev was not about to permit a liberal, democratic, pro-American state to emerge on the Soviet Union's western border. On November 4, 1956, Khrushchev ordered 2,500 tanks and a Soviet infantry division into Budapest. Bloody street fighting erupted immediately, and Hungarians died by the thousands. They did not have a chance.

Premier Imre Nagy appealed for military assistance from the Western powers, and a debate ensued in Washington, D.C., over the merits of the proposal. In the end, President Dwight D. Eisenhower* vetoed the idea. Hungary was clearly within the Soviet sphere of influence, and Eisenhower was not ready to risk World War III. Soviet troops crushed the rebellion, Nagy went into exile in the Yugoslav embassy, and 150,000 refugees fled to Austria and from there to West Germany, France, Great Britain, and the United States. A new Soviet puppet state was installed under the premiership of Janos Kadar.

SUGGESTED READING: Meray Tibor, *Thirteen Days That Shook the Kremlin*, 1959.

THE HUNTLEY-BRINKLEY REPORT. The *Huntley-Brinkley Report* premiered on NBC television in October 1956. It was a nightly, fifteen-minute news show coanchored by journalists Chet Huntley and David Brinkley. At the time, television news was more like a holdover of radio news. Former radio newscasters like John Cameron Swazy dominated television news, reading copy while showing newsreels or even staged reproductions of actual events. Huntley and Brinkley paved the way for modern telejournalism by showing on-the-spot footage filmed by NBC cameramen. Huntley handled the main news stories, while Brinkley focused on political events from Washington, D.C. Compared to the bland tradition of television news shows, Huntley and Brinkley added sardonic humor, opinion, moralism, and informed competence. Although ratings for the first two years were awful, NBC stayed with the *Huntley-Brinkley Report*, even expanding it to a thirty-minute format. In 1960 it became the number-one news show in terms of nightly viewers. In 1962 CBS followed suit with its *Evening News*, starring Walter Cronkite. The *Huntley-Brinkley Report* remained on the air until 1970. The conclusion of their last broadcast was like the conclusion of their first: "Good Night, Chet"; "Good Night, David."

SUGGESTED READINGS: Hollis Alpert, "TV's Unique Tandem: Huntley-Brinkley," *Coronet* 49 (February 1961), 162–69; "The Evening Duet," *Time*, October 19, 1959, 92.

HYDROGEN BOMB. During World War II, U.S. scientists and technicians in the Manhattan Project successfully developed the catastrophically destructive atomic bomb,* two of which were dropped on Japan in August 1945. Their destructiveness, and President Harry Truman's* willingness to employ them, brought World War II to a swift conclusion. Japan sued for peace within days of the second blast.

No sooner had the radioactive dust settled on Japan than a new debate about nuclear weapons developed. The atomic bombs dropped on Japan were based on the principle of nuclear fission, in which the nuclei of uranium atoms are bombarded with neutrons from magnetized coils. Eventually, the uranium atoms are split apart, and the split releases enormous amounts of energy. When contained in a bomb, the energy has unprecedented destructive potential. But physicists also realized the theoretical possibilities of nuclear fusion and the creation of a hydrogen bomb, or H-bomb, that would be infinitely more powerful than the bombs dropped on Nagasaki and Hiroshima, Japan. Whereas the fission process splits, the fusion process combines, converting small amounts of matter into enormous amounts of energy. Physicists identified deuterium as the best element for fusion since it is a heavier version of the hydrogen molecule.

Some physicists opposed the development of the hydrogen bomb. J. Robert Oppenheimer,* who had directed the Manhattan Project, was the leading opponent of the hydrogen bomb. When he first witnessed the detonation of the test atomic bomb at Alamogordo, New Mexico, in July 1945, Oppenheimer recalled a passage from an ancient Hindu poem, "I am death, destroyer of worlds." Enrico Fermi, another Manhattan Project physicist, shared Oppenheimer's concerns.

Other scientists disagreed. Led by physicist Edward Teller, they argued that the United States should develop the hydrogen bomb because it was only a matter of time before some other country did. Teller argued that it was foolhardy to oppose technological development. President Truman and other leading American policy makers listened carefully to the debate but were willing to postpone development until a scientific consensus had been reached.

It was easy to wait because the United States had a monopoly on nuclear weapons. In 1949, however, when the Soviet Union detonated an atomic bomb of its own, the abstract scientific debate suddenly became quite concrete. In order to maintain military superiority, President Truman decided to cut short the debate and move forward with development of the hydrogen bomb. The fact that U.S. intelligence had reported Soviet progress in developing an H-bomb of its own only made Truman's decision more imperative. He assigned the Atomic Energy Commission to develop the bomb, and Edward Teller was put in charge of the project. It was a crash program, and late in 1952 a bomb was ready. On November 1, 1952, American scientists exploded a hydrogen bomb at the tiny island of Eniwetok, one of the Marshall Islands in the Pacific Ocean. A fireball more than three miles wide suddenly blossomed over Eniwetok. The blast, with the equivalent power of 10 million tons of dynamite, was at least 500 times bigger than the bomb dropped on Hiroshima.

The military superiority provided by the H-bomb proved to be frighteningly temporary. In August 1953 Soviet physicists, led by Igor Kurchatov and Andrei Sakharov, detonated a thermonuclear device of their own. In August 1954, the United States tested three more hydrogen bombs at Bikini Atoll in the Marshall Islands. Seventeen more U.S. hydrogen bombs were exploded in 1955. Both the United States and the Soviet Union launched crash programs to build as many hydrogen bombs as possible, and the nuclear arms race, which would last for the next two generations, was under way. U.S. and Soviet politicians would soon possess the power to destroy human life on the planet. When journalists asked Princeton physicist Albert Einstein* about the weapons he thought might be employed in World War III, he replied, "I don't know about World War III, but I do know about World War IV: sticks and stones."

SUGGESTED READING: Richard Rhodes, *Dark Sun: The Making of the Hydrogen Bomb*, 1995.

I

I LED THREE LIVES. *I Led Three Lives*, a syndicated television series, premiered in September 1953. A perfect television* symbol of the Red Scare,* *I Led Three Lives* was loosely based on the exploits of Herbert Philbrick,* a double agent for the Federal Bureau of Investigation* (FBI). Philbrick, a Boston advertising executive, joined a local chapter of the Communist party in order to supply the FBI with information about party activities. The series made it appear that Communists could be found in every corner of American life, exactly what demagogues like Senator Joseph McCarthy* of Wisconsin were claiming. In the television series, which eventually included 117 separate episodes, Richard Carlson played Philbrick, and every week he foiled Communist attempts at sabotage, treason, espionage, drug dealing, and propaganda. The last episode was broadcast in the summer of 1956.

SUGGESTED READINGS: Tim Brooks and Earle Marsh, *The Complete Directory to Prime Time Network and Cable TV Shows, 1946–Present*, 1995; Herbert A. Philbrick, *I Led Three Lives*, 1952.

I LOVE LUCY. *I Love Lucy* launched the situation comedy as a staple of American television* and went on to become the most successful series in broadcasting history. During the late 1930s and throughout the 1940s, Lucille Ball performed in a series of successful "B" films and earned the sobriquet "Queen of the Bs." In 1950 executives of CBS offered her the lead in a weekly television series to be loosely based on her successful radio program *My Favorite Husband*. Ball insisted that her husband, Desi Arnaz, a Cuban-born crooner and big band leader, get the lead as her husband. She also made television history by insisting that their production company, known as Desilu, retain "residual" rights, or the ability to charge a fee for repeated airings. At the time, of course, television was so new that there was no such thing as "reruns," and Ball's decision would eventually make her the richest woman in show business.

Ball and Arnaz also decided to use first-class production techniques. At the time, television shows were filmed by primitive kinescope cameras, and the programs did not survive for very long because the kinescope tapes deteriorated. Ball and Arnaz insisted that skilled cinematographers, using three 35-mm cameras, film the weekly program. They also filmed the show before a live studio audience, which gave the program authenticity and kept the actors on their creative toes.

The first show aired in the fall of 1951. Lucille Ball played the zany Lucy Ricardo, wife of Ricky Ricardo, a Cuban-born bandleader who played at the Tropicana night club in New York City. Much of the humor played off the challenges of marriage and family life, especially within the context of an immigrant Hispanic husband with traditional role expectations for his wife, and a highly independent woman using whatever means she could to assert her own way, especially in her obsessive desire to break into show business. In supporting roles were William Frawley and Vivian Vance as Fred and Ethyl Mertz, the Ricardo's best friends, landlords, and next-door neighbors. Fred had a deadpan sarcasm and Ethyl was always a co-conspirator in Lucy's comedic schemes. By the end of its first season, *I Love Lucy* had captured 60 percent of the viewing audience. Cameo appearances by major film stars and celebrities became regular occurrences on the show.

Desilu eventually produced 179 episodes of *I Love Lucy*. The last one appeared at the end of the 1957 season. In 1953, when Lucille Ball gave birth to a son, scriptwriters wrote her pregnancy into the program, and the episode in which she gave birth to "Little Ricky" garnered more than 92 percent of all television viewers. No program since has ever come close to that viewership figure. The last episode broadcast in 1957 became a pop culture event in America, much like the last broadcast of *The Fugitive* in 1967, *M*A*S*H* in 1983, and *Seinfeld* in 1998.

Television historians trace the popularity of *I Love Lucy* to the tensions of the times. The decade of the 1950s was a time of the Red Scare,* the Cold War,* and the threat of nuclear annihilation. Watching *I Love Lucy* each week allowed Americans to forget their concerns for thirty minutes. There was more to the program's success than mere escapism. Lucille Ball's comedy enjoyed a universal appeal that transcends time and culture. The show is still seen in reruns today around the world.

SUGGESTED READINGS: Lucille Ball, *Love, Lucy*, 1996; Jess Oppenheimer, *Laughs, Luck—and Lucy: How I Came to Create the Most Popular Sitcom of All Time*, 1996.

I MARRIED JOAN. *I Married Joan*, a popular situation comedy of the early 1950s, premiered on NBC on October 15, 1952, starring Jim Backus as Judge Bradley Davis and Joan Davis as his unpredictably daffy wife, Joan. The judge, who presided over domestic court in each episode, tried to settle family disputes by commiserating over the antics of his own wife, who schemed to get more money to spend, to trick the judge into doing things her way, and who constantly conspired with her friend Minerva, played by Hope Emerson. The last episode of *I Married Joan* was broadcast on April 6, 1955.

SUGGESTED READING: Tim Brooks and Earle Marsh, *The Complete Directory to Prime Time Network and Cable TV Shows, 1946–Present*, 1995.

I WAS A COMMUNIST FOR THE FBI. During the early 1950s, *I Was a Communist for the FBI* was a popular radio espionage series. Based on the real exploits of Matthew Cvetic, an employee of the Federal Bureau of Investigation* who had joined the Communist party to work as a counterspy, the program was the work of Frederick Ziv and starred Dana Andrews as Matt Cvetic. A total of 78 episodes were produced, and by 1953, when the Red Scare* in the United States reached its peak, more than 600 radio stations carried the program in syndication. By 1954, after Senator Joseph McCarthy* had lost credibility and the Red Scare had begun to abate, *I Was a Communist for the FBI* faded as well and was cancelled.

SUGGESTED READING: John Dunning, *On the Air: The Encyclopedia of Old-Time Radio*, 1998.

INHERIT THE WIND. *Inherit the Wind*, a three-act play by Jerome Lawrence and Robert E. Lee, opened at the National Theater in New York City on April 21, 1955. Built around the famous evolution, or "Monkey," trial in Dayton, Tennessee, in 1925, *Inherit the Wind* starred Karl Light as Bertram Cates, a high school biology teacher accused of violating state laws against teaching evolution. Light, of course, is the mirror image of William Scopes, the real biology teacher in Dayton. Paul Muni played Henry Drummond, a front for famed defense attorney Clarence Darrow, who comes to defend Light. To assist the prosecution, the famous politician Matthew Brady, played by Ed Begley, arrives in town. Begley is, of course, William Jennings Bryan. Tony Randall played E. K. Hornbeck, a sarcastic reporter resembling H. L. Mencken.

The trial becomes a three-ring circus, with the press examining every word and Drummond eventually reducing Brady, who takes to the witness stand to defend the Bible, to not much more than a blithering idiot. *Inherit the Wind* exposed narrow-mindedness and intellectual bigotry. It had a run of 806 performances on Broadway and was later made into a film starring Spencer Tracy.*

SUGGESTED READINGS: Gerald Bordman, *The Oxford Companion to American Theater*, 1992; *New York Times*, April 22, 1955.

INTERCONTINENTAL BALLISTIC MISSILE. Throughout U.S. history, Americans have felt a great sense of security because of their geographic isolation behind two oceans. Until World War II, with a few exceptions, Americans had also valued an isolationist foreign policy aimed at keeping the United States clear of Old World disputes.

The advent of the Cold War* and nuclear weapons, because of their huge destructive potential, put an even larger premium on the significance of geographic isolation. Until 1957 the United States had a decided nuclear strategic advantage over the Soviet Union. American B-52 bombers, armed with high-yield nuclear weapons, were stationed at U.S. air bases in Alaska, Greenland, Iceland, Japan, Morocco, Spain, Saudi Arabia, and Turkey, and their range could carry them throughout much of the Soviet Union. The Soviets did not enjoy similar bomber access to U.S. targets.

To deal with their strategic disadvantage, the Soviet Union invested enormous resources in missile technology. Germany had already pioneered the idea of military rockets. German scientists, by the end of World War II, had developed the V-1 and then the V-2 rockets, which they launched from France and used to rain conventional explosives on London in 1945. A rocket armed with hydrogen-bomb* warheads constituted an unprecedented weapon of mass destruction.

In August 1957, the Soviets successfully tested an intercontinental ballistic missile (ICBM), flying it across thousands of miles of Soviet territory. The missile, known as the "Sapwood Rocket," was soon operational, with a range of 6,000 miles. The key to the Soviet design was staging systems. Rockets require enormous volumes of fuel to achieve liftoff, but after liftoff, they require relatively little energy. The Soviet ICBM jettisoned the fuel and engine stage of the rocket as soon as the missile had achieved sufficient altitude, after which the warhead could be targeted by the force of gravity and relatively small directional adjustments.

At first, U.S. policy makers ridiculed the announcement as just another example of Communist propaganda, but Soviet technology could no longer be dismissed after October 4, 1957. Soviet space scientists launched a rocket into space and placed a satellite in orbit around the earth. The satellite, named *Sputnik*,* made it abundantly clear that the Soviet Union could fire rockets and drop nuclear bombs on the United States. The United States still had a vast superiority in its nuclear arsenal—2,200 warheads to the Soviet Union's 250—but America's long-held sense of geographic isolation and security were gone forever.

Fears of nuclear annihilation soon became endemic to formal U.S. strategic policy and to American popular culture. Such novels as *Level Seven* (1956), *On the Beach* (1959), and *Alas Babylon* (1962) became best-sellers, and Americans launched a building boom, constructing bomb shelters* in their backyards. The arms race escalated, with the United States and the Soviet Union competing to build larger and larger nuclear warheads and more and more ICBMs.

SUGGESTED READING: Trevor Illtyd Williams, *Science: A History of Discovery in the Twentieth Century*, 1990.

INVISIBLE MAN. *Invisible Man* is the title of Ralph Ellison's highly influential 1952 novel. What set *Invisible Man* apart in modern American literature was the fact that the author, as well as the novel's major characters, were all African Americans. Naturalistic and surreal, the novel was based on the premise that black people in the United States are not perceived as human beings, or much else for that matter, by white people and white institutions. The main character is an anonymous black man who is raised in the rural South, moves to Harlem as a young man, attends an all-black college, and shifts intellectually from ignorance to Booker T. Washington accommodation to communism, concluding in the end that American society offers him no identity and that he had never developed one of his own. In that sense, the novel reflected the twentieth-century history of black people, who traded the racism of the South for the racism of the North. *Invisible Man* was the first and the last novel of Ralph Ellison, who died in 1994.

SUGGESTED READING: Ralph Ellison, *Invisible Man*, 1952.

IRAN. In 1951 Muhammad Mussadegh, national premier and leader in Iran's national legislature, passed legislation nationalizing the British-owned Anglo-Iranian Oil Company. London immediately launched a boycott of Iranian oil until Iran reversed the law. Great Britain also pressured President Harry Truman* to support the boycott. Truman had extremely mixed feelings. He wanted to support the British, but at the same time he did not want to interfere in the internal affairs of a sovereign state. Since Iran had once been part of the British empire, the British had no such misgivings.

In January 1953, Dwight D. Eisenhower* became president of the United States, and he was worried that if the United States and Great Britain did not intervene, Muhammad Mussadegh might lead Iran into the Soviet orbit. The Soviets were only too anxious to gain a political and economic foothold in the Persian Gulf. Eisenhower consulted with British Prime Minister Winston Churchill, and they decided to take joint action.

Agents from British intelligence and the Central Intelligence Agency (CIA) began to plot a secret coup d'etat against the Mussadegh government. Once the coup got under way, Muhammad Reza Shah Pahlevi, the Iranian monarch who secretly sympathized with British concerns, dismissed Mussadegh. Mussadegh refused to leave Tehran, and anti-shah rioting erupted in the streets. The shah fled to Rome. The CIA then organized anti-Mussadegh factions to rebel, and civil war erupted in the streets of Tehran. The shah then returned in triumph and established a military dictatorship.

Under the shah's authority, Iran changed the name of the Anglo-Iranian Oil Company to British Petroleum, and although the company remained under nominal Iranian ownership, it had for all intents and purposes been returned to its British owners. The shah remained in power until 1979, when the Ayatollah Khomeini and Muslim fundamentalists staged a coup of their own against him.

SUGGESTED READING: Mark Lytle, *Origins of the Iranian-American Alliance, 1941–1953*, 1987.

I'VE GOT A SECRET. *I've Got a Secret* was a popular quiz and audience participation show of the 1950s. Garry Moore served as the emcee during the 1950s, and the show consisted of four panelists questioning an individual to determine what his or her secret was. The secret was flashed on the screen so the viewing audience would know what the panel was trying to find out. The most popular panelists included Orson Bean, Jayne Meadows, Bill Cullen, Kitty Carlisle, Henry Morgan, and Laraine Day. *I've Got a Secret* debuted on CBS on June 19, 1952, and it remained on the air until April 1967.

SUGGESTED READING: Tim Brooks and Earle Marsh, *The Complete Directory to Prime Time Network and Cable TV Shows, 1946–Present*, 1995.

J

THE JACK BENNY SHOW. Jack Benny became a star performer in vaudeville during the 1920s, and in 1932 his radio show became a hit. Benny was a dead-pan comic who built his humor around his renowned stinginess and vanity about his age, which he left at a perpetual "thirty-nine"; his humor was understated, self-deprecating, and gentle. He easily made the transition to television* when CBS first broadcast *The Jack Benny Show* on October 28, 1950. CBS aired the show ten times as a special in the 1950–1951 season, and ten times more in 1951–1952 season. From September 13, 1953, to June 1960, *The Jack Benny Show* was broadcast every other week. Weekly broadcasts were produced from 1960 to the last episode in September 1965.

Featured with Jack Benny on the show were Eddie "Robinson" Anderson, who played Benny's African-American valet, and Don Wilson, the announcer. Irregular appearances were made by such actors and comedians as Mel Blanc, Dennis Day, and Artie Auerbach. By the time the show was canceled in 1965, Benny had become the dean of American comedy. He died in 1974.

SUGGESTED READINGS: Jack Benny, *Sunday Nights at Seven: The Jack Benny Story*, 1991; Mary Benny, *Jack Benny*, 1978; Tim Brooks and Earle Marsh, *The Complete Directory to Prime Time Network and Cable TV Shows, 1946–Present*, 1995.

THE JACKIE GLEASON SHOW. Jackie Gleason had starred on the DuMont television network's *Cavalcade of Stars* show, but in 1952 CBS offered him an unheard of $8,000 a week to jump to CBS. *The Jackie Gleason Show* was first broadcast on CBS on September 20, 1952. Art Carney, Gleason's friend and the actor who played Ed Norton in the popular "Honeymooners" sketch, moved to CBS too, as did the June Taylor dancers and the orchestra of Ray Bloch. Gleason was a gifted comic, and his sketches as Ralph Kramden, Reggie Van Gleason III, the Loudmouth, and Rudy the Repairman earned him a faithful television* viewing audience. His favorite catch phrases on the show—"And awa-a-aay we go" and "How sweet it is!"—entered the American pop culture lexicon. In 1955 CBS took *The Jackie Gleason Show* off the air and replaced it with *The Honeymooners*. *The Honeymooners* went off the air as an independent situation comedy after its first season, and Jackie Gleason was not on the air in 1957–1958. CBS reprised the show as a half-hour variety program in 1958, but it lasted only three months. In the 1960s, however, *The Jackie Gleason Show* returned to CBS television and had a successful six-year run.

SUGGESTED READINGS: Tim Brooks and Earle Marsh, *The Complete Directory to Prime Time Network and Cable TV Shows, 1946–Present*, 1995; William Henry, *The Great One: The Life and Legend of Jackie Gleason*, 1993; Audrey Meadows, *Love, Alice: My Life as a Honeymooner*, 1994.

JENCKS V. UNITED STATES (1959). During the 1950s, the Red Scare* targeted a variety of political dissidents for harassment, but none received more attention from Congress and the Federal Bureau of Investigation* (FBI) than individuals suspected of being members of the Communist party. The Smith Act of 1950* made it a federal crime to form any group that advocated the overthrow of the U.S. government. Since Marxism-Leninism postulated the collapse of the U.S. government and anxiously awaited that day, most active Communists fell under the rubric of the Smith Act. They protested, of course, claiming that the Smith Act was a gross violation of their First Amendment civil liberties, especially freedom of speech and freedom of the press.

Those prosecuted under the law knew that the FBI maintained extensive files on suspected Communists, and in 1957 Alan Jencks filed suit, demanding access to the FBI file on him. He was being prosecuted under the Smith Act, and he argued that he needed the file to plan his trial defense. The FBI refused. The case made its way through the federal courts, and in 1959, the U.S. Supreme Court ruled in Jencks's favor. Accused Communists should be given access to any FBI files on them as a means of preparing a legal defense. FBI director J. Edgar Hoover* howled in protest but to no avail. The highest court in the land had spoken.

SUGGESTED READING: Richard G. Powers, *Secrecy and Power: The Life of J. Edgar Hoover*, 1987; Stanford J. Unger, *The FBI*, 1976.

JOHNSON, LYNDON B(AINES). Lyndon Baines Johnson was born in Stonewall, Texas, on August 27, 1908. His father, Sam Johnson, was a highly respected state legislator, and the younger Johnson was raised on a steady diet of national, state, and local politics. He graduated from Southwest Texas Teachers College in 1930, after having taken a leave of absence to teach school in Cotulla, Texas. Johnson taught public school briefly in Houston before joining, in 1931, the staff of Congressman Richard Kleberg. In 1934 Johnson was appointed director of the state branch of the National Youth Administration, a post that allowed him to dispense government jobs and build a political base for himself.

In 1937 he was elected as a Democrat to the House of Representatives, where he was a staunch defender of President Franklin D. Roosevelt and the New Deal. During World War II, Johnson served in the U.S. Navy.

After the war, he returned to Texas and resumed his political career, winning a seat in the U.S. Senate in 1948. The election had been closely contested, and charges of election fraud in that race followed Johnson for the rest of his life. In 1949 Johnson took the Senate by storm. He was a political animal who had an uncanny instinct for finding the source of power. In just two years—an unprecedentedly short period in Senate history—he won election as majority whip, and in 1953 he became minority leader, even though he was still in his first term. Johnson was reelected in 1954, and when the Senate organized itself early in 1955, he was named majority leader. He then reformed the seniority system to make sure that every senator—senior senators as well as first-termers—received some important committee assignments. Johnson soon had the entire Senate dependent upon him.

As majority leader, Johnson proved to be a pragmatic individual capable of working with Democrats and Republicans. President Dwight D. Eisenhower* could count on Johnson to be fair and bipartisan. The majority leader played a key role in securing the Civil Rights Act of 1957* and the Civil Rights Act of 1960, both of which made modest gains in bringing civil rights to African Americans and Mexican Americans. In 1960 Johnson made a run for the Democratic presidential nomination, but Senator John F. Kennedy* of Massachusetts secured it instead. Kennedy then asked Johnson to become his vice-presidential running mate. They narrowly defeated Republican nominee Richard M. Nixon.*

Johnson proved to be a loyal vice president, although he hated the office, which lacked any real power and was largely ceremonial. On November 22, 1963, when Kennedy was assassinated, Johnson became president. He pushed his Great Society programs of antipoverty and civil rights legislation, and he was largely successful until the escalating Vietnam War* destroyed his presidency. Johnson decided not to seek reelection in 1968, and in 1969 he returned to Texas. He died on January 22, 1973.

SUGGESTED READINGS: Robert Caro, *The Years of Lyndon Johnson: The Path to Power*, 1982; Paul Conkin, *Big Daddy from the Pedernales: Lyndon Baines Johnson*, 1986; Doris Kearns, *Lyndon Johnson and the American Dream*, 1976.

JORGENSEN, CHRISTINE. Christine Jorgensen came to national and world attention in 1952 when she went public with the news of her sex change operation. A native of the Bronx in New York City, Jorgensen, born as George Jorgensen, had enjoyed a normal boyhood of school, sports, and a stint in the U.S. Army. Throughout his adolescence and young adulthood, George had felt confused sexually, always wondering why he had not been born a woman since so many of his inclinations and tastes leaned in that direction. At the time, there was no such thing as trans-sexuality, although experimental surgeries had been tried as early as the 1920s to assist men and women in coming to terms with confused sexual identities.

After World War II, however, a number of prominent Danish endocrinologists and surgeons combined their disciplines to assist individuals like Jorgensen. To change men into women, they surgically removed the penis and the testicles, fashioned a vagina, and injected female hormones. In 1950 Jorgensen moved to Denmark to receive the treatment. Over the course of two years, he underwent five major operations and received more than 2,000 hormone injections.

In 1952 several enterprising journalists from the United States caught up with Jorgensen, now known legally as Christine Jorgensen, and interviewed her. She made no secret of the operation, and upon returning to the United States she announced, "I'm happy to be home. What American wouldn't be?" Her story made headlines, but at the time the United States was in the post–Kinsey Report* era. In 1949 the Kinsey Report had scandalized the country with its description of sexual diversity in the United States, and Jorgensen's story, within that context, did not seem so terribly surprising. Many Americans had gone beyond sexual shock. Today, a transgender civil rights movement works to end discrimination against men and women who have undergone sex change operations, and leaders of the movement hail Christine Jorgensen for "coming out" and beginning the process of demystifying their lifestyle.

SUGGESTED READING: Leslie Feinberg, *Transgender Warriors: Making Hits from Joan of Arc to Dennis Rodman*, 1996.

JUVENILE DELINQUENCY. During the 1950s, the problem of juvenile crime became a near obsession among teachers, psychologists, middle-class parents, and law enforcement officials. As early as 1953, J. Edgar Hoover,* director of the Federal Bureau of Investigation,* reported that in the United States, young people under the age of eighteen were responsible for nearly 54 percent of all car thefts, 49 percent of all burglaries, 18 percent of all robberies, and 16 percent of all rapes. With the baby boom* generation just a few years from reaching the teenage years, Hoover preached, the United States could expect the problem to get worse before it got better.

The popular culture also reflected the concern. In 1955 James Dean,* in the film *Rebel Without a Cause*,* provided young people with a new icon of teenage anomie and alienation. Dressed in his white T-shirt, leather jacket, Levi's, and loafers, with a cigarette dangling from his lips, Dean personified the restless insolence that many adults detected in the younger generation. A host of other films took advantage of these fears, including *Blackboard Jungle** (1955), *Riot in Juvenile Prison* (1956), and *The Cool and the Crazy* (1957), all of which convinced many Americans that juveniles were smoldering with rebellion.

A host of explanations were offered to explain the phenomenon of juvenile crime. A few extreme conservatives accused Communists of exploiting youthful confusion to take over the country. Other conservatives targeted comic books, movies, television, divorce, the decline of the American family, and rock-and-roll* music as the culprits. Liberals blamed the rise of a consumer culture,* arguing that teenagers saw no meaning to life beyond consumption, and it left many with a sense of hopelessness. None of the explanations really explained much, and within a few years those same teenagers had grown up to become college students and the most idealist generation in recent American history— a group committed to civil rights and peace.

SUGGESTED READING: Mark Thomas McGee, *The J.D. Films: Juvenile Delinquency in the Movies*, 1982.

K

KEFAUVER COMMITTEE. The Kefauver Committee, more formally known as the Senate Special Committee to Investigate Organized Crime in Interstate Commerce, was headed by Senator Estes Kefauver,* Democrat from Tennessee. Off and on for decades, Americans had expressed concern about organized crime, but in April 1950 the murder of two gangsters in a Democratic clubhouse in Kansas City, Missouri, reignited concern. Republicans made the most of the killings, since they took place in President Harry Truman's* home state. To take some of the steam out of the Republican accusations of scandal, the Senate appointed Kefauver to head the investigation. The hearings began on May 26, 1950.

During 1950 and 1951, the committee conducted hearings in major cities throughout the country, listening to testimony from judges, police, district attorneys, convicted criminals, and corrupt public officials. The Kefauver Committee concluded that organized crime in the United States was dominated by two syndicates. One was based in Chicago and the other in New York City. The committee also tried to prove that both syndicates were under the control of Mafia head Charles "Lucky" Luciano. Although the syndicates trafficked in drugs, prostitution, and labor racketeering, most of their money came from illegal gambling, and they had bought off a legion of police, judges, and prosecutors to avoid action against them.

The hearings also became a media event because they were televised over major networks, the first time in U.S. history that a congressional investigation had ever received such attention. Millions of Americans followed the hearings on television.* Senator Kefauver wrote a widely read series of articles that appeared in the *Saturday Evening Post* about organized crime, and his book *Crime in America* (1951) became a best-seller. The Kefauver hearings made concern about organized crime and the Mafia a national concern.

SUGGESTED READINGS: Estes Kefauver, *Crime in America*, 1951; William Howard Moore, *The Kefauver Committee and the Politics of Crime*, 1974.

KEFAUVER, ESTES. Estes Kefauver was born in Madisonville, Tennessee, on July 26, 1903. He graduated from the University of Tennessee in 1924 and then earned a law degree at Yale. He practiced law in Chattanooga for more than a decade before he was elected to Congress in 1938. Kefauver served five terms in the House before being elected to the U.S. Senate in 1948. It was a remarkable electoral victory because Kefauver was widely considered a liberal, at least in terms of Southern politics. In 1942 he had enraged other Southern congressman when he voted for an anti–poll tax amendment to the Constitution. In 1948 his opponents tried to smear him by calling him a "Communist" or a "Communist sympathizer." Kefauver won anyway.

He burst into the national limelight in 1950 when he chaired the Senate investigation into organized crime. Some of those hearings were broadcast on television,* and many were held in cities across the country, giving Kefauver a national exposure few freshman U.S. senators ever experience. The so-called Kefauver Committee* exposed a number of underworld families and demonstrated their links to many prominent Democratic urban political machines.

Now a national figure, Kefauver decided to run for president in 1952. He contested the Democratic party nomination with Governor Adlai E. Stevenson* of Illinois, but Stevenson won the nomination. Kefauver's organized crime investigation had alienated the urban machine politicians in the Democratic party, and they essentially vetoed his nomination. Kefauver tried again in 1956, but Stevenson prevailed again. This time, however, he selected Kefauver as his vice presidential running mate. The Democratic ticket was easily defeated by incumbent President Dwight D. Eisenhower.* Kefauver returned to the U.S. Senate, where he earned even more respect as the South's most liberal Democrat. He was reelected in 1960 but died on August 10, 1963, before finishing his term.

SUGGESTED READINGS: Charles Fontenay, *Estes Kefauver: A Biography*, 1980; Joseph Gorman, *Kefauver: A Political Biography*, 1971; *New York Times*, August 11, 1963;

KELLY, GRACE. Grace Kelly was born in 1925 to a prominent family in Germantown, Pennsylvania. Her father was a Philadelphia businessman who had inherited a family business—Kelly for Bricks—and built it into a major construction firm. He indulged his daughter's desire to become an actress. She attended the American Academy of Dramatic Arts in New York City in 1947 and did some modeling on the side. Kelly also made a few commercials, and one for Ipana toothpaste helped her break into films. Kelly, a fine actress, was a tall, beautiful blonde and had a screen presence that combined innocence with smoldering sexuality. Her performances in *High Noon* (1952), *Dial M for Murder* (1954), and *Rear Window* (1954) earned her millions of fans. For her performance in *The Country Girl* (1954), she won an Academy Award for best actress. Kelly's face, which appeared in magazines and newspapers nearly every day, became one of the most recognizable in the country.

In 1955, while Kelly was in Europe for the Cannes Film Festival, she agreed to visit Monaco, the tiny European principality, and be photographed in the palace with Prince Rainier and the royal family. She became close friends with Prince Rainer III, a 32-year-old bachelor. Later in the year, Rainier proposed marriage, and Kelly accepted. She completed filming *High Society* (1956), and the marriage took place on April 19, 1956. The Roman Catholic ceremony was beamed to a worldwide television* audience of more than thirty million people. For Americans, the marriage was a fairy tale, almost a Cinderella story–a beautiful actress becomes a real-life princess. She left behind her film career, lived the rest of her life in Europe, raised three children, and spent her time in philanthropy and charity work. Grace Kelly died in an automobile accident in 1982.

SUGGESTED READING: Gant Gaither, *Princess of Monaco: The Story of Grace Kelly*, 1957.

KENNAN, GEORGE. George Frost Kennan was born in Milwaukee, Wisconsin, on February 16, 1904. He attended Princeton and after graduating joined the foreign service. Kennan filled a variety of State Department posts, including membership in the first U.S. mission to the Soviet Union between 1933 and 1936. He was posted in Prague and Berlin immediately before the outbreak of war in Europe. During World War II, Kennan served as a counselor in Lisbon, Portugal, from 1943 to 1944, then as minister-counselor in Moscow from 1944 to 1946. Between 1947 and 1949, Kennan served as director of the policy planning staff in the State Department, where the containment policy* originated and evolved.

In 1947 under the pseudonym "X," Kennan wrote a highly influential article outlining the containment policy in the journal *Foreign Affairs*. An expert in Soviet affairs, he argued that the United States should accept the political alignment of Europe as it existed at the end of World War II, with the Soviet Union dominating Eastern Europe, but that any attempts made by the Soviets to expand beyond those 1945 political and military boundaries should be "contained." In the beginning, containment was primarily a nonmilitary policy. Focusing on economic and technical assistance, it was embodied in such programs as the Marshall Plan of 1948 to rebuild the European economies and the Truman Doctrine of 1947 to provide the funds to Greece and Turkey for their fight against Communist guerrillas. As the Cold War* escalated in the late 1940s, however, containment took on new global, military dimensions. Its first real test came in 1948 when the Soviet Union sealed off West Berlin in hope of starving the city into submission and incorporating it into the Eastern Bloc. President Harry Truman* mounted the Berlin airlift to keep the city fed and supplied until the Soviet Union backed down.

After the fall of China in 1949, containment came to imply the encirclement of the People's Republic of China and the Soviet Union with a network of

military alliances: the North Atlantic Treaty Organization, the Baghdad Pact,*
the Southeast Asia Treaty Organization, and the enormous military buildup
of the 1950s and 1960s. When the North Koreans invaded South Korea in
1950, the United States intervened in the conflict in the name of containment.
Containment reached its peak during the Dwight D. Eisenhower* years and the
tenure of Secretary of State John Foster Dulles* (1953 to 1959).

When the French were expelled from Indochina after the Battle of Dien Bien
Phu* in 1954, the United States began increasing its commitment to prevent a
Communist takeover. American policy makers were applying the containment
doctrine to Vietnam, assuming that Soviet and Chinese aggression were behind
the North Vietnamese crusade to reunite the country. The domino theory* and
the containment policy fit nicely together in the 1950s and early 1960s. Not
until the mid-1960s, however, when American policy makers began to see that
communism was not a single, monolithic movement orchestrated from Moscow,
did the application of containment to Vietnam begin to seem counterproductive.
Ho Chi Minh,* the leading Communist in Vietnam, was not an external, foreign
invader of the country but a nationalist committed to liberating Vietnam of
French imperial authority. In applying the containment doctrine to Indochina,
the United States made a fundamental miscalculation that led to the disastrous
Vietnam War.* By the late 1960s and early 1970s, American policy makers
accepted the importance of colonialism and nationalism in the history of the
anti-French and anti-American movements in Vietnam. By that time as well,
American policy makers realized that communism was a polycentric movement
requiring creative, individual responses.

After a tour as U.S. ambassador to the Soviet Union in the 1950s, Kennan
accepted a position as professor of historical studies at the Institute for Advanced
Studies at Princeton. A prolific writer, Kennan was the author of many books,
including *American Diplomacy 1900–1950* (1951), *Soviet-American Relations,
1917–1941* (1956), *Soviet Foreign Policy Under Lenin and Stalin* (1961), *Re-
alities of American Foreign Policy* (1966), and *Memoirs, 1925–1950* (1968).

During the Vietnam War, it was natural that supporters and opponents of
American policy there would seek out Kennan's opinion. Essentially, the domino theory, when applied to Asia, was essentially an extrapolation from Kennan's containment notions. Kennan, however, disagreed with such an application
of his ideas and believed that American policies in Vietnam were misguided.
The dominating force in Asia, he believed, was nationalism, not communism.
The John F. Kennedy* and Lyndon B. Johnson* administrations had erred in
committing themselves to a hopelessly corrupt regime in South Vietnam. It
would be difficult, if not impossible, for the United States to defeat the Vietcong* militarily and politically, and in any event such a victory would mean
little, since the region was not directly connected to America's national security.
In February 1966, Kennan said as much before the Senate Foreign Relations
Committee, which was investigating U.S. policies in Indochina. He recom-

mended the withdrawal of American forces as soon as possible. Since then, Kennan has continued to lecture and teach.

SUGGESTED READINGS: John L. Harper, *America's Vision of Europe: Franklin D. Roosevelt, George F. Kennan, and Dean G. Acheson*, 1994; George F. Kennan, *Memoirs, 1925–1950*, 1968, and *At the Century's End: Reflections*, 1996; X, " The Sources of Soviet Conduct," *Foreign Affairs*, 25 (July 1947), 566–582.

KENNEDY, JOHN F(ITZGERALD). John Fitzgerald Kennedy was born May 29, 1917, in Brookline, Massachusetts, a suburb of Boston. His father, Joseph Kennedy, had made a fortune in the banking business, and his mother, Rose Fitzgerald Kennedy, was connected to one of the state's most influential political families. After he graduated from Harvard in 1940, he wrote his first book, *Why England Slept*, a study of the British reaction to the rise of Adolf Hitler in Germany. During World War II, he served in the U.S. Navy and was decorated for bravery when his patrol boat was sunk during fighting in the Solomon Islands. Because of a back injury sustained in battle as well as a case of malaria, he was discharged from the Navy early in 1945.

Since his father had decided that John would become the first Irish Catholic president of the United States, the younger Kennedy embarked on a political career and won a seat as a Democrat in Congress in 1946. He was reelected in 1948 and 1950, and in 1952 he defeated incumbent Henry Cabot Lodge for a seat in the U.S. Senate. Throughout the 1950s, Kennedy behaved in the Senate as if he were preparing for a run at the presidency. He staked out moderate ground and avoided controversy at all costs, whether it had to do with domestic affairs, like the civil rights movement,* or foreign policy, like the Cold War.* Kennedy knew that to win the White House, a candidate had to try to be "all things to all people," and he followed his own advice assiduously. In 1960 he defeated Vice President Richard M. Nixon* and won election as president of the United States.

As president, Kennedy continued to pursue a careful political course, always projecting an attractive image that compensated for some of his failures in public policy. He carefully negotiated the tightrope of civil rights, almost brought the world to nuclear war in the Cuban missile crisis of 1962, and then launched detente—or rapprochement with the Soviet Union—with the Nuclear Test Ban Treaty of 1963. Kennedy's administration, and his life, were cut tragically short on November 22, 1963, when he was assassinated in Dallas, Texas.

SUGGESTED READINGS: Herbert Parmet, *Jack: The Struggles of John F. Kennedy*, 1981, and *JFK: The Presidency of John F. Kennedy*, 1983.

***KENT V. DULLES* (1958).** The State Department denied a passport to Rockwell Kent because of his membership in the Communist party and because his travel might inflict injury on the United States. Kent sued on First Amendment grounds, naming Secretary of State John Foster Dulles* in the suit. The U.S.

Supreme Court decided the case on June 16, 1958, but avoided the constitutional issue and argued on statutory grounds that since Congress had not legislated prohibitions on the foreign travel of Communists, the State Department had no right to deny passports to individuals because of their political beliefs.

SUGGESTED READING: 357 U.S. 116 (1958).

KEROUAC, JACK. Jack Kerouac was born in Lowell, Massachusetts, on March 12, 1922. His parents, who were French Canadians, had immigrated to New England to work in the textile mills. In 1940 he won a football scholarship to Columbia University, but he found the discipline of academic life unsuitable to his free-spirited nature. An injury forced him to quit the team, and he had little patience for the rigors of scholarship. He left Columbia in 1943 and joined the U.S. Navy. His military career was even shorter than his football and academic careers. The Navy discharged Kerouac six months after he joined, citing mental instability. Whenever he was asked to march in close-order drill, Kerouac simply marched off in odd directions, all by himself, driving his drill instructors to distraction. Kerouac returned to New York City and got a dingy apartment in Morningside Heights near Columbia.

He soon began to keep company with Allen Ginsberg* and William Burroughs, who were the leading lights in the emerging Beat* movement, which rejected the conventions of middle-class consumer culture.* They protested the insistence of modern society that happiness could be found only in monogamous heterosexuality, conformity, and consumption. They introduced Kerouac to drugs and the bohemian lifestyle of the Beats.

Kerouac did have a talent for creative writing, and he published his first novel in 1950—*The Town and the City*. It tells the story of a troubled young man who abandons small-town life and its stultifying conventions to find his identity in the city. That identity is discovered among hipsters of the Beat generation, who want a life of spontaneity and feeling, not conformity.

In 1957 Kerouac published his second novel, *On the Road*, which features Sal Paradise and Dean Moriarty, two hipsters who drive back and forth across America living the lives of hipsters. Although Kerouac had labored for years on the novel, Beat promoters hailed it as an icon to spontaneity, claiming that Kerouac had written it in one sitting during an amphetamine-induced creative blitz. They even claimed that he had written it on one continuous strip of teletype paper to avoid the distractions of removing paper one sheet at a time from the typewriter. *On the Road* quickly became the Bible for the Beat generation.

The rest of Kerouac's life was an anticlimax. He continued to write, but his novels, *Subterraneans* (1958) and *Dharma Bums* (1958), never reached the critical or creative heights of *On the Road*. He also became a victim of his own ideas. During the 1960s, Kerouac confused spontaneity with drugs and alcohol, which sapped the rest of his creativity and turned him into a nasty recluse. He died on October 21, 1969, a caricature of the spontaneous rebel he had once claimed to be.

SUGGESTED READINGS: Ann Charter, *Kerouac: A Biography*, 1973; Dennis McNally, *Desolate Angel: Jack Kerouac, the Beat Generation, and America*, 1979; Michael White, ed., *Safe in Heaven Dead: Interviews with Jack Kerouac*, 1990.

KHRUSHCHEV, NIKITA. Premier of the Soviet Union between 1958 and 1964, Nikita Khrushchev was born on April 17, 1894, in Kalinovka, Ukraine, Russia, and gradually rose to power in the Communist party after joining it in 1918. Khrushchev was a loyal follower of Joseph Stalin,* became a member of the Central Committee in 1934, and joined the Politburo in 1939. After Stalin's death in 1953, Khrushchev carefully maneuvered himself into a position to succeed the dictator as chief of state of the Soviet Union. In 1953 he was picked as the first secretary of the Central Committee of the Communist party, a position that made him the most powerful person in the country. Khrushchev bided his time, but in February 1956, during a secret meeting of the 20th Communist Party Congress held in Moscow, he delivered a four-hour speech which shook the Soviet Union to its foundations. Departing from classical Marxist theory that class warfare was inevitable, as was eventual war between the Soviet Union and the capitalist United States, Khrushchev said war could be, and should be, avoided, especially in the nuclear age. He then regaled party members with his views that Stalin had been a brutal dictator, a criminal, and a murderer. In a country where the "cult of personality" reigned, and V. I. Lenin and Stalin had been all but deified, Khrushchev's speech came as a shock. But it also paved the way for a liberalization of Soviet foreign policy and a modest but nevertheless discernable easing of tensions with the United States. Over the course of the next several months, he saw to the release of more than eight million political prisoners locked up in Stalin's gulag prison camps. Although he worked to normalize relations between the Soviet Union and the United States, he was often misunderstood. When, for example, he predicted, "We will bury you," he meant that communism would eventually bury capitalism in productivity, but too many Americans interpreted the remark as a nuclear threat.

In 1956, when anti-Communist rebels in Hungary tried to lead their country out of the Soviet orbit, Khrushchev ruthlessly crushed them, further solidifying his political standing in Moscow (*see* Hungarian Rebellion).

Pro-Stalinist elements in the Soviet Communist party immediately began plotting against Khrushchev, even planning his assassination. The conspirators were led by Vyacheslav Molotov, Georgy Malenkov, and Lazar Kagnovich. Khrushchev, however, was better at political intrigue than his enemies, and he foiled the attempt on his life. He subsequently purged the trio from the party and exiled them to eastern Russia. In 1958 Khrushchev further consolidated his power when he became the premier of the Soviet Union.

He was ultimately removed as premier in 1964, primarily because of continuing Soviet problems with the People's Republic of China, terrible agricultural harvests, and the apparent diplomatic defeat of the Soviet Union in the Cuban missile crisis of 1962. Khrushchev was troubled by the increasing American commitment to the Vietnam War* during the early 1960s, but he genuinely did not want to see a major military conflict in Southeast Asia, primarily because he had no idea what role China would play in it. In 1964, when the North Vietnamese came to Moscow with requests for huge increases in military support, Khrushchev agreed, but only if the North Vietnamese would consider a negotiated settlement with the United States. When Khrushchev was removed from office in October 1964, all hopes for negotiations died. Khrushchev then lived in obscurity until his death in 1971.

SUGGESTED READINGS: Michael R. Beschloss, *The Crisis Years: Kennedy and Khrushchev*, 1991; Nikita Khrushchev, *Khrushchev Remembers*, 1970.

THE KING AND I. *The King and I*, based on the book *Anna and the King of Siam* written by Margaret Landon, was one of the most popular and enduring plays in Broadway history. The product of the fertile collaboration of Oscar Hammerstein II,* who wrote the lyrics, and Richard Rodgers,* who composed the music, *The King and I* opened at the Saint James Theater in New York City on March 29, 1951. It featured Gertrude Lawrence as Englishwoman Anna Leonowens, a teacher hired to instruct the children of the king of Siam. The king, played by Yul Brynner, is an arrogant tyrant with a soft spot in his heart for his children and his subjects. Anna works to soften the king's heart, and eventually she succeeds, even witnessing the king's deathbed confession in which he acknowledges the superiority of her value system. *The King and I* produced a bevy of musical hits that entered American popular culture, including "I Whistle a Happy Tune," "Getting to Know You," "We Kiss in a Shadow," "Something Wonderful," "Hello Young Lovers," and "Shall We Dance." *The King and I* eventually had a run of 1,246 performances and was made into a hit film starring Yul Brynner in 1956.

SUGGESTED READINGS: Gerald Bordman, *The Oxford Companion to American Theater*, 1992; *New York Times*, March 30, 1951.

KING, MARTIN LUTHER, JR. Martin Luther King, Jr., was born on January 15, 1929, in Atlanta, Georgia. His parents first named him Michael Luther King, but when he was six they changed it to Martin Luther King, Jr., after his father Martin Luther King, who was pastor of the Ebenezer Baptist Church in Atlanta. His mother was a schoolteacher. The younger King graduated from Morehouse College in 1948 and the Crozer Theological Seminary in 1951, and then earned a Ph.D. in theology from Boston University in 1955. At all three colleges, he was active in the National Association for the Advancement of Colored People (NAACP), but during those years, he concluded that the NAACP's tactic of fighting discrimination and segregation in the federal court system was insufficient, or at least would take too long, to achieve equality for black people. After carefully studying Mohandas Gandhi's successful rebellion against the British empire in India, in which nonviolent civil disobedience was employed, King became committed to that tactical approach for the civil rights movement* in the United States.

King rocketed into the national consciousness as the leader of the Montgomery bus boycott* in 1955 and 1956. The local affiliate of the NAACP decided to challenge the city ordinance requiring segregated seating on public buses, and Rosa Parks* became the woman to challenge the law. In 1955 she refused to move to the back of the bus as city ordinances required, and she was arrested. King then led a successful black boycott of the buses, which soon brought the city transportation system to the verge of bankruptcy. King's role in the bus boycott attracted wide media attention and made him a national figure.

In 1957 he established the Southern Christian Leadership Conference to fight segregation and discrimination. In 1960 King was one of the founding members of the Student Nonviolent Coordinating Committee, which decided to focus its attention on registering black voters in the Southern states. To achieve his objectives, King employed demonstrations, sit-ins, boycotts, and protest marches. His insistence on nonviolence, as well as his constant refrain that all black people wanted was to be treated equally under the law, resonated with millions of white voters, who came to support his movement. King's speech in 1963 in front of the Lincoln Memorial during the march on Washington was among the most eloquent in U.S. history. When Congress passed the Civil Rights Act of 1964 and the Voting Rights Act of 1965, it was largely in response to the moral crusade generated by King in the United States.

That probably was the high-water mark of King's career. In 1965 his leadership of the civil rights movement was challenged by black power advocates, who had little patience for his nonviolent civil disobedience philosophy. Many of them regarded King as too willing to suffer abuse patiently. King's opposition to the Vietnam War* also took some steam out of the civil rights movement. He was deeply disturbed by the effect of the draft on the black community and the inordinately large numbers of casualties black soldiers were sustaining in 1965 and 1966. In 1967 he openly protested the Vietnam War and linked the civil rights and antiwar movements together, a step that earned him the ire of President Lyndon B. Johnson* and most civil rights leaders, who worried that linking the two movements would only dissipate the force of the campaign for equality. Eventually, most Americans came to agree with King about the war. His life was ended by an assassin's bullet on April 4, 1968, in Memphis, Tennessee.

SUGGESTED READINGS: David J. Garrow, *Bearing the Cross*, 1986; Stephen B. Oates, *Let the Trumpet Sound: The Life of Martin Luther King, Jr.*, 1982.

KINSEY REPORT. In 1948 Alfred C. Kinsey, head of the Institute of Sex Research at Indiana University, published *Sexual Behavior in the Human Male*, a study that scandalized the United States. Kinsey's data claimed that adultery, premarital sex, and homosexuality were far more common in the United States than most people had assumed. In 1953 Kinsey published the companion volume—*Sexual Behavior in the Human Female*. As the first major study of female sexual behavior, it was equally controversial.

Kinsey based his findings on interviews with 5,940 female volunteers. Of the women interviewed, half had experienced sexual intercourse before they were married. Among married women, more than 25 percent of them had committed adultery before they turned forty. Kinsey also claimed that women did not reach their sexual peak until the late twenties, compared to men, who reached that level in their late teens.

What angered critics, however, was not so much Kinsey's data as his interpretation of them. Since sexual behavior was so inconsistent with the existing moral code, Kinsey suggested the abandonment of those values. Perhaps, he claimed, young people should be encouraged to experiment sexually before marriage, and society's condemnation of extramarital affairs should be toned down. Other critics also attacked Kinsey's methodology. His report on male sexuality had attracted so much media attention, they argued, that the female volunteers who asked to be interviewed did not reflect a cross section of American women. Kinsey's results, therefore, could not be generalized and applied to the entire female population of the country.

SUGGESTED READING: James H. Jones, *Alfred C. Kinsey: A Public/Private Life*, 1997.

KITCHEN DEBATE. The term "Kitchen Debate" was coined by journalists to describe the internationally televised verbal confrontation between Vice President Richard M. Nixon* and Soviet Premier Nikita Khrushchev* in Moscow in July 1959. Nixon had traveled to Moscow to open the American National Exhibition, a display of U.S. consumer goods and technology. Khrushchev was in no mood to be a good host. The U.S. Congress had recently passed the Captive Nations Resolution condemning the Soviet Union for establishing an iron political grip on Eastern Europe and for abolishing civil liberties there.

Before the public meeting, the two men had an angry encounter. Khrushchev described the Captive Nations Resolution as something that "stinks like fresh horseshit, and nothing stinks worse than horseshit." Nixon came back with a vicious analogy, since Khrushchev's parents had been pig farmers. "There is something that stinks worse than horseshit," shouted Nixon, "and that is pigshit." They then strolled into a press conference and took a walking tour with Western journalists. Khrushchev confidently told the reporters that the Soviet Union would soon surpass the United States in its technological strengths. "In passing you, we will wave to you," he told Nixon. Nixon shot back: "You don't know everything." Khrushchev then retorted, "If I don't know everything, you don't know anything about Communism, only fear of it."

Later in the tour, when they stopped at an exhibition of an American kitchen complete with all the latest appliances, Khrushchev ridiculed it as "capitalist, consumer nonsense." Nixon then pointed his finger at Khrushchev's chest and defended capitalism. The exchange continued for several minutes before the two regained control of the encounter. At home, photographs of Nixon pointing at Khrushchev made the front pages in newspapers throughout the United States and strengthened his political standing.

SUGGESTED READINGS: Stephen E. Ambrose, *Nixon: The Education of a Politician, 1913–1962*, 1987; Michael R. Beschloss, *The Crisis Years: Kennedy and Khrushchev*, 1991; Nikita Khrushchev, *Khrushchev Remembers*, 1970.

KOREAN WAR. At the end of World War II in August 1945, troops of the Soviet Union occupied northern Korea and accepted the surrender of Japanese forces there. The Soviets considered control of the Korean peninsula central to their strategic interests in Asia. Ever since the 1890s, Japan had used Korea as a staging area for economic, military, and diplomatic activities in Manchuria and Siberia. To remove Japan's foothold in mainland Asia and to prevent future incursions in the region, the Soviet Union decided to establish a puppet Communist government in northern Korea—the Democratic Republic of Korea. North Korea and South Korea were separated at the 38th parallel.

Between 1945 and 1950, the Soviet Union consolidated its political control of North Korea. Soviet and North Korean policy makers then decided to unite the two Koreas under Communist authority. Only then could the Soviet Union rest assured that Japan, or for that matter the United States, would not be able to position itself on the Korean peninsula.

Early in the morning of June 25, 1950, the North Korean People's Army, equipped and trained by the Soviet Union, staged a massive invasion across the 38th parallel. In a matter of weeks, North Korean troops steamrolled across South Korea, overrunning the capital city of Seoul and forcing the government of President Syngman Rhee to flee. President Harry Truman* interpreted the invasion in classical, Cold War* terms and decided to contain the Communist expansion. On June 27, 1950, the United Nations Security Council met to consider multilateral action against North Korea. By accident, the Soviet delegation did not attend the meeting that day, and the Security Council, without the threat of a Soviet veto, voted to deploy UN forces to roll back the invasion.

Truman then named General Douglas MacArthur* as commander of the UN security forces. At the time, MacArthur was in Japan supervising American occupation forces. By the time he arrived in South Korea, UN and South Korean forces had been isolated to a small beachhead at Pusan in far southeastern Korea. The general had a huge ego and a penchant for erratic behavior, but at times he could be a brilliant tactician. On September 15, 1950, he staged a risky but highly successful amphibious landed invasion of UN forces at Inchon, on the northwestern coast of South Korea. From Inchon he invaded east, crossing the peninsula, liberating Seoul, and trapping hundreds of thousands of North Korean soldiers.

Inspired by MacArthur's victory, Truman announced his attention to reunite the two Koreas. UN forces invaded North Korea in October 1950 and captured the capital city of Pyongyang. MacArthur then turned his army north, setting his sights on the North Korean-Chinese border. President Truman, however, was worried about how China would react to the onslaught of so many UN and U.S. troops. In 1949, after decades of bloody civil war, Mao Zedong* and the Communists had prevailed, proclaiming the People's Republic of China and driving Chinese nationalist forces into exile on Taiwan. MacArthur reassured the president that the Chinese, still weak after so many years of internal conflict and war, did not possess the resources to resist UN troops.

General MacArthur could not have been more wrong, and Mao Zedong proved it by launching an armed invasion of North Korea. More than 275,000 top Chinese troops swept across the border, and in December they recaptured Pyongyang. On December 31, 1950, Chinese forces crossed the 38th parallel into South Korea and captured Seoul on January 4, 1951. MacArthur managed to stall and then halt the Chinese offensive just south of Seoul. Eventually, China committed more than 2.1 million troops to the conflict.

A set of serious choices faced the United States. Some advocated "total war," fighting the Chinese and North Koreans like the United States had fought the German and the Japanese during World War II. Such an approach, however, was fraught with political difficulties. Most Americans did not see the war in Korea as a life-and-death struggle, at least not like World War II had been, and they would not be willing politically to make the sacrifices that they had made then. For President Truman, it would be difficult to find the political support for such an all-out effort in Korea.

Others urged all-out nuclear warfare—dumping atomic bombs on North Korea and China until they surrendered. Critics responded that such an escalation might, at the worst, lead to a thermonuclear war between the United States and the Soviet Union. If such a disaster did not occur, at the very least clouds of deadly radiation would blanket much of the world, injuring America's allies as well as its enemies. President Truman rejected that option.

Instead, Truman chose to fight a "limited conventional war," one designed to expel the North Koreans and the Chinese from South Korea without bringing the Soviet Union into the conflict. It would prove to be a political tightrope for Truman, especially when General MacArthur became involved in the politics of the war.

Anxious to redeem himself after the successful Chinese offensive, MacArthur advocated an all-out offensive against the Chinese, including, if necessary, the bombing of targets in Manchuria. For President Truman, who was desperate to maintain the Korean War as a limited conflict and prevent it from escalating into a superpower confrontation, MacArthur's position was folly. When MacArthur went public with his opinion, Truman found him intemperate at best and disloyal at worst. Citing his constitutional authority as commander in chief, Truman ordered MacArthur to keep silent on policy issues. Early in April 1951, when MacArthur again expressed his opinions to the press, Truman unceremoniously relieved him of his command. Truman replaced MacArthur with General Matthew Ridgway, who simply wanted to push the Chinese troops back above the 38th parallel into North Korea.

MacArthur tried to make the most politically of his firing. Privately he had harbored hopes of a political career, perhaps even a run at the White House, and upon his return to the United States, he let no opportunity pass to criticize the president. Like a politician on the campaign trail, he spoke widely throughout the United States and testified before a joint session of Congress, concluding his remarks with the melodramatic, "Old soldiers never die, they just fade away." Fade away he did. Although MacArthur enjoyed a temporary popularity while newspapers pilloried President Truman, the American public eventually came around to the president and to the Constitution, agreeing that MacArthur, even if he had been correct in his assessment of the military situation in Korea, had overstepped his bounds in publicly criticizing the president.

For a while in 1951 Truman second-guessed his firing of MacArthur. Chinese and North Korean troops launched a counteroffensive, and on January 4, 1951, they re-occupied Seoul, sending UN troops into a full-scale retreat. Ridgway managed to dig in and stop the invasion, and in February he launched a counteroffensive of his own and reached the 38th parallel on March 31, 1951. The war had arrived at a stalemate, and neither side was prepared to escalate it further. In July, while fighting continued, UN and Communist military commanders began discussing a possible armistice.

The negotiations proceeded at a snail's pace because of two issues: how to resolve the question of prisoners of war (POWs) and where to draw a truce line. The U.S. and UN forces wanted only "voluntary repatriation." They held 132,000 North Korean and Chinese POWs, and they wanted to repatriate only those who wanted to return home. The North Koreans and Chinese insisted on forced repatriation of all POWs, whether or not they wanted to return home. As for the truce line, the Communists wanted it drawn at the 38th parallel, which had divided North Korea from South Korea before the war. The United States wanted the truce line to be at the existing battle front, which sat north of the 38th parallel.

Talks dragged on into 1952 and early 1953, without much progress. By June 1953, however, a tentative agreement had been reached. The Chinese and North Koreans accepted the UN demand for a truce line along existing battle lines, and both sides agreed to establish a neutral commission to address the issue of POWs who did not want to be repatriated. At the last minute, however, President Syngman Rhee of South Korea tried to scuttle the peace process and allowed 25,000 North Korean POWs to "escape" into South Korea. Enraged Communist forces launched a bloody counteroffensive, and the United States all but forced Rhee to sign an armistice. The final documents were signed on July 27, 1953.

The war had proven to be one of the bloodiest events in the bloody twentieth century. Biostatisticians estimate that more than four million people died in the conflict, including 900,000 Chinese and 54,000 American soldiers.

SUGGESTED READINGS: Bruce Cumings, *The Origins of the Korean War*, 1981; Rosemary Foot, *The Wrong War*, 1985; D. Clayton James, *Refighting the Last War: Command and Crisis in Korea, 1950–1953*, 1992; Burton Kaufman, *The Korean War*, 1986; William Stueck, Jr., *The Korean War: An International History*, 1981; John Toland, *In Mortal Combat: Korea, 1950–1953*, 1992.

KUKLA, FRAN & OLLIE. During the early 1950s, *Kukla, Fran & Ollie* was a popular children's puppet show. The three puppets sang songs, told stories, pulled pranks, and joked with one another and the audience. The show, the creation of WBKB-TV in Chicago, premiered on NBC on November 29, 1948, and was broadcast Monday through Friday from 7:00 to 7:30 P.M. In November 1951, NBC cut it back to a fifteen-minute program. In June 1952, NBC moved *Kukla, Fran & Ollie* from prime time to Sunday afternoons. In June 1954, NBC canceled the series, but ABC picked it up and returned it to its fifteen-minute, daily prime-time spot. The show survived until August 31, 1957, when ABC broadcast the last episode.

SUGGESTED READING: Tim Brooks and Earle Marsh, *The Complete Directory to Prime Time Network and Cable TV Shows, 1946–Present*, 1995.

L

LADY CHATTERLEY'S LOVER. *Lady Chatterley's Lover*, based on the famous novel by D. H. Lawrence, was one of the most controversial films of the 1950s. Directed by Marc Allegret, the film was released in July 1959 but only after a bitter court challenge. In 1958 the New York State Board of Regents had declared the film *Lady Chatterley's Lover* obscene on the grounds that it portrayed adultery as a proper form of behavior. The film's producer, Kingsley International Corporation, sued, and the case reached the U.S. Supreme Court in 1959. In *Kingsley International Corporation v. Board of Regents,* the Court unanimously overturned the Board of Regents ban as unconstitutional. Although the film contained controversial material that might offend public morality, the justices decided that its purpose was not to arouse lust. When the film was finally released, reviewers wondered what all the fuss had been about since the four-letter words and steamy love scenes from the novel had never been reproduced on screen. Actually, the controversy gave the film loads of free publicity and guaranteed its box-office success.

SUGGESTED READING: *New York Times*, July 11, 1959.

LANCASTER, BURT(ON). Burton Stephen Lancaster was born in New York City on November 2, 1913. He grew up in a tough neighborhood on the Upper West Side and began acting in productions at the Union Settlement House. Lancaster attended New York University on an athletic scholarship but quit to tour as an acrobat with the Ringling Brother's and Barnum and Bailey circuses. He was on the road with them from 1932 to 1939, when an injured finger ended his career as an acrobat. Lancaster served with the army special entertainment services during World War II. A talent scout noticed his performance in an off-Broadway play, and producer Hal Wallis signed him to perform in the film *The Killers* (1946). In *The Killers*, based on a short story by Ernest Hemingway,* Lancaster played the first of many tough guy roles. In fact, in most of his early films, including *Desert Fury* (1947), *Brute Force* (1947), and *I Walk Alone* (1948), he continued in that type cast.

In 1948 Lancaster bought out his contract with Hal Wallis and set up his own independent production company—Norma Productions. *The Flame and the Arrow* (1951) was the company's first financial success. That same year, Lancaster played a memorable role as Native American athlete Jim Thorpe in *Jim Thorpe: All American*. The decade of the 1950s and early 1960s made Lancaster one of Hollywood's most bankable stars. His athleticism and charisma transformed him into the perfect leading man. Among his best performances during these years were *Come Back, Little Sheba* (1952), *From Here to Eternity* (1953), *The Rose Tattoo* (1955), *The Rainmaker* (1956), and *Run Silent, Run Deep* (1958). His performance as the troubled preacher in *Elmer Gantry* (1960) earned him an academy award nomination. Lancaster also had a number of notable films in the early 1960s, including *Judgment at Nuremburg* (1961), *Birdman of Alcatraz* (1962), and *Seven Days in May* (1964).

Lancaster began to experience health problems in the 1970s and 1980s, but he continued to work, embellishing his reputation as one of the country's most consistent actors. In his later years, he played older and often broken-down men, and in doing so displayed the considerable acting skills he had acquired over the course of his career. The most memorable films of his later career are *Atlantic City* (1981), *Local Hero* (1983), and *Field of Dreams* (1989). Lancaster suffered a serious stroke in 1990 and died on October 21, 1994.

SUGGESTED READINGS: Gene Fishgall, *Against Type: The Biography of Burt Lancaster*, 1995; *New York Times*, October 22, 1994.

LASSIE. *Lassie* was one of the most enduring and popular series in American television* history. Lassie, a superbly well-trained collie dog, was the best friend of a little boy named Jeff Miller, played by Tommy Rettig. Jeff lived on a farm near a small town named Calverton with his mother, Ellen, played by Jan Clayton, and his grandfather, "Gramps," played by George Cleveland. The plots of the episodes revolved around Lassie's weekly good deeds—thwarting evil, rescuing the helpless, and protecting Jeff. The tried-and-true theme of a little boy and his faithful dog resonated with audiences, and *Lassie* became standard Sunday night fare on CBS television from 1954 to 1971. Over the years the dog and the actors changed, but the themes did not. In watching *Lassie*, American viewers thought they were viewing their country's values—families, farms, small towns, little boys, and their dogs. The last episode of *Lassie* was broadcast on September 12, 1971. Episodes of the show were aired in reruns for years.

SUGGESTED READING: Tim Brooks and Earle Marsh, *The Complete Directory to Prime Time Network and Cable TV Shows, 1946–Present*, 1995.

THE LAWRENCE WELK SHOW. On July 2, 1955, *The Lawrence Welk Show* premiered on ABC television. It quickly became the anchor of ABC's Saturday evening lineup. Welk, an immigrant bandleader, offered up a steady diet of old favorites to his audiences. In an age of rock-and-roll,* Welk's program featured accordion and organ favorites, polkas, dance tunes, and dramatic readings. Audiences loved the Lennon Sisters, a singing group, and dancers Bobby Burgess and Barbara Boylan. *The Lawrence Welk Show* aired for two hours every Saturday night on prime-time television* for sixteen years, a record unrivaled in television history. ABC finally canceled the show in 1971 because its viewing audience had grown too old—at least for the sponsors, who desired younger viewers more willing to spend money. Welk, however, took the show into syndication, and it remained on the air for another eleven years.

SUGGESTED READING: Coyne S. Sanders, *Champagne Music: The Lawrence Welk Show*, 1987.

LEAVE IT TO BEAVER. *Leave It to Beaver*, one of the most beloved situation comedies in American television* history, premiered on CBS on October 4, 1957. The program revolved around the Cleavers, a quintessential middle-class, stable family, who lived in Mayfield, U.S.A. Ward Cleaver, played by Hugh Beaumont, was an accountant who earned a good living, and his wife, June, played by Barbara Billingsley, was an always impeccably well-dressed stay-at-home mother. The feature character was Theodore "Beaver" Cleaver, a seven-year-old when the show began. Jerry Mathers played "The Beaver," and his older brother, Wally, was played by Tony Dow. Wally was good looking, smart, and athletic; Beaver was the typical underachieving little brother. Wally dealt with teenaged problems, and Beaver tried to survive boyhood and adolescence. The Cleavers were a perfect American family—kind, prosperous, and white— perfect at least for America in the 1950s. The last program was broadcast on September 12, 1963.

SUGGESTED READINGS: Irwyn Applebaum, *The World According to Beaver*, 1998; Jerry Mathers, *And Jerry Mathers as the Beaver*, 1998.

LERNER, ALAN JAY. Alan Jay Lerner was born to a prominent, wealthy, New York City family on August 31, 1918. He graduated from Harvard in 1940, and in 1943 the teamed up with Frederick Loewe,* a musical composer. Together they wrote the musical *What's Up*, which sank quickly. They failed again in 1945 when *The Day Before Spring* bombed commercially. In 1947, however, the team that became known as Lerner and Loewe, with Loewe supplying the music and Lerner the lyrics, scored a huge success with the musical comedy *Brigadoon*, which had a Broadway run of 581 consecutive performances and featured several hit songs: "Almost Like Being in Love," "Come to Me, Bend to Me," and "The Heather on the Hill." Their *Paint Your Wagon* was a hit in 1951. Lerner and Loewe's greatest collaboration was their adaptation of George Bernard Shaw's *Pygmalian*, which opened in 1956 as *My Fair Lady*.* With such hit songs as "Get Me to the Church on Time," "I've Grown Accustomed to Her Face," "I Could Have Danced All Night," and "On the Street

Where You Live," *My Fair Lady* had a run of 2,717 performances. After their last collaboration, *Camelot* (1960), Loewe retired. Lerner, however, remained professionally active for the rest of his life. With composer Burton Lane, he wrote *On a Clear Day You Can See Forever* (1965) and *Carmelina* (1979), and he teamed up with Andre Previn to produce *Coco* (1969). He wrote *1600 Pennsylvania* (1976) with Leonard Bernstein and *Dance a Little Closer* (1983) with Charles Strouse. Lerner died in 1986.

SUGGESTED READING: Alan Lerner, *The Street Where I Live*, 1978.

LEVITTOWN. After World War II, ten million soldiers mustered out of the military forces of the United States and resumed their lives. Most of them married shortly after their return, and they soon began raising children. The demand for housing boomed, and federal government policies made it relatively easy for families of veterans to purchase homes of their own. Both the Veterans Administration (VA) and the Federal Home Administration (FHA) guaranteed the loans of banks lending money to home buyers, and both agencies required minimal down payments. The VA allowed veterans to purchase homes with only $1 down.

For construction entrepreneurs, the opportunities to make money were unprecedented, and one man became associated with the suburban housing boom of the late 1940s and 1950s. William J. Levitt had spent World War II building houses on naval bases, and he decided that a fortune was to be made in mass-produced housing. He purchased thousands of acres of land on Long Island, subdivided them into 60 by 100 foot lots, and built the necessary roads, water, and sewage facilities. Levitt then built thousands of homes, each with an identical floor plan, and included a television* set and a washing machine in each home. He also planted five trees for every two lots. Soon an incorporated town appropriately named Levittown appeared on Long Island. The city had a population of more than 10,000 people. Levitt was featured on the cover of the July 3, 1950 issue of *Time* magazine. Levitt then duplicated his Long Island effort outside Philadelphia and in New Jersey. Other builders took their cue from William Levitt, and similar projects appeared throughout the United States.

Journalists coined the term "suburbia"* to describe the bedroom communities sprouting outside major American cities. In 1950 more than 1.4 million houses were constructed nationwide. That pace continued throughout the decade. The suburban housing tracts became symbols of the conformist pressures of the 1950s. The houses were identical, except for external colors. So were the residents. The suburbs attracted middle-class, white residents. Jews, blacks, and Hispanics tended to remain behind in urban areas. The suburbs also depended upon automobile access to the cities, which prompted a road-building boom to upgrade highways. Suburbs stimulated the construction of shopping malls, restaurants, libraries, schools, movie theaters, and churches.

SUGGESTED READINGS: Richard Horn, *Fifties Style, Then and Now*, 1985; Kenneth T. Jackson, *Crabgrass Frontier: The Suburbanization of America*, 1985; Douglas

T. Miller and Marion Nowak, *The Fifties: The Way We Really Were*, 1977; Gwendolyn Wright, *Building the Dream: A Social History of Housing in America*, 1981.

LEWIS, JERRY LEE. Jerry Lee Lewis was born in Ferriday, Louisiana, on September 29, 1935. A talented musician, Lewis absorbed country and western music, especially the work of Jimmie Rodgers, gospel sounds from his local Assembly of God church, and rhythm and blues from local black clubs. In 1950 he was expelled from a Bible school in Waxahachie, Texas. Because he could combine rhythm and blues with gospel and country, and because he was white, Sam Phillips of Sun Records* in Memphis, Tennessee, signed him to a contract in 1956. Sun Records switched Lewis to rock-and-roll,* and in 1957 his song "Whole Lotta Shakin' Going On" was a runaway hit, reaching number three on the pop charts. An invitation to perform on Steve Allen's Sunday night variety show gave Lewis enormous exposure, and his performance—marked by pounding piano rhythms and acrobatics on the piano bench—pushed the sales of "Whole Lotta Shakin' Going On" past the six million mark. His "Great Balls of Fire" later in the year sold five million copies and hit number two on the charts. In 1958 Lewis released "Breathless" and "High School Confidential," which were also top hits.

Lewis's career nose-dived as quickly as it had skyrocketed. In December 1957 he married his thirteen-year-old cousin, and the press coverage ruined him. Top promoters did not want the negative publicity that now accompanied him, and Lewis had to hit the road playing minor club bookings to make a living. Late in the 1960s, he dumped rock-and-roll for country and managed to put together more than a dozen hits, but his personal life was always in shambles. He developed drug and alcohol problems and saw both of his sons die in accidents. His fourth wife, from whom he was separated, drowned in a swimming pool under circumstances that raised legal eyebrows, and his fifth wife was discovered dead in the couple's home just two months after the wedding. Various addictions and problems with the IRS have plagued Lewis in the 1990s.

SUGGESTED READING: Nick Tosches, *Hellfire!: The Jerry Lee Lewis Story*, 1998.

THE LIFE AND LEGEND OF WYATT EARP. Westerns had long been a staple of pulp fiction, B movies, and radio in America, and television* in the 1950s featured no fewer than 30 Westerns. One of them, *The Life and Legend of Wyatt Earp*, ostensibly about the career of U.S. Marshal Wyatt Earp, premiered on ABC television on September 6, 1955, starring Hugh O'Brian as Wyatt Earp. The creation of playwright Frederick Hazlitt Brennan, *The Life and Legend of Wyatt Earp* was unlike another other Western in that its story developed the characters and their friends and family relationships over the entire course of the show's six-year run. Each new episode was connected to its predecessor. Brennan brought other characters into the story line, including Bat Masterson, Doc Holliday, Virgil and Morgan Earp, and Ned Buntline. Earp presided over law and order in Dodge City, Kansas. In 1959–1960, the show shifted to

Tombstone, Arizona Territory; and in the last episode, broadcast on September 26, 1961, the epic gunfight took place at the OK Corral.

SUGGESTED READING: Tim Brooks and Earle Marsh, *The Complete Directory to Prime Time Network and Cable TV Shows, 1946–Present*, 1995.

LIFE CAN BE BEAUTIFUL. *Life Can Be Beautiful*, one of radio's more popular soap operas during the late 1940s and early 1950s, premiered on NBC radio on November 4, 1938, went off the air in 1940, and then returned on June 24, 1946, broadcasting Monday though Friday afternoons for fifteen minutes. The program revolved around ghetto-born Carol Conrad, or "Chichi," who, while escaping the clutches of the dastardly Gyp Mendoza, stumbled into the bookstore of Papa David Solomon, who dispensed wisdom and shelter. Chichi fell in with the crippled but brilliant Stephen Hamilton, a law student, and they had a tempestuous relationship—just what soap listeners wanted. They married after several years, but the relationship was still convoluted and flawed, providing endless fodder for the show's writers. The only stable force in the show was Papa David Solomon, who tried to keep Chichi from making fatal mistakes in her life. The last episode aired on June 25, 1954.

SUGGESTED READING: John Dunning, *On the Air: The Encyclopedia of Old-Time Radio*, 1998.

LIFE WITH LUIGI. *Life with Luigi*, a popular CBS radio situation comedy, aired weekly from September 21, 1948, to March 3, 1953. J. Carrol Nash starred as Luigi Basco, a Rome-born Italian immigrant trying to survive in Chicago's Little Italy. Luigi made his living from an antique store. The plots revolved around clash-of-culture themes as Luigi tried to cope with strange American ways. The Italian dialects were good enough to attract an Italian audience, but not so thick as to alienate non-Italian listeners. Much of the humor came from the relentless efforts of Pasquale, owner of Pasquale's Spaghetti Palace, to get Luigi to marry his obese daughter Rosa.

SUGGESTED READING: John Dunning, *On the Air: The Encyclopedia of Old-Time Radio*, 1998.

LITTLE ANTHONY AND THE IMPERIALS. Little Anthony and the Imperials was one of early rock-and-roll's* best so-called doo-wop* groups. The group formed in New York City in 1957, with Anthony Gourdine as lead vocalist, Ernest Wright as second tenor, Tracy Lord as first tenor, Nate Rogers as bass, and Clarence Collins as baritone. Gourdine had formed several rock groups before the Imperials, and Alan Freed* gave him the spotlight on his television show. The group's first hit came in 1958 with "Tears on My Pillow." Their next hit, "Shimmy, Shimmy, Ko-Ko Bop," came in 1960. The group then broke up, but Gourdine re-formed them in 1964, dropping Lord and Rogers and adding Sammy Strain. They had several quick hits—"Goin' out of My Head" (1964),

"Hurt So Bad" (1965), and "Take Me Back" (1965). The group then went into a permanent decline.

SUGGESTED READING: Patricia Romanowski and Holly George-Warren, *The Encyclopedia of Rock & Roll*, 1995.

LITTLE RICHARD. *See* PENNIMAN, RICHARD WAYNE.

LITTLE ROCK, ARKANSAS. In September 1957, the city of Little Rock, Arkansas, found itself at the vortex of the desegregation* debate in the United States. Although the U.S. Supreme Court had declared segregated schools unconstitutional in *Brown v. Board of Education of Topeka, Kansas** in 1954, Arkansas and other Southern states bitterly resisted the court order. When federal courts ordered the desegregation of Little Rock's public schools, nine black children registered to attend Central High School.

On September 2, 1957, the day before the school year began, Governor Orval Faubus* of Arkansas announced that he would not offer police protection to black children entering public schools. The black children, now dubbed the "Little Rock Nine" by journalists, were prepared to attend classes and integrate the high school. Even though the black children faced possible threats to their lives, they want to Central High School on September 4, 1957. The Arkansas National Guard surrounded the school and would not let them enter.

President Dwight D. Eisenhower,* who was trying to avoid a constitutional crisis, met with Governor Faubus and convinced him to remove the troops. When the nine black students tried again on September 23 to attend school, an angry mob gathered outside the school and threatened the students. When the mob refused to disperse the next day, Eisenhower nationalized the Arkansas National Guard, which put the troops under his command, and sent in troops from the 101st Airborne Division to protect the black students. The "Little Rock Nine" began their first day of school on September 25. So many white students left Central High School that the school was closed for the year. Faubus tried to start a system of private schools for white students, but the movement never gained enough support. In 1959 Central High School opened as an integrated high school.

To everybody and anybody who would listen to him in Arkansas, Faubus complained that the president had exceeded his authority and violated states' rights. To most Americans, Faubus was a symbol of racism and a bygone era, but to most white people in Arkansas, he was a hero. He was reelected three more times.

SUGGESTED READINGS: Elizabeth Huckaby, *Crisis at Central High School: Little Rock, 1957–1958*, 1980; Robert Sherrill, *Gothic Politics in the Deep South: Stars of the New Confederacy*, 1968.

LOBOTOMY. During the 1930s and 1940s, the lobotomy was a relatively popular surgical procedure to treat mental illness. Its most powerful advocate was Dr. Walter Jackson Freeman of George Washington University. Freeman performed more than 1,000 lobotomies in the 1930s and 1940s. He called for lobotomies to treat patients with chronic depression, schizophrenia, anxiety disorders, manic behaviors, and violence. Freeman, who claimed it was a "simple" procedure, typically performed it with a sterile ice pick. He pushed the instrument through the patient's eye socket into the frontal lobe of the brain, where emotions supposedly were generated and controlled, and wiggled the probe in and out and back and forth, dislodging brain tissues. Lobotomies were commonly used in mental hospitals to control disruptive patients. In his novel *One Flew over the Cuckoo's Nest* (1962), Beat* writer Ken Kesey brought the procedure into widespread popular disrepute. Lobotomies were also dangerous. Four of Freeman's patients died of surgical complications in 1951 while Freeman was promoting the treatment.

Critics in the 1950s began to take issue with Freeman. Lobotomies, they argued, were imprecise surgical assaults that often left patients permanently listless, careless, and childlike. The treatment left them less violent but even less able to function as normal adults. The development of such tranquilizers as thorazine and meprobomate made Freeman's procedure seem even more barbaric. Psychiatrists and psychoanalyists urged physicians to abandon lobotomies in favor of drug treatment and psychotherapy. By the late 1950s and early 1960s, Freeman was persona non grata in the medical community, completely disdained by colleagues who considered him a dangerous charlatan. By that time, lobotomies had been abandoned as treatments for emotional disorders.

SUGGESTED READING: David Shutts, *Lobotomy: Resort to the Knife*, 1982.

LOEWE, FREDERICK. Frederick Loewe was born in Berlin, Germany, on June 10, 1901 to a musical family. His father was a leading figure in German opera. The family moved to New York City in 1924, but for many years Frederick could not make a living as a composer. He did odd jobs to keep himself fed and solvent. In 1935 his song "Love Tiptoes Through My Heart" found its way into the play *Petticoat Fever*. Loewe did the complete score for *Great Lady* (1938), but the show was a flop commercially. He teamed up with lyricist Alan Lerner* in 1943, and they wrote the unsuccessful musical *What's Up*. They failed again in 1945 when *The Day Before Spring* bombed commercially. In 1947 Lerner and Loewe, with Loewe supplying the music and Lerner the lyrics, scored a huge success with the musical comedy *Brigadoon*, which ran on Broadway for 581 consecutive performances and included such hit songs as "Almost Like Being in Love," "Come to Me, Bend to Me," and "The Heather on the Hill." Their *Paint Your Wagon* was a hit in 1951. Lerner and Loewe's greatest collaboration, however, was their adaptation of George Bernard Shaw's *Pygmalion*, which opened on Broadway in 1956 as *My Fair Lady*.* With such hit songs as "Get Me to the Church on Time," "I've Grown Accustomed to Her Face," "I Could Have Danced All Night," and "On the Street Where You Live,"

My Fair Lady had a run of 2,717 performances. The last Lerner and Loewe collaboration was *Camelot* in 1960, another hit show featuring "Camelot" and "If Ever I Would Leave You." Loewe retired in 1960 and died in 1988.

SUGGESTED READING: Gene Less, *Inventing Champagne: The Worlds of Lerner and Loewe*, 1990.

LOLITA. *Lolita*, a highly controversial novel written by Vladimir Nabokov, was published in 1955. The novel concerns the lust and infatuation of a middle-aged man, Humbert Humbert, for a preteen American girl. A Russian emigré, Nabokov could not find a publisher in Great Britain or the United States. Editors knew it would generate too much controversy. The novel was actually less pornographic than it was satirical and farcical, a parody of sexual desire, but prudish American readers did not get the joke. A Paris publishing house finally marketed *Lolita*, and all the free publicity made the book a best-seller. In 1962 director Stanley Kubrick made a film of the book starring James Mason as Humbert Humbert. With the money from book and movie royalties, Nabokov retired to Switzerlannd.

SUGGESTED READING: Vladimir Nabokov, *Lolita*, 1955.

THE LONE RANGER. *The Lone Ranger*, one of radio's most popular and long-running series, was first broadcast locally over WXYZ Radio in Detroit in 1933, and additional stations quickly signed on to the program. Those stations—which included WGN in Chicago, WOR in New York, and WLW in Cincinnati—soon merged into the Mutual Radio Network and used *The Lone Ranger* as its foundation program. Beginning in 1944, ABC picked up *The Lone Ranger*, and they continued broadcasting it until 1956. The lead character in *The Lone Ranger* was a Texas Ranger who had survived an ambush, donned a mask, and, along with his Indian sidekick Tonto and his horse Silver, rode the range fighting for truth and justice. The show was a huge success in the 1930s, and promotional appearances of the "masked man" and his horse drew thousands of listeners. The opening signature of each program—"a fiery horse with the speed of light, a cloud of dust and a hearty Hi-Yo, Silver! The Lone Ranger!"—became the most well-known phrase in America. The Lone Ranger himself was known for being the ultimate do-gooder, and parents tuned in not only to enjoy Western drama but to have values taught to their children. The last episode of *The Lone Ranger* was broadcast on May 25, 1956. Because of the program's success in radio, ABC television had launched *The Lone Ranger* on September 15, 1949. The television show starred Clayton Moore as the Lone Ranger and Jay Silverheels as his sidekick and scout Tonto. ABC eventually produced 221 episodes of *The Lone Ranger*, and it was televised throughout the 1950s. The last episode was broadcast on September 18, 1960.

SUGGESTED READINGS: John Dunning, *On the Air: The Encyclopedia of Old-Time Radio*, 1998; Vincent Terrace, *The Complete Encyclopedia of Television Programs, 1947–1979*, 1988.

THE LONELY CROWD. *The Lonely Crowd* is the title of sociologist David Riesman's highly influential book, which was written with Nathan Glazer and Reuel Denney. Published in 1950, *The Lonely Crowd* set the intellectual tone for the decade. An indictment of the middle-class consumer culture* and the pressures for conformity that so characterized the 1950s, *The Lonely Crowd* claimed that most Americans were "other-directed" rather than "inner-directed"—they were dominated by the expectations of consumer-obsessed peers, as expressed by advertisers in the mass media, rather than by individualistic needs. One might think that "other-directed" people could fit into groups better and that society would be more cooperative, but in actuality, it led to alienation because people did not cooperate out of personal conviction but only out of an empty need to belong to the group.

Both of these terms became part of the pseudo-scientific social science literature of the 1950s. When the youth rebellion occurred in the 1960s, journalists and pop culture observers resurrected *The Lonely Crowd* to provide an explanation for the phenomenon of rebellion—the conformist, anti-individualistic, vacuous consumer culture* stifled creativity and robbed life of its meaning. By the 1970s and 1980s, *The Lonely Crowd* had lost much of its earlier cachet. Modern consumerism had not led to the faceless, meaningless society they had predicted.

SUGGESTED READING: David Riesman, Nathan Glazer, and Reuel Denney, *The Lonely Crowd*, 1950.

LONG DAY'S JOURNEY INTO NIGHT. Written by Eugene O'Neill, *Long Day's Journey into Night*, a four-act play, opened on November 7, 1956, at the Helen Hayes Theater in New York City. Part autobiographical and part the product of O'Neill's depressive introspection, *Long Day's Journey into Night* is set in New England at the summer home of James Tyrone, played by Frederic March. Tyrone is an aging, miserly actor who takes no career risks. Instead he performs over and over again in a popular, if seamy, melodrama. His wife, Mary, played by Florence Eldridge, is a drug addict, and the oldest son, James Jr. (Jason Robards), is an unsuccessful failure pathologically jealous of his younger brother, Edmund (Bradford Dillman). During one long evening, family members reveal all of their mutual hatreds, resentments, depressions, and bitterness, and the play ends with Mary, hopelessly depressed and distracted, donning her wedding dress in an attempt to block out the misery of the present for the nostalgia of the past. Theater historians consider *Long Day's Journey into Night* a seminal work in American literary history, but the play was simply too depressing for audiences to give it a long run. The play enjoyed 390 performances before its cancellation.

SUGGESTED READINGS: Gerald Bordman, *The Oxford Companion to American Theater*, 1992; *New York Times*, November 8, 1956.

LOOK HOMEWARD, ANGEL. Playwright Ketti Frings adapted Thomas Wolfe's novel *Look Homeward, Angel* for the stage, and it opened on November

28, 1957, at the Ethel Barrymore Theater in New York City. The play revolves around the psyche of Eugene Gant, played by Anthony Perkins, who lives in his family's boardinghouse. His father (Hugh Griffith) is a drunken, abusive n'er-do-well, and his mother (Jo Van Fleet) is a dominating, controlling woman. Eugene falls in love with a boarder, Laura James (Frances Hyland), but his feelings for her are unreciprocated. Eugene's world comes apart when his little brother, Ben, dies. At the end of the play, Eugene heads off for college, hoping to pick up the pieces of his life and make something of himself. *Look Homeward, Angel* enjoyed a run of 564 performances on Broadway.

SUGGESTED READINGS: Gerald Bordman, *The Oxford Companion to American Theater*, 1992; *New York Times*, November 9, 1956.

LORD OF THE FLIES. *Lord of the Flies*, William Golding's enormously popular and influential novel, was published in Great Britain in 1954. The novel takes a dark view of human nature, one consistent with world attitudes in the wake of the unprecedented carnage of World War II and the potential of the hydrogen bomb* to wipe out the human race. In recalling the development of his ideas, Golding remembered, "When I was young, before the war, I did have some airy-fairy views about man. But I went through the war, and that changed me." Optimism about human nature turned into despair on the battlefields of Asia, Africa, Europe, and the Pacific, not just for Golding but for hundreds of millions of other people as well. *Lord of the Flies* perfectly captured that despair.

The novel tells the story of a group of British schoolboys who survive a plane crash on a remote, deserted island. In the absence of law, order, and civilization, the boys quickly revert to a state of nature, and for Golding, nature was the reality of competition and survival of the fittest. Within a matter of weeks, the boys have divided themselves into two armed camps and have reverted to a state of murder and savagery. Humanity, Golding was convinced, was inherently evil, prone to fear, rivalry, and destruction.

Golding was inspired by R. M. Ballantine's *The Coral Island*, published in 1858. But the mid-nineteenth century was still caught in the age of Romanticism, and the boys on Coral Island live lives of propriety, decency, and cooperation. In *Lord of the Flies*, on the other hand, the boys almost destroy themselves in an orgy of violence. Only the arrival of a naval vessel and the presence of an adult naval officer prevent their complete destruction. The book became an instant best-seller on both sides of the Atlantic. It indirectly warns readers that if human nature is prone to disintegration and destruction, the advent of nuclear weapons has put the entire world at risk. By the 1960s, *Lord of the Flies* was being read in schools and universities throughout the world. The novel earned Golding the Nobel Prize for literature in 1983.

SUGGESTED READINGS: William Golding, *Lord of the Flies*, 1954; John S. Whitley, *Golding: Lord of the Flies*, 1970.

LUCE, HENRY. Henry Robinson Luce was born to Presbyterian missionary parents in Shantung Province of China on April 3, 1898. He graduated from

Yale in 1920 with an intense interest in journalism. He studied briefly at Oxford University in England before joining the staff of the *Chicago Daily News*, where he worked under the tutelage of Ben Hecht. In 1923, with Yale classmate Briton Hadden and $83,000 in investment money, he founded *Time*, a weekly news magazine. The first issue sold 12,000 copies, and circulation grew steadily. Hadden died in 1929, and Luce went ahead without him and launched *Fortune*, a weekly business magazine. *Time* and *Fortune* became the foundation of the world's most successful publishing venture. During the 1930s, Luce branched out into radio and book publishing, although magazines remained the staple. In 1936 he began to publish *Life* magazine, which was the first major periodical to exploit the power of photographic images. *Sports Illustrated* followed in 1954. The first issue of *Sports Illustrated* sold 550,000 copies. A devoted conservative Republican and intense supporter of the Cold War,* Luce used his publishing venues to express his own political point of view, and in the process he became one of the most influential men in the world in the 1950s. He was a close adviser to such prominent Republicans as Thomas Dewey, John Foster Dulles,* Dwight D. Eisenhower,* and Richard M. Nixon.* Henry Luce died on February 28, 1967.

SUGGESTED READINGS: John Kobler, *Luce: His Time, Life, and Fortune*, 1968; W. A. Swanberg, *Luce and His Empire*, 1972.

LUX RADIO THEATER. *Lux Radio Theater*, the most popular dramatic series in American radio history, premiered on the Blue Network on October 14, 1934, with an hour time slot every Sunday evening. CBS picked up the show on July 29, 1935, and kept it on the air until September 14, 1954, when NBC optioned it. The last episode of *Lux Radio Theater* was broadcast on June 7, 1955. The show began as anthologies of Broadway plays, but as theater plots played out, the show shifted to movie themes, basing its weekly broadcasts on popular films. In 1936 Cecil B. DeMille, the famed Hollywood director, took over directorship of *Lux Radio Theater*, and its ratings skyrocketed. DeMille attracted Hollywood's best talent to the program, and the show attracted the attention only certifiable celebrities can attract. Clark Gable,* Marlene Dietrich, Gary Cooper,* Frederic March, Robert Taylor, John Wayne,* and a host of others appeared at DeMille's request. DeMille left the *Lux Radio Theater* in 1946, and although the show remained a ratings success, it no longer attracted the audiences it had once enjoyed. The advent of television* also undermined audience interest in audio repeats of films.

SUGGESTED READING: John Dunning, *On the Air: The Encyclopedia of Old-Time Radio*, 1998.

M

MACARTHUR, DOUGLAS. The child of a military family, Douglas MacArthur was born on January 26, 1880, on an army base near Little Rock, Arkansas.* His father was a career army officer who had won great distinction during the Civil War. The younger MacArthur attended the West Texas Military Academy in San Antonio from 1893 to 1897 and graduated from the U.S. Military Academy at West Point in 1903. He then served with distinction in the Philippines and Mexico. During World War I, he earned the rank of colonel and became chief of staff to the 42nd Infantry, the so-called Rainbow Division. In 1918 he received a wartime promotion to brigadier general and assumed command of the Rainbow Division's 84th Brigade. In combat, MacArthur won two purple hearts for wounds and a distinguished service medal.

In 1919, after the end of the war, MacArthur became the commandant of West Point. He completed his tour of duty at West Point in 1922 and spent the rest of the 1920s in several corps commands and on assignment in the Philippines, where he became head of the army department. In 1930 MacArthur was promoted to general and became chief of staff of the U.S. Army. In 1935 he went to the Philippines as a military adviser. MacArthur retired from active duty in 1937 to become a field marshal in the Philippine army, and he remained in the post until 1941, when he was recalled to active duty in the U.S. Army with the rank of lieutenant general and command of U.S. Army forces in the Far East. He was in that position when Japan bombed Pearl Harbor in December 1941. MacArthur remained in the Philippines until March 1942, when President Franklin D. Roosevelt ordered his evacuation to Australia. The Philippines fell to Japanese forces in May 1942.

During the rest of World War II, MacArthur served as commander of the southwest Pacific area and led the U.S. counteroffensive on New Guinea and the Philippines. In October 1944, when he launched the American attack on the island of Leyte in the Philippines, MacArthur received his fifth star and promotion to the rank of the general of the army. In September 1945 he presided over the official Japanese surrender ceremony that took place aboard ship in Tokyo Bay. From 1945 to 1950, MacArthur served as supreme commander of the Allied powers in Japan; he virtually ruled Japan as head of the occupation forces. He drafted the new Japanese constitution and then implemented a democratic government and economic revival.

When North Korea launched its surprise invasion of South Korea in 1950, President Harry Truman* gave MacArthur command of the United Nations forces in South Korea (*see* Korean War). In a campaign of tactical and strategic brilliance, MacArthur staged the amphibious invasion at Inchon, which trapped large numbers of North Korean troops in South Korea. Inspired by MacArthur's victory, Truman announced his intention to reunite the two Koreas. UN forces invaded North Korea in October 1950 and captured the capital city of Pyongyang. MacArthur then turned his army north, setting his sights on the North Korean–Chinese border. President Truman worried about how China would react to the onslaught of so many UN and U.S. troops. In 1949, after decades of bloody civil war, Mao Zedong* and the Communists had prevailed, proclaimed the People's Republic of China, and drove Chinese nationalist forces into exile on Taiwan. MacArthur reassured the president that the Chinese, still weak after so many years of internal conflict and war, did not possess the resources to resist UN troops.

General MacArthur could not have been more wrong, and Mao Zedong proved it by launching an armed invasion of North Korea. More than 275,000 Chinese troops swept across the border, and in December they recaptured Pyongyang. On December 31, 1950, Chinese forces crossed the 38th parallel into South Korea, capturing Seoul on January 4, 1951. MacArthur managed to stall and then halt the Chinese offensive just south of Seoul. Eventually, China committed more than 2.1 million troops to the conflict.

Some serious choices faced the United States. Some advocated "total war," fighting the Chinese and North Koreans like the United States had fought the Germans and the Japanese during World War II. Such an approach, however, was fraught with political difficulties. Most Americans did not see the war in Korea as a life-and-death struggle, at least not like World War II, and they were not politically willing to make the sacrifices that they had made then. Others urged all-out nuclear warfare—dumping atomic bombs on North Korea and China until they surrendered. Critics responded that such an escalation might, at the worst, lead to thermonuclear war between the United States and the Soviet Union. If such a disaster did not occur, at the very least clouds of deadly radiation would blanket much of the world, injuring America's allies as well as its enemies. President Truman rejected that option. Instead, Truman chose to fight a "limited conventional war," one designed to expel the North Koreans and the Chinese from South Korea without bringing the Soviet Union into the conflict. It would prove to be a political tightrope for Truman, especially when General MacArthur became involved in the politics of the war.

Anxious to redeem himself after the successful Chinese offensive, MacArthur advocated an all-out offensive against the Chinese, including, if necessary, the bombing of targets in Manchuria. For President Truman, who was desperate to maintain the Korean War* as a limited conflict and prevent it from escalating into a superpower confrontation, MacArthur's position was folly. When Mac-Arthur went public with his opinion, Truman ordered him to keep silent on policy issues. Early in April 1951, when MacArthur again expressed his opinions to the press, Truman unceremoniously relieved him of his command. Truman replaced MacArthur with General Matthew Ridgway, who simply wanted to push the Chinese troops back above the 38th parallel into North Korea. Mac-Arthur then retired from the army.

During the remainder of his life, MacArthur frequently advised Presidents Dwight D. Eisenhower* and John F. Kennedy* concerning military matters. In the early 1960s, he strongly opposed U.S. military involvement in South Vietnam. Before his death on April 5, 1964, MacArthur frequently expressed to his associates, as well as to President Kennedy, his misgivings about the United States becoming involved in a protracted guerrilla war in Southeast Asia. When his advisors called for the injection of regular U.S. ground troops in Vietnam, Kennedy repeatedly told them, "If you can get General MacArthur to agree, I'll think about it."

SUGGESTED READINGS: William Manchester, *American Ceasar: Douglas MacArthur, 1880–1964*, 1978; John W. Spanier, *The Truman-MacArthur Controversy and the Korean War*, 1959.

MAKE ROOM FOR DADDY. First known as *The Danny Thomas Show*, *Make Room for Daddy* was one of the most popular situation comedies of the 1950s and early 1960s. ABC first telecast the program on September 29, 1953. Four years later, ABC scuttled the comedy, but CBS picked it up and kept it in prime time for the next eight years. American audiences fell in love with *Make Room for Daddy* because they watched the family grow up and change before their eyes. Danny Thomas played Danny Williams, a night club entertainer in New York City. During the course of the show, Williams became a widower, re-married, raised his children, and watched them get married, all on screen.

SUGGESTED READING: Tim Brooks and Earle Marsh, *The Complete Directory to Prime Time Network and Cable TV Shows, 1946–Present*. 1995.

MAMA. *Mama* was one of the most beloved series on early television.* Part comedy, part drama, it was based on Kathryn Forbes's novel *Mama's Bank Account*, which produced a successful stage play in 1944 and a film in 1948, both of which were entitled *I Remember Mama*. The series, which premiered on CBS television on July 1, 1949, revolved around the Hansens, a family of Norwegian immigrants. "Papa" Lars Hansen, played by Judson Laire, was a poor but hardworking carpenter, and "Mama" Marta Hansen, portrayed by Peggy Wood, was a homemaker and the emotional heart and soul of the family.

They had three children: Katrin (Rosemary Rice), Nels (Dick Van Patten), and Dagmar (Robin Morgan). The program remained on the air until its last episode, which was broadcast on July 27, 1956, and Americans watched the Hansen family grow up and older. Each week, a different family member was featured, and Mama always rounded things out with her advice, wisdom, and a hot cup of coffee. Millions of second-generation Americans, the children of immigrants, saw touches of the Old World and the adjustment to the New World in each episode, and because of that, *Mama* had a unique appeal.

SUGGESTED READING: Tim Brooks and Earle Marsh, *The Complete Directory to Prime Time Network and Cable TV Shows, 1946–Present,* 1995.

THE MAN IN THE GRAY FLANNEL SUIT. Sloan Wilson's novel *The Man in the Gray Flannel Suit,* which became a best-seller in 1955, concerns the fictional Rath family, who try to find happiness in the conformist world of post–World War II America, where corporate and suburban values frown on dissent and individuality. At first the Raths try to live in a society where consumerism—"keeping up with the Joneses"—is one of society's core values. Rath works for a large company where middle managers are expected to wear gray flannel suits, long-sleeved white dress shirts, conservative ties, and nondescript, polished black shoes. Eventually, Tom and Betsy Rath tire of the emptiness of it all and conclude that the values of corporate and suburban America are hollow and, in the long run, very unsatisfying.

SUGGESTED READING: Sloan Wilson, *The Man in the Gray Flannel Suit,* 1955.

MANTLE, MICKEY. Mickey Mantle was born in Spavinaw, Oklahoma, on October 20, 1931. A gifted athlete, Mantle signed a baseball contract in 1949 with the New York Yankees,* receiving a $1,500 bonus and $140 a month. Two years later, he broke into the major leagues when he replaced the legendary Joe DiMaggio in center field at Yankee Stadium. A switch hitter almost as good right-handed as he was left-handed, Mantle hit for power and for average. He had an outstanding throwing arm and good speed. Mantle was also able to play through pain, a dedication that earned him the undying respect of baseball fans in New York and throughout the country. He was the American League's Most Valuable Player in 1956, 1957, and 1962. Mantle won the coveted Triple Crown in 1956—most home runs, most runs batted in (RBIs), and highest batting average. In 1957, while suffering from a severe case of shin splints, he hit .365, with 94 RBIs and 34 home runs. When he finally retired in 1968, Mantle had hit 536 career home runs and had 1,509 RBIs. His career batting average was .298.

After his retirement, Mantle remained a highly popular figure, even though he suffered from a severe case of alcoholism. He eventually conquered the addiction, but by then his liver had been all but destroyed. He received a liver transplant in 1997, but critics charged that he had managed to scratch his way up to the top of the transplant recipient lists, even though other candidates were more worthy. The transplant did not save Mantle's life. His liver cancer returned two months after the transplant, and he died on August 12, 1997.

SUGGESTED READINGS: Phil Berger, *Mickey Mantle*, 1998; Mickey Mantle, *The Quality of Courage*, 1999; *New York Times*, April 12–14, 1997.

MAO ZEDONG. Mao Zedong, who grew up to become the legendary, and some say infamous, Communist leader of the People's Republic of China, was born in 1893. During his late teens, still a student, he moved to Beijing to work in the national library, and while meeting and mixing with students there, he developed a radical political consciousness. Soon after the Bolshevik Revolution in Russia in 1917, Mao declared himself a Marxist.

He did not long remain wedded to the Russian version of Marxism, which was theoretically built on the backs of industrial workers, who were deemed the vanguard of the revolutionary struggle. Since the Industrial Revolution had not yet reached China, Mao Zedong constructed his theoretical edifice on the peasant masses, who numbered in the hundreds of millions and suffered from desperate poverty. Mao identified the exploited peasants as the revolutionary vanguard. During the 1920s he began writing about his theory and developing a constituency of dedicated Communists, and by the early 1930s, he had emerged as the leader of Chinese communism. After the famous Long March of 1934–1935, Mao used Yenan in northwest China as his base of operations. During World War II, he led Communist forces in a series of bloody, successful battles against Japanese occupation forces and became a folk hero throughout much of China. In 1949 Mao and his Communist forces seized political control of China.

During the 1950s, Mao Zedong came to symbolize all that Americans feared in communism. His aggressive foreign policies found expression in the invasion of Tibet* in 1950 and its subsequent occupation, the bloody Korean War,* and periodic saber rattling over Formosa, Quemoy, and Matsu (*see* Matsu-Quemoy Crises). The fact that he controlled the world's most populous country with an iron hand stood as proof that the international Communist conspiracy was succeeding. Mao Zedong seemed a threat to the rest of Asia, and more than any other factor, his foreign policy gave rise to the domino theory* in Washington, D.C.

At first, most U.S. policy makers viewed Mao as just another facet of the Soviet Union's plan for global revolution, but it was not until the late 1960s that prominent Americans began to realize that he functioned quite independently of the Soviet Union. In fact, Mao viewed the Soviet Union as a greater threat to China's Asian hegemony than the United States. In the 1960s the United States began to deal with Mao Zedong and the People's Republic of China as an independent world power in its own right. That vision was reflected in the decision of President Richard M. Nixon* to visit China in 1972 and to begin the process of normalizing diplomatic relations. Mao Zedong died in 1976.

SUGGESTED READINGS: Hedda Garza, *Mao Zedong*, 1988; Rebecca Stefoff, *Mao Zedong: Founder of the People's Republic of China*, 1996.

MARCIANO, ROCKY. Rocco "Rocky" Marciano was born Rocco Marche-giano in Brockton, Massachusetts, on September 1, 1923. A gifted athlete, he played baseball and football in high school, and while in the U.S. Army during World War II, he won several boxing matches. He returned home and joined the amateur ranks, losing only one fight in two years. In 1947, now billing himself as Rocky Marciano, he turned professional and won a string of fights, mostly by knockout.

In 1951, at the age of twenty-nine, Marciano stepped into the ring and delivered a brutal beating to former heavyweight champion Joe Louis. Critics charged that Louis was an old man, only a shell of the former champion, but the fight set Marciano up for a shot at the heavyweight title, then held by Jersey Joe Walcott. What he lacked in speed and power, Marciano made up for with grit and determination. He was a bull and bruiser, indefatigable in his pursuit of an opponent, and Walcott learned that lesson on September 23, 1952. Marciano knocked him out in the thirteenth round. In the rematch eight months later, Walcott did not survive the first round.

Marciano proved to be a popular, hardworking champion. Undefeated in 49 professional fights, he retired in 1956 after defeating heavyweight challenger Archie Moore. He had become a working-class icon in the United States. He spent his retirement in a variety of business activities and died in a plane crash on August 31, 1969.

SUGGESTED READINGS: *New York Times*, September 1, 1969; Everett M. Skehan, *Rocky Marciano: The Biography of a First Son*, 1977.

MARSHALL, THURGOOD. Thurgood Marshall was born on July 2, 1908, in Baltimore, Maryland. The great-grandson of a slave, Marshall was raised in relative comfort by a father who worked as a Pullman car porter and a mother who was a schoolteacher. In 1930 he graduated from Lincoln University but was denied admission to the University of Maryland Law School because of his race. He matriculated at Howard University Law School in Washington, D.C., where he studied under Charles Hamilton Houston, the man who instilled in Marshall a passion for civil rights litigation. In 1933 Marshall graduated at the top of his law school class.

Acting on Houston's counsel, Marshall went to work for the National Association for the Advancement of Colored People (NAACP), and in 1940 he was appointed head of its legal defense and education fund. Indefatigable in his work habits and in his opposition to all forms of racial segregation and discrimination, Marshall put 50,000 miles a year on his car, driving throughout the South to defend black clients. A gifted specialist in civil rights issues, he led the NAACP's campaign against de jure segregation in education, public facilities, housing, and voting. Among his most important early victories were *Smith v. Allwright* (1944), in which the U.S. Supreme Court outlawed the so-called white primary elections in the South, and *Shelley v. Kraemer* (1948), in which the

Court overturned restrictive racial covenants designed to exclude blacks from housing developments and neighborhoods.

Marshall's most spectacular victory came in the *Brown v. Board of Education of Topeka, Kansas** case. In 1954 it was one of five cases dealing with the legality of forced racial segregation in public schools. Lower courts had rejected all of the lawsuits, but Marshall had appealed each of them all the way to the highest court in the land. He argued all five cases before the court, and *Brown* was the first to be heard. The case concerned Linda Brown, an eleven-year-old black girl who had to cross a railroad yard to attend a segregated school for blacks, even though another public school was located across the street. Her father filed the lawsuit, claiming that such school rules and the laws behind them were inherently discriminatory and therefore violated the Fifth and Fourteenth Amendments to the U.S. Constitution. In its decision, the Supreme Court held that *Plessy v. Ferguson* (1896), which had authorized racially segregated, if equal, public facilities, was unconstitutional. Segregated public schools, the Court unanimously decided, are inherently discriminatory. The court then ordered desegregation* of the public schools "with all deliberate speed."

The victory made Marshall the most prominent civil rights attorney in the United States and a hero in the black community. President John F. Kennedy* named Marshall to the Court of Appeals for the Second Circuit in 1961, and in 1965 President Lyndon B. Johnson* appointed him solicitor general of the United States. Marshall was the first African American to hold that office. In 1967 Johnson made Marshall the first African-American justice of the U.S. Supreme Court. Soon after, however, Chief Justice Earl Warren* retired, and the Supreme Court, under a series of judicial appointments made by President Richard M. Nixon,* grew more conservative. Marshall found himself as part of a liberal minority, often writing dissenting opinions. He favored affirmative action programs, opposed the death penalty, and worked to protect the rights of criminal defendants. His health failing, Marshall retired from the Supreme Court in 1991. He died on January 24, 1993.

SUGGESTED READINGS: Richard Kluger, *Simple Justice*, 1976; Mark V. Tushnet, *Making Constitutional Law: Thurgood Marshall and the Supreme Court, 1961–1991*, 1997.

MARY MARGARET McBRIDE. *Mary Margaret McBride* was one of the most popular radio talk shows in American history. Mary McBride had been a well-known writer in the 1920s, and on the air she parlayed that cachet into interviews with the rich and the famous. The show was broadcast three times a week on CBS from 1937 to 1941, and then every week day on NBC from 1941 to 1950. ABC picked up *Mary Margaret McBride* in 1950 and broadcast it until the show was canceled in 1954.

SUGGESTED READING: John Dunning, *On the Air: The Encyclopedia of Old-Time Radio*, 1998.

MASSIVE RETALIATION. In January 1954, Secretary of State John Foster Dulles* coined the term "massive retaliation" to describe a new U.S. foreign policy and military initiative: the United States would be willing to use thermonuclear weapons to deal with threats to national security. The policy was part of President Dwight D. Eisenhower's* New Look* defense plan.

THE MATCHMAKER. *The Matchmaker,* a two-act comedy written by Thornton Wilder, premiered on December 5, 1955, at the Royale Theater in New York City. Actress Ruth Gordon played Dolly Levi, a matchmaker who is trying to find a wife for Horace Vandergelder (Loring Smith), a rich, uppity businessman, and to prevent Vandergelder's niece from eloping with an artist. Actually, Dolly has set her sights on marrying Vandergelder herself. She brings all of the interested parties together at a New York club, and in the end finds herself betrothed to Vandergelder. *The Matchmaker* had a run on Broadway of 486 performances.

SUGGESTED READINGS: Gerald Bordman, *The Oxford Companion to American Theater,* 1992; *New York Times,* December 6, 1955.

MATHIS, JOHNNY. John Royce (Johnny) Mathis was born in San Francisco, California, on September 30, 1935. His parents were both domestics. Blessed with a talented, almost nasal tenor voice, he took opera lessons as a teenager. While attending San Francisco State College, he sang in local jam sessions at several clubs. One evening George Avakian, an executive with Columbia Records, heard Mathis sing at the 440 Club, signed him to a record contract and sent him to New York City to record several songs. Columbia kept Mathis away from jazz in favor of popular ballads, and in July 1957 he had his first hit, "Wonderful Wonderful," which reached number fourteen on the charts. He followed that up with a second hit that reached number five—"It's Not for Me to Say." In November 1957 Mathis's "Chances Are" reached number one on the pop charts. Between 1958 and 1963, Mathis had several more hits, including "The Twelfth of Never" (1958), "Misty" (1959), and "What Will Mary Say" (1963). In 1958 he released an album, *Greatest Hits,* which remained on the album charts for nearly ten years and made Mathis a multimillionaire. An African American, Mathis projected a squeaky-clean image that appealed to white audiences. In the 1990s he was still selling out concert engagements in Atlantic City and Las Vegas; most of the ticket buyers were aging, middle-class baby boomers.*

SUGGESTED READING: Patricia Romanowski and Holly George-Warren, *The New Encyclopedia of Rock & Roll,* 1995.

MATSU-QUEMOY CRISES (1954–1955, 1958). On September 3, 1954, the artillery shelling of the Chinese Nationalist–held offshore islands groups, including Matsu (Madzu) and Quemoy (Jinmen), intensified. Both were part of a series of island groups sprinkling the southern coast of China's mainland, from

Shanghai to Hainan Island. Several of the island groups, located less than five miles from the Chinese coast, were vulnerable to artillery shells, propaganda, and, potentially, invasion from forces of the mainland Chinese Communist government. They remained under the control of the military forces of the Republic of China (ROC) and its president Chiang Kai-shek (Jiang Jieshi) of the Nationalist Party or Kuomintang (KMT) (Guomindang) (GMD).

The Nationalist government had lost political and military control of mainland China in 1949 when the People's Republic of China (PRC) was founded. After fleeing to the island province of Taiwan, located 200 miles across the Taiwan Straits from the mainland, the Nationalist government proclaimed itself to be the de jure government of all of China. According to the Nationalists, the island groups, including Matsu and Quemoy, were important for military and propaganda reasons. Psychologically they were a symbol to the approximately two million Chinese who had fled with Chiang Kai-shek that the mainland would be reclaimed and China would be "liberated" from communism. The "loss of China" to communism fostered a sense of betrayal among the American people and catapulted the country into its second Red Scare* of the twentieth century. In hopes of containing the spread of communism in Asia, the United States did not grant formal recognition to the PRC, embargoed trade with the PRC, and manipulated voting in the United Nations to prevent the Chinese government from occupying its seat in the General Assembly and the Security Council. Rather, the United States renewed military, economic, and humanitarian aid to the Nationalists, whom it supported in the United Nations and recognized as the de jure government of China. Late in 1950, after PRC troops intervened in the Korean War,* President Harry S. Truman* ordered the U.S. Seventh Fleet to patrol the waters of the Taiwan Straits to prevent a widening of the Korean conflict, hence protecting Nationalist-controlled territory. The PRC, in turn, engaged in intense shelling of Matsu and Quemoy to test the depth of the American commitment to Taiwan.

Upon his inauguration in January 1953, President Dwight D. Eisenhower* announced what was popularly referred to as the "unleashing" of Chiang. The Seventh Fleet would continue to protect the Nationalists from the Chinese Communists but would not hinder Nationalist military incursions against the mainland. The unleashing resonated with American public opinion at the time but likely encouraged Chiang to enforce an economic embargo of the mainland by bombing and intercepting international and Chinese ships plying their wares along the southern coast of China. Indeed, the Nationalists were not blameless in the events that resulted in the increased shelling of the offshore islands in September 1954.

The ensuing Matsu-Quemoy crisis became one of the flashpoints in the history of the Cold War*; it ended as it began with no clear aggressor and no clear winner. The crisis resulted in the signing of a Mutual Security Treaty between the United States and the ROC in December 1954, which was similar to those ultimately signed with South Korea, Japan, and South Vietnam. The public part of the treaty bound the United States to defend only Taiwan and its nearest island chain, the Pescadores. The unpublished notes exchanged at the signing, however, "re-leashed" Chiang. Eisenhower left it to his own discretion to determine the circumstances under which the United States would defend the offshore islands from future attacks. Chiang was forced to abandon many of the offshore islands but retained control of Matsu and Quemoy. Although Chiang survived on Taiwan due to the generosity of American funding, he was no puppet, and he refused American enticements to withdraw completely from all the offshore islands. Chiang was not happy, however, that the crisis resulted in an opening of direct talks between the United States and the PRC. The talks, which continued in Warsaw, were primarily an exercise in Cold War invective. The United States demanded that the Chinese renounce the use of force to recover Taiwan, and the Chinese Communists called on the United States to end its occupation of Taiwan.

Flare-ups over Quemoy and Matsu recurred in 1958 and 1960, but neither was a serious attempt by the Chinese Communists to recover Taiwan. The 1958 crisis ended with a rather bizarre arrangement: the islands were bombed on alternate days in order to allow the delivery of supplies. Clearly, the PRC did not want control of the offshore islands since this would have led to a clear delineation of one Taiwan and one China—a solution along the lines of two Germanys or two Koreas. The Chinese Communists preferred the offshore islands to remain under Nationalist control despite the sporadic military incursions launched from the islands. Both the Nationalists and the Communists agreed that there was only one China; a two China solution was not acceptable to either. In Cold War lore, the Matsu-Quemoy crises symbolized a precarious peace that could easily erupt in nuclear conflagration. This was confirmed in the spring of 1955 when Eisenhower's secretary of state, John Foster Dulles,* told *Life* magazine that in Korea, Dien Bien Phu, and Matsu-Quemoy, the threat of nuclear weapons forced the enemy to back down. Dulles talked about going to the "brink" of war, hence the term "brinkmanship" was coined.

SUGGESTED READINGS: Foster Rhea Dulles, *China and America: The Search for a New Relationship*, 1973; Alexander L. George and Richard Smoke, *Deterrence in American Foreign Policy*, 1974; Kwan Ha Yim, *China and the United States, 1955–1963*, 1973.

Tracy Steele

MAU MAU. The so-called Mau Mau insurgency, a violent, nationalist movement in Kenya in the early 1950s, originated in the late 1940s among the Kikuyu people who were determined to rid the country of white people and British imperial power. The Mau Mau rebels relied on terrorist tactics—guerrilla warfare and the random murder of whites—and the British resorted to equal violence of their own to crush the rebellion. By the time the rebellion was finally settled, the British had killed 11,503 rebels. The Mau Mau rebellion convinced Great Britain to extend independence to its African colonies as crushing similar insurgencies in other colonies would be financially impossible.

In the United States, the Mau Mau rebellion coincided with the early stirring of the civil rights movement,* and white Southerners who opposed extending full equality to black people exploited the rebellion in Kenya. Mau Mau rebels committed twenty-six random murders of whites, and Southern racists loudly predicted that similar violence would soon visit the South unless the civil rights movement were crushed. In fact, the term "American Mau Mau" was frequently applied to African-American activists in the 1950s.

SUGGESTED READINGS: D. B. Barnett, *Mau Mau from Within*, 1966; Robert Edgerton, *Mau Mau: An African Crucible*, 1989.

MAVERICK. Maverick, a very popular television adventure series of the 1950s, was first broadcast by ABC on September 22, 1957, starring James Garner as Bret Maverick and Jack Kelly as his brother, Bart. Bret was a wisecracking card shark with an eye for a pretty woman, while Bart was the more serious of the two. The show was unlike any other Western. The Mavericks did see to the demise of a fair share of desperadoes, but the scripts were too offbeat to fit into the genre. Bret fumbled his pistol all the time, and he was not above cheating at cards when he needed to. Sometimes, when a showdown with a gunman loomed, the two simply sneaked out of town, avoiding a fight so they could play cards and date women another day. Garner played the role for laughs, adding satire to his lines. Sometimes the scripts were parodies of other popular Westerns, like *Gunsmoke** and *Bonanza.** The show began to fail when Garner left in a dispute with the producers. The last episode of *Maverick* was broadcast July 8, 1962.

SUGGESTED READING: Tim Brooks and Earle Marsh, *The Complete Directory to Prime Time Network and Cable TV Shows, 1946–Present*, 1995.

MAYS, WILLIE. Willie Mays was born in Westfield, Alabama, on May 6, 1931. He learned baseball by playing stickball in the streets of New York City. After a stint in the Negro Leagues, he broke into the majors in 1951 to play center field for the New York Giants. At the time, baseball was in the early stages of integration, and Mays received a stiff dose of racist harassment. But he endured the humiliation, which occasionally became dangerous, especially when opposing pitchers intentionally threw fast balls at his head. Leo Durocher, who managed the Giants in 1951, mentored Mays and reassured the young player when he went 0 for 26 at the plate during his first seven games. The slump ended with the eighth game, when Mays hit an enormous home run that some pundits claimed traveled upward of 600 feet. Of his next nine hits, six were home runs. By the end of his rookie year, Mays was widely regarded as one of the game's most all-around players.

In the field and at the plate, he could do it all. He hit for power and average, and he was fast on the bases. He was also an extraordinary outfielder. In the first game of the 1954 World Series between the Giants and the Cleveland Indians, Indian Vic Wertz blasted a 440-foot-deep shot into center field. Mays raced toward the wall at breakneck speed, with his back to home plate, and caught the ball over his shoulder. Baseball historians consider it the greatest catch of all time.

Mays eventually hit 660 career home runs and was the first player in baseball history to hit 30 home runs and steal 30 bases in the same season. By the end of his career, Mays had earned his way to the top-ten list of virtually every major category of performance. He may very well have been the best player of all time.

SUGGESTED READINGS: Charles Einstein, *Willie's Time: A Memoir*, 1979; Willie Mays, *Say Hey: The Autobiography of Willie Mays*, 1988.

McCARTHY, JOSEPH. Joseph Raymond McCarthy was born in Grand Chute, Wisconsin, on November 14, 1908. He grew up on a farm near Appleton, Wisconsin, and eventually took a law degree at Marquette University. In 1939 he was elected judge of the tenth judicial circuit in Wisconsin, but he took a leave of absence from the post in 1942 to join the Marine Corps. In 1946, by grossly exaggerating his exploits in the army during World War II, McCarthy won a seat in the U.S. Senate as a Republican from Wisconsin. As a freshman senator, he labored in obscurity, becoming known as the "Pepsi Cola Kid" because of his ties with soft-drink lobbyists. By 1949 he began worrying about his reelection chances, since he would have to run again in 1952. McCarthy began casting about for an issue, and he noticed that Congressman Richard M. Nixon,* who headed the House Un-American Activities Committee (HUAC), had garnered a great deal of media attention through his investigation of Communists in the film industry. With the fall of China to Mao Zedong* and the Communists in 1949, along with the Soviet Union's successful detonation of an atomic bomb,* the American fear of Communist aggression abroad had reached a state of paranoia (*see* Red Scare), and McCarthy suspected that the fear of internal Communist subversion could be exploited.

In a speech made at Wheeling, West Virginia, on February 9, 1950, McCarthy claimed to have a list of 205 names of confirmed Communists who worked for the State Department. The wire services picked up the story, giving McCarthy headline coverage in newspapers throughout the country. In subsequent speeches made on the Senate floor and at other sites across the country, McCarthy fudged on the numbers, claiming to know of 57 or 65 or 110 or 205 Communists in the State Department. When journalists or other congressmen asked him to be more specific, McCarthy demurred, claiming, "It would be improper to make the names public until the appropriate Senate committee can meet in executive session and get them." He maintained his stance even though critics claimed he was either lying or badly misinformed. The public, however, believed the Wisconsin senator, and he quickly became one of the most powerful individuals in the country. Rival politicians soon became intimidated and refused to take a public stand against McCarthy's excesses.

In 1951 Senator Millard Tydings, a Democrat from Maryland, convened special subcommittee hearings on McCarthy's charges, and Roy Cohn, McCarthy's legal counsel, claimed that Professor Owen Lattimore of Johns Hopkins University, who also served as a State Department consultant, was a Communist, and that the Truman administration harbored other subversives. Tydings eventually charged McCarthy with perpetrating a "fraud and a hoax." Senator Patrick McCarran, a Republican from Nevada, convened hearings of his own and decided that McCarthy's claims could be substantiated and that Lattimore was an "instrument of the Soviet conspiracy." McCarthy got what he wanted; in 1952 he easily won election for a second term in the U.S. Senate.

Early in 1953, as the new chairman of the Senate Committee on Government Operations, McCarthy continued his investigations, and he soon led the Permanent Investigations Subcommittee. In 1954 McCarthy charged that the U.S. Army leadership was riddled with Communists, and he opened an investigation. The hearings were televised nationwide, and McCarthy met his match in Joseph Welch, the U.S. Army counsel. When McCarthy made irresponsible allegations, Welch condemned him before a nationwide audience, and McCarthy's public reputation began a steady decline. Other senators, Republican and Democrat, smelled blood and moved in, condemned McCarthy, and stripped him of his major committee assignments. By 1956 McCarthy's health had deteriorated badly. He had long suffered from alcoholism, and on May 2, 1957, he died. Since then, his name has become synonymous with political rumor mongering, exaggeration, and abuse of individual civil liberties.

SUGGESTED READINGS: Fred Cook, *The Nightmare Decade: The Life and Times of Joe McCarthy*, 1971; William Bragg Ewald, Jr., *Who Killed Joe McCarthy?* 1984; Richard Fried, *Men Against McCarthy*, 1976; David M. Oshinsky, *A Conspiracy So Immense: The World of Joe McCarthy*, 1983.

McCLELLAN COMMITTEE. During the 1950s, many Americans, especially conservatives, became extremely concerned about corruption and radicalism within the American labor movement. The concern was rooted in primal fears. Early in the 1950s, the United States endured another Red Scare,* in which fear of Communists assumed paranoid proportions. A number of unions—such as the Fur and Leather Workers Association, the American Communications Association, and the United Electrical, Radio and Machine Workers—were riddled with Communists. Concern about organized crime was also a preoccupation of the 1950s, since a sizable number of union leaders had been convicted of graft and corruption. Concern about corruption in the 1.4 million–member Teamsters* Union was particularly acute.

In 1957 Senator John L. McClellan of Arkansas, who chaired the Senate Select Committee on Irregular Activities in the Labor-Management Field, opened a formal congressional investigation of radicalism and corruption in labor unions. McClellan's chief counsel was Robert F. Kennedy. Kennedy went after the Teamsters Union with a passion and exposed enough corruption to precipitate the union's expulsion from the AFL-CIO.* In many unions, it soon became clear, union officials were stealing membership dues, siphoning off money through sweetheart deals with corporations, taking kickbacks from management for agreeing to certain negotiating terms, and extorting money from businessmen.

The committee achieved important results. David Beck, head of the Teamsters Union, was indicted for corruption and eventually was convicted and imprisoned, and the AFL-CIO expelled from its ranks the Teamsters Union, the Laundry Workers Union, and the Bakers Union. The McClellan Committee enacted tight oversight within the Justice Department over labor union finances. Congress passed the Labor-Management Reporting and Disclosure Act of 1958, which guaranteed the right of workers to influence union decision making and required unions to report regularly on finances and membership.

SUGGESTED READINGS: Steven Brill, *The Teamsters*, 1978; John L. McClellan, *Crime Without Punishment*, 1962.

McDONALD'S. In the early 1950s, Ray Kroc had an exclusive national distributorship of the Multimixer, a machine capable of simultaneously mixing five milkshakes. Kroc marketed the Multimixer to fast-food restaurants around the country. In 1954, during a sales trip to San Bernardino, California, he tried to sell the Multimixer to a hamburger stand owned by two brothers, Richard and Maurice McDonald. Kroc was impressed with their assembly-line operation and the fact that the McDonald brothers had turned a roadside hamburger stand into a business grossing $200,000 a year. In April 1955 Kroc opened a hamburger restaurant himself in Des Plaines, Illinois, a suburb of Chicago. Anxious to sell more of his Multimixers, Kroc talked the McDonald brothers into giving him the right to license the McDonald's name and their production methods nationwide. In the process, he created the idea of franchising fast-food restaurants.

Kroc soon realized that the real money was in selling hamburgers, french fries, and shakes, not Multimixers. He sold the Multimixer distributorship and focused all of his attention on McDonald's franchises. By 1961, 200 McDonald's restaurants operated nationwide. By employing military precision in making hamburgers and fries, with each product an exact copy of every other, Kroc built a huge following. By the 1990s, McDonald's franchises covered the entire globe, and the company was by far the largest food retailer in the world. Kroc became a billionaire in the process.

SUGGESTED READING: John F. Love, *McDonald's: Behind the Golden Arches*, 1995.

McLAURIN V. OKLAHOMA STATE REGENTS **(1950).** After World War II, G. W. McLaurin, an African-American student, began to work on his doctoral degree in education at the University of Oklahoma. At the time, the university was racially segregated. The University had admitted McLaurin to graduate school, but university officials then segregated him in school classrooms, the cafeteria, and the library. McLaurin filed a civil rights lawsuit, claiming that racial segregation in a public school violated his Fourteenth Amendment right to equality and due process. In June 1950, the U.S. Supreme Court agreed and ordered that all students, once admitted, "must receive the same treatment at the hands of the state as students of other races." *McLaurin v. Oklahoma State Regents* was a milestone in the desegregation* of public education in the United States.

SUGGESTED READING: 339 U.S. 637 (1950).

MEANY, GEORGE. George Meany was born in Harlem in New York City on August 16, 1894. His father, a plumber, had been elected president of the Bronx, New York, chapter of the Plumbers International Union, and Meany followed in his footsteps. He became an apprentice plumber first and a journeyman in 1915. Meany remained active in local union politics, and in 1923 he was elected to a full-time union administrative post: secretary-treasurer of the New York Building Trades Council. Tough, honest, and a skilled negotiator, Meany quickly earned the trust of his associates. He became president of the New York State Federation of Labor in 1933.

Workers had suffered during the Great Depression, and when President Franklin D. Roosevelt pushed the National Labor Relations Act of 1935 through Congress, Meany showed his appreciation by throwing the full support of the plumbers union behind Roosevelt's reelection. In 1939 Meany was elected national secretary-treasurer of the American Federation of Labor (AFL). He became AFL president in 1952.

An inveterate foe of communism, Meany opposed extremists of all kinds in the AFL, left-wing radicals as well as right-wing extremists. He also fought corruption in the union. Meany's position on political issues was highly calculated. If the labor movement were to keep its influential position in American politics, it had to adhere to the mainstream and avoid at all costs being tied to extremists and criminals. When the AFL and the Congress of Industrial Organizations merged in 1955, Meany was elected president of the 14.6 million–member AFL-CIO* union. From that post, he supported the New Frontier of President John F. Kennedy* and the Great Society of President Lyndon B. Johnson.*

He became one of the most powerful individuals in the United States. He spoke to presidents the same way he spoke to apprentice plumbers—direct, tough, and honest. He was not above calling senators and congressmen to lobby for pending pro-worker legislation, and he could deliver campaign financing and votes to back up his requests. He could be counted on to oppose conservative opponents to the federal bench and to support civil rights and antipoverty legislation. In December 1979, after nearly a quarter of a century, Meany stepped down as president of the AFL-CIO. George Meany died on January 10, 1980.

SUGGESTED READINGS: *New York Times*, January 11–12, 1980; Archie Robinson, *George Meany and His Times*, 1981.

MELBOURNE OLYMPIC GAMES. The Helsinki Olympic Games of 1952 became entangled in Cold War* politics, and the Melbourne, Australia, Olympic games of 1956 became even more politicized. The Soviet Union had invaded Hungary in 1956, and many Western nations were up in arms. Spain, Switzerland, and the Netherlands decided to boycott the Melbourne games in protest of the Soviet invasion. When the International Olympic Committee (IOC) invited the Republic of China (Taiwan) to compete, the People's Republic of China withdrew from competition. Norway then asked the IOC to ban South Africa from competing at Melbourne because of South Africa's racist apartheid policies. War had erupted in the Middle East during the Suez crisis,* and Egypt decided not to compete because of the presence of the Israeli team. Because France, Great Britain, and Israeli had attacked Egypt, Iraq decided to boycott the games. During the games, forty-five Hungarian athletes found their way to the U.S. embassy and defected. Dozens of athletes form other Eastern Bloc countries defected as well.

SUGGESTED READINGS: Christopher R. Hill, *Olympic Politics*, 1992; Martin Barry Vinokur, *More than a Game: Sports and Politics*, 1988.

THE MICKEY MOUSE CLUB. A creation of the Walt Disney Studio, *The Mickey Mouse Club* premiered on ABC television on October 3, 1955. It quickly became the most popular program on daytime television. The show was broadcast daily, Monday through Friday, between 5:00 and 6:00 P.M. By the 1956 season, it had twenty million daily viewers. The show was introduced each day by Mickey Mouse, and animated Disney cartoon characters sang the opening song. With a cast of child stars like Annette Funicello, Doreen Tracy, Tommy Cole, and Cubby O'Brien, the show featured cartoons, musical skits, comedy routines, inspirational stories, and travelogues. The show also inculcated values, wasting no opportunity to tell viewers to obey their parents, study hard at school, and obey the law. The final episode of *The Mickey Mouse Club* aired in September 1959.

SUGGESTED READINGS: Richard Schickel, *The Disney Version*, 1968; Steven Watts, *The Magic Kingdom: Walt Disney and the American Way of Life*, 1997.

MILITARY-INDUSTRIAL COMPLEX. Because of the onset of the Cold War* in 1946, the American economy continued to produce large volumes of military weapons, even though a formal state of war did not exist. The Soviet threat made it imperative for the United States to maintain a well-equipped, well-trained military, and throughout the 1950s, defense spending steadily increased, often constituting half of the entire federal budget. Also, in order to maintain the military in a state of readiness with the most advanced technologies, the defense contractor companies had to be kept in business. If the federal government scaled back its orders, the companies would have to cut back production, lay off workers, and downsize their physical plants, all of which would have impacted military readiness. To prevent that, the Department of Defense continued to place orders for state-of-the-art equipment and kept the companies in business.

It soon became obvious that a good portion of the U.S. economy had become dependent on the defense industry. That reality concerned President Dwight D. Eisenhower,* who worried that a symbiotic relationship between the military and private industry was potentially dangerous. In order to sustain company profits and employment, the companies might actually lobby for a more aggressive foreign policy on the part of the United States. In an impassioned speech delivered in 1961, Eisenhower warned the United States about the existence of a "military-industrial complex" that was growing in power and had the potential of affecting American foreign policy. The idea that there was an important relationship between the military and private industry was not new. During the 1930s, Senator Gerald P. Nye of North Dakota had charged that munitions manufacturers were responsible for getting the United States involved in World War I. Eisenhower argued, however, that the Cold War* with the Soviet Union had created huge and permanent defense expenditures and that the military and the industries producing the weapons had a vested interest in the continuation of international tensions. Since Eisenhower's speech, the term military-industrial complex has continued to be used by those who oppose massive defense spending.

SUGGESTED READINGS: Paul A. C. Koistinen, *The Military-Industrial Complex: A Historical Perspective*, 1980; Roger W. Lotchin, *Fortress California, 1910–1961: From Warfare to Welfare*, 1992; Ann R. Markusen, *The Rise of the Gunbelt: The Military Remapping of Industrial America*, 1991.

MILLER, ARTHUR. Arthur Miller was born in New York City on October 17, 1915. His father was a successful businessmen until the Great Depression, when he went bankrupt. After graduating from high school in 1933, Miller went to work in order to make enough money to go to college. He attended the University of Michigan. At Ann Arbor, Miller began to show his talent for writing, especially plays. His most celebrated work, *The Death of a Salesman*, was published in 1949. The hero of the play, Willy Loman, is a washed up, elderly salesman who loses his career and his identity. The play was an indictment of middle-class American values. In 1953 Miller wrote *The Crucible*, a play allegedly about the Salem witch trials of the 1690s but actually an attack on the hysteria, innuendo, and guilty-by-association assumptions so characteristic of American society during the Red Scare* of the early 1950s. In 1955 Miller wrote *A View from the Bridge*. In retaliation for his liberal leanings, the House Committee on Un-American Activities subpeoned Miller in 1956 and charged him with contempt of Congress. He appealed the conviction and won. Miller's later works grew even more pessimistic. In *The Misfits* (1961), *After the Fall* (1964), and *The Price* (1968), he presents a morally ambiguous world where human beings are alienated from the universe and from themselves. People exist in hopelessly corrupt circumstances.

SUGGESTED READING: James J. Martine, ed., *Critical Essays on Arthur Miller*, 1979.

THE MILLIONAIRE. *The Millionaire*, which premiered on CBS television on January 19, 1955, was a dramatic anthology with a simple premise: each week billionaire John Beresford Tipton instructed his personal secretary, Michael Anthony (Marvin Miller), to deliver a cashier's check for $1 million to an unsuspecting party. The plot of the program was what the recipient did with the money, whether they would use it for good or ill, and how it changed their lives. The last episode was broadcast on September 28, 1960.

SUGGESTED READING: Tim Brooks and Earle Marsh, *The Complete Directory to Prime Time Network and Cable TV Shows, 1946–Present*, 1995.

MR. CHAMELEON. *Mr. Chameleon*, a popular CBS radio program, premiered on July 14, 1948, and featured actor Karl Swenson as "Mr. Chameleon," a detective adept at wearing disguises. His home base was known as Central Police Headquarters, and every week he foiled criminals and con artists. Mr. Chameleon had a sidekick named Dave Arnold, who did little more than ask obvious questions that the Chameleon could answer so the audience would be able to follow the plot. The program was so full of clichés that it resembled a soap opera more than a dramatic detective series. *Mr. Chameleon* lasted until the broadcast of its last episode on August 7, 1953.

SUGGESTED READING: John Dunning, *On the Air: The Encyclopedia of Old-Time Radio*, 1998.

MR. PRESIDENT. *Mr. President*, a modestly popular radio program presented by ABC radio, premiered on June 26, 1947, and starred Edward Arnold, who each week portrayed a different president of the United States. The plot revolved around little-known events in the lives of American presidents, and viewers were supposed to try to guess the identity of the character before the end of the program. Although *Mr. President*'s ratings were only modest, the show survived on the radio until September 23, 1953.

SUGGESTED READING: John Dunning, *On the Air: The Encyclopedia of Old-Time Radio*, 1998.

MONROE, MARILYN. Marilyn Monroe was born Norma Jean Mortensen in Los Angeles, California, on June 1, 1926. She later changed her name to Norma Jean Baker. Her mother was an unmarried, mentally unstable film editor who spent long periods of time committed to mental institutions. Throughout her life, Norma Jean worried about succumbing to mental illness herself. Although she never exhibited the manic characteristics of her mother, she nevertheless fought an ongoing battle against clinical depression.

Norma Jean never knew her father. She was raised in a succession of orphanages and foster homes, where she was raped several times, and at the age of sixteen, to escape the chaos of her personal life, she married James Dougherty, an aircraft factory worker. When World War II broke out, she went to work in the defense industry in Los Angeles. To supplement her income, she also began posing for calendar photographs and pinups.

Blonde and busty, she exuded sexuality, and her photographs began appearing in national publications. Talent scouts at 20th-Century Fox signed her to a film contract, and she took the stage name Marilyn Monroe. She flopped at Fox and switched to Columbia Pictures, where two 1950 films—*The Asphalt Jungle* and *All About Eve*—attracted considerable attention. That year, she signed a new seven-year contract with Fox, and her career took off, especially after nude photographs of her appeared on 1951 calendars. In 1953 Fox released three Monroe films—*Niagara, Gentlemen Prefer Blondes*, and *How to Marry a Millionaire*—in which she demonstrated her talent as an actress and as a comedian.

Monroe became a pop culture icon in the 1950s. During the 1930s and 1940s, Americans had become accustomed to sex symbols whose beauty was juxtaposed with innocence, even if the innocence was feigned. Betty Grable pinups, which might have insinuated a great deal but showed very little, had sustained a generation of World War II GIs. Marilyn Monroe's sexuality was more overt, magnified by nude photos, low-cut dresses, and an endless list of double entendres. She gave countless interviews, posed for countless photographs, and steadily during the 1950s became the most popular, recognizable woman in the world. Her 1954 marriage to Yankee baseball slugger Joe DiMaggio only exaggerated her fame, as did their stormy divorce a year later.

By that time Monroe had left Fox. She went to New York City and studied for a year at the Actors' Studio. She returned to Hollywood with a $100,000 per film contract and prior approval of all directors of her films. Her next film, *Bus Stop*, was a critical success, as was her next film, *Some Like It Hot*. In 1956 Monroe married playwright Arthur Miller,* but the marriage was doomed. Her own depressions and demons ruined relationships, and she could never transcend the sex symbol she had become. During the early 1960s, rumor had it that she was having affairs with President John F. Kennedy* and with his brother Attorney General Robert F. Kennedy. Her last film was *The Misfits* (1962). By then she was trying to forget her miseries in alcohol and prescription drugs. On August 5, 1962, she died of an overdose of barbiturates. The debate over whether her death was a suicide continues today.

SUGGESTED READINGS: James Haspiel, *Marilyn: The Ultimate Look at the Legend*, 1991; Norman Mailer, *Marilyn: A Biography*, 1973; *New York Times*, August 6–8, 1962.

MONTGOMERY BUS BOYCOTT. Ever since the years of Reconstruction, legal statutes throughout the Southern states required racial segregation in all forms of public transportation. In Montgomery, Alabama, local ordinances required black people to sit in the backs of buses. No African American was ever allowed to sit in the same row of seats or in any row in front of white riders. In fact, no black under any circumstances could sit in the front rows of a bus, and they had to give up their seat in a middle row and move farther back if a white person needed the seat.

The local branch of the National Association for the Advancement of Colored People (NCAAP) decided to test the ordinance legally, and Rosa Parks, a 43-year-old seamstress, volunteered. On December 1, 1955, she refused to give up her seat to a white rider. Even though the bus driver tried to get her to move back, she refused and was arrested. She was fined $10 for her actions.

The NAACP then organized a boycott. Black people, who constituted 75 percent of the city's bus riders, stopped riding the buses. NAACP leaders promised to continue the boycott until black riders were treated with courtesy, more black bus drivers were hired, and the ordinance was repealed. They did not demand repeal of the ordinance requiring blacks to sit in the back of the bus, only that once on the bus, a black person would not have to give his or her seat to a white. All but a few of Montgomery's 48,000 black residents joined the boycott.

The boycott produced a monumental reaction. Several NAACP leaders had their houses firebombed, blacks walking to work were beaten, and white supremacists fired handguns and rifles at black riders. The boycott also produced one of the greatest leaders in American history—the Reverend Martin Luther King, Jr.*—a 26-year-old preacher who assumed leadership of the boycott. Bright, charismatic, passionate, and courageous, King managed to sustain the boycott, despite its dangers and inconveniences. In the meantime, the NAACP took the segregation ordinance to court. The boycott lasted more than a year, and it brought the city's transportation system to the brink of financial ruin. In 1956 the U.S. Supreme Court ended the boycott by declaring racial segregation in public transportation facilities unconstitutional.

SUGGESTED READINGS: David J. Garrow, *Bearing the Cross*, 1986; Stephen B. Oates, *Let the Trumpet Sound: The Life of and Times Martin Luther King, Jr.*, 1982.

MOUNT EVEREST. At 29,028 feet, Mount Everest in the Himalayas of Nepal is the highest point on earth. During the years of British imperial authority in India and Nepal, Sir George Everest had surveyed the Himalayas, and the tallest peak was named in his honor. A number of mountaineering teams had tried and failed to make the ascent. In 1924 a British expedition came within 900 feet of the summit before disappearing, probably off a mountain ledge or into a deep crevice. In 1934 Michael Wilson attempted a solo assault on the peak, but he died of exhaustion in subzero weather.

In 1950, however, political changes made the mountain more accessible. Nepal decided to open the country to foreign tourists, and New Zealand mountaineer Edmund Hillary immediately began planning an expedition. By going through Nepal, he would have access to Mount Everest's south side, a much less dangerous route than the northern side of the peak, which earlier mountaineers had tried and failed to breech. Hillary relied on the cooperation and assistance of Sherpas, a Nepalese ethnic group thoroughly familiar with and conditioned to the Himalayas and high altitudes. The expedition was headed by John Hunt, and Hillary and his Sherpa guide, Tenzing Norkay, were tapped to make the final ascent. They did so on May 29, 1953, becoming the latest and probably last in a great series of British adventurer heroes. Around the world, Hillary was hailed as a man of courage, stamina, and determination, and his feat inspired tens of millions of people.

SUGGESTED READING: *New York Times*, May 30–31, and June 1, 1953.

MOVIES. During the 1950s, the film industry experienced challenges unknown since the advent of talking pictures three decades before. Part of the challenge was legal. In 1948 the Justice Department had filed an antitrust lawsuit that eventually forced the Hollywood studios to sell their theaters. The federal government did not believe that the production and distribution of films should be concentrated in so few hands. In 1951 the studios sold their theaters.

The decision had a triple impact on the industry. First, the studios had to cut back on the number of films they produced each year. During the 1940s, they had averaged from 350 to 400 films a year, but in the 1950s, that number dropped to 125 per year. Also, the content of movies began to change. When studios controlled production and distribution of films, they were able, through the Motion Picture Producers and Distributors of America (MPPADA), to control completely the moral tone of films—sexuality, language, cruelty, violence, and so on. But once the studios lost control over distribution, some producers pushed the moral envelope on films, introducing themes and images that would have been completely unacceptable just a few years before. Such films as *A Streetcar Named Desire* (1951), *The French Line* (1954), and *Baby Doll* (1956) were just a few examples. Finally, the separation of production and distribution led to a proliferation of independent producers not connected to the major studios.

Many of the industry's problems were demographic. Several million World War II veterans came home, married, and had children. With young children to tend to, they were less inclined to go out in the evenings, preferring to stay at home. Also, the rise of housing in suburbia* changed moviegoing practices. Most movie theaters were located downtown, and it required a long drive to get to them. At the same time, downtown areas were deteriorating, and moviegoers worried about crime and safety issues. Finally, the rise of television* provided entertainment at home, eliminating the need to go to the movies. As a result, movie attendance plummeted in the early 1950s.

The Hollywood studios engaged in a desperate search for ways to attract audiences back to the movies. One solution was technological. Cinemascope* and VistaVision were both based on a simple principle: enlarge the screen in movie theaters to make movie watching more different from watching television. The conventional ratio of a movie screen was 1.33 times as wide as it was high, but in Cinemascope, the screen was 2.5 times as wide as it was high. In 1953 20th-Century Fox released *The Robe*,* the first film to be projected in Cinemascope. Cinemascope was highly popular with movie audiences and soon became a staple of the industry. The big screen allowed the production of swashbuckling spectacles complete with elaborate sets, lavish musicals, and castings in the thousands, none of which really worked as well on small television screens.

Another technological development was three-dimensional, or 3-D,* projection. The concept had been tried in 1922, but technical difficulties made it impossible for 3-D to survive then. Similar problems doomed it in the 1950s. The real innovation of 3-D was its ability to provide viewing audiences with on-screen depth perception. During the shooting, cameramen used several cameras to film a scene from different angles. When the film was shown in a theater, two projectors had to project the film simultaneously, from different angles, onto a screen. To watch the movie, ticket buyers donned special colored glasses that synchronized the two images. Non-Biblical exhibitions included *The Greatest Show on Earth* (1952) and *Giant** (1956).

With the assistance of these new technologies, producers began making large-scale spectacles. Many of them were based on the Bible, including *David and Bathsheba* (1951), *The Robe* (1953), *The Ten Commandments* (1956), *Ben Hur** (1959), and *Solomon and Sheba* (1959). The Biblical films attracted to theaters people who were not accustomed to going to movies.

Films in the 1950s also addressed social concerns. *The Blackboard Jungle** (1955) focused on problems in urban schools, and *Rebel Without A Cause** (1955) dealt with youth rebellion and social anomie. *All About Eve* (1950) tackled the issue of mental illness; *On the Waterfront* (1954) concerned labor racketeering; and *The Wild One** (1954) dealt with motorcycle gangs.

Because of the Cold War,* the Red Scare,* and the threat of nuclear weapons, Americans became concerned with science, technology, conspiracies, and invasion. Horror movies dealt with invasions by unusual creatures: *The Day the Earth Stood Still* (1951), *The Thing from Another World* (1951), *War of the Worlds* (1953), *It Came from Outer Space* (1953), *Them!* (1954), *Creature from the Black Lagoon* (1954), *Tarantula* (1955), *Forbidden Planet* (1956), *Invasion of the Body Snatchers* (1956), *I Was a Teenage Werewolf* (1957), *The Fly** (1958), and *The Blob** (1958).

The 1950s was also the last decade for the genre of the musical film in all of its glory. Musicals fell out of favor in the 1960s, when Americans began to view them as irrelevant compared to all of the pressing problems of the day, but in the 1950s, Americans still enjoyed escaping into them. Many of them were film versions of Broadway musicals. The most prominent musicals of the decade were *Annie Get Your Gun* (1950), *Show Boat* (1951), *Kiss Me Kate* (1953), *Call Me Madam* (1953), *Brigadoon* (1954), *Oklahoma!* (1955), *The King and I** (1956), and *South Pacific** (1958).

Most of Hollywood's efforts proved worthwhile. 3-D did not survive; it was simply beset with too many technological problems. But Cinemascope and VistaVision did survive, and theater construction in the suburbs made moviegoing more convenient. Televison did not destroy the film industry, as many had predicted.

SUGGESTED READINGS: Pauline Kael, *5001 Nights at the Movies*, 1982; David Shipman, *The Great Movie Stars: The International Years*, 1972.

MURROW, EDWARD R. Edward R. Murrow was born in Greensboro, North Carolina, on April 25, 1908. He graduated from Washington State College in 1930 with a strong interest in journalism. Between 1929 and 1932, he served as president of the National Student Federation and then assistant director of the Institute for International Education. In 1935 Murrow joined the staff of CBS radio, beginning a career that would make him the world's first premier telejournalist. In 1937 Murrow was assigned by CBS to move to Europe, and in 1938, when Adolf Hitler forced the *anschluss* on Austria, which essentially made Austria a German puppet state, Murrow began sending weekly broadcasts back home. He delivered his first broadcast on March 13, 1938. His report, which was accurate and powerful, was enriched by his deep, resonating voice. Murrow became a household name in the United States in 1940 when he reported the Battle of Britain. Each broadcast would begin with his signature, "This is London." During the next five years, tens of millions of Americans listened to Murrow report on the people and the events of World War II.

He returned to the United States in 1945 as CBS vice president for public affairs, but he returned to the air in 1947. In 1950 his weekly radio show *Hear It Now* became a hit. In 1951 Murrow made the jump to television* with *Hear It Now* by changing its name to *See It Now*. His weekly televison news and interview show was broadcast at 6:00 P.M. on Sundays. He addressed hard news topics, such as race relations, poverty, and nuclear weapons. In March 1954, Murrow invited Senator Joseph McCarthy* to appear on the show. Murrow loathed the senator and his Red Scare* tactics, and the portrait that appeared on *See It Now* was highly unfavorable. Many historians consider the program a watershed in McCarthy's career because it convinced millions of Americans that McCarthy was little more than a bully.

Later in the 1950s, Murrow started a lighter weekly shows of interviews with personalities and *CBS Reports*, a series of documentaries. Among them was "Harvest of Shame," which exposed the plight of migrant workers in the United States. In 1960, however, *See It Now* was canceled for low ratings. The decision embittered Murrow, who in 1961 accepted President John F. Kennedy's* appointment as director of the U.S. Information Agency. Edward R. Murrow died on April 27, 1965.

SUGGESTED READINGS: William Boddy, *Fifties Television: The Industry and Its Critics*, 1990; Joseph E. Persico, *Edward R. Murrow: An American Original*, 1988.

THE MUSIC MAN. *The Music Man* opened at the Majestic Theater on Broadway on December 19, 1957. A product of the genius of Meredith Wilson, who wrote the two-act musical, the play tells the story of Harold Hill, played by

Robert Preston, who is a con man out to bilk the town of River City by selling it band instruments. His scheme is flawless until he confronts Marion Paroo (Barbara Cook), the town librarian, who from the beginning is suspicious of his promises. She threatens to expose him unless he delivers on his promise, and Hill waits until the instruments arrive, after which he puts on a band concert, even though he cannot read music. Although the concert is more noise than music, the parents of the band members find it melodious. In the process, Hill falls in love with Marion. *The Music Man* produced several pop music hits, including "Seventy-Six Trombones," "Goodnight, My Someone," "Rock Island," and "Trouble." *The Music Man* enjoyed a run of 1,375 performances.

SUGGESTED READINGS: Gerald Bordman, *The Oxford Companion to American Theater*, 1992; *New York Times*, December 20, 1957.

MY FAIR LADY. *My Fair Lady*, based on the play *Pygmalion* by George Bernard Shaw, premiered as a Broadway musical in 1956. Alan Jay Lerner* wrote the lyrics, and Frederick Loewe* composed the music. Moss Hart directed the musical. Julie Andrews starred as Eliza Doolittle, the poor, Cockney flower girl, and Rex Harrison played Henry Higgins, a linguistics professor determined to teach Eliza proper English and assume the airs of a duchess. Lerner and Loewe provided a string of classic songs, including "I Could Have Danced All Night," "I've Grown Accustomed to Her Face," "Get Me to the Church on Time," "On the Street Where You Live," and "The Rain in Spain." *My Fair Lady* ran for 2,717 consecutive performances, making it one of the most successful plays in American theater history.

SUGGESTED READING: Kurt Ganzl, *The Encyclopedia of the Musical Theater*, 1994.

MY FRIEND IRMA. *My Friend Irma*, a popular radio program of the late 1940s and early 1950s, premiered on CBS radio on April 11, 1947, starring Marie Wilson as Irma Peterson, who posed as a classic "dumb blonde." As such, she followed in the footsteps of other radio comediennes, such as Gracie Allen and Jane Ace. Irma was hopelessly uninformed, without guile, innocent, and naive. The funniest plots involved her work as a stenographer for her curmudgeon of a boss, Mr. Clyde, and her roommate, Jane Stacy. Jane had a huge crush on Mr. Clyde, and she always tried to warn Irma about Al, a Brooklyn con man who always managed to get Irma into hilarious, if innocent, scrapes. The last episode of *My Friend Irma* was broadcast on August 23, 1954. Producer Hal Wallis took the program to television.*

SUGGESTED READING: John Dunning, *On the Air: The Encyclopedia of Old-Time Radio*, 1998.

MY SON JOHN. *My Son John*, released by Paramount Pictures in 1951, constituted a popular cultural expression of the anticommunist paranoia so common in the United States. Bosley Crowther, film critic for the *New York Times*, described the movie as being "so strongly dedicated to the purpose of the American Anti-Communist purge that it seethes with the sort of emotionalism and illogic that is characteristic of so much thinking these days." The film stars Dean Jagger as Dan Jefferson, Helen Hayes as his wife Lucille, and Robert Walker as their son John. Dan Jefferson is a patriotic, Bible-reading veteran who loves America and loathes communism. Helen Hayes shares her husband's passions. They also have two other boys, both high school football stars who march off to the Korean War together.

Their son John, however, is an enigma. He ridicules his father's flag-waving patriotism, questions his mother's devotion to the Bible, and fails to come home from Washington, D.C., to see his brothers off to war. His parents start to worry about his loyalties, about whether he is being seduced into communism, and their fears take on new urgency when they learn that the Federal Bureau of Investigation* has him under investigation, primarily because of his relationship with a young woman accused of being a Soviet spy. Robert solemnly assures his mother, with his hand on the Bible, that he is not a Communist. He is lying, of course, and the film ends with his murder near the Lincoln Memorial. John Jefferson leaves behind a posthumous message confessing his communism and recanting his loyalty to it. Though saddened by their son's death, the Jeffersons are grateful for his reconversion to American and Christian values. He can meet his maker with peace of mind.

Film historians are hard put to find a movie more symbolic of the worst elements of the Red Scare* of the early 1950s. Hearsay is elevated to truth and bigotry to virtue. Self-righteousness is confused with piety and patriotism with fascism. One viewing of *My Son John* tells almost as much about Joseph McCarthy* as one of the senator's most vitriolic speeches.

SUGGESTED READING: *New York Times*, April 9, 1952.

N

NASSER, GAMAL ABDEL. Gamal Abdel Nasser was born on January 15, 1918 in Alexandria, Egypt. His father was a village postal clerk. He was educated at the Egyptian Military Academy and joined the Egyptian army, where as an officer he quickly became frustrated with the power the British wielded in Egypt over King Farouk. The disastrous Arab war with Israel in 1948 enraged Nasser, who decided that the king had to be overthrown. Nasser formed a secret society of army officers dedicated to Farouk's demise, and in 1952 they staged a successful rebellion. In 1953 Nasser became the first Egyptian to rule Egypt since the time of the pharoahs.

Convinced that his people had been exploited by European imperial powers, Nasser set his sights on the Suez Canal, which had been owned and managed by an Anglo-French conglomerate. Nasser created a one-party state and began moving toward a socialist economy. He also turned away from the West and purchased agricultural goods and weapons from the Soviet Union. He also made a public show of his refusal to join the Baghdad Pact,* as well as a regional, anti-Soviet alliance.

The United States and Great Britain reacted angrily to Nasser's new anti-Western posture, and they pulled financing from his coveted Aswan Dam construction project, which would dam the Nile and provide hydroelectric power to much of Egypt. Nasser retaliated by announcing that Egypt had decided to nationalize the Suez Canal (*see* Suez crisis). Ever since its completion nearly a century before, the Suez Canal had been a vital route for the British navy making its way from Atlantic and Mediterranean ports to India and East Asia. Losing the canal to Egyptian control constituted a severe strategic reversal for Britain. With the revenues from canal tolls, Nasser could finance the Aswan Dam himself.

Enraged at Nasser's impunity, Great Britain and France conspired with Israel to invade Egypt across the Sinai Peninsula. The British and French would then use the war as a pretext to occupy the canal zone. Israel invaded Egypt on October 29, 1956 and British bombs then wiped out the Egyptian air force. French and British paratroopers took control of Port Faud and Port Said, key canal outposts.

President Dwight D. Eisenhower* was outraged. The French, British, and Israelis had acted without consulting the United States, and the conflict threatened to escalate into a superpower confrontation. The Soviets, anxious to cement their budding relationship with Nasser, expressed similar outrage. Soviet and American officials sent troops to force a cease-fire on the combatants. The war came to an end within a week, with 2,700 Egyptians and 140 Israelis dead. When the dust had settled on the war, Egypt retained control of the Suez Canal, and the Soviet Union helped finance construction of the dam. Nasser was a hero in the Arab world.

In 1958 Nasser played a key role in the formation of the United Arab Republic (UAR), a union of Egypt and Syria that reflected Nasser's desire to build a Pan-Arab movement and to secure some advantages, from either the Soviet Union or the United States, in the Cold War.* New coalitions began to appear. Yemen officially affiliated with the UAR and formed the United Arab States. For a time, other Arab states—particularly Lebanon, Saudi Arabia, and Iraq—gravitated toward the UAR without establishing any formal connections.

But just as soon as it appeared that Pan-Arabism might be securing a foothold in the Middle East, old rivalries surfaced again. Iraqi dictator Abdul Karim Kassem had a falling out with Nasser, and the Syrians decided Nasser was behaving too autocratically. The Saudi Arabians and Yemenis eventually rejected Nasser's socialism. In 1961, after just three years, the UAR ceased to exist when Syria seceded. In moving Egypt toward socialism, Nasser earned the undying devotion of Egypt's poor classes, but the reforms failed to rescue the country from serious economic decline. In 1967 the Six Day War with Israel was a humiliating defeat for Nasser. Nasser died suddenly of a heart attack on September 28, 1970.

SUGGESTED READINGS: R. Hrair Dekmejian, *Egypt Under Nasir: A Study in Political Dynamics*, 1971; Joachem Joesten, *Nasser: The Rise to Power*, 1974; Mary Shivanandan, *Nasser: Modern Leader of Egypt*, 1973.

NATIONAL ASSOCIATION FOR THE ADVANCEMENT OF COLORED PEOPLE V. ALABAMA EX REL. PATTERSON (1958). In 1956 the state of Alabama decided to outlaw the National Association for the Advancement of Colored People (NAACP) and demanded that the NAACP turn over its membership list to the state attorney general. NAACP leaders refused, and the organization was fined $100,000 for contempt. The NAACP appealed the decision, and the U.S. Supreme Court decided it on June 30, 1958. The Court decided in favor of the NAACP, arguing that inherent in the First Amendment right to free association is a right to privacy. In other words, members of the NAACP, and other organizations, have the right to associate with one another without fear of coming under government scrutiny.

SUGGESTED READING: 357 U.S. 449 (1958).

NATIONAL COMMITTEE FOR A SANE NUCLEAR POLICY. During the 1950s, Americans became increasingly concerned about the threat nuclear weapons posed to the future of the world. Because the United States and the Soviet Union engaged in Cold War* rhetoric that frequently employed references to nuclear weapons, those concerns escalated, and when the Soviets launched *Sputnik** in 1957, concerns about nuclear annihilation reached a fever pitch. In 1957 Normal Cousins, editor of the *Saturday Review* magazine, founded the National Committee for a Sane Nuclear Policy. Cousins was joined in the effort by such luminaries as television performer Steve Allen, musician Pablo Casals, composer Leonard Bernstein,* pediatrician Benjamin Spock,* and black writer James Baldwin.* Employing petition-signing campaigns and public demonstrations, the group worked diligently to outlaw the atmospheric testing of nuclear weapons and to reduce the number of nuclear warheads. They eventually endorsed the idea of world disarmament. In 1969 the National Committee for a Sane Nuclear Policy changed its name to SANE: A Citizens' Organization for a Sane World.

SUGGESTED READING: Milton Katz, *Ban the Bomb*, 1987.

NATIONAL DEFENSE EDUCATION ACT OF 1958. The Soviet Union's success in putting *Sputnik,** an artificial satellite, into orbit around the earth in 1957 sent the United States tumbling into a national identity crisis. Suddenly, the United States seemed to be technologically behind the Soviet Union. Critics who blamed the country's public education system argued that the Soviet school system had more discipline, more emphasis on science and mathematics, and more single-mindedness. President Dwight D. Eisenhower* called for educational reform and the postponement of school construction in favor of an investment in science, mathematics, and technological education.

Congress reacted to the criticism by passing the National Defense Education Act (NDEA) of 1958. The NDEA provided a low-interest loan program worth $295 million for college students; provided $300 million to assist public schools in science, mathematics, and foreign language education; and established NDEA fellowships for college students planning careers in public education. Subsequent amendments to the legislation strengthened and expanded the federal government's support for science and mathematics in the public schools.

SUGGESTED READINGS: Homer D. Babbidge, Jr., and Robert M. Rosenzweig, *The Federal Interest in Higher Education*, 1962; Barbara Clowse, *Brainpower for the Cold War: The Sputnik Crisis and the National Defense Education Act of 1958*, 1981.

NATIONAL HIGHWAY ACT OF 1958. The Soviet Union's successful launching into orbit of the artificial satellite *Sputnik** created a technological identity crisis in the United States. Concern about the economy, as well as America's ability to ward off the Communist threat, intensified. To integrate the economy and make the movement of goods and people, including military arms and troops, more efficient, Congress passed the Federal Interstate of Defense Highway Act, also known as the National Highway Act, in 1956.

The National Highway Act envisioned a nationwide highway system of limited access freeways where automobiles could travel at speeds of 70 mph without the delays of traffic lights, small towns, and farm equipment. The east-west highways would be numbered by tens. The most southern highway, for example, was Interstate 10, which runs from Los Angeles, California, to Jacksonville, Florida. The north-south highways would be numbered by fives. Interstate 5, for example, links San Diego, California, with Seattle, Washington. Interstate 95 runs up the east coast from Florida to Maine. Each major city would be circled by a freeway traffic loop, or beltway, so that truck traffic would not have to go through downtown areas. The loops also allowed for the diverting of hazardous materials around major population centers.

The interstate highway system eventually linked the entire country into a single transportation system. Trucking firms saved enormous amounts on fuel and travel time, which reduced shipping costs and led to large-scale productivity gains in the industry. Completion of the system, first launched during the Dwight D. Eisenhower* administration, took 25 years and hundreds of billions of dollars, but it created the most modern transportation system in the world and made the American economy a single marketplace.

Critics charged that the money was badly misspent. Putting hundreds of billions of dollars into good rural roads and state-of-the-art urban mass transit would have made greater sense, they argued. According to them, the National Highway Act exacerbated America's dependence on the automobile and rendered the development of alternate transportation systems all but impossible.

SUGGESTED READINGS: James J. Fink, *The Car Culture*, 1975; Mark Rose, *Interstate Express Highway Politics, 1939–1989*, 1991.

NSC-68. *See* NATIONAL SECURITY COUNCIL MEMORANDUM-68.

NATIONAL SECURITY COUNCIL MEMORANDUM-68. In 1949, in response to the escalation of the Cold War* accompanying the fall of China to Mao Zedong* and the Soviet Union's successful detonation of an atomic bomb,* the Harry Truman* administration embarked on a dramatic reevaluation of U.S. defense policy. In April 1950, Paul Nitze, head of policy planning in the State Department, delivered National Security Council Memorandum-68 to the president. NSC-68 became the foundation of post–World War II U.S. foreign policy. It postulated a bipolar world in which the United States stood for freedom and democracy and the Soviet Union stood for oppression. The memorandum urged massive increases in defense spending, development of a hydrogen bomb,* establishment of a worldwide system of anti-Soviet regional alliance systems, and military threats to stop Soviet expansionism. NSC-68 downplayed the need for diplomatic negotiations with the Soviet Union because the Soviets understood only raw military power.

SUGGESTED READINGS: Stephen E. Ambrose, *Eisenhower: The President*, 1984; James Gilbert, *Another Chance: Postwar America, 1945–1968*, 1981.

NATIVE AMERICAN CHURCH V. NAVAJO TRIBAL COUNCIL (1959). The Navajo Tribal Council objected to the presence and activities of the Native American Church on the Navajo reservation. The Native American Church combined Christian and traditional Native American religious beliefs and practices. The use of peyote, a hallucinogenic drug derived from the mescal cactus, was a central part of the religious ceremony of the Native American Church. The Navajo Tribal Council prohibited the use, sale, or possession of peyote on the reservation and also prohibited the Native American Church from practicing there.

The Native American Church claimed that their right to use peyote and practice their religion without prosecution was protected by the First Amendment to the Constitution. The Tenth Circuit Court of Appeals disagreed. The First Amendment did indeed protect the right to freedom of religion, but the protection applied only to acts of Congress. The Fourteenth Amendment extended those same restrictions only to actions by the states. The Navajo Tribal Council, although created under congressional action, was not restricted by either the First or Fourteenth Amendments. The court ruled that Indian tribes occupied a level of their own between the states and the federal government and had unique legal standings. As such, federal courts did not have jurisdiction over tribal rulings.

SUGGESTED READINGS: Monroe E. Price, *Law and the American Indian: Readings, Notes and Cases*, 1973; John R. Wunder, *"Retained by The People": A History of American Indians and the Bill of Rights*, 1994.

USS NAUTILUS. In January 1954, the U.S. Navy, from its base in New London, Connecticut, launched the USS *Nautilus*, the world's first nuclear-powered submarine. Named after the submarine piloted by Captain Nemo in Jules Verne's novel *Twenty Thousand Leagues Under the Sea*, the USS *Nautilus* was largely the work of Admiral Hyman Rickover, who ran the Naval Reactors Branch of the Atomic Energy Commission. General Dynamics Corporation built the USS *Nautilus* for $30 million. At 319 feet in length with a crew of 95, the USS *Nautilus* dwarfed all other submarines. Its cruising speed of 20 knots per hour was double that of other submarines. Because of its nuclear reactor and uranium fuel, it had a virtually unlimited range, was able to cruise for years at a time, if necessary, and was able to remain submerged for long periods.

In January 1955, the USS *Nautilus* made its maiden voyage to great fanfare. It sailed underwater all the way from New London to Puerto Rico. In 1958 the USS *Nautilus* captured even more public attention by sailing underwater all the

way from Point Barrow, Alaska, to the Greenland Sea, under the Arctic ice cap. The *Nautilus* sailed directly beneath a 35-foot-thick ice sheet at the North Pole.
SUGGESTED READING: William R. Anderson, *Nautilus 90 Degrees North*, 1959.

NELSON, RICK. Rick Nelson was born Eric Hilliard Nelson in Teaneck, New Jersey, on May 8, 1940. His father, Ozzie Nelson, was a famous big band leader, and during the early 1950s Rick and his older brother, David, grew up before tens of millions of Americans, who weekly tuned into *The Adventures of Ozzie and Harriet*,* one of the country's most popular television* programs. Ricky was a wisecracking adolescent who grew up into a teen idol on screen. When he launched his singing career in 1957, he had a built-in audience of millions. His first song—"I'm Walkin'," an older Fats Domino* tune—rocketed to number four on the pop charts after Rick performed it on the television show. The song eventually sold more than one million records. Its flip side, "A Teenager's Romance," hit number two. Nelson followed those up with more than twenty top-forty hits in the next four years, including "Be-Bop Baby" (1957), "Stood Up" (1958), "Waitin' in School" (1958), "Believe What You Say" (1958), "My Bucket's Got a Hole in It" (1958), "Poor Little Fool" (1958), "It's Late" (1959), "Lonesome Town" (1960), "Hello Mary Lou" (1961), and "Travelin' Man" (1961). His last hit, "For You," came in 1964, and *The Adventures of Ozzie and Harriet* was canceled at the end of the 1966 season. Nelson appeared in several films, including *The Sons of Katie Elder* (1961) with John Wayne,* but he spent the rest of his life touring and performing what became known as country rock songs. He died in a plane crash in DeKalb, Texas, on December 31, 1985.
SUGGESTED READINGS: Philip Bashe, *Teenage Idol, Travelin' Man: The Complete Biography of Rick Nelson*, 1992; *New York Times*, January 2, 1986; John Selvin, *Rick Nelson: Idol for a Generation*, 1992.

NEW LOOK. The term "New Look" was used during the 1950s to describe a shift in U.S. foreign and military policy. The policy took shape after 1953, when incoming President Dwight D. Eisenhower* named Admiral Arthur Radford* as his new chairman of the joint chiefs of staff. Radford had spent his naval career with aircraft carriers, and he was a strong proponent of airpower. Airpower, Radford believed, was a cost-efficient way of protecting U.S. national security. In an age of nuclear weapons, Radford was convinced that the United States needed the capability to deliver weapons of mass destruction anywhere in the world. U.S. policy makers also needed to have the will to use such weapons if necessary.

Arthur Radford's convictions played into Secretary of State John Foster Dulles's* concerns. Dulles believed in the reality of an international Communist conspiracy and in the need for the United States to be able to resist that conspiracy everywhere, but he was also convinced that fighting small brush fires around the world was financially impossible, especially if conventional forces were being used. For Dulles, nuclear weapons posed a cheap alternative. In

January 1954 he announced the central doctrine of the New Look policy: massive retaliation.* Henceforth, he announced, the United States would display "a great capacity to retaliate, instantly, by means and at places of our choosing." By threatening the use of nuclear weapons, he hoped, he could deter the Soviet Union and the People's Republic of China from fomenting Communist revolutions in Third World areas. As a result of the New Look policy, the U.S. Air Force and naval airpower thrived, receiving disproportionate shares of the Defense Department budget, but the U.S. Army and Marine Corps, which revolved around conventional tactics, suffered in comparison.

The New Look policy was riddled with logical weaknesses. Some critics accused Dulles of "bluffing," doubting whether the United States would employ nuclear weapons in dealing with minor political and military skirmishes around the world. Others argued that massive retaliation would be impossible in some areas. To use nuclear weapons in Europe, for example, would deliver deadly radiation to American allies. Because of that reality, massive retaliation would not be employed, and with U.S. conventional forces weakened by the New Look policy, the U.S. military would not be able to respond at all to many situations.

Late in the 1950s, critics gained ground against the New Look. General Maxwell Taylor of the U.S. Army published the book *An Uncertain Trumpet* (1960), in which he argued that the United States was unprepared to deal with national security threats around the world. Instead of the New Look, he proposed "flexible response." The U.S. military, according to Taylor, should be equally able to fight nuclear wars, conventional wars, and guerrilla wars. Senator John F. Kennedy* of Massachusetts read *An Uncertain Trumpet*, and when he became president, he named Taylor chairman of the joint chiefs of staff, effectively ending the New Look defense policy.

SUGGESTED READINGS: Stephen E. Ambrose, *Eisenhower: The President*, 1984; James Gilbert, *Another Chance: Postwar America, 1945–1968*, 1981.

NEW YORK YANKEES. Beginning in the 1920s and 1930s, with the baseball diamond exploits of Babe Ruth and Lou Gehrig, the New York Yankees became the premier professional sports franchise in the United States. Because New York City was becoming the world's media center at the same time, the Yankees generated a national reputation that overshadowed that of any other sports team. With the advent of television* in the 1950s, their reputation for athletic skill and financial success became unrivaled. When Joe DiMaggio retired in 1951, a number of commentators predicted the decline of the franchise, but a new generation of extraordinary talent soon appeared, led by Yogi Berra as catcher, Whitey Ford and Don Larsen on the pitching mound, Phil Rizzuto at shortstop, and Mickey Mantle and Roger Maris in the outfield. The Yankees won the World Series in 1949, 1950, 1951, 1952, 1953, 1956, and 1958, and they played and lost in the World Series in 1955 and 1957. No other baseball team before or since has ever enjoyed such dominance.

SUGGESTED READINGS: Dean Chadwin, *Those Damn Yankees: The Secret History of America's Greatest Sports Franchise*, 1999; George Sullivan, *The Yankees: An Illustrated History*, 1997.

NEWPORT JAZZ FESTIVAL. Until 1954 most Americans viewed jazz as an exotic musical genre rooted in African-American culture. For decades it had been confined to bars, nightclubs, and whorehouses, and its pulsating rhythms and often suggestive lyrics alienated most whites. Few whites, outside of rare aficionados, had any appreciation for it, even though contemporary musicologists had already recognized jazz as a uniquely creative contribution to modern music.

In 1954, however, with the advent of the Newport Jazz Festival, jazz left the fringes of American popular culture and began to move into the mainstream. Elaine and Louis Lorillard, scions of Newport, Rhode Island, society and jazz enthusiasts, sponsored the festival, which opened in July 1954 at the Newport Casino. Thousands of people flocked to Newport and heard performances by the leading lights of jazz, including Eddie Condon, Pee Wee Russell, Wild Bill Davison, Dizzy Gillespie, Oscar Peterson, and Gerry Mulligan. The Newport Jazz Festival quickly became a premier event in American music. More than 25,000 people attended the 1955 festival, and the numbers continue to grow.

SUGGESTED READING: Whitney Balliett, "Jazz at Newport," *Saturday Review* 38 (July 30, 1955), 48–49.

NIXON, RICHARD M(ILHOUSE). Richard Milhouse Nixon was born on January 9, 1913, in Yorba Linda, California. He graduated from Whittier College in 1934 and then took a law degree at Duke in 1937. Nixon practiced law in Whittier, California, between 1937 and 1942, and he was active in the naval reserve during World War II. He won a seat in Congress, as a Republican, in 1946 and then rose to prominence in 1949 by pushing the treason case against Alger Hiss* for the House Un-American Activities Committee. A conservative, anticommunist Republican, Nixon won a seat in the U.S. Senate in 1950. In 1952 Dwight D. Eisenhower* selected Nixon as his vice-presidential running mate, and Nixon survived a controversy over personal use of campaign funds to become vice president of the United States. As vice president, Nixon proved to be a loyal supporter of the president. Eisenhower respected Nixon's experience in the House and the Senate and used him to help push administrative measures through Congress. Nixon also played a key role in securing congressional passage of the Civil Rights Acts of 1957 and 1960. Eisenhower did believe, however, that Nixon was a bit too strident on foreign policy issues, and he knew that Nixon was widely disliked by the press. In 1956 some Republicans tried to launch a "Dump Nixon" movement and convince Eisenhower to select another running mate, but the president valued loyalty too much, and he stayed with the vice president.

Nixon's stock with public rose considerably after the so-called Kitchen Debate* of July 1959. Nixon had traveled to Moscow to open the American National Exhibition, a display of U.S. consumer goods and technology. Nikita Khrushchev* was in no mood to be a good host. The U.S. Congress had recently passed the Captive Nations Resolution condemning the Soviet Union for establishing an iron political grip on Eastern Europe and for abolishing civil liberties there.

Before the public meeting, the two men had an angry encounter. Khrushchev described the Captive Nations Resolution as something that "stinks like fresh horseshit, and nothing stinks worse than horseshit." Nixon came back with a vicious analogy, since Khrushchev's parents had been pig farmers. "There is something that stinks worse than horseshit," shouted Nixon, "and that is pigshit." They then strolled into a press conference and walking tour with Western journalists. Khrushchev confidently told the reorters that the Soviet Union would soon surpass the United States in its technological strengths. "In passing you, we will wave to you," he told Nixon. Nixon shot back: "You don't know everything." Khrushchev then retorted, "If I don't know everything, you don't know anything about Communism, only fear of it."

Later in the tour, when they stopped at an exhibition of an American kitchen complete with all the latest appliances, Khrushchev ridiculed it "as capitalist, consumer nonsense." Nixon then pointed his finger at Khrushchev's chest and defended capitalism. The banter continued for several minutes before the two regained control of the encounter. Back home, photographs of Nixon pointing at Khrushchev made the front pages in newspapers throughout the United States and strengthened his political standing.

In 1960 Nixon lost a narrow election for president to Democrat John F. Kennedy,* and in 1962 he lost a bid for the governorship of California to incumbent Democrat Pat Brown. Most observers assumed Nixon's political career was over, but while practicing law, he spoke widely on behalf of Republican candidates and causes and revived his political career. In 1968 he won the GOP presidential nomination. By then the Democratic party was self-destructing over the Vietnam War,* and in the general election, promising a new plan to end the war, Nixon narrowly defeated Hubert Humphrey.

Although Nixon's political career had taken on a hard-line ideological tone over the years, especially in foreign policy, he proved to be a pragmatic president willing to explore a variety of initiatives. Until 1967 he had supported the American commitment in Vietnam, but he became more critical as the election politics of 1968 heated up. By the time he took office in 1969, Nixon, along with his national security adviser, Henry Kissinger, was convinced that the war must come to an end. But they did not wanted a unilateral withdrawal. Anything less than an "honorable" peace would compromise their grand design to reach an accommodation with the People's Republic of China and the Soviet Union without abandoning traditional allies. In the end, Nixon adopted what he called "Vietnamization," which gradually withdrew American troops and turned the war over to South Vietnam. With the Paris Peace Accords of 1973, the war came to an end. Two years later, North Vietnam conquered South Vietnam and reunited the country.

After that, the Watergate quagmire gradually destroyed the Nixon presidency. During the election campaign of 1972, zealous subordinates had authorized a break-in at the Democratic party headquarters in the Watergate complex in Washington, D.C. They botched the break-in and were arrested by Washington, D.C., police. A few days later, when Nixon learned about the arrest, he initiated a cover-up and tried to block formal investigation of the crime. During the next two years, the president consistently denied that he had engaged in such a cover-up, but when White House tapes revealed his complicity in August 1974, he resigned the presidency in disgrace. Only a pardon from President Gerald Ford kept him out of prison.

During the next ten years, Nixon almost went into hiding; he gave few interviews and said little about public policy. Most Republican politicians wanted little to do with him because of the stigma attached to his administration. But late in the 1980s, Nixon slowly reentered public life, gave more interviews, delivered selected lectures, and wrote articles and books about public affairs. He died on April 21, 1994.

SUGGESTED READING: Stephen A. Ambrose, *Nixon*, 3 vols., 1987–1991.

NO TIME FOR SERGEANTS. *No Time for Sergeants*, a two-act comedy written by Ira Levin and based on a novel by Mac Hyman, premiered at the Alvin Theater on October 20, 1955. Andy Griffith played Will Stockdale, a country bumpkin who joins the air force and immediately earns the wrath of Sergeant King, played by Myron McCormick. King tries to make life miserable for Stockdale, giving him KP and latrine duty, but Stockdale remains hopelessly pleasant and without guile, doing whatever the sergeant asks and doing it well, much to McCormick's frustration, who wants nothing less than to drive Will out of the military. *No Time for Sergeants* ends with Will inadvertently flying through, and surviving, an atomic explosion. The play had a run of 796 performances on Broadway.

SUGGESTED READINGS: Gerald Bordman, *The Oxford Companion to American Theater*, 1992; *New York Times*, October 21, 1955.

NUCLEAR POWER. Although the great investment in nuclear energy during the 1950s revolved around creation of nuclear weapons, the reality of Atoms for Peace, or the peaceful use of nuclear energy, became a reality as well in the 1950s. Argonne National Laboratories, at the behest of the Atomic Energy Commission, had constructed a power station at Arco, Idaho, and in 1951 an experimental reactor at the facility generated enough power to run the lab's own lighting system. Similar research was going on in other developed countries. In 1954 the Soviet Union opened the first civilian nuclear energy plant, a small, five-megawatt facility. In 1956 the British opened a full-sized, 40-megawatt industrial nuclear power plant.

As other nuclear power plants sprouted up around the world in the late 1950s and 1960s, nuclear energy enthusiasts predicted a future without the burning of fossil fuels and without skies full of smog. But such predictions proved naive and premature. Nuclear power plants had built-in dangers, some of them catastrophic. That became abundantly clear in 1952 at the Chalk River Atomic Energy Research Center in Ontario, Canada. An unplanned power surge brought about the release into the atmosphere of a radioactive cloud and the contamination of nearly one million gallons of water in the reactor. Safety standards were improved after the Chalk River accident, but concerns remained. In the late 1960s, nuclear energy collided head-on with the environmental movement, which was concerned about the possibilities of catastrophic accidents occurring in nuclear plants—which could pollute vast regions—and the problem of storing radioactive waste materials.

SUGGESTED READING: Fred Clements, *The Nuclear Regulatory Commission*, 1989.

O

OKLAHOMA SOONERS. The great college athletic dynasty of the 1950s was the football team of the University of Oklahoma. Coached by Bud Wilkinson, the Oklahoma Sooners won eight games in 1951 and lost only two. The 1952 season was a better year. The Sooners lost only one game. They lost to Notre Dame in 1953 and tied a game with the University of Pittsburgh. The 9-1-1 season left Oklahoma fourth in the national polls. In 1954 Oklahoma went undefeated, winning all ten games and finishing third in the polls. UCLA and Ohio State had also gone undefeated. Wilkinson's team went undefeated again in 1955, defeating Maryland in the Orange Bowl and winning the national championship. The Sooners were undefeated again in 1956, stretching their winning streak to 40 games, a record still unmatched in college football. The winning streak had reached 47 games when Notre Dame defeated the Sooners 7-0 in the 1957 season. Between 1948 and 1958, the Sooners won 107 games, lost 8, and tied 2.

SUGGESTED READING: Harold Keith, *Forty-Seven Straight: The Wilkinson Era at Oklahoma*, 1984.

ON THE WATERFRONT. Released in July 1954, the film *On the Waterfront* is a gripping tale of corruption, labor racketeering, politics, and crime on the wharfs of New York City. During the early 1950s, America was concerned about organized crime and corrupt, powerful labor unions, and *On the Waterfront* underlined that concern. Marlon Brando* starred as a blue-collar longshoreman unwilling to submit to bureaucrats, lawyers, and racketeers. The film, directed by Elia Kazan, was based on a series of Pulitzer prize–winning newspaper articles by Malcolm Johnson. Brando won an academy award for his performance.

SUGGESTED READING: *New York Times*, July 29, 1954.

ONE MAN'S FAMILY. *One Man's Family*, a popular radio serial, premiered on NBC radio on April 29, 1932. Broadcast for fifteen minutes each weekday evening, the program revolved around the lives of the Barbour family of Sea Cliff, a San Francisco community. The program, the brainchild of Carlton E. Morse, who based it loosely on John Galsworthy's *The Forsyte Saga*, starred J. Anthony Smythe as Henry Barbour. *One Man's Family* traced Barbour's family from the time he was a young, ambitious middle-class business executive to his life as an elderly grandfather. The Barbour family had its ups and downs, full of disagreements and strife, but they also cared about each other, and listeners could identify with many of its themes. Children were born, grew up, left home, and started families of their own. In 1950 *One Man's Family* left CBS for NBC, where it remained until its last broadcast on May 8, 1959.

SUGGESTED READING: John Dunning, *On the Air: The Encyclopedia of Old-Time Radio*, 1998.

OPPENHEIMER, J(ULIUS) ROBERT. J. Robert Oppenheimer was born on April 2, 1904, in New York City, to German immigrant parents. His father was a successful importer-exporter. A brilliant young man, the younger Oppenheimer graduated from Harvard in 1925 with a degree in chemistry. He then studied physics under Max Born at the University of Göttingen and received his Ph.D. there in 1927. After brief periods of research at Harvard, the University of Utrecht, and the California Institute of Technology, he joined the physics faculty at the University of California at Berkeley. His brilliance earned him a full professorship in 1936 and membership in the National Academy of Sciences in 1941.

In 1942, when the United States launched the Manhattan Project to develop an atomic bomb,* Oppenheimer was appointed coordinator of fast-neutron research. At Los Alamos, New Mexico, he directed the laboratory that designed and fabricated the world's first nuclear weapon. After the successful detonation of the first atomic bomb in New Mexico, in July 1945, Oppenheimer resigned from the project. By that time, he was afflicted with serious concerns about the long-term impact of nuclear weapons and the role he had played in their development.

Oppenheimer rejoined the faculty at UC Berkeley and decided to devote his attention to the peace-time benefits of nuclear power. Between 1947 and 1953, he served as a member of the General Advisory Committee to the U.S. Atomic Energy Commission (AEC). Also in 1947, he was appointed director of the Institute for Advanced study at Princeton University. He was appointed president of the American Physical Society in 1948.

Oppenheimer then fell victim to the Red Scare* of the late 1940s and early 1950s. After World War II, he had helped draft the Acheson-Lilienthal proposal, which advocated control of all nuclear weapons by an international body and the free sharing of all atomic secrets with all nations. Conservatives rejected the proposal out of hand. On technical and humanitarian grounds, Oppenheimer openly opposed the development of the hydrogen bomb,* and he earned the wrath of most political conservatives. In 1953 Senator Joseph McCarthy* targeted Oppenheimer as a security risk for his political views, and the AEC voted in 1953 to revoke Oppenheimer's security clearance. The scientific community protested the decision, but Oppenheimer could not win the battle. He remained at the Institute for Advanced Study until his retirement in 1966. Oppenheimer died on February 18, 1967.

SUGGESTED READINGS: Charles Pelham Curtis, *The Oppenheimer Case*, 1955; Nuel Pharr Davis, *Lawrence and Oppenheimer*, 1968; Peter Goodchild, *J. Robert Oppenheimer: Shatterer of Worlds*, 1981.

THE ORGANIZATION MAN. *The Organization Man* is the title of William Whyte's scathing attack on modern American society. Published in 1956, the book asserts that because of corporate values, bureaucracy, and the conformity of suburban life, America had lost touch with its Puritan roots and the ethic of hard work, self-reliance, and innovation. Modern society, Whyte argued, destroyed individual initiative in the name of group cooperation, which inevitably led to rigid, highly structured institutions whose primary goal was self-perpetuation. Although Whyte acknowledged that cooperation was necessary in society, he also feared that the demands of corporations and bureaucracies stifled initiative, creativity, and the expression of individual values.

SUGGESTED READING: William Whyte, *The Organization Man*, 1956.

OUR GAL SUNDAY. *Our Gal Sunday*, which premiered on CBS radio on March 29, 1937, survived as a daily 15-minute weekday melodrama for the next 22 years, broadcasting its last episode on January 2, 1959. It was based on the most improbable of stories, which is probably why it survived so long on radio. The lead character, a young woman named Sunday, an orphan, comes from a poverty-stricken background and marries Lord Henry Brinthrope, a rich English aristocrat whose family owns silver mines. They settle in Virginia and raise two adopted sons, but their lives are complicated by blackmailers, kidnappers, con men, imposters, and the insane. The series survived throughout the 1950s, but as daily soap operas became staples of daytime television,* *Our Gal Sunday* lost listeners.

SUGGESTED READING: John Dunning, *On the Air: The Encyclopedia of Old-Time Radio*, 1998.

OUR MISS BROOKS. *Our Miss Brooks*, which premiered on CBS radio on July 19, 1948, was a 30-minute weekly situation comedy that was broadcast on Monday nights and then on Sunday nights. The show featured Eve Arden* as Connie Brooks, who taught English at Madison High School. The other players were Gale Gordon as school principal Osgood Conklin, Jeff Chandler as biology teacher Philip Boynton, and Richard Crenna as scatterbrained student Walter Denton. Witty and sarcastic, but with a heart of gold, Miss Brooks endeared herself to millions of Americans. She spent her time chasing Mr. Boynton, who never succumbed to her charms, tormenting Mr. Conklin, and shepherding her students. By 1952 *Our Miss Brooks* was one of the most popular radio shows in the country. On October 3, 1952, CBS brought *Our Miss Brooks* to weekly television.* Eve Arden, Gale Gordon, and Richard Crenna reprised their roles from the radio program, and their minor idiosyncrasies endeared them to tens of millions of Americans. The last episode of *Our Miss Brooks* was broadcast on September 21, 1956.

SUGGESTED READINGS: Tim Brooks and Earle Marsh, *The Complete Directory to Prime Time Network and Cable TV Shows, 1946–Present*, 1995; John Dunning, *On the Air: The Encyclopedia of Old-Time Radio*, 1998.

P

PAJAMA GAME. *Pajama Game*, a two-act musical comedy, opened on Broadway at the St. James Theater on May 13, 1954. The musical, based on a book by George Abbot entitled *7 1/2 Cents*, features music and lyrics by Richard Adler and Jerry Ross. The play revolves around Babe Williams (Janis Paige), a worker at the Sleep-Tite Pajama Factory, who serves on the union grievance committee. She falls in love with Sid Sorokin (John Raitt), the factory's new superintendent, but refuses to date him because he represents management. Finally, Sid agrees to a 7.5 cent hourly pay raise for workers, and Babe becomes his girlfriend. *Pajama Game*'s most memorable songs are "Hernando's Hideaway," "Hey There," and "Steam Heat." *Pajama Game* enjoyed a run of 1,063 performances on Broadway.

SUGGESTED READINGS: Gerald Bordman, *The Oxford Companion to American Theater*, 1992; *New York Times*, May 14, 1954.

PALEY, WILLIAM. William Paley was born in Chicago, Illinois, on September 28, 1901. His family owned the Congress Cigar Company of Chicago, and Paley joined the business. During the 1920s, the business bought considerable advertising time from the Columbia Phonograph Broadcasting System, a small radio network with its headquarters in Philadelphia. Paley bought the company, which had 16 affiliate stations, for $500,000 in 1928, changed its name to the Columbia Broadcasting System (CBS), and quickly increased the number of affiliate stations to 49 altogether. Throughout the 1930s, Paley expanded the business, signing on such prominent performers as Kate Smith, Bing Crosby, George Burns, Gracie Allen, Jack Benny, Al Jolson, Nelson Eddy, and Fred Allen.

At first, Paley had little interest in television.* He started up WXAB, an experimental station in New York City in 1931, but he did little to build it up. Not until late in the 1940s, with millions of dollars in bank loans, did Paley begin to entice popular performers to appear on CBS television. By the early 1950s, he was signing up affiliate stations all over the country because of a stable of stars that included Jack Benny, Red Skelton, Edgar Bergen,* Frank Sinatra,* and *Amos 'n Andy*.* During the 1950s, he built his television empire around such situation comedies as *I Love Lucy** and variety shows like *The Ed Sullivan Show*.* Paley also took great pride in CBS News, which was headlined by Edward R. Murrow* and such programs as *See It Now* and *CBS Reports*. Paley eventually built the premier news establishment in the country, which included such prominent journalists as Eric Sevareid, William Shirer, Howard K. Smith, and Walter Cronkite. William Paley, one of the most influential figures in American television history, died on October 26,1990.

SUGGESTED READINGS: *New York Times*, October 27, 1990; William S. Paley, *As It Happened: A Memoir*, 1979; Sally Bedell Smith, *In All His Glory: The Life of William S. Paley*, 1990.

PARKER, CHARLES. Charles "Charlie" Parker was born in Kansas City, Missouri, on August 29, 1920. From as early as he could remember, music fascinated him, and he possessed an amazing, creative talent. He began to play the alto saxophone when he was thirteen, and by the time he was seventeen he was performing brilliantly. Music critics today consider Parker to have been the greatest alto saxophonist in the history of jazz. His music was so melodic and so pure that he earned the nickname "Birdie" or "Yardbird." Dizzie Gillespie, a major light in the jazz world himself, acknowledged Parker as the "greatest who ever lived." Gillespie also credited Parker with inventing bebop, which dominated jazz expression throughout the 1950s and 1960s. In 1949, to honor Parker's genius, a prominent jazz club on Broadway in New York City was renamed Birdland. In 1954, when the Newport Jazz Festival* pushed jazz into the mainstream of American popular music, Charlie Parker gained a fame he had not known before.

He gained notoriety as well. Throughout his life, he fought alcoholism and drug addictions, as well as a clinical depression that worsened after the death in 1954 of his two-year-old daughter. The depression was so severe at one time that he tried to commit suicide and was placed in the psychiatric ward of Bellevue Hospital in New York. He was released for a furlough after two months, but Parker could no longer cope with life. He was only 34 years old, but he already had an advanced case of cirrhosis of the liver, complicated by bleeding ulcers. A heart attack on March 9, 1955, finally took his life.

SUGGESTED READINGS: Lawrence O. Koch, *Yardbird Suite: A Compendium of the Music and Life of Charlie Parker*, 1988; Robert George Reisner, *Bird: The Legend of Charlie Parker*, 1975.

PARKS, ROSA. Rosa Parks was born Rosa Louis McCauley on February 4, 1913, in Tuskegee, Alabama. She grew up Pine Level, Alabama, a hotbed of Ku Klux Klan activity, and attended Alabama State College in Montgomery.

Growing up in Tuskegee, where Booker T. Washington had established the Tuskegee Institute, and KKK-dominated Pine Level gave Parks a strong sense of personal identity and a hatred for racial discrimination. As a young mother in Montgomery, Alabama, she became activie in civic affairs. In 1943, Parks was elected secretary of the Montgomery branch of the National Association for the Advancement of Colored People (NAACP), and held the post until 1956. She also worked as a seamstress.

Parks came to national attention in 1955–1956 when the NAACP staged a boycott of Montgomery's segregated public transportation system. Black riders were required by law to ride at the back of the bus, In 1955 Parks agreed to precipitate an incident by refusing to move to the back of the bus. She was arrested, and the NAACP announced a black boycott of the city's buses until desegregation was implemented. The Rev. Martin Luther King, Jr. assumed leadership of the boycott, which ultimately succeeded in achieving desegregation on December 20, 1956. Rosa Parks was widely considered the heroine of the boycott. She did, however, lose her job because of her activism and moved with her family to Detroit. After several years in Detroit, Parks went to work for Congressman John Conyers, Jr. Today, she lives in Chicago, Illinois, and was recently hailed by President Bill Clinton as one of America's greatest civil rights leaders.

SUGGESTED READINGS: Eloise Greenfield, *Rosa Parks*, 1995; Rosa Parks, *I Am Rosa Parks*, 1997.

PASSENGER JET. Toward the end of World War II, Nazi aerospace engineers developed jet engine prototypes and installed them in fighter aircraft. The jet fighters had superior speed and maneuverability compared to standard diesel-engine fighters. The technology continued to develop during the 1950s, creating more powerful jet engines that were capable of flying larger aircraft. The U.S. military made the adjustment quickly; there really was no other choice. In October 1947 test pilot Chuck Yeager, flying Bell Aircraft's X-1 rocket plane, broke the sound barrier of 760 miles an hour and achieved a maximum speed of 964 miles per hour. By the time of the Korean War,* the United States had deployed the Lockheed P-80 "Shooting Star," the North American F-86A "Sabre," the Grummon F9F-2 "Panther," and the Boeing B-47 and B-52, both of which were strategic jet bombers.

Commercial airlines at first steered clear of jet technology, primarily because they feared the long-term reliability of the engines, the possibility of stress fractures of aircraft parts at such high speeds, and the fact that at such high speeds the margin for error, pilot or equipment, narrowed substantially, which posed a threat to passenger safety. The possibilities of commercial jet aviation were also highly tempting because of the ability to deliver passengers and freight to distant locations in previously impossible times. Boeing developed the Boeing 707 passenger jet. The first viable version of the 707, the Boeing 367–80, flew nonstop at 592 miles per hour from Seattle to Washington, D.C., on July 15,

1954. The return trip averaged 567 miles per hour and took only four hours and eight minutes. Douglas Aircraft also entered the race to develop a commercial jet aircraft. The Douglas DC-8's maiden flight took place on October 13, 1955. On November 8, 1955, the breakthrough arrived when Pan American Airways purchased thirty 707s and twenty DC-8s.

In October 1958, the British Overseas Airways Corporation began the first transatlantic passenger jet service. Its Havilland Comet IV jet flew from London to New York. The flight took six hours and twelve minutes, compared to the more than twelve-hour flight of propeller aircraft. Three weeks later, Pan American Airways began a similar service. In 1958 Douglas Aircraft's DC-8 and Boeing's 707 began carrying passengers cross country and across the Atlantic as well.

Passenger jet service had a dramatic impact on American life. Well-to-do Americans were sometimes called "jet-setters" because they could now fly anywhere, even for just a day or two. Businessmen were able to travel, in a matter of hours, distances that used to take days, making them infinitely more efficient. Professional sports franchises, which formerly had been confined to the East Coast and Midwest, proliferated and spread across the country, led by the decision of the Brooklyn Dodgers* to relocate to Los Angeles and the New York Giants to San Francisco.

SUGGESTED READINGS: Walter J. Boyne and Donald S. Lopez, eds., *The Jet Age: Forty Years of Jet Aviation*, 1979; Michael J. H. Taylor and David Mondey, eds., *Milestones of Flight*, 1983.

PAYOLA. Payola, a term coined by journalists to describe a prominent scandal of the early 1950s, refers to a series of kickbacks paid by record-producing companies to disc jockeys who played their songs. Disc jockeys in major media markets wielded enormous power, and they could make or break a new release. Such kickbacks were considered illegal—a form of bribery and a misdemeanor. Investigations swept the country, and eventually more than 200 radio employees were convicted of accepting such bribes, including prominent New York City disc jockey Alan Freed.* Freed was also found guilty of income tax evasion. Together with the quiz show scandals,* the college basketball scandals,* and the West Point scandal,* payola convinced many Americans that the nation was caught in the midst of a moral crisis. It underwrote a prevailing sense among many older, middle-class Americans that rock-and-roll* had corrupted the nation's youth.

SUGGESTED READING: Gerry Cagle, *Payola*, 1998.

PEALE, NORMAN VINCENT. Norman Vincent Peale was born in Bowersville, Ohio, on May 31, 1898, to a very religious family. His father was a Methodist minister. In 1920 Peale graduated from Ohio Wesleyan College, worked as a journalist for a year in Ohio and Michigan, and then entered Boston University to study for the ministry. He became a full-time minister in 1924 with a small congregation in Brooklyn, New York. Peale was an instant success, drawing more and more people to hear his weekly sermons and raising lots of money in contributions. Within three years, the congregation of 3,000 was meeting in a new sanctuary. In 1927 Peale took the pastorship of the University Methodist Church in Syracuse, New York, and he added a radio ministry in 1932. He was unrivaled at raising money and attracting new church members.

Late in 1932, Peale accepted the pulpit of the Marble Collegiate Church in New York City, a decrepid, poorly maintained former chapel of the Reformed Church. A new radio program, *The Art of Living*, made Peale a household name in the 1930s. Peale became a regular columnist for *Reader's Digest*, a popular speaker on the lecture circuit, and, in 1952, with his book *The Power of Positive Thinking*, a best-selling author. He was perfect for the popular culture of the 1950s, which emphasized family values, financial success, and conservatism. Critics charged Peale with confusing religion with success, but he remained a popular clergymen during the turbulent 1960s, a beacon of stability in a troubled time. In 1984 he wrote his twenty-second book, *The True Joy of Positive Living*, an autobiography. Norman Vincent Peale died on December 24, 1993.

SUGGESTED READINGS: Carol George, *God's Salesman: Norman Vincent Peale and the Power of Positive Thinking*, 1994; *New York Times*, December 25, 1993; Norman Vincent Peale, *The True Story of Positive Living*, 1984.

"PEANUTS." After studying cartooning by taking a correspondence course, Charles Schultz, a native of Minneapolis, Minnesota, launched a comic strip titled "Lil Folks." United Features decided to syndicate the comic strip but insisted on changing its name to "Peanuts," after the so-called Peanut Gallery audience of kids watching the *Howdie Doodie Show* every Saturday morning on television.* "Peanuts" debuted in seven newspapers on October 2, 1950, with a cast of characters perfect for the schizophrenic 1950s. Schultz had a theory that "happiness does not create humor. There's nothing funny about being happy," and his characters host a variety of personal problems. Charlie Brown is pathetically insecure, a bundle of neuroses; Lucy is bossy and domineering. The dog Snoopy is an egocentric daydreamer, and Linus, the thoughtful skeptic, is able to see through every pretense. The troupe worries about school, relationships, the Cold War,* nuclear weapons, and a host of other problems. The series became a runaway hit, rivaled in popularity only by the comic creations of Walt Disney. By the end of the decade, "Peanuts" was a daily feature in hundreds of newspapers, and it made Charles Schultz a millionaire many times over. The series continued until Schultz's death in 2000.

SUGGESTED READING: Robert Short, *The Gospel According to Peanuts*, 1965.

PENNIMAN, RICHARD WAYNE. Richard Wayne Penniman, who came to be known by stage name of "Little Richard," was born in Macon, Georgia, on December 5, 1932. A rebellious adolescent who early on acknowledged his homosexuality, Penniman was expelled from his devout Seventh Day Adventist home when he was thirteen years old. He was also a talented musician and performer who loved the piano, rhythm and blues, and rockabilly music. He was raised by a white family who owned the local Tick Tock Club, and Penniman began performing there. His pompadour hairdo and thick mascara, along with his high-pitched falsetto voice, dripped rebellion and sexuality. For many years he toured the black night club circuit in the South. In 1955, Penniman, now known as "Little Richard," signed with Specialty Records in Los Angeles, and his first release with them, "Tutti Frutti," was a top-twenty hit. Little Richard soon released a string of pop hits, including "Long Tall Sally" (1956), "Rip It Up" (1956), "Lucille" (1957), "Jenny, Jenny" (1957), "Keep a Knockin'" (1957), and "Good Golly, Miss Molly" (1958). He also appeared in several popular teen films—*Don't Rock the Clock* (1957), *That Girl Can't Help It* (1958), and *Mister Rock 'n' Roll* (1959).

At the peak of his popularity, Little Richard underwent a religious conversion and dropped out of the rock-and-roll* scene. He attended Oakwood College in Huntsville, Alabama, and became an ordained minister. He tried to make it on the gospel musical circuit, but his recordings stirred little interest. In 1964 he returned to rock-and-roll, but the so-called British invasion—such groups as the Beatles and the Rolling Stones—were already changing rock music. He remained, however, a popular performer on the club circuit with small concert bookings.

SUGGESTED READING: Charles White, *The Life and Times of Little Richard*, 1984.

PERRY MASON. The weekly dramatic series *Perry Mason*, which premiered on CBS television on September 21, 1957, became one of the most successful programs in television* history. The series, based on Earle Stanley Gardner's murder mysteries, starred Raymond Burr as defense attorney Perry Mason, Barbara Hale as his assistant Della Street, William Hopper as private investigator Paul Drake, and William Talman as District Attorney Hamilton Burger. Every week, Perry Mason represented in criminal court an individual wrongly accused of murder, and every week, Perry Mason rescued the accused from the misguided clutches of the prosecution. The series lasted in prime time until its final broadcast in September 1966. CBS resurrected the series briefly in 1973 and 1974.

SUGGESTED READINGS: Tim Brooks and Earle Marsh, *The Complete Directory to Prime Time Network Shows: 1946–Present*, 1992; David Marc, *Demographic Vistas: Television in American Culture*, 1984.

PEYTON PLACE. *Peyton Place* is the title of Grace Metalious's best-selling novel. At a time when American popular culture, on television* and in films, idealized the squeaky-clean, consumer-driven, conservative suburban family, *Peyton Place* told a quite different story. The novel is set in a small, prosperous New England town where extramarital affairs, crime, pettiness, and banal superficialities characterize social life. The novel is steamy and the sex scenes graphic, at least by 1950s' standards. Metalious had a difficult time finding a publisher; the major New York houses all rejected the manuscript. It was eventually picked by Messner publishing and released in 1956. Dell, a small paperback firm, released it soon after, and the book sold twelve million copies, putting Dell on the publishing map and making Metalious a multimillionaire. Critics panned the novel as soap opera at best and sleazy trash at worst, but *Peyton Place* was by far the decade's most successful publishing venture. In the 1960s, it was made into a popular prime-time dramatic series.

SUGGESTED READINGS: Grace Metalious, *Peyton Place*, 1956; Emily Toth, *Inside Peyton Place: The Life of Grace Metalious*, 1981.

PHILBRICK, HERBERT. Herbert Philbrick was born in Boston, Massachusetts, in 1915. As a college student, Philbrick studied mechanical engineering, but he ended up in the advertising business, selling copy to a variety of business and government agencies. In 1940 he visited the Massachusetts Youth Council, which coordinated the activities of several youth groups, including some that had Communist affiliations. He became affiliated with the Communist party, but his sympathies dissipated quickly. He was especially concerned that the Communist party was misleading people by sponsoring such youth groups as front organizations. He reported his concerns to the Federal Bureau of Investigation* (FBI).

The FBI asked Philbrick if he would agree to remain active in the Massachusetts Youth Council and the Communist party but report their activities to the FBI. Philbrick agreed to be an official informant of the FBI. For the next eight years, he supplied the FBI with information and documents about Communist activities in New England. In 1948, when the FBI arrested twelve leading Communists for violating the Smith Act of 1950,* Philbrick was asked to testify against them. He was reluctant about "blowing his cover," but he agreed. The testimony, which took place in April 1949, made Philbrick a household name in the United States. In 1952 he wrote his best-selling memoirs *I Led Three Lives.** The book inspired a popular television series, starring Richard Carlson as Herbert Philbrick, which weekly portrayed Philbrick foiling Communist attempts at subversion.

SUGGESTED READING: Herbert A. Philbrick, *I Led Three Lives*, 1952.

PICNIC. Picnic, a three-act play written by William Inge, opened on February 19, 1953, at the Music Box in New York City. The play is set in a small Kansas town when a drifter, Hal Carter (Ralph Meeker), walks into the backyard of the Owens family. His presence soon turns the family upside down. Young, handsome, and arrogant, Carter flirts with tomboy daughter Millie (Kim Stanley), and she develops a terrific crush on him. At the same time, he seduces older daughter Madge (Janice Rule) and convinces her to run away with him. He also talks Millie's spinster sister Rosemary (Eileen Heckart) into marrying a gentleman acquaintance. *Picnic* stood in sharp contrast to the idealized American families appearing on television* situation comedies. Unlike Ozzie and Harriet Nelson and Ward and June Cleaver, the Owens family is riddled with dysfunctional frustrations. In the end, Carter destroys the family. *Picnic* had a run of 477 performances.

SUGGESTED READINGS: Gerald Bordman, *The Oxford Companion to American Theater*, 1992; *New York Times*, February 20, 1953.

THE PILL. Ever since the 1920s, Margaret Sanger,* the eventual founder of Planned Parenthood, had campaigned for the development of better birth control devices and better birth control education in America. At the root of her crusade was a powerful conviction that until women gained control over their reproductive cycles, they would never become truly liberated. Her ultimate goal, of course, was a safe, easy to use, and reliable method of birth control that the individual woman could control.

In 1951 two biologists, Gregory Pincus and M. C. Chang, approached Sanger with the results of their research. The two scientists had developed a pill that could disrupt the normal production cycles of estrogen and progesterone in a woman's body, which would either prevent her from ovulating or prevent a fertilized egg from planting itself in the lining of the uterus. Sanger immediately realized the potential of their discovery, and she approached Katherine McCormick, her friend and heir to the McCormick farm machinery fortune, for financial assistance. McCormick came up with $2 million to finance more research. The research yielded synthetic hormones, which had the potential of being included in a pill, to be taken in daily doses by women wishing to avoid pregnancy.

In 1955 G. D. Searle Company took over the project from Pincus, and in 1956 they conducted clinical trials on 15,000 women in Puerto Rico and Haiti. The results produced undeniable proof that a convenient, reliable, and safe oral contraceptive had been developed. The Food and Drug Administration then conducted trials of is own, and in 1960 the pill was approved for use in the United States.

SUGGESTED READINGS: Virginia Coigney, *Margaret Sanger: Rebel with a Cause*, 1969; Madeline Gray, *Margaret Sanger: A Biography of the Champion of Birth Control*, 1978; David Kennedy, *Birth Control in America: The Career of Margaret Sanger*, 1970.

PLAYBOY. After finishing college, while working for *Esquire* magazine, Hugh Hefner had an idea for another men's magazine. At the time, *Esquire* published sexually suggestive photographs, but nothing as explicit as those that appeared in the so-called stag magazines. Raised in a religious, straight-laced family, Hefner wanted to rebel against his upbringing, and he thought money could be made in rebellion. But he did not want to traffic in the sleaze of cheap pulp publications. His idea was to produce a glossy, high-production quality men's magazine comparable to *Esquire* that included explicit photographs of nude women. Hefner wanted men to be able to purchase the magazine without being embarrassed. He also envisioned a magazine that would include sophisticated articles of general interest.

In 1953 he produced the first issue. He had intended to title the magazine *Stag Party*, but at the last minute he changed it to *Playboy*. He also had made a shrewd decision to purchase a nude photograph of actress Marilyn Monroe.* Monroe had posed for the calendar shot before she became a Hollywood sensation, and by 1953 her status as a sexual icon had already been established. Hefner used the photograph as *Playboy*'s first centerfold, and the issue, 53,000 copies, sold out in a matter of days. In that first issue of the magazine, Hefner projected what became known as the *Playboy* philosophy: affluence and individual sexual freedom as positive virtues. When Hefner was later asked to sum up the *Playboy* philosophy, he remarked, "If you had to sum up the idea of *Playboy*, it is anti-puritanism. Not just in regard to sex, but the whole range of play and pleasure." By the magazine's fourth issue, Hefner was already in the black financially, and the construction of the *Playboy* empire began. In 1954 circulation reached 100,000 copies, and by December 1956, it topped 600,000 copies. Hefner was a rich man, and the *Playboy* empire—complete with mansions, clubs, and nude, willing women—was established.

SUGGESTED READING: Frank Brady, *Hefner*, 1974.

POLIO. Polio, or infantile paralysis, was the most feared disease of the 1950s. It struck people of all ages and races. It could cripple or kill, if respiratory muscles were attacked. Although the disease had been known for thousands of years, it was not until 1908 that scientists identified the virus that caused the disease. The virus was breath-born and entered the patient's bloodstream. It then took one of two routes through the body. If it entered the large intestine, it caused a brief illness similar to the common cold and was then excreted; but if it entered the central nervous system, it entered the brain stem and/or the spinal cord and caused paralysis or death.

Polio gained national attention in 1921 when Franklin D. Roosevelt, soon to be governor of New York and then president of the United States, came down with the disease. In 1939 Roosevelt founded the National Foundation for Infantile Paralysis. During the 1950s, polio reached epidemic proportions. More than 150,000 cases were reported in 1950, and that number jumped to nearly 300,000 in 1952. In some parts of the country, concern assumed almost the dimensions of panic. Parents kept children home from school, avoided parks and swimming pools, and played only in small groups with the closest of friends. Cases seemed to increase in the summer.

Scientists raced for a cure. At the University of Pittsburgh, researcher Jonas Salk had developed three vaccines based on the three separate polio viruses (*see* Salk vaccine). He dipped the polio viruses in formaldehyde, which killed them, and then injected the dead virus into the bloodstream. It caused the body to develop antibodies that protected against the disease. He delivered the vaccine in three shots over the course of six weeks. The federal government approved clinical trials, and in the spring of 1954, 440,000 children were vaccinated. Children receiving the placebo were 3.5 times more likely to get polio than those receiving the vaccination. At the urging of President Dwight D. Eisenhower,* Congress passed the Poliomyelitis Vaccination Act, and by the end of 1958 more than 200 million Salk vaccinations had been administered.

But there were problems with the Salk vaccine. Salk soon learned that the triple vaccination endowed immunity for only thirty months, at which point a booster vaccination was needed. The four necessary vaccinations were cumbersome. Also, since the vaccination was based on a live virus, some recipients fell victim to polio after being vaccinated because the formaldehyde had not killed the virus. They had been injected with living virus.

Albert Sabin of the University of Cincinnati developed an alternative vaccine, which he announced to the world in October 1956 (*See* Sabin Vaccine). He developed a disabled live polio virus that was too weak to cause illness but was strong enough to trigger the body's immune system to manufacture antibodies. The Sabin vaccine was an easily administered oral medicine. The Salk and Sabin discoveries had a dramatic effect on polio. The incidence of the disease fell from 37.2 cases per 100,000 people in 1952 to 1.8 cases per 100,000 in 1960.

SUGGESTED READINGS: Alton L. Blakeslee, *Polio and the Salk Vaccine*: *What You Should Know About It*, 1956; Richard Carter, *Breakthrough*: *The Saga of Jonas Salk*, 1967.

POLISH REBELLION. After World War II, Soviet troops did not withdraw from Eastern Europe as Joseph Stalin* had promised. Actually, Stalin had no intention of pulling Soviet troops back across the border. After two world wars, both of which had inflicted severe losses on Russia and the Soviet Union, Stalin wanted to keep a buffer zone between his own country and Germany, France, and Great Britain. That buffer zone, which the West nicknamed the "Iron Curtain," included Poland, Latvia, Lithuania, Estonia, Czechoslovakia, Hungary, Yugoslavia, and Bulgaria. More than one million Soviet troops occupied those countries, and Stalin set up puppet Communist regimes in all of them.

When Joseph Stalin died on March 5, 1953, hopes soared throughout Eastern Europe, and Soviet Premier Nikita Khrushchev's* modest liberalization campaign in 1954 and 1955 fostered that hope. In October 1956, Polish nationalists, led by students and trade union leaders, rebelled against the Soviet-backed puppet regime. Soviet troops invaded Warsaw, and Khrushchev flew to Warsaw to negotiate a settlement. At the time, he hoped to avoid an outright military confrontation, and he quickly struck a deal with Wladysla Gomulka, leader of Poland's liberal faction. Soviet troops would pull back from Warsaw, and the Soviet Union would allow Poland a greater measure of political independence. That agreement ended the Polish rebellion, but the Polish rebels had inspired an even more volatile Hungarian rebellion.*

SUGGESTED READING: George Blazynski, *Flashpoint Poland*, 1979.

POLLOCK, JACKSON. Jackson Pollock was born in Cody, Wyoming, on January 12, 1912. In 1932 he moved to New York City to study art under Thomas Hart Benton at the Art Students' League. He was almost literally a "starving artist" during the 1930s, scratching out a living with the art program of the Works Progress Administration. During World War II and the late 1940s, Pollock worked for the Museum of Non-Objective Painting where he decorated men's ties and lipstick cases for the gift shop. In 1946 he began the stylistic innovations that eventually earned him a national reputation. He dripped paint onto canvas in multilayered, multicolored patterns that made no pretension of definitive meaning, leaving interpretation completely up to the viewer. In doing so, he became one of a few abstract impressionists in the United States.

Pollock rocketed from obscurity to celebrity status in 1949 when Clement Greenberg, art critic for *The Nation*, described him as a genius. Most art critics accused Greenberg of exaggeration and hyperbole. One critic even sarcastically described Pollock as "Jack the Dripper." *Life* magazine gave Pollock mountains of free publicity with its 1949 article "Jackson Pollock: Is He the Greatest Living Painter in the United States?" Pollock established a studio in East Hampton, Long Island, that become a gathering place for the rich and famous. By the early 1950s, he was cranking out one painting per day and selling it for upward of $10,000.

Notoriously rude in his personal life, he was given to alcoholism and reckless sexual promiscuity. Most people excused his behavior as the downside of genius, which gave him more excuses for his self-destructive behavior. On August 10, 1956, Pollock left a bar so drunk that he could barely walk, and he drove off a winding road and died in the crash. His death instantly drove up the price of his paintings.

SUGGESTED READINGS: Steven Naifeh and Gregory Smith, *Jackson Pollock: An American Saga*, 1989; *New York Times*, August 11–12, 1956.

THE POWER ELITE. *The Power Elite* is the title of a highly influential book written by C. Wright Mills, a prominent sociologist and theorist at Columbia University. The book was published in 1956 to rave reviews from intellectuals and social theorists. In *The Power Elite*, Mills describes how political and economic power is wielded in the United States. He claims that America is run by a high profile network of lawyers, corporate leaders, Washington, D.C., bureaucrats, high-ranking military officers, and Ivy League intellectuals. These individuals control access to the corridors of power, freezing out other constituencies in American society. Mills did not claim that any sinister conspiracy existed to wield such power, only that it occurred because the influential leaders and their institutions had so much contact with one another that cooperation was inevitable. In 1960, when President Dwight D. Eisenhower* warned of the implications of a military-industrial complex,* he was taking his intellectual cue from *The Power Elite*.

Many social historians look back on *The Power Elite* as a precursor to the anti-institutional culture that flourished in America in the 1960s. During the Vietnam War,* millions of Americans concluded that Mills had put his finger on the greatest problem in American society—rule by an isolated elite whose own self-confidence knew no bounds. The only solution, Mills argued, was more widespread participation in the political process. During the 1960s, the student movement and groups like Students for a Democratic Society promoted the notion of participatory democracy, which had its roots in Mills's theories. Mills did not live long enough to see that impact of his work. A heavy drinker and smoker, and plagued with hypertension, he died of a heart attack in 1962.

SUGGESTED READINGS: David Halberstam, *The Fifties*, 1993; Irving L. Horowitz, *C. Wright Mills: An American Utopian*, 1983; Rick Tilman, *C. Wright Mills: A Native Radical and His American Intellectual Roots*, 1984.

PRESLEY, ELVIS. Elvis Aaron Presley was born in Tupelo, Mississippi, on January 8, 1935, to dirt poor but loving parents. A twin brother was stillborn that day. The family moved to Memphis, Tennessee, in 1948. He was, at best, an average student, but he had musical talents that found expression in his guitar and a unique singing voice. After school, Elvis hung out at the office of Sun Records,* where owner Sam Phillips was searching for the "perfect talent—a white man who can sing black rhythm and blues." At the time, rhythm and blues was confined exclusively to African-American performers and African-American audiences. Presley did part-time odd jobs for Phillips and occasionally fooled around in the recording studio. Phillips listened to some of Presley's work, and in 1954 had him record "That's All Right Mama," a song written by black blues artist Arthur Crudup. Phillips put a country song on the flip side— "Blue Moon of Kentucky." Phillips released the record in July 1954, and it sold 25,000 copies in its first six months.

Phillips had discovered exactly what he had been looking for—a white artist who could sing rhythm-and-blues music who could appeal to both white and black audiences. He sent Presley on tour to promote the record, and news of his talent spread throughout the industry. In September 1954, Presley performed in Nashville on the *Grand Ole Opry*,* a mecca for country and western musicians. Phillips had a certifiable star on his hands. Over the next year, Presley recorded eight more songs for Phillips and became the most recognizable figure in popular music.

In 1955 Presley signed Colonel Tom Parker as his agent, and Parker, who had a shrewd nose for the music business, began negotiating with RCA records, trying to convince them to make Sam Phillips an offer for the rights to Presley's music. Phillips then made an extraordinary business miscalculation. He sold all rights to Elvis Presley's music for $35,000, and within a matter of months, RCA was selling 75,000 copies of Elvis Presley records every day. Such records as "Hound Dog," "Love Me Tender," and "Jailhouse Rock" made Presley the king of rock-and-roll.* Parker also pioneered ancillary celebrity businesses, licensing Elvis Presley merchandise, including teddy bears, fan magazines, hound dogs, and books. By the time Elvis turned 21, he was a multimillionaire.

In September 1956, just two years after his appearance on *Grand Ole Opry*, Presley earned a prime time spot on *The Ed Sullivan Show*,* America's premier television* variety show. Three appearances earned Presley $50,000, and the audience ratings were the highest in television history. To appease older viewers, Sullivan's cameras focused on Elvis's torso, as some found his hip gyrations offensive. Moral critics lamented the fact that someone like Elvis Presley could inspire such devotion among so many millions of American young people. Colonel Parker also navigated Presley into a movie career. In the 1950s, Presley starred in four films: *Love Me Tender* (1956), *Jailhouse Rock* (1957), *Loving You* (1957), and *King Creole* (1958). He sang in all four films, and they were all box-office hits. Presley's estimated income in 1957 was $10 million.

Ironically, for someone who symbolized so much rebellion, Elvis Presley was remarkably conservative in his personal life. He was an obedient child who was devoted to his parents, especially to his mother, and he was a believing church-going Christian. He was not really a political animal, but the convictions he did express tended to be conservative. He was also extremely patriotic and un-ashamed about expressing such values. But Elvis Presley was not an icon to patriotism or conservatism in the 1950s. He was on the cutting edge of the baby boom* generation, and although he was certainly not the cause of the youth rebellion of the 1950s, he was a catalyst. By the end of the decade, Elvis Presley was probably the most recognizable individual in the country.

Being on the cutting edge of a youth rebellion also has a downside, including the seeds of its own destruction. Teenagers quickly become young adults, and new icons appear. The watershed in Presley's career came in March 1958 when he was drafted into the U.S. Army. He demanded no special treatment and served out much his tour of duty in West Germany with an armored division. He recorded no music, made no personal appearances, and tried to be like the other GIs. He mustered out of the army in 1960.

During the 1960s, Presley continued to record music and make personal appearances, but he was no longer on the cutting edge of rock-and-roll. Compared to the rock stars of the 1960s—such as the Beatles and the Rolling Stones—Presley appeared almost bland. His music, films, and performances became more stylized and predictable, and he became almost formulaic. By the 1970s, he was an overweight, aging rock star who had become a caricature of his former self. Bedecked in a tight-fitting, rhinestone-twinkling jumpsuits that exposed every roll of fat, Presley became a regular on the Las Vegas circuit in the 1970s, performing before audiences that had become middle-class and middle-aged. He died in a drunken stupor on August 16, 1977.

SUGGESTED READINGS: Albert Goldman, *Elvis*, 1981; Peter Guralnick, *Last Train to Memphis: The Rise of Elvis Presley*, 1994; Robert Hall, *Elvis Presley*, 1986.

PRISONER OF GOD. *Prisoner of God: Letters and Papers from Prison* is the title of Dietrich Bonhoeffer's highly influential 1951 theological treatise. In the wake of World War II, theologians had to come to terms with the magnitude of evil represented by Adolf Hitler and the Nazis. During the war, German Protestants and their churches had become co-conspirators in Hitler's madness. Churches accepted Nazi-imposed bishops and pastors, purged non-Aryans from their congregations, and incorporated Nazi values into their doctrine and liturgies.

As early as 1937, Pastor Dietrich Bonhoeffer criticized German Protestants for having lost their moral compass and acquiescing and even cooperating in Nazism's crimes against humanity. He was a leading figure in the establishment of the Confessing Church, which went underground, acknowledging only the authority of God, not the state, and actively opposing the Holocaust and Nazi rule. In 1943 Bonhoeffer was arrested and jailed for sedition. Before he was executed in 1945 for plotting Hitler's assassination, Bonhoeffer wrote *Prisoner of God: Letters and Papers from Prison.*

First published in 1951, *Prisoner of God* proposes a "religionless Christianity"—devoid of any bureaucracies, liturgies, denominations, and even theology—based simply on emulating the life of Jesus by reaching out to the poor, the oppressed, and the suffering. Bonhoeffer acknowledged the moral ambiguity of the modern world, argued that ethics must devolve from Christlike deeds, and admitted that a belief in God was purely a leap of individual faith. *Prisoner of God* inspired a vigorous, ongoing debate at seminaries and divinity schools in the 1950s and prepared the ground for the social activism of many Protestant denominations in the 1960s.

SUGGESTED READING: Charles Marsh, *Reclaiming Dietrich Bonhoeffer: The Promise of His Theology*, 1994.

PUBLIC LAW 277 (1953). The question of Indian alcohol abuse had long troubled many non-Indians, who often nurtured the most vicious stereotypes of Indian alcohol consumption. Many states prohibited the sale of alcohol beverages to Indians, a law that smacked of discrimination to many people. During World War II, Indian soldiers purchased alcohol around the world, and when they returned to the United States, the prohibition seemed particularly irritating to veterans. In 1946 the Bureau of Indian Affairs sponsored legislation permitting the sale or gift of alcohol to Indians outside reservations. The bill, however, maintained the prohibition against alcohol consumption or possession on reservations. The bill never passed, but in 1953 the Dwight D. Eisenhower* administration sponsored Public Law 277. The bill passed Congress on August 15 of that year. Public Law 277 lifted the restriction against selling alcohol to Indians off the reservations and allowed tribal governments to decide whether alcohol could be sold on the reservations.

SUGGESTED READING: Wilcomb E. Washburn, *Red Man's Land, White Man's Law*, 1995.

PUBLIC LAW 280 (1953). Almost since the beginning of the history of the United States, a great debate has raged over the relationship between Indian nations and reservations and the states. Disputes have been common as to when state laws could and should be applied on the reservations. The U.S. Congress tried to resolve this problem in 1953 with the termination* program.

Public Law 280 requires certain states, and allows others on an optional basis, to assume legal jurisdictions on the Indian reservations. The states would have jurisdiction over criminal actions taking place on the reservations, but only with laws that apply to the entire state. States are not permitted to pass special laws for the Indian reservations alone or to regulate taxation or water rights.

Public Law 280 had no provision for Native American consent for granting the states jurisdiction over reservation criminal law enforcement. President Dwight D. Eisenhower* complained about this even as he signed the bill into law. Although the Western states had demanded the passage of Public Law 280, the federal government granted them no funds to pay for the necessary law enforcement expenses. The reservations were given whatever law enforcement each state chose to provide, sometimes with little or no protection being offered to the Indians. The law also made it difficult for the states to try to remove the sovereignty of the Indian tribes altogether. The nature of Public Law 280, requiring the state laws to have general application, forced the state to treat all self-governing groups, such as counties, cities, and towns, equally.

The reaction to Public Law 280 was not favorable within the Indian community. Native Americans worried about discrimination from state officials, and the states worried about how to pay for the newly required law enforcement services. Several of the optional states declined to assume jurisdiction over Indian country.

SUGGESTED READINGS: Russel Lawrence Bars and James Youngblood Henderson, *The Road: Indian Tribes and Political Liberty*, 1980; Frederick J. Stefon, "The Irony of Termination: 1943–1958," *Indian Historian* 11 (Summer 1978), 1–13; John R. Wander, *"Retained by The People": A History of American Indians and the Bill of Rights*, 1994.

PUBLIC LAW 291 (1952). Under the leadership of Dillon S. Myer in the early 1950s, the Bureau of Indian Affairs (BIA) moved ahead with its plans to terminate federal responsibility over Indian tribes in favor of state control. Early in 1952, House Resolution 698 asked Myer to report on the status of the Bureau of Indian Affairs and to draw up a list of BIA services that could be ended outright or transferred to the states. Most Indians opposed both ideas, worrying about the loss of federal funding and becoming subject to local political authority, where white majorities would have significantly more power. Myer told Congress that one federal service that could be transferred to the states was health care, particularly the BIA hospitals serving Indian communities. In April 1952, Congress acted on Myer's suggestion and passed Public Law 291, which transferred BIA hospitals to state jurisdiction. Public Law 291 was one of the earliest steps in the termination* movement.

SUGGESTED READINGS: James S. Olson and Raymond Wilson, *Native Americans in the Twentieth Century*, 1984; Frederick J. Stefon, "The Irony of Termination: 1943–1958," *Indian Historian* 11 (Summer 1978), 1–13.

PUBLIC LAW 568 (1954). During the 1950s, the Bureau of Indian Affairs (BIA) enthusiastically promoted the termination* program ending federal responsibility over Indian tribes in favor of state control. Early in 1952, House Resolution 698 asked Dillon S. Myer, head of the Bureau of Indian Affairs, to report on the status of the BIA and to draw up a list of BIA services that could be ended outright or transferred to the states. Myer soon reported that health care could be transferred. In April 1952, Congress acted on Myer's suggestion and passed Public Law 291,* which transferred BIA hospitals to state jurisdiction. Congress followed up Public Law 291 with Public Law 568 which, passed on August 5, 1955, transferred the entire Indian health program to the U.S. Public Health Service. The transfer involved 3,600 employees and more than $40 million in property.

SUGGESTED READINGS: James S. Olson and Raymond Wilson, *Native Americans in the Twentieth Century*, 1984; Frederick J. Stefon, "The Irony of Termination: 1943–1958," *Indian Historian* 11 (Summer 1978), 1–13.

Q

QUEEN FOR A DAY. *Queen for a Day*, a popular radio program, premiered on the Mutual Radio Network on April 30, 1945. It was broadcast daily Monday through Friday with a simple premise: select an individual woman and try to fulfill her dreams. Each day five women were selected from the studio audience. They explained their wishes to the studio audience, who then voted for one of them. The woman selected was dubbed "Queen for a Day." She was then dressed in the latest fashions, showered with wonderful gifts, and entertained in New York's fanciest night spots. The show became especially popular when Jack Bailey took over as emcee. The final broadcast of *Queen for a Day* took place on June 10, 1957.

SUGGESTED READING: John Dunning, *On the Air: The Encyclopedia of Old-Time Radio*, 1998.

QUIZ KIDS. *Quiz Kids*, a popular television show of the 1950s, premiered on NBC television on March 1, 1949, with a simple format. It had its origins as a radio program at WNBQ in Chicago in 1940, where the producers located brilliant children and adolescents and built a quiz show with them as contestants. NBC carried the television show from 1949 to 1953 when CBS picked it up. Although the show was never a top-rated, huge money maker, it did well enough to stay on the air until its last broadcast on September 27, 1956.

SUGGESTED READING: Tim Brooks and Earle Marsh, *The Complete Directory to Prime Time Network and Cable TV Shows, 1946–Present*, 1995.

QUIZ SHOW SCANDALS. During the 1950s, when Americans hailed the virtues of their own society and excoriated those of communism and the Soviet Union, a series of scandals rocked them with a crisis of faith. Cadets at West Point, the U.S. Military Academy, were accused of cheating on examinations (*see* West Point Scandal); many disc jockeys were convicted of accepting illegal kickbacks in the payola* scandal; and a number of college basketball players were found guilty of shaving points in order to allow professional gamblers to win bets (*see* College Basketball Scandal).

The most notorious scandal of all involved the major television networks. Quiz shows had became familiar fare on American television,* but in the late 1950s two prime-time quiz shows, *The $64,000 Question* and *Twenty-One*, became especially popular. Contestants answered arcane, detailed, complex, questions, impressing viewers with the volume of their erudite knowledge. Producers made sure that contestants represented a cross section of American life, not just Ivy League intellectual elitists who knew everything. Soon the shows were in television's top ten.

In 1959 the quiz show scandals exploded into the public consciousness. On *Twenty-One*, producers had put Herbert Stempel, a brilliant, extremely well-read blue-collar man from a working-class family against Charles Van Doren, a Columbia University English professor and scion of a prominent intellectual family. Stempel had been the "champion" on *Twenty-One* for several weeks and had won tens of thousands of dollars and became a national celebrity. After a two-month string of victories on *Twenty-One*, he lost to Van Doren.

Upset with the way he had been treated, Stempel went to the press and revealed that he had been supplied with the questions and answers in advance of each show, and that he had even been coached how to act, talk, and behave in front of the camera. Journalists elevated the story into a full-blown scandal, precipitating a congressional investigation. Congress passed legislation outlawing deceptive practices on quiz shows. The networks quickly canceled *Twenty-One* and *The $64,000 Question*.

SUGGESTED READING: Richard S. Tedlow, "Intellect on Television: The Quiz Show Scandals of the 1950s," *American Quarterly* 28 (Fall 1976), 183–95.

R

RACKETS. During the late 1940s and early 1950s, the term "rackets" was used widely by journalists and criminal justice officials to describe organized crime. *See* KEFAUVER, ESTES and THE KEFAUVER COMMITTEE.

RAISIN IN THE SUN. *Raisin in the Sun*, a three-act play by Lorraine Hansberry, opened on Broadway at the Ethel Barrymore Theater on March 11, 1959. A classic now in American theater history, *Raisin in the Sun* focuses on a black family's dream. Lena Younger, played by Claudia McNeil, has received a $10,000 life insurance payment after the death of her hardworking husband. She wants to use the money to move her family out of the ghetto to suburbia* where there will be less crime and more opportunity for her children and grandchildren. Her son Walter wants to use the money to invest in a liquor store business, so that he can quit his job as a chauffeur and do better for his own children. Walter and his mother argue about the money. He eventually takes the money against her will and makes the investment, only to find that his so-called business partner absconds with the funds. When Lena tries to move to the suburbs anyway, she runs into opposition from white neighbors, who do not want their neighborhood to become integrated. In the end, they are able to make the move. *Raisin in the Sun* exposed the depth of racism in the white communities of the North, where many Americans assumed that racism did not exist. Also about family, determination, and resiliency, critics hailed it. *Raisin in the Sun* had a run of 530 performances.

SUGGESTED READINGS: Gerald Bordman, *The Oxford Companion to American Theater*, 1992; *New York Times*, May 12, 1959.

RAMAR OF THE JUNGLE. *Ramar of the Jungle* was a popular children's adventure program of the early 1950s. It was produced in syndication, with 52, 30-minute episodes, and it first aired on October 10, 1952. It starred Jon Hall as Dr. Tom Reynolds, a medical missionary who wore khakis and a pith helmet and served in darkest Africa. He was the all-wise white man, a father figure to ignorant, childlike Africans. The show was produced on a shoestring budget with indoor sets supposedly depicting the wilds of Africa. Most adults hated the show, but children loved it. Even after the last episode was produced in 1953, *Ramar of the Jungle* remained for years as a staple of Saturday morning children's television.

SUGGESTED READING: Tim Brooks and Earle Marsh, *The Complete Directory to Prime Time Network and Cable TV Shows, 1946–Present*, 1995.

RAND, AYN. Ayn Rand was born on February 2, 1905, in Saint Petersburg, Russia. She immigrated to the United States in 1926 after receiving her undergraduate degree in history from the University of Leningrad. The Bolshevik Revolution had an indelible impact on Rand's thinking. Totalitarian bureaucracies that destroyed individual initiative were certain, she believed, to ultimately destroy civilization as well. She became a naturalized U.S. citizen in 1931.

Rand published her first book in 1936—*We the Living*, a novel of the Russian Revolution. She followed it up with a series of successful and influential books: *The Fountainhead* (1943), *Atlas Shrugged* (1957), *The Virtue of Selfishness* (1965), *Capitalism: The Unknown Ideal* (1966), and *The New Left: The Anti-Industrial Revolution* (1970). During the peak of the 1960s and its faith in the ability of big government to ameliorate social problems, Rand became the godmother to conservatives and libertarians who believed only in the power of capitalism, the individual, and the market. Her heroes were brave men who defied the demands of bureaucracies, whether corporate or political. New Left critics labeled her a fascist. Ayn Rand died in New York City on March 6, 1982.

SUGGESTED READINGS: Barbara Branden, *The Passion of Ayn Rand*, 1986; Sid Greenberg, *Ayn Rand and Alienation*, 1977; Douglas J. Uyl and Douglas B. Rasmussen, eds., *The Philosophic Thought of Ayn Rand*, 1984.

RAND CORPORATION. At the end of World War II, a number of major defense contractors became concerned about corporate profits. Government orders for research, development, and weapons production had fallen off dramatically, but at the same time, the Cold War* and the Red Scare* were intensifying, providing potential new economic opportunities. Hoping to take advantage of the rise in tensions between the United States and the Soviet Union, and to generate more revenues for the company, Douglas Aircraft Company, a defense contractor in Santa Monica, California, founded the Rand Corporation. The name was an acronym based on "research and development." Rand split from Douglas in 1948. During the early 1950s, Rand conducted research to evaluate the effectiveness of major American weapons systems under contracts with the Department of Defense. It also handled such civil defense issues as the social and economic impact of nuclear warfare on the United States. Later in the decade, Rand broadened out into economics as well by securing contracts to analyze and evaluate resource allocation as it related to national security issues.

SUGGESTED READING: L. R. Smith, *The Rand Corporation*, 1966.

THE REAL McCOYS. *The Real McCoys* was the first in a genre of so-called rural television programming that eventually produced such huge hits as *The Andy Griffith Show*, *Beverly Hillbillies*, *Petticoat Junction*, and *Green Acres*. Producers Irving Pincus and Norman Pincus had a difficult time selling the concept. Most sponsors worried that urbanites would find little to interest them in the program, since the scripts revolved around a fictional rural family. In the show, a poor West Virginia family moves to a small ranch in California. The family was presided over by Grandpa Amos McCoy, played by Walter Brennan, with Richard Crenna playing his son Luke McCoy, and Kathy Nolan playing Luke's wife Kate. It was a situation comedy that struck television* gold; first broadcast on ABC on October 3, 1957, it rocketed to the top of the Nielsen ratings and remained there for years. The last episode was broadcast on September 22, 1963. After that, the show remained in daytime reruns for many years.

SUGGESTED READING: Tim Brooks and Earle Marsh, *The Complete Directory to Prime Time Network and Cable TV Shows, 1946–Present*, 1995.

REBEL WITHOUT A CAUSE. Released in October 1955, *Rebel Without a Cause* starred James Dean,* Natalie Wood, and Sal Mineo as troubled teenagers.* Raised by hardworking, well-meaning, middle-class parents, they are without social moorings or life goals. They are given to racing cars in death-defying, and sometimes death-causing, "chicken races" and fighting with switchblade knives. Dean played Jim Stark, a teenaged boy ridden with angst and tormented by a sense of alienation that he cannot understand. He rebels against his parents, teachers, police, and the world at large, but not for any purpose except rebellion as an end in itself. His costume for the film—an open leather jacket over a white T-shirt, blue jeans, and boots—caught the fancy of millions of American teenagers, who saw in Jim Stark an alter ego for their own growing restlessness with the conformity of the 1950s. The film resonated with social commentators worried about juvenile delinquency* in America. Three weeks before the film's release, Dean got into his new Porsche, revved it up to 115 miles per hour, and collided with another car. He was killed instantly. Dean's death guaranteed huge moviegoing audiences, and he all but became a saint in American popular culture, worshiped in death by millions of teenagers. Since then, *Rebel Without a Cause* has become a popular cult film and a symbol of the 1950s.

SUGGESTED READINGS: David Dalton, *James Dean: The Mutant King*, 1983; Joe Hyams, *James Dean: Little Boy Lost*, 1992; *New York Times*, October 27, 1955.

RECORDS. During the 1950s, record technology improved dramatically. Ever since Thomas Edison had invented the record player, Americans had been fascinated with listening to recorded music, but record technology, even late into the 1940s, was quite poor. Records made of shellac were played at 78 revolutions per minute (rpm). Each side of a record played four minutes of music, and the record itself wore out quickly with continued play, scratched easily, and was very brittle, breaking when dropped. Sound quality was poor, at least compared to contemporary standards. In spite of these problems, Americans purchased 350 million records in 1947, at an average price of $1.50 each.

RCA-Victor and Columbia Records were the leading record manufacturers, and in June 1947 new technologies appeared on the market. Columbia Records introduced a new ten- or twelve-inch record made from scratch-resistant vinyl. They were not nearly as brittle as the old 78s, and they were advertised as long-playing records, or "LPs," because each side contained 25 minutes of music. Early in 1949 RCA-Victor introduced the 45-rpm record. Also made of vinyl, it had superior sound quality and sold for only 79 cents. Its downside was that it contained only four to five minutes of music. RCA-Victor advertised it as a perfect vehicle for recently released pop music hits, and it sold well.

The new records had a dramatic economic impact on the industry. Within a matter of 18 months or so, the old 78s had become obsolete, along with more than 16 million 78-rpm record players. Record sales dropped to less than 200 million in 1949 because consumers did not want to have to purchase new record players. The sales slump lasted for several years, but then record player sales jumped. Consumers bought 830,000 new record players in 1950, 1.2 million in 1951, and 1.5 million in 1952. They hit 3 million in 1959. Improvements in record player technology spurred sales. The "hi-fi," or high-fidelity sound player, was a vast improvement over earlier models.

SUGGESTED READING: Lawrence C. Goldsmith, "War in Three Speeds," *Nation* 168 (May 7, 1949), 523–25.

RED MONDAY. With the onset of the Cold War* after the end of World War II and the rise of the Soviet Union as a nuclear power, fear of communism escalated dramatically in the United States, and fear of domestic Communists was especially intense. Congress passed the Smith Act of 1950* making it a federal offense to advocate the overthrow of the U.S. government or to form an organization dedicated to its overthrow. In 1951, in its *Dennis v. United States*ence* decision, the U.S. Supreme Court upheld the constitutionality of the Smith Act, even though civil libertarians roundly condemned it.

By the late 1950s, however, the Red Scare* had subsided, and the philosophical complexion of the Supreme Court had changed. Under the direction of Chief Justice Earl Warren,* the Court had taken a decidedly liberal turn, and a series of civil liberties cases reached the Court in 1957.

On June 17, 1957, a day conservatives and anticommunists labeled "Red Monday," the U.S. Supreme Court handed down a number of important decisions concerning civil liberties, in particular the extent to which an individual could be punished for maintaining radical or revolutionary political views. *Service v. Dulles** was one of those cases. William Service had been fired from his job in the State Department because several of his superiors considered his political opinions dangerously "liberal." The State Department's Internal Loyalty Board investigated the allegations and concluded that Service was not a security risk. Secretary of State John Foster Dulles* fired him anyway. Service filed a civil rights lawsuit, claiming that the State Department had violated his constitutional right to free speech. The U.S. Supreme Court agreed with Service. His firing had been arbitrary, and the State Department had contradicted its own regulations depriving Service of due process.

In the case of *Sweezy v. New Hampshire*,* a college professor had admitted to the New Hampshire legislature that he was a member of the left-wing Progressive party but then refused to identify other party members. Because he would not "name names," the state legislature held him in contempt. He filed a lawsuit claiming that his constitutional rights had been violated. The U.S. Supreme Court agreed with Sweezy and overthrew the contempt citation.

*Watkins v. United States** was similar to *Sweezy v. New Hampshire*. In *Watkins*, a union member admitted to the House Un-American Activities Committee that he was a member of the American Communist party but refused to identify other party members. Because he would not "name names," Congress held him in contempt. He filed a lawsuit claiming that his constitutional rights had been violated. The U.S. Supreme Court agreed with Watkins and overthrew the contempt of Congress citation. The Court's reason held that such a compromise of the Fifth Amendment was not justified, especially given the fact that Watkins had never advocated the overthrow of the U.S. government.

The final decision made on Red Monday, was *Yates v. United States*,* a test of the Smith Act. Yates had been prosecuted under the Smith Act, but he sued, claiming that the conviction violated his civil rights. On this occasion, the Court distinguished between mere speech—discussing the merits of overthrowing the government—as opposed to concerted attempts to do so. For the Court, discussion was different from behavior and was protected by the First Amendment, which imposed a critical limit on the Smith Act. Yates's conviction was overturned.

Civil libertarians hailed the four decisions of Red Monday for restoring the credibility of the Bill of Rights, but conservatives like J. Edgar Hoover,* director of the Federal Bureau of Investigation,* accused the Court of promoting the Communist cause in the United States.

SUGGESTED READINGS: Richard G. Powers, *Secrecy and Power: The Life of J. Edgar Hoover*, 1987; Athan Theoharis, *Spying on Americans: Political Surveillance from Hoover to the Huston Plan*, 1978; Stanford J. Unger, *The FBI*, 1976.

RED SCARE. During the late 1940s and early 1950s, the United States endured the second "Red Scare" of the twentieth century. The first had occurred in the wake of World War I and the Bolshevik Revolution in Russia. The second one was a product of World War II and the rise of the Soviet Union to a position of military and political dominance in Eastern Europe. After the war, Premier

Joseph Stalin* refused to withdraw Soviet troops from Poland, Lithuania, Latvia, Estonia, Czechoslovakia, Hungary, Yugoslavia, and Bulgaria, even though the Yalta Accords of 1945 had promised free elections in Allied-occupied countries. Anticommunists claimed that Soviet intransigence on the issue was simply one stage in communism's grand design to take over the world. Many historians argued that the Soviet Union, twice burned in the twentieth century by invasions from Western powers, was only creating a military buffer zone to protect itself from future assaults.

In any event, President Harry Truman* opted for a containment policy,* which was designed to keep the Soviet Union from extending its political and military influence into Central and Western Europe. To protect Greece and Turkey from Communist insurgents, Truman implemented the Truman Doctrine, a program of financial and military assistance to Greece and Turkey. To prevent an economic meltdown in Western Europe that Communists might exploit, Truman instigated the Marshall Plan, a $10 billion economic assistance program for Western Europe. All of these programs cost money, and to push them through Congress, Truman warned Americans again and again of the threat of communism, whipping up an anticommunist frenzy. That frenzy escalated in 1949 when Mao Zedong* and the Chinese Communists seized control of China and the Soviet Union detonated its first atomic bomb.*

Soon, fear of Communist expansion abroad turned into fear of Communist infiltration at home. The issue first surfaced in a major way with the activities of the House Un-American Activities Committee (HUAC). The Hollywood Ten* was a group of prominent film industry people cited in 1947 by HUAC for contempt of Congress. In 1947 the HUAC had conducted hearings into the Communist infiltration of the film industry. Between October 28 and 30, 1947, the HUAC subpoened 41 people, but 10 of them refused to answer the following question: "Are you now or have you ever been a member of the Communist Party?" Each was cited for contempt of Congress, fined $1,000, and sentenced to jail terms of from six months to one year. They appealed the citations, but in 1950 they had to serve their prison terms.

Concerned about protecting the industry from intense public scrutiny and criticism, the heads of the major studios developed the blacklist which banned the Hollywood Ten and any other Communists and Communist sympathizers from working in the industry. On November 26, 1947, the Motion Picture Association of America released the following announcement: "We will forthwith discharge or suspend without compensation those in our employ and will not reemploy any of the ten until such time as he is acquitted or has purged himself of contempt and declares under oath that he is not a Communist. . . . We will not knowingly employ a Communist or a member of any party or group which advocates the overthrow of the Government of the United States by force, or by any illegal or unconstitutional methods."

The next major episode in the Red Scare was the Alger Hiss* case. Whitaker

Chambers,* a former Communist and an editor at *Time* magazine, testified before the HUAC that, during the 1930s, he had been a member of a Communist cell in New York City. He told the HUAC that several current government officials were also members of that cell, including Alger Hiss, head of the Carnegie Endowment for International Peace. Hiss denied the charges and sued Chambers for libel. Chambers then charged Hiss, under oath, with having passed government documents to Soviet agents, which escalated the controversy from simple Communist party membership to treason and espionage. Chambers delivered to Congressman Richard M. Nixon,* who headed the HUAC hearings, five rolls of microfilm. Chambers claimed that Hiss had given him the microfilm. Because the statute of limitations had expired on the crime of treason, Hiss was indicted for perjury. Hiss went on trial in 1949, but the case ended in a hung jury. Early in 1950; a second perjury trial resulted in Hiss's conviction. He was sentenced to five years in prison, and his incarceration began on March 22, 1951.

Liberals came to Hiss's defense, claiming that people like Nixon and Senator McCarthy* had created a political atmosphere in America that guaranteed miscarriages of justice and that Hiss had been railroaded. Hiss eventually served three years and eight months of the sentence. Chambers became the darling of conservatives and wrote the best-selling book *Witness* in 1952.

Senator Joseph McCarthy, a Republican from Wisconsin, provided the Red Scare's most notorious episode. In 1950 he expressed concern about getting reelected; he needed an issue that would galvanize voters. Fear of communism seemed perfect. The Soviet juggernaut had gobbled up much of Eastern Europe, and Mao Zedong had proclaimed the People's Republic of China. Fear of communism was at a fever pitch, and McCarthy decided to exploit it. On February 9, 1950, he had a speaking engagement in Wheeling, West Virginia. Before a small crowd of listeners, he pulled out a sheaf of papers and said that he had a list of 205 Communists who had infiltrated the State Department. When journalists pressed him for evidence, McCarthy hedged on the numbers and refused to name names, but his charges received extraordinary media attention. Almost overnight, McCarthy became famous and infamous, a hero and a demigod, depending upon one's perspective.

As chairman of the Government Committee on Operations of the Senate, McCarthy turned his attention on a variety of Americans and launched a witch-hunt. Leftists of every persuasion—liberals, Socialists, Communists, and labor leaders—were labeled "dupes" or "fellow travelers." He trafficked in rumor and innuendo, not in truth or evidence, and thousands of Americans lost their jobs and found their reputations besmirched by coming under the glare of McCarthy's spotlight. Red Scare crusaders targeted the rich and famous as well as the obscure. In 1953 actor Charlie Chaplin, a British subject, was denied readmission into the United States because many considered him a dangerous left-winger. J. Robert Oppenheimer,* who had played the key role in the Manhattan Project, which developed the atomic bomb during World War II, lost his government security clearance in 1953 because he opposed the development of a hydrogen bomb.*

Senator McCarthy was one of the most powerful men in the country until 1954 when he overstepped his bounds. He accused the U.S. Army of harboring card-carrying Communists. In nationally televised hearings, McCarthy went toe-to-toe with Joseph Welch, the Army's special counsel. When McCarthy accused one of Welch's associates of being a Communist, Welch lashed back. "Until this moment, Senator, I think I never really gauged your cruelty or your reck-lessness. . . . If it were in my power to forgive you for your reckless cruelty, I would do so . . . but our forgiveness will have to come from someone other than me." When McCarthy persisted in his accusations, Welch cut him off. "Senator. You've done enough. Have you no sense of decency, sir? At long last, have you left no sense of decency?" At that point, the Senate chamber erupted in applause, and the spell McCarthy had cast over the American people was broken. In September 1954, Edward R. Murrow,* on his Sunday evening television show *See It Now*, denounced Senator McCarthy as an irresponsible witch-hunter.

The Red Scare particularly targeted labor unions, where suspicions about rad-ical loyalties ran very high. During 1949 and 1950, the Congress of Industrial Organizations (CIO), in order to protect itself from the wrath of right-wing conservatives convinced that all unions were Communist infiltrated, turned on its most radical components. The CIO expelled eleven member unions, including the Fur and Leather Workers Association and the American Communications Association, for harboring Communists. In 1955 the Subversive Activities Con-trol Board in the Department of Justice declared that the United Electrical, Radio and Machine Workers had been badly infiltrated by Communists. In November 1956 the attorney-general accused 14 leaders of the International Union of Mine, Mill and Smelter Workers Union with being Communists.

Nor did American education escape the Red Scare's insidious wrath. If, as Senator Joseph McCarthy charged, Communists had infiltrated the State De-partment, surely they must have burrowed their way into the public education system, where they could corrupt the minds of America's youth. Teachers every-where found their loyalties carefully examined and, in many cases, challenged outright. Earl McGrath, the U.S. commissioner of education, warned in 1950 of the dangers of Communists teaching in the public schools, and in July 1950 the National Education Association purged its membership of known Communists. Loyalty oaths became common for public school employees throughout the country. In New York City, so many teachers were fired that teacher shortages appeared throughout the city's schools.

The most notorious case revolved around the so-called New York Eight— eight New York City public schoolteachers who were suspended without pay in 1950 for being Communists. Even though a formal investigation could produce no evidence of their Communist party membership, all eight were dis-missed. Similar firings occurred in school districts across the country. Throughout the country, supposedly "subversive" materials were purged from public school libraries and removed from public school curricula.

The most celebrated and most controversial case of the Red Scare era involved Julius and Ethyl Rosenberg.* In 1950 the Federal Bureau of Investigation* identified them as spies who had passed secrets of the atomic bomb to the Soviet Union. Although the Rosenbergs vehemently proclaimed their innocence, they were indicted and brought to trial late in March 1951. The prosecution employed highly questionable techniques, accusing the Rosenbergs of treason even though they were not being tried for that crime. The Rosenbergs took the Fifth Amendment when asked if they were Communists, which did not help their cause. The jury convicted them and they were sentenced to death. The sentence was carried out on June 19, 1953.

The deaths of the Rosenbergs and the self-destruction of Senator Joseph McCarthy seemed to take some of the steam out of the Red Scare. When President Dwight D. Eisenhower* took office in January 1953, he conveyed a sense of peace and calm to a troubled country. The end of the Korean War* later in 1953 also eliminated a source of political tension in the United States.

SUGGESTED READINGS: Michael R. Belknap, *Cold War Political Justice: The Smith Act, the Communist Party, and American Civil Liberties*, 1977; Bernard Dick, *Radical Innocence: A Critical Study of the Hollywood Ten*, 1988; Richard Fried, *Nightmare in Red*, 1990; Victor Navasky, *Naming Names*, 1980; Kenneth O'Reilly, *Hoover and the Un-Americans: The FBI, HUAC, and the Red Menace*, 1983; David M. Oshinsky, *A Conspiracy So Immense: The World of Joe McCarthy*, 1983; Walter Schneir and Miriam Schneir, *Invitation to an Inquest: A New Look at the Rosenberg-Sobell Case*. 1983; Athan G. Theoharis and John Stuart Cox, *The Boss: J. Edgar Hoover and the Great American Inquisition*, 1988; Allen Weinstein, *Perjury: The Hiss-Chambers Case*, 1978.

THE RED SKELTON SHOW. Red Skelton may be the most enduring comedian in the history of television.* He came from a family that lived on the Barnum and Bailey Circus tour, in which his father performed as a clown. During the 1940s, Skelton achieved national fame as a radio comedian, and he brought his talent to NBC televison when *The Red Skelton Show* premiered on September 30, 1951. Although billed as a comedy and variety program, *The Red Skelton Show* was more comedy than variety, and Skelton himself provided most of the laughs. He had a gentle, self-deprecating humor, and his regular comedy sketches, such as "Freddy the Freeloader," "Clem Kadiddlehopper," "Cauliflower McPugg," "Willie Lump-Lump," and "San Fernando Red," became hits among television viewers. At the end of each show, Skelton signed off by thanking his viewers and the studio audience and saying, "And may God bless." The last episode of *The Red Skelton Show* was broadcast on August 29, 1971.

SUGGESTED READING: Arthur Marx, *Red Skelton*, 1979.

RELOCATION. After World War II, assimilationists once again came into control of U.S. Indian policy, and they were convinced that the continued existence of reservations as home to hundreds of thousands of American Indians would only perpetuate poverty and cultural alienation. One solution, the reformers believed, was to move Indians off the reservation and into larger cities, where they would work in industrial jobs and send their children to public schools. In 1947 Congress appropriated money for a Labor Recruitment and Welfare Program on the Navajo and Hopi reservations to train people to work in Denver, Los Angeles, Phoenix, and Salt Lake City. The Hoover Commission soon called for an ambitious relocation program to drain surplus labor off the reservations.

In 1949 the Bureau of Indian Affairs established urban job bureaus for Native Americans. After the terrible blizzards of 1949–1950, Congress passed the Navajo-Hopi Rehabilitation Act of 1950, which provided funds to relocate thousands of Indians to cities where they could find jobs. By 1952 the Bureau of Indian Affairs was providing job training, moving expenses, housing location assistance, and a 30-day subsistence allowance to Indians willing to leave the reservations and relocate to the cities. By 1960 more than 35,000 Indians had been relocated to Denver, Phoenix, Albuquerque, San Francisco, Dallas, Los Angeles, Oklahoma City, Tulsa, and Chicago.

The program did not live up to the expectations of its promoters. Few reservation Indians trusted the government enough to participate willingly in the program, and most Indians felt comfortable on the reservations. City life had little appeal to most of them. Urban life, with its materialism, anonymity, and emphasis on individual aggrandizement, proved to be a cultural shock to most relocated Indians. Also, most relocated Indians experienced a new kind of poverty in the cities. On the reservations, they were accustomed to free medical care and subsidized rent and utility bills, but in the cities they found themselves without that safety net, trying to make a living with low-paying, unskilled, and often seasonal employment. More than 10,000 of the Indians who relocated under the program eventually returned to the reservations.

SUGGESTED READINGS: Joan Ablon, "American Indian Relocation: Problems of Dependency and Management in the City," *Phylon* 26 (Winter 1965); Larry W. Burt, *Tribalism in Crisis: Federal Indian Policy, 1953–1961*, 1982; Elaine M. Neils, *Reservation to City: Indian Migration and Federal Relocation*, 1971.

REUTHER, WALTER. Walter Phillip Reuther was born on September 1, 1907, in Effingham, Illinois. He moved to Detroit, Michigan, in 1926 and went to work for the Briggs Manufacturing Company. He soon took a job with Ford Motor Company. He became active in union organizing activites, and in 1932 Ford fired him. By then Reuther was absolutely committed to the labor union movement for automobile workers, and he became widely known among workers in May 1937, when he handed out leaflets outside Henry Ford's River Rouge manufacturing facility outside of Detroit, Michigan. Ford's goons assaulted Reuther. When Reuther emerged from the hospital a week later, he had become the most widely known union organizer in the automobile industry. The fact that he was also a skilled negotiator elevated him in union politics and labor-management relations.

Although Reuther had been a committed socialist early in his career, he had abandoned the political philosophy by the late 1930s, trading it in for a virulent anticommunism. During World War II and in the late 1940s, Reuther purged the United Automobile Workers of its Communist members. Nevertheless, Reuther never lost faith in the welfare state or for the need to have the federal government actively engaged in the economy in order to protect the poor, the sick, and the elderly.

During the 1950s, along with George Meany,* Reuther helped engineer the merger of the American Federation of Labor and the Congress of Industrial Organizations. The AFL-CIO,* with 14.6 million members, was by far the largest labor union in the country. Meany became president of the new AFL-CIO and Reuther became vice president. Together, they used the union's resources to improve wages, working conditions, and benefits, and they also threw their support behind a succession of pro-union Democratic party candidates at the local, state, and national levels.

During the 1960s, Reuther backed the Great Society of President Lyndon B. Johnson* because he supported its civil rights and antipoverty programs. As for the Vietnam War,* Reuther backed Presidents Johnson and Richard M. Nixon,* as did large numbers of union workers, whose own service in World War II and the Korean War* made them sympathetic with Vietnam servicemen and Vietnam veterans. Reuther died in a plane crash on May 9, 1970.

SUGGESTED READINGS: John Barnard, *Walter Reuther and the Rise of the Auto Workers*, 1983; *New York Times*, May 10–11, 1970.

REVISED STANDARD VERSION (BIBLE). On September 30, 1952, the *Revised Standard Version* (RSV) of the Bible was published under the auspices of the National Councils of Churches of Christ. It was the work of 32 Biblical scholars who had labored for 15 years to bring it to press. Most Protestants hailed the RSV and it became an instant best-seller. In fact, it remained so consistently at the top of best-seller lists that in 1955 major book-sellers decided not to list it any more. Critics questioned the National Council of Churches of Christ for its sincerity, since the organization reaped huge royalties from sales of the RSV. Conservative Protestants were upset with the modern language of the RSV, when compared to the King James Bible, and they worried about the doctrinal implications of some of the RSV changes. For example, the RSV substituted "the young woman" for virgin in several places, which some decided was an assault on the doctrine of the virgin birth of Jesus Christ.

Other revisions of the Bible also appeared in the 1950s. Hebrew University published the *Jerusalem Bible* in 1953, which constituted the first revision by Jewish scholars of sacred Hebrew texts. In 1958 the Catholic Church published the *Catholic Bible* in Saint Peter's Edition.

SUGGESTED READING: Gilbert Cassidy, *Compare and See: A Comparison of the Authorized and Revised Standard Versions of the Bible*, 1956.

RICHARDSON, J(ILES) P(ERRY). Jiles Perry (J. P.) Richardson, known professionally as "The Big Bopper," was born in Sabine Pass, Texas, on October 24, 1930. Soon after high school, he went to work as a disc jockey at KTRM radio in Beaumont, Texas. He also performed country and western and rockabilly music himself, and in 1957 Mercury Records signed him to a contract. Richardson's 1958 song "Chantilly Lace" had been a runaway hit, selling more than a million copies and going to the top of the pop music charts. He followed that up with two modest hits, "Little Red Riding Hood" and "The Big Bopper's Wedding." In order to promote "The Big Bopper's Wedding," he went on tour. He signed on with Winter Dance Party, a touring rock-and-roll* show that catered to rural audiences in the Midwest. Buddy Holly* and Richie Valens* were the tour's other attractions. Severe winter weather all but canceled the tour. On February 2, 1959, Holly chartered a private plane to fly his band from Clear Lake, Iowa, to the next show in Moorhead, North Dakota. At the last minute, to avoid a long ride in a tour bus, Valens and Richardson hitched a ride on the plane. Soon after midnight, on February 3, the plane crashed in fog and heavy snow. The three rock stars were killed instantly.

SUGGESTED READING: *New York Times*, February 5, 1959.

THE RIFLEMAN. During the 1950s, dramatic series based on the history of the Old West became staples of prime-time televison.* One of the more popular series in this genre was *The Rifleman*, featuring Chuck Connors as Lucas McCain, a farmer in North Fork, New Mexico Territory, in the 1880s. A widower, McCain is raising his son Mark (Johnny Crawford) and helping Sheriff Micah Torrance (Paul Fix) protect North Fork from a succession of desperadoes. McCain's trademark was his specially designed Winchester rifle and its large ring, which allowed him to cock the weapon as he drew it. ABC first broadcast the series on September 30, 1958, and it remained on the air until its last episode on July 1, 1963.

SUGGESTED READING: Tim Brooks and Earle Marsh, *The Complete Directory to Prime Time Network and Cable TV Shows, 1946–Present*, 1995.

ROBBINS, JEROME. Jerome Robbins was born Jerome Rabinowitz in 1918 in New York City. Fascinated with movement and the human form, Robbins studied ballet under Anthony Tudor and in the late 1930s won several parts on Broadway. His real talent, however, was as a choreographer, not as a performer. In 1944 he created the dances for *On the Town*. Dance historians consider his "Mack Sennett Ballet" for *High Button Shoes* (1947) to be a classic. Robbins followed that up with the choreography for *Look, Ma, I'm Dancin'* (1948), *Miss Liberty* (1949), *Call Me Madam* (1950), and *The King and I** (1951). Robbins directed *The Pajama Game*,* which opened in 1954. He then directed and choreographed a string of hits, including *Bells Are Ringing* (1956), *West Side Story* (1957), *Gypsy* (1959), and *Fiddler on the Roof* (1964). Robbins then changed his focus and dedicated himself to creating dances for major ballet companies. He returned to the theater in 1989 with his autobiographical *Jerome Robbins' Broadway*.

SUGGESTED READING: Christina Schlundt, *Dance in the Musical Theater: Jerome Robbins and His Peers, 1934–1965*, 1989.

THE ROBE. *The Robe* was one of Hollywood's first experiments with Cinemascope,* a wide-screen projection system designed to attract viewers away from television sets and back to movie theaters. Released in September 1953, *The Robe* starred Richard Burton as an arrogant Roman tribune who presides over the crucifixion of Jesus Christ but eventually becomes obsessed with Christ's robe and converts to Christianity. Critics had high praise for Cinemascope, which was especially good for action and spectacle films. The wide, narrow screen was an immediate hit with moviegoers.

SUGGESTED READING: *New York Times*, September 17, 1953.

ROBINSON, JACKIE. John Roosevelt (Jackie) Robinson was born near Cairo, Georgia, on January 31, 1919, to a family of poor sharecroppers. His father left the family soon after Jackie's birth, and his mother moved the family to Pasadena, California. A bright, articulate young man, Jackie was also a gifted athlete. He attended Pasadena Junior College and then UCLA, where he lettered in four varsity sports. Commissioned a first lieutenant, he served in the U.S. Army during World War II. A proud man, Robinson was unwilling to quietly accept second-class racial status, and his outspoken protests led to a court-martial. He survived the trial, however, and was honorably discharged.

In 1945 Robinson signed with the Kansas City Monarchs, a professional baseball franchise in the Negro Leagues. At the time, Branch Rickey, the general manager of the Brooklyn Dodgers,* was committed to integrating baseball, and he was looking for the right black athlete to pioneer the process. He needed an individual who was smart, articulate, talented, and highly disciplined. Dodger scouts told him that Jackie Robinson, shortstop for the Kansas City Monarchs, would probably fill the requirements. After conducting extended discussions with Robinson, Rickey agreed, and he signed Jackie to a contract and sent him to the Montreal Royals, a AAA Dodger farm team. Robinson played second base for the Royals, and in 1947 Rickey brought him up to the majors, starting him at first base for the Dodgers.

Robinson faced a storm of racist protest, on the field and off, but he handled it all with stoic determination. On the road, he was often denied access to hotels and restaurants. On the field, his athleticism was undeniable, and he was named Rookie of the Year. The Dodgers moved him to second base in 1948. The next year, he won the award as the National League's best fielding second baseman, and he won the batting title. That year, he was also named the league's most valuable player. Robinson played for the Dodgers through the 1956 season, when he was traded to the New York Giants. He decided to retire in 1957, with a lifetime batting average of .311 and a hand in winning six National League pennants for the Dodgers.

Historians look back upon Jackie Robinson as a leading figure in the modern civil rights movement.* His athletic gifts won him a national spotlight, and his intelligence and demeanor won the respect of millions of white people, who decided that segregation in sports had no place in American life. When Martin Luther King, Jr.,* launched the modern civil rights movement in the 1950s, in which he announced that segregation and discrimination in any walk of life was unconstitutional, he enjoyed some political momentum that Jackie Robinson had set in motion. After his retirement from baseball, Robinson became an executive with the Chock Full O'Nuts restaurant company. He died of a heart attack on October 24, 1972.

SUGGESTED READING: Jules Tygiel, *Baseball's Greatest Experiment: Jackie Robinson and His Legacy*, 1983.

ROBINSON, SUGAR RAY. "Sugar" Ray Robinson was born May 3, 1921, in Detroit, Michigan, but he grew up in Harlem. A gifted athlete, Robinson decided to go into boxing because it promised a lucrative career. He fought his first professional fight in 1940. During World War II, Robinson joined the U.S. Army and spent most of the duration putting on boxing exhibitions. In 1947, because he had neglected to report a bribe attempt, he was suspended from the ring. Eventually, Robinson was reinstated, and he got a shot at the middleweight championship in 1951. Although he was thirty years old, he delivered a thirteenth-round technical knockout (TKO) to Jack LaMotta. He became a hero to the African-American community and an icon comparable to Joe Louis. Boxing historians consider him one of the greatest, perhaps the greatest fighter—pound for pound—in the history of the sport.

Four months later, Robinson learned how fleeting fame can be. Overconfident and undertrained, he lost a title defense to Randy Turpin. Turpin did not have much staying power either. On September 12, 1951, Robinson regained the middleweight title. Americans admired his talent and his perseverance.

On June 25, 1952, Robinson gambled and fought for the light heavyweight championship against Joe Maxim. Although he was winning the fight according to all the judges, Robinson collapsed in the thirteenth round, weakened by dehydration. He then retired from the ring, switching to a show business career.

In 1956 he returned to the ring. Now 34 years old, Robinson fought middleweight champion Bobo Olson and won. On January 2, 1957, he lost the title again, this time to Gene Fullmer. In their rematch, fought on May 1, 1957, Robinson defeated Fullmer and became the only champion in boxing history to win a title four times. He lost the title in 1958 to Paul Pender, who also won the rematch. Robinson retired from the ring in 1965. By then he was a virtual pauper, having squandered more than $4 million in gate receipts. Sugar Ray Robinson died April 13, 1989.

SUGGESTED READINGS: *New York Times*, April 14, 1979; Ray Robinson, *Sugar Ray*, 1970.

***ROCHIN V. CALIFORNIA* (1952).** On January 2, 1952, the U.S. Supreme Court decided the *Rochin v. California* case. Police officers had arrested an individual on suspicion of drug possession and then forcibly pumped out the contents of his stomach, which revealed the presence of drugs. The defendant claimed that his Fourth Amendment protection from unreasonable searches had been violated, and the Court agreed by an 8 to 0 margin, citing a violation of constitutional rights. The *Rochin v. California* decision of the Vinson Court presaged many similar decisions by the Warren Court.

SUGGESTED READING: 342 U.S. 165 (1952).

ROCK-AND-ROLL. Rock-and-Roll was perhaps the most significant cultural development of the 1950s and certainly was the most important development in the popular culture of the era. There was an irony to it. While white parents debated the merits of school desegregation,* with many insisting that the races should not mix in the classroom, the dance floor, or the bedroom, rock-and-roll would bring black and white children together, at least in terms of musical tastes.

In terms of demographics, rock-and-roll was rooted in the postwar, baby boom* generation. The GIs returned from World War II, married their sweethearts, and began raising children. The first of the so-called baby boomers were born in 1946, and by the mid-1950s they had entered the years of self-conscious adolescence. Raised amidst plenty, without memories of the Great Depression or the two world wars, they enjoyed a previously unknown sense of social security and shared few of the values that rooted their parents. They quickly came to resent the conformist pressures of the decade. The youth rebellion, which sprouted fully in the 1960s, germinated in the 1950s, and rock-and-roll music was like water on a dry plant. Popular music became the primary vehicle in which most teenagers* expressed rebellion and discontent, and, not surprisingly, conservative parents felt threatened by the music and its implications.

During the 1950s, their parents had listened to and danced to the music of Frank Sinatra,* Vic Damone, Peggy Lee, Pat Boone,* Perry Como, Rosemary Clooney, and Dinah Shore, all talented performers to be sure, but teenagers found the music inhibited and cautious, lacking primal impulses and any tinge of rebelliousness. They wanted music they could dance to and even perform if they so chose. The music of the older generation was a bit too sophisticated for that, requiring highly talented musicians, orchestras, and vocalists. Rock-and-roll did not require elaborate instrumentation, only a rhythm guitar, a bass guitar, drums, and a singer whose voice was less important than the primal, emotional ways he or she expressed feelings. Having "soul" meant infinitely more than talent. Rock-and-rollers reduced music to a few fundamental chords, some simple melodies, and some basic arrangements.

Rock-and-roll developed from the rhythm-and-blues (R & B) traditions of Southern blacks and whites. Among blacks, R & B had emerged from the trauma of slavery, the music of the black church, and the poverty and pain of the black experience. In small Southern towns, of course, blacks and whites listened to R & B. Rock-and-roll also had its roots in the blues music of Southern whites, which many Americans labeled "hillbilly" music. It too expressed pain and suffering, employed simple musical constructions, and could often be hokey and highly sentimental. Sometimes the boundaries between black blues music and hillbilly music were exceedingly fine.

In terms of marketing, rigid parameters confined black R & B to the black community and isolated pockets of Southern whites. White record stores did not carry black R & B records, jukeboxes in white restaurants and nightclubs did not include black R & B songs, and white disc jockeys did not play black R & B music. Sam Phillips, a record producer in Memphis, Tennessee, knew he could become a millionaire if he could find a white man who could effectively perform in the black rhythm-and-blues tradition.

While Sam Phillips, who founded Sun Records,* was looking for the perfect crossover white band or white performer, Alan Freed,* a disc jockey in Cleveland and later New York City, began experimenting by having black R & B groups perform in front of white audiences. Whites responded well to the performances. Freed also noticed that the record "Shake, Rattle, and Roll" by William (Bill) Haley* and the Comets climbed to the top of the pop music charts when it was released as the theme song for the 1955 film *Blackboard Jungle*.* Freed began playing black R & B music on late night broadcasts primarily to white listeners. Freed called the music rock-and-roll, and characterized it as part country, part R & B, and part performance. Soon Freed's rock-and-roll broadcasts attracted huge audiences, and sponsors bought up the airtime to sell their products.

Until Elvis Presley,* however, rock-and-roll remained confined to isolated music markets in the United States. In 1954 Sam Phillips signed Elvis to a recording contract. Presley's first record, "That's All Right Mama" with "Blue Moon of Kentucky" on the flip side, was released in July 1954 and sold 25,000 copies by the end of the year. Phillips had what he had been searching for—a white man who could sing black R & B music in ways that would appeal to black and white listeners. Over the next year, Presley recorded eight more songs for Phillips and became the most recognizable figure in popular music. When he appeared before a national audience on *The Ed Sullivan Show*,* CBS cameras focused on his torso and head because many considered his hip gyrations obscene. Teenaged and preteen girls, however, screamed their delight.

Elvis Presley was not the only white performer who could perform successfully for a biracial audience. Others who succeeded were Jerry Lee Lewis* from

Memphis, Tennessee; Buddy Holly* from Lubbock, Texas; and Eddie Cochran from Nashville, Tennessee. Along with Elvis Presley, they paved the way for black R & B groups to cross over and succeed with white audiences. By the late 1950s, such African Americans as Chuck Berry,* Little Richard,* Chubby Checker, Wilson Pickett, and Otis Redding had become certifiable national stars in their own right and as popular among whites as they were among blacks.

Rock-and-roll is also credited with saving radio during the 1950s. Because of the advent of television,* Americans abandoned radio programming in droves, and some critics wondered whether radio would survive as a communications medium. When the radio stations began to play rock-and-roll music, however, audiences returned in droves, and the audiences tended to be somewhat younger.

The speed with which rock-and-roll conquered American popular culture caught many Americans off-guard. The music troubled them for many reasons, including its biracial roots, its visceral performances, and its inherent rebelliousness. Critics condemned rock-and-roll for corrupting the morals of America's youth, undermining the school system, and causing juvenile delinquency.* Elvis Presley's gyrations and James Dean's* sullen distance, as well as his rejection of adult values, troubled most parents.

In 1957, disc jockey Dick Clark launched *American Bandstand** on ABC television. It was a daily, after-school broadcast in which local Philadelphia teenagers danced to rock-and-roll music and watched rock-and-roll performers sing. Dick Clark, a wholesome, squeaky-clean host, dressed in a conservative business suit and reassured an older generation that rock-and-roll was not sinister and dangerous but actually good clean fun that could fit comfortably into American middle-class culture.

By the end of the 1950s, after only five years in the national consciousness, rock-and-roll had become a permanent fixture in American popular culture and was set to spread to teenage audiences throughout the world. It had also become a huge business. Within one year of Elvis Presley's performance on *The Ed Sullivan Show*, record sales had jumped from $231 million to $331 million annually; by the end of the decade, they went past $1 billion.

SUGGESTED READINGS: Carl Belz, *The Story of Rock*, 1972; Colin Escott, *Good Rockin' Tonight: Sun Records and the Birth of Rock and Roll*, 1991; Charlie Gillett, *The Sound of the City: The Rise of Rock and Roll*, 1983; Peter Guralnick, *Last Train to Memphis: The Rise of Elvis Presley*, 1994; John A. Jackson, *Big Beat Heat: Alan Freed and the Early Years of Rock 'n' Roll*, 1991; David P. Szatmary, *Rockin' in Time: A Social History of Rock and Roll*, 1991; Ed Ward, *Rock of Ages: The Rolling Stone History of Rock and Roll*, 1987.

RODGERS, RICHARD. Richard Charles Rodgers was born in New York City on June 28, 1902. He attended Columbia University, where he met Oscar Hammerstein II.* They later formed one of the most fertile writing teams in American theater history. Rodgers's talent for composition became evident during his undergraduate days at Columbia, and after graduation, he collaborated with lyricist Lorenz Hart. Together, they produced material for *Poor Little Ritz Girl* (1925), *Dearest Enemy* (1925), *The Girl Friend* (1926), *A Connecticut Yankee* (1927), *Present Arms* (1928), *Spring Is Here* (1929), *Simple Simon* (1930), *Jumbo* (1935), *On Your Toes* (1936), *Babes in Arms* (1937), *I'd Rather Be Right* (1937), *I Married An Angel* (1938), *The Boys from Syracuse* (1938), and *Pal Joey* (1940).

Rodgers then broke up with Hart, and in 1943 he teamed up with Hammerstein, and together they became the most successful team of composers in theater history. They created nine shows, the first of which was *Oklahoma!* (1943). An extraordinary hit that had a run of 2,212 performances on Broadway, *Oklahoma!* featured such popular hits as "Oh, What a Beautiful Morning," "People Will Say We're in Love," and "The Surrey with the Fringe on Top." Two years later, their *Carousel* opened on Broadway and had a run of 890 performances. Among its hit songs were "If I Loved You," "June Is Bustin' Out All Over," "Soliloquy," and "You'll Never Walk Alone." Their last collaboration during the 1940s was *South Pacific* (1949), which had a run of 1,925 consecutive performances. *South Pacific* produced a remarkable number of hit songs, including "Bali Ha'i," "I'm Gonna Wash That Man Right Outa My Hair," "Some Enchanted Evening," "There Is Nothin' Like a Dame," "A Wonderful Guy," and "Younger Than Springtime."

The decade of the 1950s was even more productive. In addition to *Me and Juliet* (1953), *Pipe Dream* (1955), and *Flower Drum Song* (1958), they wrote two of Broadway's greatest hits—*The King and I** (1951) and *The Sound of Music* (1959). The most memorable songs from *The King and I* are "Getting to Know You," "Shall We Dance?", "Hello, Young Lovers," and "I Whistle a Happy Tune." *The Sound of Music* included "Climb Every Mountain," "Do-Re-Mi," "The Sound of Music," and "My Favorite Things." Hammerstein's retirement left Rodgers feeling somewhat adrift, and his subsequent work did not have the success he had earlier enjoyed. Richard Rodgers died in 1979.

SUGGESTED READING: Richard Rodgers, *Musical Stages*, 1975.

ROSENBERG, JULIUS AND ETHYL. During the early 1950s, Julius and Ethyl Rosenberg found themselves in the vortex of the Red Scare* that was sweeping across the United States. In 1950 the quiet, mild-mannered couple lived with their two sons in a small apartment on the Lower East Side of Manhattan in New York City. Julius Rosenberg had been born on May 12, 1918, and his wife, Ethyl Greenglass, on September 28, 1915, both in New York City. Julius had graduated from the City College of New York with a degree in electrical engineering. They married in 1939.

The couple made no secret of their Communist party sympathies and their conviction that Karl Marx's writings would prove correct and bring about proletariat revolutions throughout the developed world. Julius had joined the Young Communist League in 1934, and Ethyl had been active in the International

Seamen's Union, well known for its Marxist sympathies. Such opinions were not uncommon in New York City in the 1940s.

The onset of the Red Scare after World War II elevated the Rosenbergs, who would otherwise have been considered harmless "lefties," to the status of infamous traitors. The Soviet Union's successful detonation of an atomic bomb* in 1949 terrorized millions of Americans, who had thought the United States had a monopoly on nuclear weapons. Many wondered how the Soviets had managed to produce such a weapon so quickly, since the United States had spent billions of dollars and taken several years in the Manhattan Project to do the same. Suspicions that Communist spies had somehow supplied nuclear secrets to the Soviet Union found their way into newspaper headlines.

In 1950 the Federal Bureau of Investigation* identified Julius and Ethyl Rosenberg as those spies. Klaus Fuchs, a German-born physicist who had worked on the Manhattan Project, confessed to FBI leaders that he had spied for the Soviet Union and had supplied them with nuclear secrets. His plea-bargain earned Fuchs a fourteen-year prison sentence, and he implicated chemist Harry Gold as a co-conspirator. In return for a light sentence, Gold implicated David Greenglass, a Manhattan Project machinist who had worked at the Los Alamos, New Mexico, laboratory. In return for a fifteen-year sentence, Greenglass confessed and told the FBI that he had passed atomic secrets to his sister Ethyl Rosenberg and brother-in-law Julius Rosenberg, and that the two of them had passed them on to Soviet contacts in New York. Because of holes in their case, the FBI charged the Rosenbergs with conspiracy to commit espionage rather than treason.

Although the Rosenbergs vehemently proclaimed their innocence, they were indicted and brought to trial late in March 1951. The prosecution employed highly questionable tactics and accused the Rosenbergs of treason even though they were not being tried for that crime. The Rosenbergs insisted on taking the Fifth Amendment when they were asked if they were Communists. The jury convicted them. Judge Irving Kaufman handed down the death penalty, claiming that their crime was "far worse than murder" because "putting into the hands of the Russians the A-bomb has already caused, in my opinion, the Communist aggression in Korea, with the resultant casualties exceeding 50,000 and who knows but what that millions more innocent people may pay the price of your treason."

The Rosenberg case became a cause célèbre in American politics. Conservatives insisted on their guilt and said that the electric chair was too good for them. Liberals claimed that the Rosenbergs were innocent victims of a great American witch-hunt—a malignant crusade that would some day rival in infamy the Saiem witch trials.

As their execution date approached in 1953, a worldwide furor erupted over their death sentences. The couple had two little boys to raise, and the case against them was considered weak by most legal analysts. The Rosenbergs appealed their conviction to the U.S. Supreme Court, but by a 6–3 vote, the justices upheld the guilty verdict and the sentence. On June 19, 1953, the Rosenbergs were strapped into the electric chair at New York's Sing Sing prison and executed. Conservatives hailed the execution, arguing that the Rosenbergs got exactly what they deserved, while liberals tried to make them martyrs of the Red Scare.

SUGGESTED READINGS: Alvin H. Goldstein, *The Unquiet Death of Julius and Ethyl Rosenberg*, 1975; *New York Times*, June 18–25, 1953; Ronald Radosh and Joyce Milton, *The Rosenberg File: The Search for the Truth*, 1983; Joseph F. Sharlitt, *Fatal Error: The Miscarriage of Justice That Sealed the Rosenbergs' Fate*, 1989.

ROTH V. UNITED STATES (1957). In the case of *Roth v. United States* in 1957, the U.S. Supreme Court under Chief Justice Earl Warren* reached a major decision on the issue of censorship. The federal government had prosecuted Samuel Roth, who owned a pornographic bookstore. Roth claimed that his Fifth and Fourteenth Amendment rights to due process had been violated, and that his First Amendment right to freedom of expression had been denied. He filed the *Roth v. United States* lawsuit.

The Supreme Court used the case to establish new standards on obscenity and censorship. Justice William Brennan* wrote the majority opinion, which upheld the right of the government to outlaw obscene materials. He wrote, "All ideas having even the slightest redeeming social importance . . . have the full protection of the guarantees of the First Amendment . . . but implicit in the history of the First Amendment is the rejection of obscenity as utterly without redeeming social importance." That was the easy part. Brennan then had to define obscenity. In doing do, he came up with the following statement, which continues to drive federal law today: "Whether to the average person, applying contemporary community standards, the dominant theme of the material taken as a whole appeals to prurient interests." The definition, of course, satisfied few people, since it was so open to interpretation, but it remains today the guiding legal force in censorship controversies.

SUGGESTED READING: 354 U.S. 476 (1957).

THE ROY ROGERS SHOW. *The Roy Rogers Show* premiered on the Mutual Radio Network on November 21, 1944, and then switched to NBC in 1946. It starred Roy Rogers, the singing cowboy who was a veteran of dozens of B Western films during the 1930s and early 1940s. He had a palomino horse named Trigger, his dog Bullitt, a sidekick Brady played by veteran actor Gabby Hayes, and his wife Dale Evans. Each week Rogers foiled robbers, rescued damsels, and sang a few songs. Audiences were overwhelmingly adolescent boys, and in the 1950s the program could not survive television.* NBC canceled the series in 1955. By that time, Rogers had a weekly Saturday morning television show of the same name.

SUGGESTED READINGS: John Dunning, *On the Air: The Encyclopedia of Old-Time Radio*, 1998; Roy Rogers, *Happy Trails: Our Life Story*, 1994.

RUSSELL, WILLIAM (BILL). William "Bill" Russell was born in Monroe, Louisiana, on February 12, 1934. He attended the University of San Francisco on a basketball scholarship and led the team to two NCAA championships (1955 and 1956). They suffered only one loss during that streak. At 6 feet 10 inches, Russell played center and virtually dominated the inside game. Because of Russell's unrivaled skills as a rebounder, the NCAA decided to widen the foul lane from 6 feet to 12 feet. The change was made after his sophomore year, but it did little to inhibit Russell's game. In 1956 Russell led the U.S. Olympic team to a gold medal at the Melbourne Olympic Games.*

After graduating from USF, Russell signed with the Boston Celtics* of the National Basketball Association (NBA). He won the NBA's Most Valuable Player award in 1958, and during Russell's thirteen seasons with the Celtics, he led them to eleven NBA championships. An intelligent, articulate, well-educated man, Russell also spoke openly about racism in professional sports. That became especially apparent in 1958 when Russell won the MVP award. White sportswriters did not select him to the All-NBA team. He also complained about racism in the city of Boston. Eventually, however, Russell earned the respect and then the admiration of Boston fans. They could not deny his talent, and his outspoken courage became a point of admiration. After his retirement in 1961, Russell spent his time in a number of business ventures and as a broadcaster for professional basketball.

SUGGESTED READINGS: Bill Russell, *Second Wind: The Memoirs of an Opinionated Man*, 1979; Mike Shapiro, *Bill Russell*, 1991.

RYDELL, BOBBY. Bobby Rydell was born Robert Ridarelli in Philadelphia, Pennsylvania, on April 26, 1942. Along with Frankie Avalon,* Pat Boone,* and Fabian,* Bobby Rydell became one of rock-and-roll's* clean-cut white entertainers. A talented musician, he sang and played the drums. In 1951 he began performing on *Teen Club*, a local Philadelphia television show. In 1959 Rydell's "Kissin' Time" reached number eleven on the pop music charts, and during the next four years he had a number of other top hits, including "Volare," "Sway," "Swingin' School," "Wild One," and "Forget Him." Rydell starred in the film *Bye Bye Birdie* in 1961, but his career then plummeted and did not survive the advent of the Beatles. Rydell continues to perform today on the resort club circuit, with Fabian and Frankie Avalon, as one of the "Golden Voices."

SUGGESTED READING: Patricia Romanowski and Holly George-Warren, *The Encyclopedia of Rock & Roll*, 1995.

S

SABIN VACCINE. During the 1950s, the most feared disease was polio,* which had reached epidemic proportions. Polio was caused by three viruses that entered the body through the mouth. When the virus made its way into the central nervous system and from there into the brain stem and spinal cord of a victim, it brought about paralysis and sometimes death. Jonas Salk, director of the Virus Research Laboratory at the University of Pittsburgh, first developed a vaccine, which went into clinical trials in 1954 (*see* Salk Vaccine). He took live polio virus, killed it with formaldehyde, and then manufactured a vaccine. When injected into human beings, the dead virus triggered an immune response, and the body manufactured antibodies that warded off live polio viruses. The short-comings of the Salk vaccine involved the fact that it had to be delivered in three separate vaccinations and followed up thirty months later by a booster vacci-nation. Also, dozens of children receiving the Salk vaccine actually came down with polio because the virus ingested had not been completely killed by the formaldehyde. Other researchers were pursuing a superior vaccination.

Albert Sabin, a virologist at the University of Cincinnati, was the first scientist to generate a better vaccine to fight polio. Sabin cultivated the three virus strains in monkey kidney tissues, then weakened the virus by allowing it to infect research animals. He then recultivated the virus strains and developed them into a solution that could be administered orally. When the U.S. government refused to begin clinical trials, Sabin went to the Soviet Union, where he administered the vaccine to millions of children in 1957 and 1958. The vaccine proved to be a great success, and its advantages were obvious. It did not require multiple injections, and recipients were not at risk of receiving a full-fledged, living polio virus. In 1961, the U.S. Public Health Service licensed the Sabin vaccine for use in the United States.

SUGGESTED READINGS: Alton L. Blakeslee, *Polio and the Salk Vaccine: What*

You Should Know About It, 1956; Richard Carter, *Breakthrough: The Saga of Jonas Salk,* 1967.

SAINT LAWRENCE SEAWAY. From the fifteenth to the eighteenth centuries, adventurous European explorers engaged in a quest for the maritime holy grail—the elusive Northwest Passage, a rumored water passage in North America linking the Atlantic and Pacific oceans. The Northwest Passage, of course, did not exist, but in 1959, after a gargantuan engineering project undertaken by the United States and Canada, a northwest passage reached nearly halfway to the Pacific.

As early as 1896, the United States, Great Britain, and Canada began discussing the possibility of making the Saint Lawrence River navigable all the way from the Atlantic to the Great Lakes. Opposition to the idea quickly came from railroads and Atlantic seaports, which feared losing commercial traffic once the seaway opened. In 1932 the participating countries signed a treaty providing for the construction of the seaway, but world politics and World War II stalled it. In May 1954 Congress passed the Wiley-Donder Act, which authorized the U.S. government to enter into a cooperative agreement with Canada to construct a 27-foot deep canal connecting Montreal and Lake Ontario. Construction actually began late in 1954 when nearly 59,000 laborers went to work.

Subsequent legislation extended the construction project. The workforce spent nearly six years on the project. They dug canals, dredged river bottoms, and constructed dams, dikes, and levees along 2,300 miles of waterway. In June 1959 Queen Elizabeth II of Great Britain and President Dwight D. Eisenhower* dedicated the Saint Lawrence Seaway. Products built or harvested from the American interior could now be shipped by sea anywhere in the world. The queen hailed it as "one of the outstanding engineering accomplishments of modern times," but it was also an infrastructural improvement of momentous proportions. Commercial traffic exploded all along the waterway, as did the growth of cities and towns along the way.

SUGGESTED READING: Jacques LesStrang, *Seaway: The Untold Story of North America's Fourth Seacoast,* 1976.

SALK VACCINE. During the twentieth century, one of the most feared diseases was infantile paralysis, or polio.* Polio, a viral disease, is highly contagious, and children have been its primary victims. By making its way into the central nervous system and then into the brain stem or spinal cord, the virus can cause paralysis, muscle atrophy, and sometimes death. It is fatal if it strikes the chest muscles, making it impossible for victims to breath on their own. It became a high-profile disease in the 1930s because President Franklin D. Roosevelt had contracted it in 1921, confining him to a wheelchair for the rest of his life. It reached epidemic proportions in the 1950s, with 58,000 cases in the United States in 1952.

In 1947 Jonas Salk, a young virologist, began working on a vaccine under funding provided by the National Foundation for Infantile Paralysis. He had already helped develop a vaccine for one strain of influenza, in which an altered living strain of the virus was injected into a healthy person. The individual came down with a mild case of the disease and soon recovered, but the body developed immunities that prevented the patient from ever getting the disease again.

Salk was not comfortable with that approach for a polio vaccine because the disease was so unpredictable. Instead, he based his vaccine on a killed virus, hoping the body's immune system would recognize the virus as an alien invader and develop antibodies for it, without the patient ever actually getting sick. Salk took live polio virus and then killed it with formaldehyde. From the dead virus, he made a vaccine. He also decided to become the first guinea pig and injected himself with the vaccine. "I look upon it as ritual and symbolic. You wouldn't do unto others that which you wouldn't do unto yourself." As he perfected the vaccine, he learned that it needed to be administered in three shots, with a booster vaccination delivered thirty months after the initial shots. Large-scale clinical trials began in 1954, when more than 440,000 children participated in the study.

In 1955 the U.S. government announced that the clinical trials had demonstrated the effectiveness of the Salk vaccine. A nationwide inoculation program began, and Americans lined up by the millions to get the injection. Salk's success greatly enhanced the reputation of scientists in the United States.

SUGGESTED READINGS: Alton L. Blakeslee, *Polio and the Salk Vaccine*: *What You Should Know About It*, 1956; Richard Carter, *Breakthrough*: *The Saga of Jonas Salk*, 1967.

SAMUEL SHEPPARD TRIAL. The Samuel Sheppard trial was one of the most sensational judicial proceedings of the 1950s. Sheppard, a prominent Cleveland osteopath, was charged with the murder of his pregnant wife, Marilyn. On the evening of July 3, 1954, the Sheppards entertained friends at their home on the shore of Lake Erie. Sheppard fell asleep on the couch while the others watched television,* and the guests left around midnight. Marilyn Sheppard went to bed. Several hours later, Shepphard awoke to screams upstairs. He said that he went into the bedroom, saw a "white figure," and then blacked out. He woke up some time later to find his wife bludgeoned to death in her bed.

When news that Sheppard was having an extramarital affair came to light, the Cleveland press, in front page headlines, all but convicted Sheppard of the murder, even though no direct evidence linked Sheppard to the crime. New York gossip columnist Walter Winchell made the most of the case too, and soon most Americans believed that Sheppard was guilty. A politically ambitious judge allowed celebrity journalists from all over the country into the courtroom, and he told Dorothy Kilgallen, a New York columnist, that Sheppard was "guilty as hell." The jury convicted Sheppard of murder and sentenced him to life in prison.

Sheppard was incarcerated until 1964, when F. Lee Bailey, a young attorney, learned of the judge's comment to Kilgallen. He appealed Sheppard's conviction on the grounds of judicial misconduct and prejudice. In 1965 the U.S. Supreme Court set aside the conviction, and in a new trial, Sheppard was acquitted. He died in 1970. His son pursued the case, however, until in 1996 he secured a confession from the real killer, a man who was serving a life sentence for another killing.

SUGGESTED READINGS: F. Lee Bailey, with Harvey Aronson, *The Defense Never Rests*, 1971; Paul Holmes, *The Sheppard Murder Case*, 1961;

SANGER, MARGARET. Margaret Sanger was born Margaret Higgins on September 14, 1879, in Corning, New York. She was the sixth of eleven children. Her parents encouraged her to develop her mind and her talents, and when she was in the eighth grade, they enrolled her in the Hudson River Institute, a private school north of New York City. As an adolescent, she decided that women needed to be able to control the process of reproduction; otherwise, they were destined to lives of pregnancy, child rearing, and poor health, and the world, without birth control, would suffer from overpopulation with all of its consequences—poverty, misery, and war. Margaret also decided that her own mother's poor health was the result of having borne eleven children. After nursing her mother through a terminal case of tuberculosis, Margaret decided to become a nurse.

She met and married William Sanger, an architect, and they had three children. The three children, which arrived in rapid succession, created health problems for Sanger, and she became even more determined to help women gain control over the process of reproduction. As a nurse, Sanger often worked as a midwife, and more times than she could count, her patients asked her how they might postpone or avoid another pregnancy. Sanger decided that women were in desperate need of information about contraception.

In the early decades of the twentieth century, however, Sanger encountered a phalanx of opposition to birth control. The Comstock Act made the distribution of birth control information across state lines a federal offense, and the Roman Catholic Church lobbied state legislatures to outlaw such activities at the state level and prohibit the manufacture and sale of birth control devices. Sanger launched a one-woman crusade against these laws, speaking widely throughout the country, staging protest demonstrations, and on more than one occasion being jailed for her activities. She coined the term "birth control" and founded the Birth Control League to promote the dissemination of birth control devices and reliable information about contraception.

By the 1950s, Sanger's crusade for birth control education and the availability of birth control devices through her Birth Control League had resulted in the establishment of the International Planned Parenthood Federation, which was formally organized in 1952. She also played a key role in the development of the birth control pill.* In 1950 she met Dr. Gregory Pincus who, with an associate, had developed a pill that could disrupt the normal production cycles of estrogen and progesterone in a woman's body, which would either prevent her from ovulating or prevent a fertilized egg from planting itself in the lining of the uterus. Sanger immediately realized the potential of the discovery, and she approached Katherine McCormick, her friend and heir to the McCormick farm machinery fortune, for financial assistance. McCormick supplied $2 million to finance more research. The research yielded synthetic hormones, which had the potential of being included in a pill, to be taken in daily doses by women wishing to avoid pregnancy. The oral contraceptive was safe, simple, and convenient, and it revolutionized the lives of women around the world.

By the early 1960s, Margaret Sanger was widely recognized as the key figure in improving the lives of women in the twentieth century. In her lifetime, she had changed the climate in which Americans viewed sexuality and reproduction, not only coining the term "birth control" but rescuing it from its illegal, sleazy status and making it a useful, respectable way for women to control their bodies and their lives. Margaret Sanger died on September 6, 1966.

SUGGESTED READINGS: Virginia Coigney, *Margaret Sanger: Rebel with a Cause*, 1969; Madeline Gray, *Margaret Sanger: A Biography of the Champion of Birth Control*, 1978; David Kennedy, *Birth Control in America: The Career of Margaret Sanger*, 1970.

SARNOFF, DAVID. David Sarnoff was born in Minsk, Russia, on April 14, 1892. His family immigrated to New York City in 1900, and Sarnoff was raised on the Lower East Side of Manhattan. When he was just sixteen, he got a job as a telegrapher for American Marconi Company, a wireless telegraph operation. In April 1912, when the SS *Titanic* sank, Sarnoff stayed at his post for three straight days, broadcasting the names of survivors and the dead as the information became available. When American Marconi merged with several other wireless companies in 1919 to form the Radio Corporation of America (RCA), Sarnoff became one of the new company's most promising young executives.

Sarnoff quickly pushed the company away from transoceanic communication to commercial radio broadcasting, and he found himself on the ground floor of a booming industry. In 1926 RCA formed the National Broadcasting Company (NBC) to manage its radio business. By the time NBC named Sarnoff its president in 1930, the company was broadcasting radio programs nationwide. He soon pushed RCA into the film and phonograph industries.

Sarnoff was the first at NBC to see the potential of television.* In 1946 RCA began manufacturing television sets, and Sarnoff began manufacturing television programming at NBC. He was also a pioneer in color television. In 1953 NBC began broadcasting regular color television programming. In the beginning, the programming was limited to two hours a day. The technology was slow to catch on because color television sets were very expensive, well out of the range—at from $500 to $1,000 each—of most households, and the technology was still quite crude in the early 1950s. Viewers had to adjust the dials constantly because the image often bled and warped. Color television in the 1950s was a virtual monopoly of NBC because the network was owned by RCA, which manufactured all color picture tubes. Color television did not really catch on in the United States until the 1960s. Sarnoff retired in 1970 and died on December 12, 1971.

SUGGESTED READINGS: Kenneth W. Bilby, *The General: David Sarnoff and the Rise of the Communications Industry*, 1986; *New York Times*, December 13, 1971.

SCIENTOLOGY, CHURCH OF. In 1950 L. Ron Hubbard, a Los Angeles–based science fiction writer, published his book *Dianetics: The Modern Science of Mental Health*, which became the sacred text of his Church of Scientology. In a search for meaning to his own life, Hubbard had engaged in a long study of religious and philosophical literature but had never been able to find answers to life's greatest questions. "I found, oddly enough, that nobody could tell me what man was." In what was later described as a religious epiphany, Hubbard came to believe that the human originated from a small group of space beings banished to Earth long ago by a stellar dictator. Hubbard also claimed to have the answer for the angst of modern society. He offered psychic healing through electronics and technology. Dianetics cleansed people of emotional imbalances by "auditing" them, which involved connecting them to lie detectors, which could purge their bodies and minds of emotionally disturbing "engrams." Hubbard's new religion proved threatening to many mainstream denominations, which attacked his theology as modern-day mumbo-jumbo and accused him of profiting from the religion. In 1967 the Internal Revenue Service robbed Scientology of its tax-exempt status, which the church did not regain until 1993.

SUGGESTED READING: Brent Corydon, *L. Ron Hubbard: Messiah or Madman*, 1992.

SEA HUNT. Sea Hunt, starring Lloyd Bridges as Nelson, was one of the most popular syndicated shows in television* history. The show was based on the exploits of Nelson, a former U.S. Navy frogman now working as an underwater investigator for insurance companies, police forces, shipping companies, and the military to solve problems involving underwater searches and rescues. The show was shot on location in the Gulf of Mexico, the Pacific, and the Caribbean—wherever the water was warm—and more than half of each episode consisted of underwater scenes. For a 1950s adventure series, *Sea Hunt* had a realism that no other program approached. The first episode of *Sea Hunt* appeared in January 1958, and a total of 156 episodes were eventually produced. *Sea Hunt* went into reruns in 1961 and remained quite popular in that format throughout the 1960s.

SUGGESTED READING: Tim Brooks and Earle Marsh, *The Complete Directory to Prime Time Network and Cable TV Shows*, 1946–Present, 1995.

SEEGER, PETE. Pete Seeger was born in New York City on May 3, 1919. He was raised in a family committed to art and politics and to the importance of fusing them whenever possible. Seeger's father was a gifted musician and a dedicated pacifist. By the time Seeger entered Harvard in 1936, he already nurtured intense, left-wing political views. He found Harvard musically stultifying, however, and in 1938 Seeger dropped out and went to work for the Archives of American Folk Music in New York City. His experiences there left him with a deep and abiding interest in folk music that has remained with him throughout his life. In New York, he became close to legendary folk singer Woodie Guthrie, and together they formed the Almanac Singers.

When World War II erupted, Seeger joined the U.S. Army, but to prove his own political independence, on the same day he also joined the Communist party. Throughout the rest of the 1940s, Seeger composed and performed folk songs that supported the labor movement and the needs of the poor. In the late 1940s, Seeger formed the folk group the Weavers and recorded the hits "Goodnight Irene" and "If I Had a Hammer." By that time he had grown disillusioned with the Communist party and its capricious ideological machinations. In 1948 he quit the party.

In the intense political atmosphere of the Cold War* and the Red Scare,* Seeger was labeled a dangerous radical. J. Edgar Hoover* and the Federal Bureau of Investigation* made him a target for ongoing investigations, and recording contracts and concert bookings were difficult to come by. Seeger supported himself with steady bookings on the college concert circuit, where his left-wing views had built-in audiences. In 1955 he was subpeonaed by the House Un-American Activities Committee (HUAC), but he refused to testify and refused to invoke his Fifth Amendment protection against self-incrimination. He argued that the very existence of the HUAC violated his First Amendment rights. He was indicted for contempt of Congress in 1956, the same year his popular song "Where Have All the Flowers Gone" was released. Seeger fought the contempt citation for five years, but in 1961 he was convicted of contempt of Congress and sentenced to ten years in prison. He never served a day, however, because an appellate court overturned the conviction.

During the 1960s, Seeger was active in the civil rights movement* and the antiwar movement and became the unofficial balladeer of both crusades. His version of "We Shall Overcome" became the theme song of the civil rights movement. In 1966, on *The Smothers Brothers Comedy Hour*, he sang "Waist Deep in the Big Muddy," an antiwar song that CBS censors edited from the program. At the insistence of the Smothers brothers, Seeger was invited back to sing it again, which he did, but CBS soon canceled the program. Since then, Seeger has turned his attention to environmental concerns, crusading against a consumer culture that standardizes American life and causes so much environmental damage.

SUGGESTED READING: David King Dunaway, *How Can I Keep from Singing*: *Pete Seeger*, 1983.

SERVICE V. DULLES (1957). On June 17, 1957, a day conservatives and anticommunists labeled "Red Monday,"* the U.S. Supreme Court handed down a number of important decisions concerning civil liberties, in particular the extent to which an individual could be punished for maintaining radical or revolutionary political views. *Service v. Dulles* was one of those cases. William Service had been fired from his job in the State Department because several of his superiors considered his political opinions dangerously "liberal." The State Department's Internal Loyalty Board investigated the allegations and concluded that Service was not a security risk. Secretary of State John Foster Dulles,* worried about the Red Scare* of the early 1950s and wary of being targeted for political criticism, dismissed Service anyway.

Service filed a civil rights lawsuit, claiming that Dulles and the State Department had violated his constitutional right to free speech. On Red Monday, the U.S. Supreme Court agreed with Service. His firing had been arbitrary and the State Department had contradicted its own regulations, thereby depriving Service of due process. Civil libertarians considered the decision an enormous victory, and anticommunists roundly condemned it.

SUGGESTED READINGS: Richard G. Powers, *Secrecy and Power: The Life of J. Edgar Hoover*, 1987; Stanford J. Unger, *The FBI*, 1976.

SEUSS, DR. *See* THE CAT IN THE HAT.

THE SEVEN YEAR ITCH. *The Seven Year Itch*, a three-act comedy written by George Axelrod, premiered on November 20, 1952, at the Fulton Theater in New York City. The play featured Tom Ewell as Richard Sherman, a paperback book publisher whose runaway imagination lands him in trouble one summer when his wife and family leave town on vacation. Dreams of infidelity almost become reality when a flower pot from the balcony above his apartment almost hits him on the head. The young woman (Vanessa Brown) who occupies the apartment dropped the flower pot intentionally as an excuse to meet Sherman. Her intentions are obvious, and Sherman conducts a mental debate between his libido and his moral code. In the end, he remains loyal to his wife. *The Seven Year Itch* enjoyed a run of 1,141 performances and was later made into a film starring Marilyn Monroe and Tom Ewell.

SUGGESTED READINGS: Gerald Bordman, *The Oxford Companion to American Theater*, 1992; *New York Times*, November 21, 1952.

SHEEN, FULTON J(OHN). Fulton J. Sheen was born on May 8, 1895, in El Paso, Texas. He attended St. Paul's Seminary in Minneapolis, Minnesota, and was ordained a Roman Catholic priest in 1919. He then did graduate work at the Catholic University of America in Washington, D.C., and the Catholic University of Louvain, Belgium. He also studied at the Sorbonne in Paris as well as the Angelicum and Gregorian in Rome. After a stint as a parish priest in Peoria, Illinois, Sheen joined the faculty of the Catholic University of America. His first book, *God and Intelligence in Modern Philosophy*, was published in

1925, and he followed it up with 65 more books. His last book, *Treasure in Clay*, was published posthumously in 1980.

Although Sheen continued to write and publish widely, his fame was not to come as an academic. In 1930 he launched the *Catholic Hour* on NBC radio, and the program made him the most well-known Roman Catholic in the United States. In 1950 he became the national director of the Society for the Propagation of the Faith. Sheen's radio program became a television program in 1952, and from then until 1968 he appeared on weekly television,* primarily ABC's prime-time *Life Is Worth Living* and then *The Bishop Fulton Sheen Program*. On screen, Sheen served up common sense homilies and a conservative, anticommunist commentary on world affairs. In addition to becoming a television personality, Sheen served as the auxiliary bishop of New York City from 1951 to 1966, when he was appointed bishop of Rochester, New York. He retired from the diocese in 1969 and died on December 9, 1979.

SUGGESTED READINGS: D. P. Noonan, *Missionary with a Mike: The Bishop Sheen Story*, 1968, and *The Passion of Fulton Sheen*, 1972.

SHEPPARD, SAMUEL. *See* SAMUEL SHEPPARD TRIAL.

THE SHIRELLES. Formed in Passaic, New Jersey, in 1958, the Shirelles was one of early rock-and-roll's* so-called girl groups. The group consisted of Shirley Alston as lead vocalist, Addie Harris, Doris Kenner, and Beverly Lee. They wrote their own songs, and their first hit, "I Met Him on a Sunday," was released early in 1958. Subsequent Shirelle hits included "Dedicated to the One I Love" (1959), "Tonight's the Night" (1960), "Will You Love Me Tomorrow" (1961), "Mama Said" (1961), "Baby It's You" (1962), "Soldier Boy" (1962), and "Foolish Little Girl" (1963). After "Foolish Little Girl," the Shirelles went into a decline and broke up in the late 1960s.

SUGGESTED READING: Patricia Romanowski and Holly George-Warren, *The Encyclopedia of Rock & Roll*, 1995.

SINATRA, FRANK. Frank Sinatra was born Francis Albert Sinatra on December 12, 1915, in Hoboken, New Jersey. Blessed with a rich baritone voice and influenced by the work of Tommy Dorsey, Bing Crosby, Cole Porter, Irving Berlin, and Jerome Kern, Sinatra became America's most memorable popular singer in the twentieth century, a performer whose phrasing abilities were legendary and who could improvise with the skill of a jazz artist. He also projected an image of cool toughness and romantic innocence that audiences found irresistible. In 1937, with a group known as the Hoboken Four, Sinatra won an award on the *Major Bowes Original Amateur Hour*, and in 1939 he signed a contract with Harry James to become the lead vocalist in his orchestra. In 1940 Sinatra joined Tommy Dorsey's band. In 1943 Sinatra's song "All or Nothing at All" hit number two on the pop music charts and made Sinatra a star. During the next three years, he had seventeen top-ten hits.

After World War II, however, his career plummeted. Sales slumped and Columbia Records terminated his contract. Sinatra all but begged for a part in the film *From Here to Eternity*, and he got the role of Maggio and won an Oscar in 1953 for his performance. Capitol Records then signed him to a recording contract, and Sinatra's career took off again. Nelson Riddle began arranging for him, and Sinatra focused on ballads and swing tunes. He had a number of top-ten hits, including "Young at Heart" (1954), "Learnin' the Blues" (1955), "Hey! Jealous Lover" (1956), "All the Way" (1957), and "Witchcraft" (1958). He also appeared in several films and won critical acclaim for his performance as a heroin addict in *The Man with the Golden Arm* (1955). Although the advent of rock-and-roll* drove Sinatra from the top of the pop music business, he nevertheless remained an icon, known to millions of Americans as "The Voice" or "The Sultan of Swoon" or "The Chairman of the Board." Frank Sinatra died on May 14, 1998.

SUGGESTED READINGS: Michael Freedland, *All the Way: A Biography of Frank Sinatra*, 1997; John Lahr, *Sinatra: The Life and the Man*, 1994; *New York Times*, May 15–16, 1998.

SINGIN' IN THE RAIN. *Singin' in the Rain* is the title of the hit film musical of 1952. With Gene Kelly in the lead role, the film is set in Hollywood at the beginning of the sound era in the 1920s. Film historians consider *Singin' in the Rain* an important film in cinema history for two reasons. First, Gene Kelly's dance in the title tune—an extraordinary performance of rhythm and athleticism—became one of the most enduring images on film. Second, *Singin' in the Rain* proved to be the highwater market of the Hollywood musical, whose lavish productions had been a staple of the industry since Al Jolson first broke the sound barrier in the 1920s. Never again would musicals enjoy such elan and popularity.

SUGGESTED READING: Clive Hirschborn, *Gene Kelly: A Biography*, 1985.

***SLOCHOWER V. BOARD OF EDUCATION OF NEW YORK* (1956).** Harry Slochower, a tenured professor at Brooklyn College, invoked his Fifth Amendment right against self-incrimination when he testified before the Senate Subcommittee on Internal Security. The Senate was investigating subversive activities in higher education. The New York municipal charter forbade the invocation of the Fifth Amendment during investigations of official misconduct, and the board of education fired him. Slochower sued, claiming that his Fifth Amendment rights had been violated. The U.S. Supreme Court decided the case on April 9, 1956. By a narrow 5 to 4 margin, the Court agreed with Slochower and declared the relevant provision in the municipal charter to be unconstitutional.

SUGGESTED READING: 350 U.S. 551 (1956).

SMITH ACT OF 1950. In 1950, in the midst of Senator Joseph McCarthy's* scandalous charges and Congressman Richard M. Nixon's* allegations against

Alger Hiss,* the United States descended into a Red Scare* era, in which fear of domestic Communists reached epidemic, and paranoid, proportions. Congress responded to the fears by passing the Smith Act, which made it a federal offense to advocate the overthrow of the U.S. government or to form organizations dedicated to such an event. Civil libertarians were outraged and accused Congress of trampling the First Amendment to the Constitution, but in 1951, in the case of *Dennis v. United States*,* the U.S. Supreme Court upheld the constitutionality of the law.

Within a few years, however, the political climate had changed. The Red Scare had subsided considerably, and the Supreme Court, under the leadership of Chief Justice Earl Warren,* had become substantially more liberal. On what conservatives labeled "Red Monday"*—June 17, 1957—the U.S. Supreme Court imposed restrictions on the Smith Act. In the case of *Yates v. United States*,* the Court overturned a conviction under the Smith Act, arguing that merely talking about the overthrow of the U.S. government—without actively taking steps to implement such an overthrow—was protected by the First Amendment to the Constitution. Civil libertarians hailed the decision; conservatives and anticommunists just as passionately condemned it.

SUGGESTED READINGS: Richard Gird Powers, *Secrecy and Power: The Life of J. Edgar Hoover*, 1987; Athan Theoharis, *Spying on Americans: Political Surveillance from Hoover to the Huston Plan*, 1978.

SOUTH PACIFIC. *South Pacific* was one of the most popular Broadway musicals of the 1950s. A product of the fertile collaboration of Richard Rodgers* and Oscar Hammerstein II,* *South Pacific* opened at the Majestic Theater in New York City on April 7, 1949. Mary Martin played Nellie Forbush, a U.S. Navy nurse serving in the Pacific during World War II. A number of American servicemen stationed there are interested in Nellie, but she falls for the rich French planter Emile de Becque (Ezio Pinza), even though he has fathered some Eurasian children on the island. The play deals carefully with the theme of interracial marriage, something that seems almost quaint today but which had real immediacy in the early 1950s. Among *South Pacific*'s most memorable songs are "Some Enchanted Evening," "There Is Nothin' Like a Dame," "Bali Ha'i," "I'm Gonna Wash That Man Right Outa My Hair," and "A Wonderful Guy." *South Pacific* had a run of 1,925 consecutive performances.

SUGGESTED READINGS: Gerald Bordman, *The Oxford Companion to American Theater*, 1992; *New York Times*, April 8, 1949.

SPACE PATROL. *Space Patrol*, a popular radio series of the early 1950s, which targeted adolescent audiences, premiered on ABC radio on September 18, 1950. It related the interplanetary exploits of Commander Buzz Cory, a space gunfighter fighting desperadoes on the galactic frontiers. The series survived until March 19, 1955.

SUGGESTED READING: John Dunning, *On the Air: The Encyclopedia of Old-Time Radio*, 1998.

SPACE RACE. During the late 1950s, the competition between the Soviet Union and the United States to place artificial satellites, and eventually astronauts, into orbit around the earth reached unprecedented levels. The so-called space race became a symbol of the Cold War,* a way of measuring the superiority of the capitalist and Communist ways of life. During the 1950s, at least, the Soviets won the race. When the Soviet Union launched the satellite *Sputnik*,* on October 4, 1957, Americans underwent a technological identity crisis. The Cold War rivalry was at its peak, and both sides were committed to demonstrating the superiority of their political and economic systems. Beating the United States into space was a public relations coup for the Soviet Union, and the Russians celebrated wildly and advertised their success to the world.

In a desperate effort to close the gap between American and Soviet rocket technology, Congress in 1958 established the National Aeronautic and Space Administration (NASA) as an umbrella agency for a variety of military space programs. At first, the U.S. space program fell flat on its face. While the Soviet Union was putting increasingly heavy payloads into earth orbit, demonstrating the overwhelming superiority of its rocket thrusters, NASA presided over a series of dismal failures, most of them broadcast over national television. While Soviet rockets apparently functioned flawlessly, American rockets underwent a series of spectacular failures, blowing up on the launch pads or veering out of control like a child's Roman candle on the Fourth of July.

American credibility in space did not begin to improve until 1959, when *Vanguard* rocket launches became consistently successful. On April 10, 1959, NASA introduced the first American astronauts to the public. Project Mercury, in which an American astronaut would be squeezed into a tiny capsule and launched into space, was designed to push the United States ahead of the Soviet space program. The first seven men selected were military test pilots: John Glenn, Alan Shepard, Virgil Grissom, Wally Schirra, Donald Slayton, Gordon Cooper, and Scott Carpenter. In 1961, however, the Soviet Union put Cosmonaut Yuri Gagarin in a space capsule, fired him into earth orbit, and brought him back home alive. The U.S. space program was still behind the Soviet program.

SUGGESTED READING: Barbara Clowse, *Brainpower for the Cold War: The Sputnik Crisis and the National Defense Education Act of 1958*, 1981.

SPELLMAN, FRANCIS JOSEPH CARDINAL. Francis Joseph Spellman was born in Whitman, Massachusetts, on May 4, 1889. As a boy he decided to become a Roman Catholic priest, and he graduated from Fordham College in 1911. He was ordained in Rome in 1916 and then assigned to All Saints Parish in Roxbury, Massachusetts. Two years later, he joined the editorial staff of the *Boston Pilot*, a Roman Catholic newspaper. That job exposed his talents to the church hierarchy in Boston, and in 1922 Spellman became an assistant chancellor in the archdiocese. Between 1925 and 1932, Spellman served in the Vatican as a translator and interpreter. He was ordained a bishop in 1932 and assigned as an auxiliary bishop in Boston as well as pastor of the Sacred Heart Parish at Newton Center, Massachusetts. In 1939 Spellman was named archbishop of New York, a post that made him one of the most powerful Catholics in the United States. That status increased in 1946 when he was created cardinal.

Spellman was a fearless promoter of church causes, so much so that his political enemies labeled him "the American Pope" and referred to his Fifth Avenue home in New York City as "the Powerhouse." He openly advocated U.S. diplomatic relations with the Vatican, although most Protestants opposed the move. Spellman was also carefully wired into the Democratic party establishment, primarily because so many Irish, Polish, and Puerto Rican families were Catholics and Democrats. He was an outspoken opponent of fascism and communism, a gifted administrator, and one of the most prominent Catholics of his time. He died on December 2, 1967.

SUGGESTED READINGS: John Cooney, *The American Pope: The Life and Times of Francis Cardinal Spellman*, 1984; Robert I. Gannon, *The Cardinal Spellman Story*, 1962.

SPOCK, BENJAMIN. Benjamin McLane Spock was born on May 2, 1903, in New Haven, Connecticut. In 1929 he graduated from Yale, and four years later he received a medical degree from Columbia. Spock then specialized in pediatrics and psychiatry, and in combining those two disciplines he would become one of the most influential men in the social history of the 1950s. While on duty in the U.S. Navy during World War II, Spock wrote *The Common Sense Book of Baby and Child Care*. A best-seller soon after its publication in 1946, it became the most successful book in publishing history, appearing just when the baby boom* generation was being born. Spock offered mothers revolutionary advice on child raising. Until Spock appeared on the scene, physicians had advised mothers to raise infants on firm, strict schedules, feeding them well-defined diets and making them sleep, play, and eat at specific times. Parents were not to indulge children who wanted to break these schedules. Spock gave completely different advice. He helped mothers realize that each child was unique, that each parent was unique, and that no single, fixed schedule would work for everybody. No set of firm rules could be applied to all babies. During the late 1940s and 1950s, *The Common Sense Book of Baby and Child Care* sold millions of copies, making Spock the most powerful voice on child care in the world.

During the 1960s, Spock became active in the politics of protest. He opposed the testing of nuclear weapons because of radioactive contamination, and from 1963 to 1967 Spock headed the National Committee for a Sane Nuclear Policy.* As the Vietnam War* escalated after 1965, Spock bitterly denounced America's role in it and engaged in acts of civil disobedience to protest the war and urged young men not to register for selective service and not to report for draft physicals. He ran for president in 1972 on the People's party ticket but tallied only 78,000 votes. During the rest of his life, Spock remained politically active and a popular speaker on the lecture circuit. In February 1998, he completed a new edition of *The Common Sense Book of Baby and Child Care*. Spock died on March 16, 1998, at the age of 94.

SUGGESTED READINGS: Lynn Z. Bloom, *Doctor Spock: Biography of a Conservative Radical*, 1972; *New York Times*, March 17, 1998.

SPORTS ILLUSTRATED. Early in the 1950s, Henry Luce,* who owned *Time* and *Life* magazines, decided that television* would soon create a new market for sports spectators, and that a weekly magazine devoted to sports could succeed. On August 16, 1954, Luce published the first issue of *Sports Illustrated*, featuring Eddie Matthews, the home-run slugger of the Milwaukee Braves, on the cover. For its first few years, *Sports Illustrated* covered almost every sports activity, but by the end of the decade, Luce had learned that football, baseball, basketball, auto racing, boxing, horse racing, and golf attracted middle-class male readers and advertisers. *Sports Illustrated* became the number-one sports periodical in America and one of the country's most successful weekly magazines.

SUGGESTED READING: W. A. Swanberg, *Luce and His Empire*, 1972.

SPUTNIK. On October 4, 1957, it was announced to the world that Soviet scientists had launched an artificial satellite into orbit. The Soviets dubbed the satellite *Sputnik*, which meant "fellow traveler" in Russian. A 184-pound, 23-inch diameter aluminum sphere, *Sputnik* was the first artificial satellite in the history of the world.

For a variety of reasons, the successful launch of *Sputnik* caught the United States off guard and sent Americans reeling into a collective identity crisis. Ever since World War II, Americans had basked in the notion of their own technological superiority over the rest of the world, but *Sputnik* proved beyond doubt that the Soviet Union had moved ahead of the United States in rocket technology. Senator Henry Jackson of Washington called *Sputnik* a "devastating blow to the prestige of the United States as the leader of the scientific and technical world." President Dwight D. Eisenhower* tried to downplay the event, claiming that the launch "does not raise my apprehensions, not one iota. I see nothing at this moment, at this stage of development, that is significant in that development as far as security is concerned."

There were, nevertheless, vast national security implications to the *Sputnik* launch. Throughout U.S. history, Americans had felt a great sense of security because of their geographic isolation between two oceans. Until World War II, with a few exceptions, Americans had valued an isolationist foreign policy aimed at keeping the United States separate from of Old World disputes. In August 1957, the Soviets had successfully tested an intercontinental ballistic missile* (ICBM), flying it across thousands of miles of Soviet territory. At first, American policy makers ridiculed the announcement as just another example of Communist propaganda, but Soviet technology could no longer be dismissed after October 4, 1957. *Sputnik* proved that the Soviet Union could fire rockets and drop nuclear bombs on the United States. After *Sputnik*, the United States never again felt as secure as it once had.

Americans reacted vigorously to *Sputnik*. The National Defense Education Act of 1958* funneled hundreds of millions of dollars into the American school system, with an emphasis on mathematics, science, and technology. Congress also poured huge volumes of resources into space and rocketry programs, so that the United States could close the technology gap with the Soviet Union. Finally, the Department of Defense embarked on an accelerated nuclear weapons development program to increase the number and the yield of U.S. hydrogen bombs.* Between 1950 and 1960, U.S. research and development on weapons technology increased from $934 million to $2.1 billion. Finally, in April 1958, Eisenhower founded the National Aeronautics and Space Administration to strengthen America's space efforts.

SUGGESTED READINGS: Stephen E. Ambrose, *Eisenhower: The President*, 1984; Barbara Clowse, *Brainpower for the Cold War: The Sputnik Crisis and the National Defense Education Act of 1958*, 1981.

SPUTNIK II. In November 1957, Soviet scientists launched a second artificial satellite into earth orbit. The event was not quite as dramatic, for Americans at least, as the successful launch of *Sputnik** on October 4, 1957, but it nevertheless garnered enormous media attention. What was unique about *Sputnik II* was its size. At more than half a ton, it represented a huge payload, and its launch required a rocket of great thrust, far more powerful than anything American scientists had even put on paper. Also, the Russians put a dog named Laika aboard, complete with its own oxygen supply, in order to track its vital signs in space. The launching of *Sputnik II* made it even more obvious to Americans that the Soviet Union enjoyed substantial technological superiority over the United States.

SUGGESTED READING: Barbara Clowse, *Brainpower for the Cold War: The Sputnik Crisis and the National Defense Education Act of 1958*, 1981.

STALAG 17. *Stalag 17*, a three-act play written by Donald Bevan and Edmund Trzcinski, both of whom had been prisoners of war during World War II, opened at the 48th Street Theater on May 8, 1951. The play is set in a World War II prisoner-of-war (POW) camp in Germany, where American and British aircrews are incarcerated. One of the POWs, a man named Sefton (John Ericson), keeps his distance from the others, and when an escape attempt is foiled, they assume that he is the informer. Eventually, Sefton exposes Price (Laurence Hugo) as the real informer. When Price tries to escape, German guards kill him.

Stalag 17 resonated with the public because it appeared simultaneously with the Korean War* and the Red Scare.* When Red Chinese forces entered the Korean conflict late in 1951, hundreds of American soldiers were captured, and Americans worried about their fate. Also, because of the Red Scare of the early 1950s, federal law and congressional orders required many Americans to "name names," to identify friends and associates who had once been members of the Communist party. As such, the play had a special immediacy for theatergoers. *Stalag 17* had a run of 472 performances and was made into a movie starring William Holden* in 1953.

SUGGESTED READINGS: Gerald Bordman, *The Oxford Companion to American Theater*, 1992; *New York Times*, May 9, 1951.

STALIN, JOSEPH VISSARIONOVICH. Joseph Stalin was born in Gori, Georgia, Russia, on December 9, 1879. His father was a peasant shoemaker. Feigning religious tendencies in order to win a scholarship to a local seminary, he was soon expelled for reasons of "unreliability." In 1896 Stalin joined the Social Democrats, a radical labor organization in Georgia. Russian secret police arrested him in 1902 for labor agitation and banished him to Siberia for three years. He escaped a year later, returned to Georgia under a pseudonym, and resumed his labor activities. Stalin was arrested again in 1908 and sentenced to three years in the gulag prisons of Siberia. He managed another escape in 1908 but was arrested in Baku. Stalin repeated that process—arrest, imprisonment in Siberia, and escape—a half dozen times over the next several years, and became active in the Bolshevik party as well. In February 1917 he returned from Siberia to St. Petersburg, where he immediately emerged as a leader in the Bolshevik Revolution. With the establishment of the Soviet Union, Stalin was named minister of nationalities and a general secretary of the central committee of the ruling Communist party. When Nicolai Lenin died in 1924, Stalin consolidated his power and eventually became dictator of the country.

Paranoid and ruthless, he brooked no opposition and felt no compunction about sending literally millions of people to their deaths for defying him politically or for even possessing the potential of undermining his regime. During World War II, the United States formed an alliance with the Soviet Union, and Stalin, to defeat Germany and Japan, but the relationship was always an uneasy one. Brutal and inscrutable, with a snarl usually creasing his face in public settings, Joseph Stalin became, for most Americans, the primary symbol of the malignancy of communism and the threat it posed to the free world. Once World War II gave way to the Cold War,* Stalin replaced Adolf Hitler, in the minds of Americans, as the incarnation of evil. Americans realized that Stalin's willingness to see to the demise of tens of millions of his own people could easily translate into the destruction of millions of Americans. Once the Soviet Union acquired nuclear weapons in 1949, that threat seemed even more real. When news of Stalin's death on March 5, 1953 reached the United States, the entire country heaved a sigh of relief.

SUGGESTED READINGS: David Remnick, *Lenin's Tomb*, 1993; Adam Ulam, *Stalin: The Man and the Era*, 1973.

STARKWEATHER MURDERS. In 1958 a series of highly publicized murders in Wyoming and Nebraska electrified the nation. Charles Starkweather, an 18-year-old psychopath, pulled the trigger on eleven people over the course of two months. He fancied himself a "rebel without a cause" like actor James Dean,* but he was little more than a violent killer. On December 1, 1957, he robbed a gas station and murdered the proprietor, Robert Colvert. Early in January 1958, Starkweather went to the home of his girlfriend, Caril Ann Fugate. After an argument with her parents, he shot them both to death and then turned the gun on Caril's two-year-old sister. Afer staying in the house for several more days, the two fled in the Fugate's car.

The killings continued, usually following the same pattern. The couple robbed the victim, killed him or her, and drove off in the victim's car. The law finally caught up with them when one of his victims struggled with Starkweather and a deputy sheriff came upon the scene. Fugate ran to the deputy and begged for protection from Starkweather who, she claimed, had kidnaped her. After a high-speed chase, Starkweather was captured.

The ensuing trial made headlines across the country. Defense attorneys tried to portray Starkweather as insane, and Fugate denied that she had killed anyone or had participated willingly in the crime spree. Jurors thought otherwise. Starkweather was convicted and sentenced to death. He died in Nebraska's electric chair on June 25, 1959. Fugate was convicted of one murder and sentenced to life in prison. A model prisoner, she was paroled in 1977.

SUGGESTED READINGS: Ninette Beaver, B. K. Ripley, and Patrick Trese, *Caril*, 1974; *New York Times*, June 26, 1959.

STEEL STRIKE. Late in 1951, the United Steelworkers Union decided to impose a nationwide strike on the steel industry unless company executives agreed to substantial increases in wages and fringe benefits. The companies refused, and beginning on January 1, 1952, steelworkers still went to work, even without a contract, but the union continued to threaten a strike. For President Harry Truman,* the prospects of a strike were frightening. At the time, the United States was in the midst of the Korean War,* and the president feared that an extended strike would compromise the war effort. He tried, unsuccessfully, to secure binding arbitration of the dispute.

Early in April, when the strike appeared imminent, Truman ordered U.S. troops to seize the steel mills. The union hailed the decision but company officials denounced it. They sued in the federal courts, and in June 1952 the U.S. Supreme Court decided that Truman had acted unconstitutionally. The mills were returned to the companies, and a 53-day strike ensued. Truman's fears proved to be exaggerated. The strike did not damage the economy or the war effort, and it was settled later in the summer.

SUGGESTED READINGS: Robert Farrell, *Harry S. Truman and the Modern American Presidency*, 1983; Harold Vatter, *The U.S. Economy in the 1950s*, 1963.

STELLA DAVIS. *Stella Davis*, a heavy soap-opera melodrama broadcast on NBC radio, premiered on WEAF radio in New York City on October 25, 1937, as a 15-minute, daily broadcast Monday through Friday. The network picked it up on June 6, 1938, and continued it as a weekday, 15-minute broadcast. Anne Estner starred as Stella Davis, who had seen her beloved daughter Laurel marry into a rich, upper-class, high-society family. Stella schemes her way back into her daughter's life, even though her daughter's in-laws always viewed her as trash and would never accept her. Listeners sympathized with Stella Davis, who was a good person who had to face on-going discrimination from snobs. She was a classic underdog with whom Americans sympathized.

SUGGESTED READING: John Dunning, *On the Air: The Encyclopedia of Old-Time Radio*, 1998.

STEVENSON, ADLAI. Adlai Ewing Stevenson was born on February 5, 1900, in Los Angeles, California. He grew up in Bloomington, Illinois, and graduated from Princeton in 1922. Stevenson then spent two years at Harvard Law School without getting a degree. After leaving Harvard, he worked as managing editor of the Bloomington *Daily Pantgraph*. He finished law school at Northwestern University and received his degree in 1926. Stevenson then joined a prominent Chicago law firm and later went into private practice. He spent some time with the Agricultural Adjustment Administration in Washington, D.C., in 1933 before returning to the law firm of Cutting, Moore, and Sidley. In 1941 Stevenson became special assistant to Secretary of the Navy Frank Knox. He became assistant to the secretary of state in 1945 and worked on the formation of the United Nations. By that time Stevenson was a faithful Democrat. He served as governor of Illinois from 1949 to 1953.

As governor of Illinois, Stevenson earned a reputation as a man of unusual intelligence and grace, a liberal with courage who spoke out against the excesses of Senator Joseph McCarthy's* Red Scare.* When President Harry Truman* announced his decision not to seek another term in the White House, Stevenson was widely considered by other Democrats to be the heir apparent. Truman even asked Stevenson to run for the nomination. Stevenson had some reservations about running for the presidency, and he did not openly seek the nomination.

Several Democratic candidates for the nomination emerged. Senator Estes Kefauver* of Tennessee, a conservative, actually defeated Harry Truman in the New Hampshire primary, which influenced the president's decision not to run again. But Kefauver had enemies in the party. As a crusader against organized crime, he had exposed corrupt links between organized crime and several big city Democratic political party machines, and the bosses were determined to prevent him from getting the nomination. Stevenson emerged as the frontrunner. A well-known reformer in Illinois, Stevenson was also known for his party loyalty, and he had also earned a reputation as a friend of the labor movement, one of the Democratic party's most powerful constituencies. While Kefauver had openly criticized political corruption in the Truman administration, Stevenson had faithfully backed the president.

The Democrats held their convention in Chicago, and the maneuvering for the nomination became intense. Kefauver quickly lost control over his delegates. On the third ballot, Stevenson won the nomination. For his vice-presidential running mate, Stevenson selected Senator John Sparkman of Alabama, balancing the ticket between the Northern and Southern wings of the party.

Stevenson faced former General Dwight D. Eisenhower,* whose brilliant military leadership during World War II had made him a national hero. Because of the Cold War,* the Korean War,* and the Red Scare, most Americans had lost faith in the Democratic party. Stevenson's campaign was characterized by erudite speeches discussing major issues; Eisenhower smiled and repeated platitudes. He also promised to end the Korean War. Voters went Republican in 1952, and Stevenson lost the election.

Stevenson was back for more in 1956. The Democratic party nominated him again, and once again he faced Eisenhower. The president had had a heart attack, and Democrats hoped that voters might shy away from him, but it was not to be. Stevenson emphasized a liberal social agenda to address the problems of the poor and the elderly and called for bans on nuclear weapons. President Eisenhower won handily and sent Stevenson back to Illinois.

Stevenson returned to private practice, pursued a legal career, and assumed the mantle of elder statesman of the Democratic party. In 1961 President John F. Kennedy* named him ambassador to the United Nations. Stevenson handled the job nobly, especially during the Cuban missile crisis of 1962. Adlai Stevenson died on February 14, 1965.

SUGGESTED READINGS: Bert Cochran, *Adlai Stevenson: Patrician Among the Politicians*, 1969; Porter McKeever, *Adlai Stevenson: His Life and Legacy*, 1989.

STEWART, POTTER. Potter Stewart was born on January 23, 1915, in Jackson, Michigan, and raised in Cincinnati, Ohio, where his father's family was well known and well established. His father, James Garfield Stewart, served as mayor of Cincinnati and as a justice of the Ohio supreme court. Potter Stewart graduated from Yale in 1937 and earned his law degree there. At the time, Yale was the intellectual center of a movement to reject formal, legalistic approaches to the law and to public policy. Yale Law School left Stewart with a strong commitment to legal realism. Upon graduating from Yale in 1941, he joined a Wall Street law firm, but that career was cut short by the outbreak of World War II. Stewart was decorated for his service in the U.S. Navy.

After the war, Potter returned to Wall Street, but he soon found the work empty and stultifying. He returned to Cincinnati to practice law there. A devoted Republican, Stewart supported Senator Robert Taft's* bid for the GOP presidential nomination in 1952, but he then actively backed Dwight D. Eisenhower* in 1952 and 1956. In 1954 Eisenhower appointed him to the Sixth Circuit Court of Appeals, and in 1958, when Justice Harold H. Burton retired from the U.S. Supreme Court, the president nominated Stewart to replace him.

Stewart began his tenure as a consistent, conservative dissenter, but by the early 1960s he had moved more closely to the legal center. Legal scholars eventually had a difficult time characterizing him; some declared Stewart a liberal on a conservative court and others a conservative on a liberal court. In any event, on the court of Chief Justice Earl Warren,* Stewart was frequently the swing vote. On civil rights, Stewart could be counted on to uphold school desegregation* opinions, but he dissented on legalizing busing to achieve integration. He voted for vigorous enforcement of fair employment statutes, but he drew the line at affirmative action regulations when they appeared as racial quotas. On the issues of civil liberties for criminal defendants and prison inmates, Potter usually sided with the police. Stewart retired from the court in 1984 and died on December 7, 1985.

SUGGESTED READINGS: Jerald H. Israel, "Potter Stewart," in *The Justices of the United States Supreme Court, 1789–1969*, ed. Leon Friedman and Fred Israel, 1969; *New York Times*, December 8, 1985.

SUBURBIA. One of the most visible social and demographic changes during the 1950s was the rise of suburban housing communities. During World War II, Americans earned high wages but had relatively few consumer outlets for their money because the military enjoyed the priority use of natural resources. When the war ended, Americans had substantial savings accounts, and many decided to buy houses.

The demand for housing was enormous. When the war ended and the GIs were mustered out of the military, marriage rates skyrocketed, and so did birthrates. In 1945 the country recorded 1.6 million marriages, and the number jumped to 2.3 million in 1946. In 1947 more than 3.8 million babies were born in the United States, and between 1948 and 1953, more babies were born in the United States than in the previous 30-year period. Predictably, the U.S. population boomed too, from 150 million people in 1950 to 179 million people in 1960. Americans needed unprecedented numbers of new homes.

The federal government responded to that demand by making it easier to purchase a new home. One item of the GI Bill of Rights was home ownership, and the Veterans Administration was able to offer subsidized, 30-year fixed mortgage loans to veterans for only $1 down. Millions of servicemen took advantage of the opportunity.

Because of the demand for housing and the availability of automobiles, contractors looked outside metropolitan areas and constructed so-called bedroom communities. The U.S. Census used the term "suburb" to refer to a community that had economic ties to a large metropolitan area but existed outside the city limits. Suburban communities first appeared in the 1920s when developers began building new homes outside city limits, but the Great Depression and World

War II brought the effort to a close as other priorities crowded out individual family home needs.

The boom in suburban construction appeared after the war, with the prototype community the brainchild of Abraham Levitt, a New York real estate developer. His son William Levitt became the moving force behind the development of Levittown,* approximately 30 miles from Manhattan. Between 1945 and 1948, the Levitts purchased land on Long Island, and they then began constructing homes, completing the suburban community in November 1951 after putting up 17,447 homes. Along with the homes came schools, stores, shopping centers, hospitals, and parks. All the homes in Levittown, which were built according to several simple floor plans, received such names as the "Cape Cod" and the "Ranch." Each home cost between $6,990 and $9,500, depending upon square footage and amenities, and came equipped with a refrigerator, an electric stove, and a washing machine. The Levitts made a fortune from their idea, and across the country other developers imitated them. In 1950 more than 1.4 million houses were constructed nationwide. That pace continued throughout the decade.

Since most men who lived in the new suburbs worked in nearby cities, a boom in highway construction occurred. New York built the Long Island Expressway, a limited-access freeway running east from Manhattan out to Long Island, and during the 1950s, 1960s, and 1970s, the expressway had to be continuously extended, with new housing developments sprouting along its arteries. Eventually, the expressway became so crowded that critics labeled it the "world's largest parking lot." Similar freeway construction booms took place throughout the United States.

Critics, however, saw problems in the rise of suburbia. Suburban housing tracts became symbols of the conformist pressures of the 1950s. The houses were identical, except for external colors. The suburbs also attracted middle-class, white residents; Jews, blacks, and Hispanics tended to remain behind in urban areas. Finally, the rise of suburbs stimulated business relocations from cities to suburbs, which eventually eroded the urban tax base and left city residents, particularly the poor and undereducated, with fewer job opportunities. The urban crisis that began affecting America in the 1960s had its roots in the post–World War II suburban housing booms.

SUGGESTED READINGS: Herbert J. Gans, *The Levittowners*, 1967; Kenneth T. Jackson, *Crabgrass Frontier: The Suburbanization of America*, 1985; Harold Wattel, *The Suburban Community*, 1958; Gwendolyn Wright, *Building the Dream: A Social History of Housing in America*, 1981.

SUEZ CRISIS (1956). When Gamal Abdel Nasser* came to power in Egypt, he changed Middle East politics and the Cold War* forever. Convinced that his people had been exploited by European imperial powers, Nasser set his sights on the Suez Canal, which had been owned and managed by an Anglo-French conglomerate. In Egypt, Nasser created a one-party state and began moving toward a socialist economy. He also turned away from the West and purchased agricultural goods and weapons from the Soviet Union. He made a public show of his refusal to join the Baghdad Pact,* a regional, anti-Soviet alliance.

The United States and Great Britain reacted angrily to Nasser's new anti-Western posture, and they pulled financing from his coveted Aswan Dam construction project, which would dam the Nile and provide hydroelectric power to much of Egypt. Nasser retaliated by announcing that Egypt had decided to nationalize the Suez Canal. Ever since its completion nearly a century before, the Suez Canal had been a vital route for the British navy making its way from Atlantic and Mediterranean ports to India and East Asia. Losing the canal to Egyptian control would constitute a severe strategic reversal for Britain. With the revenues collected from canal tolls, Nasser could finance the Aswan Dam himself.

Enraged at Nasser's impunity, Great Britain and France conspired with Israel to invade Egypt across the Sinai Peninsula. The British and the French would then use the war as a pretext to occupy the canal zone. Israel invaded Egypt on October 29, and British bombs wiped out the Egyptian air force. French and British paratroopers took control of two key canal outposts—Port Faud and Port Said.

President Dwight D. Eisenhower* was outraged. The French, British, and Israelis had acted without consulting the United States, and the conflict threatened to escalate into a superpower confrontation. The Soviets, anxious to cement their budding relationship with Nasser, expressed similar outrage. Soviet and American officials sent troops to force a cease fire on the combatants. The war came to an end within a week; 2,700 Egyptians and 140 Israelis were dead. When the dust had settled on the war, Egypt retained control of the Suez Canal, and the Soviet Union helped finance construction of the Aswan Dam. Nasser's reputation in the Arab world skyrocketed.

SUGGESTED READINGS: Winthrop W. Aldrich, "The Suez Crisis: A Footnote to History," *Foreign Affairs* 45 (April 1967), 541–52; Robert W. Stookey, *America and the Arab States*, 1975.

SUN RECORDS. Sun Records was owned by Sam Phillips, a Memphis disc jockey who, in January 1950, established the Memphis Recording Service, a record production company. Phillips concentrated on a narrow niche in the record business—African-American rhythm and blues (R & B) artists. He managed to sign contracts with some of the greatest R & B artists in the country: B. B. King, Chester "Howlin' Wolf" Burnettt, Ike Turner, James Cotton, and "Little Junior" Parker. Phillips was convinced that a market for R & B music could be built outside the Southern black community. What he really hoped to find was a white artist who could perform such music and appeal to a biracial audience. In 1954, he founded Sun Records.

By 1955 Phillips had decided to pursue "rockabilly" music—a combination of country music and rhythm and blues characterized by uninhibited lyrics, performance gyration, and a dominant rhythm section in the music. Between

1954 and 1956, Phillips recorded such early rock-and-roll* icons as Carl Perkins, Roy Orbison, and Jerry Lee Lewis,* but his real coup was signing Elvis Presley.* In 1954 Presley had recorded "That's All Right Mama" and "Blue Moon of Kentucky," and Phillips released the record in July 1954. The record sold 25,000 copies in its first six months, and Phillips had a certifiable star on his hands. Over the next year, Presley recorded eight more songs for Phillips and became the most recognizable figure in popular music.

Phillips then made a huge business mistake. He sold all rights to Elvis Presley's music for $35,000, and within a matter of years he found himself out of the recording business. He had invested generously, however, in Holiday Inn,* a chain motel venture started in 1952 by his Memphis friend Kemmons Wilson. That investment eventually made Phillips a multimillionaire.

SUGGESTED READING: Colin Escott and Martin Hawkins, *Good Rockin' Tonight: Sun Records and the Birth of Rock 'n' Roll*, 1991.

SUNRISE AT CAMPOBELLO. *Sunrise at Campobello*, a three-act play by Dory Schary, opened at the Cort Theater in New York City on January 30, 1958. Campobello was the summer home of President Franklin D. Roosevelt, and the play begins in the summer of 1921, with Roosevelt taking a swim. He becomes unusually fatigued and, within hours, is afflicted with aches and pains. The next morning he is paralyzed, and the doctors soon diagnose a case of polio.* Ralph Bellamy played the part of Roosevelt and Mary Fickett, his wife, Eleanor. Roni Dengel played Roosevelt's doting mother, Anna, and Henry Jones portrayed Roosevelt's crusty political adviser Louis Howe. The play depicts Roosevelt's struggle to regain control of his life, even though he never regained control of his body. It ends at Madison Square Garden in New York in 1924, when Roosevelt is able to appear at the Democratic National Convention to nominate Governor Al Smith for president. *Sunrise at Campobello* had a run of 558 performances and was made into a movie starring Ralph Bellamy.

SUGGESTED READINGS: Gerald Bordman, *The Oxford Companion to American Theater*, 1992; *New York Times*, January 30, 1958.

SWEATT V. PAINTER (1950). *Sweatt v. Painter* was a milestone in the process by which the United States desegregated its public schools. In 1946 Herman Sweatt, an African American, applied for admission at the University of Texas (UT) Law School. The university rejected his application because he was black, and Sweatt sued, arguing that racial discrimination denied him his Fourteenth Amendment rights. In response, in order to comply with *Missouri ex rel. Gaines v. Canada* (1938), UT established a separate law school for blacks, staffed by part-time faculty. Sweatt was not satisfied; he refused to attend and continued to pursue his lawsuit. In June 1950 the U.S. Supreme Court rendered its decision, siding with Sweatt and finding UT guilty of racial discrimination. The justices of the court realized, as did everybody else, that the University of Texas would not be able to build a second law school equal in quality to its first; the decision actually violated the decision in *Plessy v. Ferguson* (1896). The decision led to the desegregation* of professional programs—medicine, dentistry, and law—throughout the country.

SUGGESTED READING: 339 U.S. 629 (1950).

***SWEEZY V. NEW HAMPSHIRE* (1957).** On June 17, 1957, a day conservatives and anticommunists labeled "Red Monday,"* the U.S. Supreme Court handed down a number of important decisions concerning civil liberties, particularly the extent to which an individual could be punished for maintaining radical or revolutionary political views. One of those cases was *Sweezy v. New Hampshire*. Sweezy was a college professor who admitted to the New Hampshire legislature that he was a member of the left-wing Progressive party, but he refused to identify any other party members. Because he would not "name names," the state legislature held him in contempt. He filed a lawsuit claiming that his constitutional rights had been violated. The U.S. Supreme Court agreed with Sweezy and overthrew the contempt citation. According to the Court, such a compromise of the Fifth Amendment was not justified, especially given the fact that Sweezy had never advocated the overthrow of the U.S. government.

SUGGESTED READINGS: Richard Gird Powers, *Secrecy and Power: The Life of J. Edgar Hoover*, 1987; Athan Theoharis, *Spying on Americans: Political Surveillance from Hoover to the Huston Plan*, 1978.

T

TAFT, ROBERT. Robert Alphonso Taft, the man a generation of politicos nicknamed "Mr. Republican," was born in Cincinnati, Ohio, on September 8, 1889. The Taft pedigree included more than its share of the famous and powerful. Taft's grandfather, Alphonso Taft, served as secretary of war under President Ulysses S. Grant and then attorney general of the United States and U.S. minister to Austria and Russia. Robert Taft's father, William Howard Taft, served as governor-general of the Philippines, secretary of war under President Theodore Roosevelt, president of the United States (1909–1913), and chief justice of the U.S. Supreme Court. Robert Alphonso Taft spent a lifetime trying to live up to that legacy.

Robert Taft was educated in the public schools of Cincinnati and in the Philippines during his father's tenure as governor-general. During his father's presidential administration, Taft shuttled back and forth between Yale and the White House and acquired an unbridled political ambition of his own. He graduated from Yale in 1910 and earned, with highest honors, a law degree from Harvard in 1913. Taft practiced law in Cincinnati until 1917, when he became assistant counsel with the U.S. Food Administration. Poor vision kept him from military service during World War I.

In 1920 Taft began a six-year stint in the Ohio legislature. He returned to Cincinnati as a senior partner with the law firm of Taft, Stettinius and Hollister in 1926. During the 1930s, he became an inveterate opponent of President Franklin D. Roosevelt and the New Deal, which he considered "completely socialistic and a threat to the future of America." In 1938, with opposition to Roosevelt increasing throughout the country, Taft ran for the U.S. Senate. He won handily and entered the Senate as a conservative Republican.

Until the Japanese attack on Pearl Harbor in December 1941, Taft led the isolationist bloc in Congress, urging Franklin Roosevelt to stay out of European conflicts while accusing the president of secretly working to draw the United

States into the war. After Pearl Harbor, he joined the patriotic throng and backed the president's war policies. In 1945, with the war over, Taft resumed his foreign policy criticisms. The Korean War,* he felt, was a terrible mistake and the consequence of military and diplomatic mismanagement on the part of President Harry Truman.* He also declared that the United Nations was a useless entity.

In terms of domestic policy, Taft led the conservative wing of the Republican party, and he played a key role in pushing the Taft-Hartley Act of 1947 through Congress. The act repealed portions of the Wagner Act of 1935 and restricted the right of labor unions to strike. Over and over again during these years, Taft expressed his belief in a "program of progress within the principles of the liberty of the individual, of state and local government and of economic freedom and not based on the New Deal philosophy of constant increase in Federal Government power and Federal Government spending."

Taft ran for the Republican presidential nomination three times—1940, 1948, and 1952—but each time he was perceived as being too conservative. In his last bid for the White House, he lost the nomination to General Dwight D. Eisenhower,* who won the presidency. Late in April 1953, Taft began complaining of pain in his abdomen, legs, and left hip. Exploratory surgery revealed metastatic malignant tumors. Taft then put his personal affairs in order and died on July 31, 1953.

SUGGESTED READINGS: *New York Times*, August 1, 1953; James T. Patterson, *Mr. Republican: A Biography of Robert A. Taft*, 1972.

TALES OF THE TEXAS RANGERS. Produced and directed by Stacy Keach, *Tales of the Texas Rangers* was a weekly dramatic radio series broadcast on NBC between 1950 and 1952. Joel McCrea, a veteran actor of dozens of B Westerns during the 1930s and 1940s, starred as a Texas Ranger, Ranger Pearson, who tracks down criminals and desperadoes. Keach managed to get full cooperation from the Texas Rangers, and most of the plots were adapted from actual Ranger cases during the 1920s, 1930s, and 1940s. In that aspect, the program resembled *Dragnet*,* whose stories were based on the crime-solving skills of the Los Angeles Police Department.

SUGGESTED READING: John Dunning, *On the Air: The Encyclopedia of Old-Time Radio*, 1998.

TALES OF WELLS FARGO. *Tales of Wells Fargo*, a popular Western of the late 1950s and early 1960s, starred Dale Robertson as Jim Hardie, an agent for the Wells Fargo Company. During the late nineteenth century, Wells Fargo was a freighting company that carried passengers, mail, and freight from town to town in the Far West. Hardie solved all kinds of problems for the company—catching thieves, fighting Indians, rescuing troubled employees, and generally helping to enforce justice in a world where vigilantism still prevailed. *Tales of Wells Fargo* premiered on NBC television on March 18, 1957, and it remained on the air until September 8, 1962.

SUGGESTED READING: Tim Brooks and Earle Marsh, *The Complete Directory to Prime Time Network and Cable TV Shows, 1946–Present*, 1995.

TEAHOUSE OF THE AUGUST MOON. *Teahouse of the August Moon*, a three-act comedy written by John Patrick based on a novel by Vern Sneider, opened at the Martin Beck Theater in New York City on October 15, 1953. Set in Okinawa after World War II, it relates the story of Captain Frisby, played by John Forsythe, who is charged with bringing democracy to the island. The villagers have little interest in his assignment, and when he tries to bring free enterprise capitalism to them, Frisby discovers that the only commodity they can manufacture is cricket cages, for which there is no export market. When Frisby decides to build a school, local villager Sakini, played by David Wayne, actually constructs a teahouse so that alcohol can be served. When the U.S. military officials begin to dismantle the teahouse, they learn that their superiors in Washington, D.C., are hailing the teahouse as an example of free enterprise acumen. The teahouse must be hastily rebuilt so that a visiting congressional delegation can admire it. *Teahouse of the August Moon* had a run of 1,027 performances.

SUGGESTED READINGS: Gerald Bordman, *The Oxford Companion to American Theater*, 1992; *New York Times*, October 16, 1953.

TEAMSTERS. The Teamsters Union, or Brotherhood of Teamsters, originated as a union of coach and wagon drivers, but in the twentieth century it evolved into a truck drivers' union. By the 1950s, the Teamsters Union dominated the American trucking industry, and its connections to organized crime had become scandalous. The business community began demanding government action to divest the Teamsters of its power and to cleanse the union of its corruption.

The union's difficulties developed in the mid-1950s when AFL-CIO* leaders, especially George Meany* and Walter Reuther,* accused Teamsters president David Beck of diverting union funds to his personal use and to the financial benefit of other union leaders. The word of possible corruption in the Teamsters Union hit the front pages of newspapers across the country. The union became a political hot potato. In March 1957, when AFL-CIO president Meany proposed that Beck be nominated as the U.S. delegate to the United Nations International Labor Organization, Secretary of Labor James Marshall refused.

In May 1957, Senator James McClellan of Arkansas launched the McClellan Committee* investigation of organized labor, which soon exposed the reality of criminal activities within the Teamsters Union. Robert Kennedy, brother of Senator John F. Kennedy,* pursued the investigation with a vengeance. When Beck appeared before the McClellan Committee, he took the Fifth Amendment more than 200 times, leading most Americans to decide that he was probably guilty of all the crimes he had been accused of committing. A few weeks later, the AFL-CIO expelled Beck from its membership.

In what the Department of Justice considered a corrupt election, James

(Jimmy) Hoffa* was elected to replace Beck as head of the Teamsters, and in his testimony before the McClellan Committee, Hoffa too took the Fifth Amendment repeatedly. Beck was soon found guilty of embezzlement, tax evasion, and grand larceny. The AFL-CIO began to distance itself from Teamsters leadership, demanding that the union clean up its act. Hoffa escaped conviction because of a hung jury, and he assumed full control of the Teamsters Union in September 1958. In 1958 the AFL-CIO expelled the Teamsters and its two million members.

The federal government, however, was not done with Jimmy Hoffa and the Teamsters. John F. Kennedy won the presidential election of 1960, and he named his brother Robert attorney general. Robert Kennedy was indefatigable in his assault on Teamsters corruption, and, in 1964, Hoffa was convicted of jury tampering. Hoffa spent four years in a federal penitentiary. President Richard M. Nixon* pardoned him in 1971. Hoffa disappeared and his whereabouts are still unknown.

SUGGESTED READING: Steven Brill, *The Teamsters*, 1978.

TEENAGERS. During the 1950s, American society first saw "teenagers"— young people between thirteen and twenty years of age—emerge as an identifiable constituency in the United States. At the root of the phenomenon was a fundamental demographic reality. During the Great Depression, birthrates had fallen, and World War II took so many men away from home that the decline continued. When the war ended and the GIs were mustered out of the military, however, marriage rates skyrocketed, and so did birthrates. Between 1948 and 1953, more babies were born in the United States than in the previous 30-year period. Predictably, the U.S. population boomed too, from 150 million people in 1950 to 179 million people in 1960.

By the mid-1950s, the number of adolescents in the population had exploded. Because of access to cars provided by the automobile industry* and to disposable income—the average teenager in 1956 enjoyed a weekly income of $10.50—young people had more freedom than any previous generation. They were no longer as dependent upon their parents for spending money, which also liberated them. Finally, they were raised during the most prosperous era in U.S. history.

To their parents, they seemed a rebellious generation, one symbolized by James Dean* in the 1955 film *Rebel Without a Cause.** In that film, Dean played Jim Stark, a teenaged boy ridden with angst and tormented by a sense of alienation that he cannot understand. He rebels against his parents, teachers, police, and the world at large, but not for any purpose other than rebellion as an end in itself. His costume for the film—an open leather jacket worn over a white T-shirt with blue jeans and boots—caught the fancy of millions of American teenagers, who saw in Jim Stark an alter ego for their own growing restlessness with the conformity of the 1950s. Dean provided young people with a new icon of teenage anomie and alienation and personified the restless insolence that many adults detected in the younger generation. A host of other films took advantage of these fears, including *Blackboard Jungle*,* *Riot in Juvenile Prison*, and *The Cool and the Crazy*. Many Americans were convinced that juveniles were smoldering with rebellion.

Americans also worried about juvenile delinquency.* The problem of juvenile crime became a near obsession among teachers, psychologists, middle-class parents, and law enforcement officials. As early as 1953, J. Edgar Hoover,* director of the Federal Bureau of Investigation* (FBI), reported that, in the United States, young people under the age of eighteen were responsible for nearly 54 percent of all car thefts, 49 percent of all burglaries, 18 percent of all robberies, and 16 percent of all rapes. With the baby boom* generation just a few years from reaching the teenage years, Hoover preached, the United States could expect the problem to get worse before it got better.

Parents also blamed the advent of rock-and-roll.* The music troubled them for many reasons, including its biracial roots, its visceral performances, and its inherent rebelliousness. Critics condemned rock-and-roll for corrupting the morals of America's youth, undermining the school system, and causing juvenile delinquency. Elvis Presley's* gyrations and James Dean's sullen distance, as well as his rejection of adult values, troubled most parents.

By the early 1960s, the so-called baby boom generation had begun entering college and universities, and their discontent, born of the high expectations bequeathed to them by prosperity and the World War II generation, fueled the youth rebellion, the civil rights movement,* the environmental movement, and the antiwar movement of the 1960s.

SUGGESTED READINGS: Landon V. Jones, *Great Expectations: America and the Baby Boom*, 1980; Elaine Tyler May, *Homeward Bound: American Families in the Cold War*, 1988; Hermann Remmers, *The American Teenager*, 1957; Ernest Allyn Smith, *American Youth Culture: Group Life in Teenage Society*, 1962.

TELEPHONE BOOTHS. The great college fad of 1959 involved stuffing as many people as possible into a standard-size telephone booth. The fad started in several South African universities and spread to Europe and the United States. All over the country in the spring of 1959, college students, primarily male, packed themselves into telephone booths and then filmed the site in order to claim a world's record. Students at Modesto Junior College in California claimed the record: 34. The fad disappeared as quickly as it had started.

SUGGESTED READING: Peter Skilnik, *Fads: America's Crazes, Fads, & Fancies*, 1978.

TELEVANGELISM. Ever since the Great Awakening of the early 1700s, American culture has produced a succession of prominent evangelists who have tried to rid the country of sin and convert the nation to their brand of Christianity. During the 1950s, the most popular of those evangelists was Billy Graham,* a young Baptist preacher from North Carolina. Since the late 1930s, when he was a teenager, Graham had worked the Southern tent-meeting revival circuit, honing his preaching skills and shaping his own religious identity. Like other prominent evangelists, Graham was blessed with a powerful, if subdued, charisma, but unlike popular preachers like Billy Sunday and Aimee Semple McPherson, his private life was above reproach. While Sunday and McPherson fulfilled the Elmer Gantry stereotypes of modern evangelists whose sexual appetites got the best of them, Graham donned a business suit and exhibited a wholesome, trustworthy earnestness. A faithful husband and devoted father, he was the perfect evangelist for the bland 1950s.

Graham's big break, and the birth of modern televangelism, came in 1950 after he conducted a series of revivals in Los Angeles. The revivals attracted a number of Hollywood celebrities, and newspaper magnate William Randolph Hearst ordered his writers to promote Graham. With such favorable press coverage, Graham launched the weekly radio show *Hour of Decision*, which soon attracted fifteen million weekly listeners. In 1951 he began televising his revivals, which played to larger and larger audiences in bigger and bigger venues. By the end of the decade, Graham was the most widely recognized religious figure in the country, a confidant to the rich and famous in politics, entertainment, and sports. Other televangelists, like Oral Roberts and Katherine Kuhlman, joined him on the airways, but none ever achieved his mainstream respectability.

SUGGESTED READINGS: William Martin, *A Prophet with Honor: The Billy Graham Story*, 1991; John Pollock, *To All the Nations of the World: The Billy Graham Story*, 1985.

TELEVISION. The most dramatic technological advance of the decade, or any other decade in American history, was the mass adoption by consumers of the television set. In 1948 less than 6 percent of American households had television sets. That number rose to 42 percent by 1952 and nearly 90 percent by 1960. In only a decade, the television had gone from luxury to necessity in American popular culture. The technology had first appeared in the 1920s, and by the 1930s, such companies as RCA were doing limited television broadcasting in select urban areas. By 1940, 23 television stations were broadcasting programming in the United States.

The onset of World War II postponed television development, but after the war the industry grew by leaps and bounds. In 1946 RCA Victor offered a 10-inch, black-and-white set for $375. Four years later, the Silvertone model could be purchased for $150. By 1950 the National Broadcasting Company (NBC), an RCA subsidiary, and the Columbia Broadcasting System (CBS) were offering regular nightly programming in most major cities. The system operated like the radio network. A local broadcaster secured a license from the Federal Communications Commission (FCC), and the FCC then assigned the station a frequency, or channel as it was called. Licensed stations then affiliated with CBS, or NBC, or later the American Broadcasting Company (ABC). The local affiliate agreed to broadcast network-supplied programming in return for a share of the advertising revenues. In addition, the stations developed their own programming, which they used to generate local advertising revenues.

Televison had an immediate and dramatic impact on other entertainment venues. Movie attendance fell, as did attendance at local sporting events. Restaurant, bar, and nightclub business fell off as well. Even library circulation declined. Americans stayed home in mass to watch television. The real victim of television, however, was radio. Americans no longer viewed radio as their primary source of entertainment. Between 1950 and 1960, radio advertising revenues grew slowly, from $605 million to only $675 million, while televison advertising revenues exceeded $1 billion.

In 1953 NBC began broadcasting regular color television programming. In the beginning, the programming was limited to two hours a day. The technology was slow to catch on because color television sets were very expensive, well out of the range—from $500 to $1,000 each—of most households, and the technology was still quite crude in the early 1950s. Viewers had to adjust the dials constantly because the image often bled and warped. Color television in the 1950s was a virtual monopoly of NBC because the network was owned by RCA, which manufactured all color picture tubes. Color television did not really catch on in the United States until the 1960s.

The marriage between sports and television during the 1950s revolutionized both. Early in the decade, television began covering boxing, wrestling, and roller derby—sports whose mechanical dynamics were suitable for one camera angle. Sports taking place on large playing fields proved extremely difficult to cover adequately at first. Cameramen gradually developed more sophisticated techniques, and by 1958 more than 800 major baseball games were telecast. Soon college football games had become staples of Saturday afternoon television. The broadcast of major league baseball games on television almost killed minor league baseball. In 1949 more than 42 million people bought tickets to minor league baseball games; in 1957 it had dropped to 15 million tickets.

Television also revolutionized the delivery of news and information to the American public. Until the 1950s, newspapers served as the source of information to the vast majority of Americans, with radio a close second. Movie theaters also ran newsreels before evening showings of films. The advent of television news changed all that. NBC pioneered television news when its New York City affiliate in 1939 began broadcasting the *Sunoco News* every weeknight, featuring world-renowned radio broadcaster and traveler Lowell Thomas. In July 1941, Sam Cuff began to broadcast network news via his program *The War As It Happens*. The familiar version of evening network news with an "anchorman" in front of the camera began in 1949 when John Cameron Swayze, who had narrated news footage off camera on his evening program *Camel Newsreel Theater*, moved in front of the camera. He became America's first primetime network news anchor.

By the mid-1950s, however, the major television news programs were no longer just reporting footage filmed by somebody else. They had become news-gathering enterprises in their own right, and NBC decided that the news anchors should be experienced reporters. That decision led to *The Huntley-Brinkley Report,** which replaced Swayze in front of the camera with Chet Huntley and David Brinkley. *The Huntley-Brinkley Report* remained on the air, for 15 minutes each weeknight, for the next 14 years. In 1963 its format was expanded to 30 minutes each night. The other networks followed suit during the 1950s, with Walter Cronkite taking over the anchor duties at CBS and John Daly at ABC.

Although television critics hailed the news programs as the best of television, some began to complain in the late 1950s that television news emphasized images over information, that no issue could really be analyzed in depth because most stories were covered in only two to three minutes. Politicians, they claimed, became devoted to brief "sound bites" which might appeal to a viewer's prejudices but which could not be examined in any detail.

Perhaps the greatest impact of television was its acceleration of the development of a national popular culture. Because of the network-affiliate system, Americans all over the country watched the same television programs at the same time on the same day, and saw the same commercials being presented by the same advertisers. By watching the same programs and purchasing the same products, Americans lost some of their regional distinctiveness. Politicians immediately took advantage of the new medium and began to appeal to voters over the airwaves. Party organizations began to decline in significance.

Critics charged that television was responsible for "dumbing down" American culture. Slapstick comedy, quiz shows, and soap operas became standard fare, appealing to the lowest common denominator of public tastes. In watching more and more television, Americans did less and less reading and less and less visiting with their neighbors. Some claimed that television had undermined neighborhoods, had led parents to spend less time with their children, and had made it more difficult for teachers to educate children.

SUGGESTED READINGS: Erik Barnouw, *Tube of Plenty: The Evolution of American Television*, 1990; William Boddy, *Fifties Television: The Industry and Its Critics*, 1990; Benjamin Rader, *In Its Own Image: How Television Has Transformed Sports*, 1984.

TV DINNER. The mass popularity of television* changed American family life during the 1950s. The dinner hour changed especially. As better programming made its way into prime time, families wanted to gather in front of the television set during dinnertime. Also, the fact that many women had remained in the workforce after World War II put a premium on rapid preparation of evening meals. In Omaha, Nebraska, in 1951, Clarke and Gilbert Swanson began marketing frozen pot pies on a national scale. That same year, Cecil Johnson, an attorney, put a trademark on the term "TV dinner." The Swansons soon purchased the trademark from Johnson, and by 1953 they were marketing complete frozen dinners in sealed aluminum trays. By 1955, the year Campbell Soups bought them out, the Swansons were selling 25 million TV dinners a year.

SUGGESTED READING: Kenneth Morris, Marc Robinson, and Richard Kroll, eds., *American Dreams: One-Hundred Years of Business Ideas and Innovation*, 1990.

***TV GUIDE*.** The growth of television* in the early 1950s, and the dramatic expansion in local and network programming, created a demand for published listings of upcoming programs. In 1952 Walter Annenberg, who published the *Philadelphia Inquirer* and the *Daily Racing Form*, decided to publish a national magazine listing televison programs—times and dates—for the upcoming week. The first issue of *TV Guide*, published in April 1953, sold more than 1.56 million copies, and in September 1.75 million were sold. By 1959 *TV Guide* consisted of fifty-three regional issues, with a total circulation of 6 million copies every week.

SUGGESTED READING: *TV Guide: The First 25 Years*, 1978.

***THE TEN COMMANDMENTS*.** First released in 1956, *The Ten Commandments*, director Cecil B. DeMille's epic film about the life of Moses, stars Charlton Heston as Moses, Anne Baxter as Nefretiri, Yul Brynner as the Pharoah Rameses, and Edward G. Robinson as Dathan. A total of 3 hours, 39 minutes in length, *The Ten Commandments* was Hollywood's biggest film, in terms of production and scale, since *Gone with the Wind*. At the time, Hollywood was trying to lure audiences away from their television* sets and back into movie theaters. *The Ten Commandments* was designed to provide viewers with scenes that could never be reproduced on a television screen. Filmed in Technicolor, with immense sets and unprecedented special effects, *The Ten Commandments* was a huge box-office smash.

SUGGESTED READING: *New York Times*, November 9, 1956.

TERMINATION. The term "termination" is used by historians to refer to a movement in the 1950s and early 1960s to end federal supervision of American Indian tribes. The termination movement had its beginnings just after World War II when conservative congressmen campaigned to eliminate the so-called trust status of Indian reservations, in which they were legally independent from all state and local taxes and criminal and civil jurisdiction. The impetus for termination came primarily from non-Indian economic interests. The postwar boom in recreational camping turned the attention of white developers to the reservations. They wanted to turn Indian land into large commercial farms or resort developments, but purchasing the land was impossible as long as reservations enjoyed trust status.

In 1950 President Harry Truman* appointed Dillon S. Myer commissioner of Indian affairs. Previously employed by the War Relocation Authority, which had incarcerated Japanese Americans into concentration camps during World War II, Myer was an assimilationist who had tried to scatter Japanese Americans among the general population in 1945. He brought that same commitment to the Bureau of Indian Affairs (BIA), hoping to dissolve the reservations and disperse Native Americans throughout the country. On August 1, 1953, Congress inaugurated the termination program by passing a series of resolutions that removed federal authority over all Indian tribes, terminated their status as wards of the United States, and granted them all the privileges of citizenship. State and local governments were to take legal jurisdiction over the reservations, and federal authority would be ended.

Termination was to take place in stages, beginning with the tribes most prepared to "go it on their own." Between 1953 and 1956, Congress terminated a number of tribes, including the Alabama-Coushattas in Texas, the Utes and Paiutes in Utah, the Klamaths in Oregon, and the Menominis in Wisconsin. Nearly 1.7 million acres of the reservation land fell into white hands between 1953 and 1960, usually because tribes could not pay state and local property taxes on the reservation land and had to generate cash. Without federal funds and with tribal corporate power negated, terminated Indians had no means of livelihood and sold their land to support themselves. The Klamaths and Menominis suffered especially heavy losses. In 1957 Ralph Nader, editor of the *Harvard Law School Record*, denounced termination, and a number of liberal journals, including *Nation*, *Christian Century*, and *Harper's*, openly criticized termination. Such Native American lobbying groups as the National Congress of American Indians, the Indian Rights Association, and the Association of American Indian Affairs condemned termination as well. By 1956 the antitermination movement had become so strong that president Dwight D. Eisenhower* halted it except at the request of individual tribes. The program became increasingly unpopular but was not reversed until 1970, when President Richard M. Nixon* implemented its repeal. Not until 1988, however, did Congress formally repeal termination when it passed the Repeal of Termination Act, which prohibited Congress from ever terminating or transferring BIA services without tribal permission.

SUGGESTED READINGS: Russel Lawrence Bars and James Youngblood Henderson, *The Road: Indian Tribes and Political Liberty*, 1980; John R. Wander, *"Retained by the People": A History of American Indians and the Bill of Rights*, 1994; Wilcomb E. Washburn, *Red Man's Land, White Man's Law*, 1971.

THIS IS YOUR FBI. *This Is Your FBI*, a radio police drama very similar to its counterpart *The FBI in Peace and War*, premiered on ABC radio on April 6, 1945, and survived until its last broadcast on January 30, 1953. During the immediate postwar years, the FBI agents foiled Nazi attempts at sabotage, but by 1947–1948, Communists were becoming the primary targets of FBI agents, who tried to prevent treason and subversion. The show became especially popular during 1951 and 1952, when the Red Scare* reached its peak in the United States. The Federal Bureau of Investigation* regularly used *This Is Your FBI* to serve its own public relations purposes.

SUGGESTED READING: John Dunning, *On the Air: The Encyclopedia of Old-Time Radio*, 1998.

THIS IS YOUR LIFE. On October 1, 1952, NBC television first aired *This Is Your Life*, which creator and host Ralph Edwards had brought to NBC radio in 1948. He also had a one-year run on CBS radio in 1950. The weekly show had a simple format. Edwards surprised unsuspecting individuals and brought them to the studio, where he had already assembled a "living" biography, including friends and relatives from the past. Edwards then reviewed those events and introduced the guest to the friends and relatives. Joyous reunions became staples of *This Is Your Life*. Sometimes the guests would be normal, ordinary people who had done something extraordinary; on other shows, Edwards featured a celebrity. Most of the time, Edwards worked, as one critic wrote, "to jerk every tear possible out of the guest and the audience." And it worked. *This Is Your Life* remained on prime-time television until its last broadcast on September 3, 1961.

SUGGESTED READING: Tim Brooks and Earle Marsh, *The Complete Directory to Prime Time Network and Cable TV Shows, 1946–Present*, 1995.

3-D. The acronym "3-D" was used during the early 1950s to describe a popular, if short lived, fad used in the movies. The advent of television* had confronted Hollywood with a real challenge. Weekly movie attendance fell dramatically in 1950 and 1951, with millions of families opting to stay at home huddled around a television set rather than venture out to a movie theater. Another problem facing the film industry was the fact that most movie houses were located downtown in urban centers, while large numbers of middle-class moviegoers had relocated to the suburbs. Many Americans simply did not want to get in the car and drive downtown at night, particularly since downtown areas of many cities had acquired a gritty, rundown appearance.

Hollywood became desperate for any gimmick or fad that might attract people back to movie theaters, and 3-D, or three-dimensional projection, was one of them. The concept had been tried as early as 1922, but technical difficulties made it impossible for 3-D to survive then. Similar problems doomed it in the 1950s. The real innovation of 3-D was its ability to provide viewing audiences with on-screen depth perception. During shooting, several cameramen using multiple cameras filmed a scene from different angles. When the film was shown in a theater, two projectors had to project the film simultaneously, from different angles, onto a screen. To watch the movie, ticket buyers donned special colored glasses that synchronized the two images.

Action films—car crashes, horse races, and fights—were ideal for 3-D, but such films tended to be more expensive simply because action sequences cost more to shoot than scenes on sets. Also, 3-D movies required more careful editing in order to make sure that the film reels were in synch. It also cost more for theaters to show 3-D films, since they had to own and maintain two state-of-the-art projectors. Finally, technical problems were very common. Projector speeds had to be exact and timing very accurate; otherwise, the film suffered from voice-image discrepancies and the special glasses could not fuse the dual images into one. Within a year or two, audiences had tired of the novelty and grown extremely critical of and frustrated with the technical problems common to 3-D. By 1955 3-D had already become a thing of the pop culture past.

SUGGESTED READINGS: Pauline Kael, *5001 Nights at the Movies*, 1982; David Shipman, *The Great Movie Stars: The International Years*, 1972.

TIBET. For centuries, the invasion route into southwestern China, and from there deep into the heart of China, had run through Tibet. A mountainous nation bordered to the south by the impenetrable Himalayan peaks, Tibet had always been a key to Chinese independence. Nineteenth- and early twentieth-century Chinese leaders had worried about control of Tibet. If British forces moved out of British India and crossed the Himalayan Mountains, they could build a staging area in Tibet for the penetration of China. So could Russians coming in from the east. China had first established political control over Tibet in the eighteenth century, but in 1912 Tibet proclaimed its independence. China had long yearned for the opportunity to retake the region.

As soon as Mao Zedong* and the Communists had proclaimed the People's Republic of China in 1949, securing control of Tibet became an objective of high priority. In October 1950, 20,000 Chinese troops from the People's Liberation Army invaded Tibet. At the time Tibet was a pure theocracy, a country ruled by the Dalai Lama, spiritual leader of millions of Lamaist Buddhists. Taking his cue from what was occurring in Korea, the Dalai Lama appealed for United Nations assistance, but few European or Asian democracies considered Tibet central to their national security. Many, in fact, had never even recognized Tibetan independence. The Dalai Lama was on his own.

At the same time, China resurrected a tried-and-true public policy regarding conquered lands. For hundreds of years, whenever China had occupied foreign territory, they had relocated tens of thousands and then hundreds of thousands of ethnic Chinese immigrants. The ethnic Chinese soon outnumbered the native inhabitants of a region, and the processes of assimilation made the natives all but disappear. In the early 1950s, thousands of Chinese began settling in Tibet. Tibetans worried that their own culture and ethnicity would eventually be overwhelmed.

In 1959 Tibetan nationalists rose up against their Communist Chinese overlords. The capital city of Llasa became a bloody battleground. Mao Zedong had recently quelled an uprising in the Kham region of Tibet, employing extraordinary brutality and raising the ire of Tibetan nationalists everywhere. Rumors circulated widely that Mao intended to arrest and then execute the Dalai Lama.

The Dalai Lama fled Tibet, set up a government-in-exile in northern India, and vowed to return to a liberated Tibet someday. The Chinese did not wait. During the next 30 years they killed 1.2 million Tibetans and destroyed 6,200 Buddhist monasteries. As late as 2000, the Dalai Lama continued to protest Chinese occupation of his homeland.

SUGGESTED READINGS: A. T. Grunfeld, *The Making of Modern Tibet*, 1987; Alastair Lamb, *The British and Tibet*, 1986.

THE TODAY SHOW. *The Today Show*, which premiered on NBC televison on January 14, 1952, was a Monday-through-Friday program that began at 7:00 A.M. and targeted people preparing their families for work and school. At the time, most network affiliates did not begin programming until after 10:00 A.M. NBC gave the job of host of *The Today Show* to David Garroway, a laid-back personality with a sharp but affable wit. The show, which consisted of news and talk with guests, was only a modest success until 1953, when a chimpanzee named J. Fred Muggs was added to the cast. Ratings jumped because children began to watch the show. *The Today Show* was on its way to becoming an American institution.

SUGGGESTED READING: Robert Metz, *The Today Show*, 1977.

THE TONIGHT SHOW. On September 27, 1954, *The Tonight Show* premiered. It was the first "talk show" in a programming genre that one day would become a staple of television.* *The Tonight Show* came on every weeknight at 11:30 P.M. in the Eastern and Pacific time zones and 10:30 in the Central and Mountain zones. Its first host was comedian Steve Allen, who offered up lighthearted comedy and interviews with celebrity guests. Allen hosted *The Tonight Show* until 1957, when Jack Paar succeeded him. Paar's humor was a bit more risque than Allen's, and he was a more skilled interviewer, occasionally asking questions that had an edge to them. Nor was Paar unwilling to address political issues. Still, he was careful not to create an adversarial relationship with guests; Paar knew instinctively that people lying in bed watching television before falling to sleep were not interested in hearing verbal sparring and seeing fights. In 1962 Johnny Carson replaced Jack Paar as host of *The Tonight Show*.

SUGGESTED READING: Tim Brooks and Earle Marsh, *The Complete Directory to Prime Time Network and Cable TV Shows, 1946–Present*, 1995.

TRACY, SPENCER. Spencer Tracy was born on April 5, 1900, in Milwaukee, Wisconsin. He acquired a love for the theater as an adolescent, and after a brief stint at Ripon College, he moved to New York City and began studying at the American Academy of Dramatic Arts. He had some minor success on Broadway, securing critical acclaim for his performance in *The Last Mile*, and he then moved to Hollywood to make his first film—*Up the River* (1930). Tracy won back-to-back best actor Oscars for his performances in *Captains Courageous* (1937) and *Boys Town* (1938). By the 1950s, he was considered one of America's finest character actors, and he secured academy award nominations three times during the decade for *Father of the Bride* (1950), *Bad Day at Black Rock* (1955), and *The Old Man and the Sea* (1958). He received best acting nominations for his performances in *Inherit the Wind* (1960) and *Judgment at Nuremburg* (1961). Tracy died on June 10, 1967, and his last film, *Guess Who's Coming to Dinner*, was released posthumously.

SUGGESTED READING: Bill Davidson, *Spencer Tracy: Tragic Idol*, 1988.

TRANQUILIZERS. During the 1950s, scientists working at a number of prominent pharmaceutical companies developed the first generation of tranquilizer drugs designed to treat medically the symptoms of depression and anxiety. The first of those drugs to be widely used, thorazine, was approved by the Food and Drug Administration in 1954. Available only by prescription, thorazine relieved some of the symptoms of anxiety disorders, but it had serious side effects, often dulling the sense of recipients to the point that they could not perform normal activities. Researchers began developing drugs that had thorazine's beneficial properties without its negative side effects.

In 1950 the pharmaceutical company Ludwig and Piech developed what became the most popular tranquilizer, the drug meprobomate, known generically as Miltown. It was marketed by Wyeth Laboratories as Equinal. Equinal and Miltown were essentially muscle relaxants that created a sense of well-being among those who took them. Tranquilizers became instantly popular, and by 1957 a total of 36 drug companies had placed 73 different tranquilizer drugs on the market. That year physicians in the United States wrote nearly 40 million prescriptions for tranquilizers, and the drug companies grossed $160 million from them. Tranquilizers were prescribed for alcoholism, drug dependency, depression, anxiety disorders, phobias, and a host of other ailments.

While the drug companies hailed tranquilizers as non–habit forming answers to life's most difficult challenges, critics charged that the popularity of tranquilizers demonstrated just how much a modern, consumer, conformist society had alienated normal men, women, and children. Americans wanted tranquilizers, the social critics argued, because their lives had no meaning. Consumerism was not a satisfying way of life and only created increasing pressures for more of the same. David B. Allman, president of the American Medical Association, warned that "modern man cannot solve his problems of daily living with a pill."

In the long run, both advocates and critics had their points. Contrary to drug company hype, tranquilizers could indeed be habit forming, and physicians prescribed them too readily, especially when patients complained of difficult to diagnose, nonspecific maladies. At the same time, the first generation of tranquilizers pioneered the way to the sophisticated antidepressants of the 1990s, which treated a number of emotional disorders rooted not in social alienation but in genetic and biochemical abnormalities.

SUGGESTED READING: Richard Hughes, *The Tranquilizing of America: Pill-Popping and the American Way of Life*, 1979.

TRANSISTOR. Until the 1950s, electronic equipment was made up of glass vacuum tubes, which allowed for electrical activity without the resistance of air inside the tubes. The components were bulky and scientists searched for an alternative. Bell Laboratories headed the research that led to success. Bell's team of William Chockley, John Bardeen, and Walter Brattain developed semiconductors constructed from the metal germanium.

The key problem with germanium, however, was its availability. The metal was extremely rare, and only thirteen pounds of it were produced worldwide in 1950. Bell scientists then figured out how to substitute silicon for germanium. The first commercially available silicon transistor appeared in 1954. The transistor led to the electronics revolution of modern history. Four years later, in 1958, scientists at Texas Instruments and Fairchild Semiconductor developed the first silicon microchip and then figured out how to develop circuits that could connect the microchips. Such miniaturization led to the computer revolution.

SUGGESTED READINGS: John Diebold, *The Innovators: The Discoveries, Inventions, and Breakthroughs of Our Time*, 1990; Michael Riordan, *Crystal Fire: The Birth of the Information Age*, 1997.

TRANSISTOR RADIO. In 1952 Sony Corporation, a Japanese company, introduced the transistor radio to American consumers. An electronics innovation that provided a pocket-sized radio, the transistor radio became an instant consumer success, and Sony sold millions of them in the United States. The transistor radio had a symbolic significance, as well, for two reasons: it highlighted the recovery of the Japanese economy from the ravages of World War II, and the transistor launched the consumer electronics revolution that would stimulate enormous economic growth throughout the world in the twentieth century.

SUGGESTED READINGS: John Diebold, *The Innovators: The Discoveries, Inventions, and Breakthroughs of Our Time*, 1990; Michael Riordan, *Crystal Fire: The Birth of the Information Age*, 1997.

TRUMAN, HARRY S. Harry S. Truman was born in Lamar, Missouri, on May 8, 1884. His father was a hardworking farmer. After graduating from high school, the younger Truman worked for several railroads and several banks; he then helped his father manage a dairy farm in Grandview, Missouri. When World War I erupted in 1917, Truman joined the Missouri National Guard and eventually saw combat in France as commander of an artillery battery. When he returned from the war, Truman started his own business selling men's clothing in Kansas City, but the business failed. Active in Democratic party politics, he rose through the ranks of Tom Pendergast's political machine and in 1922 won election as a judge in Jackson County. In 1934, with Pendergast's blessing, Truman was elected to the United States Senate.

In the Senate, Truman proved to be a faithful supporter of President Franklin D. Roosevelt and the New Deal, and late in the 1930s he also backed the president's move toward a more activist foreign policy. Truman made a name for himself during World War II as head of a senate committee investigating graft and corruption in military procurement contracts. In 1944, Roosevelt selected Truman as his vice presidential running mate. Truman took the oath of office as vice president on January 20, 1945, and he became president of the United States on April 12, 1945, upon the sudden death of Franklin D. Roosevelt. In the election of 1948, he defeated Republican nominee Thomas Dewey even though all the polls predicted defeat for Truman.

As president, Truman led America down the path to the Cold War.* To prevent Soviet expansion in southern and western Europe, he launched the Truman Doctrine in 1947, which supplied U.S. financial and military aid to anti-Communist forces in Greece and Turkey, and the Marshall Plan in 1948, which eventually supplied more than $10 billion to the countries of Western Europe to rebuild their economies and war off communist insurgencies. In 1949, when Mao Zedong* and his communists established the People's Republic of China, President Truman severed diplomatic relations and tried to isolate China, which he considered a rogue nation, from the rest of the world community. In 1950, when North Korean forces invaded Sourth Korea, Truman brought the United States into the conflict as the main contingent of a United Nations army driving the North Koreans back across the 38th parallel. When China joined the war, Truman found himself fighting a ground war in Asia, and it became the first so-called "limited war" in American history. Afraid of the possibility of Korea escalating into a larger conflagration with the Soviet Union, Truman did not use all of his military assets, and in doing so courted the criticism of political and military conservatives. He also found himself at odds with General Douglas MacArthur,* who wanted to adopt a more aggressive, all-out posture toward China. In 1951, when MacArthur publicly criticized Truman for being too cautious, the president summarily fired him. The decision earned Truman even more criticism from conservatives.

In terms of domestic policy, Truman tried to revive Roosevelt's New Deal philosophy when World War II ended. Calling his program the "Fair Deal," Truman succeeded in securing improvements in social security and the GI "Bill of Rights" for veteran education and housing, but he failed in his dream to implement a program of national health insurance. In the Employment Act of 1946, he established the Council of Economic Advisors and succeeded in making the federal government the key force in shaping national economic policy and achieving full employment and stable prices. Historians now look back on Harry Truman as a key figure in the development of the Democratic party's commitment to social justice.

When it came time to seek another term in 1952, President Truman decided not to stand for reelection. The Korean War* had proven extremely controversial, and war-time inflation irritated many Americans. Worried that he might lose the election, the president returned to private life. Until his death on December 26, 1972, he served as the elder statesman of the Democratic party.

SUGGESTED READINGS: Robert J. Donovan, *Conflict and Crisis: The Presidency of Harry S. Truman, 1945–1948*, 1977, and *Tumultuous Years: The Presidency of Harry S. Truman, 1949–1953*, 1982.

TRUTH OR CONSEQUENCES. *Truth or Consequences*, one of the most famous, long-running, and zany quiz shows in radio history, premiered on CBS radio on March 23, 1940, switched to NBC three months later, returned to CBS in September 1950, and then went back to NBC in June 1952. Ralph Edwards created and hosted the show, which posed questions to contestants who, if they answered incorrectly, were subjected to hilarious punishments, such as kissing skunks, bathing elephants, dancing with dogs, or imitating babies. It remained on the air until September 12, 1956.

SUGGESTED READING: John Dunning, *On the Air: The Encyclopedia of Old-Time Radio*, 1998.

TWENTY QUESTIONS. *Twenty Questions*, one of radio's most popular quiz shows, premiered on the Mutual Network on February 2, 1946, and survived until March 27, 1954. Fred Van Devanter of WOR radio in New Jersey created the show, which was like the famed parlor game, in which a group of players was required to identify an object by asking no more than twenty "yes or no" questions.

SUGGESTED READING: John Dunning, *On the Air: The Encyclopedia of Old-Time Radio*, 1998.

TWENTY-SECOND AMENDMENT. First proposed in 1947 and ratified in 1951, the Twenty-Second Amendment to the Constitution limited the president of the United States to two elected, four-year terms in office. An unelected president, if he or she had ever served more than half of the term of the previously elected president, was limited to one more four-year term. Until President Franklin D. Roosevelt, no American president had ever served more than two terms. Because of the crisis atmosphere of the Great Depression and World War II, however, and because of Roosevelt's charismatic personality, Americans had elected him to the presidency in 1932, 1936, 1940, and 1944. With hindsight, most Americans agreed that such service should not occur again since it would confer too much power on an individual.

SUGGESTED READING: Kermit L. Hall, ed., *The Oxford Companion to the Supreme Court of the United States*, 1992.

TWITTY, CONWAY. Conway Twitty was born Harold Lloyd Jenkins on September 1, 1933, in Friars Point, Mississippi. During the 1940s, under his given name, he formed a country music band known as the Phillips County Ramblers. After service in the U.S. Army, Jenkins renamed his band the Rockhousers and added rhythm-and-blues music to their repertoire. He also changed his name to Conway Twitty, which he selected from the names of two towns the band had traveled through on tour. In 1955 the Rockhousers made a demo record in Memphis with Sun Records,* and they had a minor hit in 1957 with "I Need Your Lovin'." Later in the year, their "Make Believe" was a smash hit, reaching number one on the pop music charts. Their "Lonely Blue Boy" in 1960 was another top-ten hit, and Twitty and the band enjoyed great success on the concert tour.

Like so many other rock-and-roll* stars, they were soon eclipsed by other groups. Twitty shifted to country music in 1964, and he signed with Decca Records in 1966. He enjoyed extraordinary success, selling more records than any other country performer until the 1990s, when Garth Brooks became a superstar. Among Twitty's most popular country hits are "Next in Line" (1968), "I Love You More Today" (1968), "To See My Angel Cry" (1969), "That's When She Started to Stop Loving Me" (1970), "Hello Darlin'" (1970), "She Needs Someone to Hold Her" (1972), "I Can't Stop Loving You" (1972), "Tight Fittin' Jeans" (1981), "The Clown" (1982), and "Don't Call Him a Cowboy" (1985). Twitty died on June 5, 1993, in Branson, Missouri.

SUGGESTED READINGS: *New York Times*, June 6, 1993; Patricia Romanowski and Holly George-Warren, *The New Encyclopedia of Rock & Roll*, 1995.

TWO FOR THE SEESAW. Written by William Gibson, *Two for the Seesaw*, a three-act, two-character play, opened on January 16, 1958, at the Booth Theater in New York City. The play is set in New York City. Jerry Ryan, played by Henry Fonda, is a resident of Omaha, Nebraska, who has become alienated from his wife. While in New York City, he becomes enchanted with Gittel Mosca (Anne Bancroft), a young, liberal Jewish woman. They fall in love, but the romance swings back and forth between their attraction for one another and the pull of loyalties to their own families. In the end, Ryan returns to Omaha and his wife. *Two for the Seesaw* had a run of 750 performances.

SUGGESTED READINGS: Gerald Bordman, *The Oxford Companion to American Theater*, 1992; *New York Times*, January 17, 1958.

U

THE UGLY AMERICAN. *The Ugly American* was one of most influential novels of the late 1950s and early 1960s. Written by William J. Lederer and Eugene Burdick, *The Ugly American*, published in 1958, spent 78 weeks on the bestseller list, sold four million copies, and was made into a major motion picture starring Marlon Brando.* The novel is set in the fictionalized Southeast Asian country of Sarkhan, where U.S. foreign policies are hopelessly ineffectual. Except for Colonel Hillandale, the lead character, most American foreign service officers in the novel are narrow-minded and short-sighted. They are political appointees unable to communicate in the language of the host country. They hear only what their interpreters want them to hear and obtain from newspapers only what their readers want them to obtain. They spend their days wining and dining American VIPs, socializing with other diplomats, and engaging the local elites. Communist diplomats, on the other hand, speak the local language and work closely with local peasants to build a political base. *The Ugly American* had a clear message: the United States was losing the Cold War* in the Third World.

SUGGESTED READINGS: William J. Lederer and Eugene Burdick, *The Ugly American*, 1958; James S. Olson and Randy Roberts, *Where the Domino Fell: America and Vietnam, 1945–1995*, 2000.

UNITED ARAB REPUBLIC. Bitter tribal and kinship rivalries have politically divided the Arab Peninsula since time immemorial. Occasionally, when external forces threaten them, the Arab peoples have managed to unite politically, but only for a short time, and as soon as the threat dissipates, they have returned to their former factionalism. Since World War II, the primary force working to unite Arabs has been the existence of the state of Israel. After the rise of Gamal Abdel Nasser* in Egypt and the disastrous Suez Canal war of 1956, some Arab statesmen tried to forge a new political reality. In 1958 Syria and Egypt joined to form the United Arab Republic (UAR) in an attempt to build a Pan-Arab movement and to secure some advantages, from either the Soviet Union or the United States, in the Cold War.*

New coalitions then appeared. Yemen officially affiliated with the UAR and formed the United Arab States. For a time, other Arab states—particularly Lebanon, Saudi Arabia, and Iraq—gravitated toward the UAR without establishing any formal connections.

Just as soon as it appeared that Pan-Arabism might be securing a foothold in the Middle East, old rivalries surfaced again. Iraqi dictator Abdul Karim Kassem had a falling out with Nasser, and the Syrians decided he was behaving too autocratically. The Saudi Arabians and Yemenis eventually rejected Nasser's socialism. In 1961, after just three years, the United Arab Republic ceased to exist when Syria seceded.

SUGGESTED READINGS: R. Hrair Dekmejian, *Egypt Under Nasir: A Study in Political Dynamics*, 1971; Joachem Joesten, *Nasser: The Rise to Power*, 1974; Mary Shivanandan, *Nasser: Modern Leader of Egypt*, 1973.

UNIVAC. UNIVAC, an acronym for Universal Automatic Computer, was America's first commercially viable computer. In 1946 two University of Pennsylvania scientists, John Eckert and John Mauchly, constructed ENIAC, an all-electronic digital computer made for the U.S. Army. They then left the University of Pennsylvania to go into business for themselves as the Eckert-Mauchly Computing Corporation. Their business skills, however, did not match their scientific know-how, and they sold their technology in 1950 to Remington Rand, one of the country's largest office supply companies. Remington Rand ran with the technology and in 1951 sold UNIVAC to the U.S. Census Bureau's Philadelphia office.

UNIVAC, which brought America into the information age, used magnetic tape to input and download data at a rate of 7,200 digits a second, far faster than bulky punch cards. It also had the capability of dealing with alphabetic characters, not just numerical characters. Its powers became particularly well known in 1952 when CBS News television used UNIVAC to cover the presidential election. UNIVAC predicted an overwhelming victory for Dwight D. Eisenhower* after only 7 percent of the votes nationwide had been actually counted. Its predictions proved to be highly accurate.

UNIVAC also revolutionized the office machine industry, which still employed mechanical machines to handle data. International Business Machines (IBM) felt threatened by Remington Rand's success and began to develop its own computers. Thomas Watson, IBM's founder, had been slow to warm up to the idea of computers, but in 1952, his son took over the company. Thomas Watson, Jr.* enthusiastically pushed IBM into the computer business. Although its 700 series machines were technologically no match for Remington-Rand's computers, IBM had an excellent sales forces that overwhelmed the market. By 1957 IBM had captured more than 50 percent of the computer market. Today, historians regard UNIVAC as the first workable model in the first generation of computers.

SUGGESTED READINGS: William Rodgers, *Think: A Biography of the Watsons and IBM*, 1969; Joel N. Shurkin, *Engines of the Mind: A History of the Computer*, 1984.

V

VALENS, RICHIE. Richie Valens was born Richard Stephen Valenzuela in Pacoima, California, on May 11, 1941. Fascinated with the guitar and with the advent of rock-and-roll,* Valens became the first popular Mexican-American rock star with the release of his song "Donna," which rocketed to number two on the pop music charts and earned Valens a billing on *American Bandstand.* He then recorded "La Bamba," a song in Spanish that had more longevity in rock history.

Early in 1959, Valens decided to go on tour. His recent success with "Donna" had to be sustained, and he wanted to promote "La Bamba." He signed on with Winter Dance Party, a touring rock-and-roll show that catered to rural audiences in the Midwest. Buddy Holly* and J. P. Richardson* ("The Big Bopper") were the tour's other attractions. Severe winter weather in February all but canceled the tour. On February 2, 1959, Holly chartered a private plane to fly his band from Clear Lake, Iowa, to the next show in Moorhead, North Dakota. At the last minute, to avoid a long ride in a tour bus, Valens and Richardson hitched a ride on the plane. Soon after midnight, on February 3, the plane crashed in fog and heavy snow. The three rock stars were killed instantly.

SUGGESTED READINGS: *New York Times*, February 5, 1959; Patricia Romanowski and Holly George-Warren, *The New Encyclopedia of Rock & Roll*, 1995.

VIETCONG. The term "Vietcong" was coined by South Vietnamese president Ngo Dinh Diem in the 1950s as a reference to "Vietnamese Communists." Coming from him, it was more epithet than definition. The Vietcong were primarily South Vietnamese Communists committed to the overthrow of the American-backed government of the Republic of Vietnam. During the late 1950s and early 1960s, the Vietcong became a formidable army in South Vietnam, supported by Russian and Chinese supplies brought to them down the Ho Chi Minh trail. The inability of South Vietnamese troops to prevail militarily against the Vietcong ultimately led to the U.S. escalation of the conflict. The Vietcong remained a powerful fighting force until the Tet Offensive of 1968, in which they suffered huge losses at the hands of American troops. After Tet, Vietnam was largely a war against North Vietnamese forces.

SUGGESTED READING: James S. Olson and Randy Roberts, *Where the Domino Fell: America and Vietnam 1945–1995*, 2000.

VIETNAM WAR. During the 1950s, the United States steadily became more and more deeply involved in Southeast Asia, and that involvement eventually led to the Vietnam War. For decades, Vietnamese nationalists had waged a guerrilla war against the French colonial empire, but the leading Vietnamese nationalists, led by Ho Chi Minh,* were Communists. In the Red Scare* atmosphere of the late 1940s, American policy makers decided that Ho, a Communist and a devotee of Karl Marx and V. I. Lenin, was a danger to national security. He was also, as he had always been, a genuine nationalist who wanted to see Vietnam independent and free of all foreign domination. But as the United States entered the years of the Cold War,* Ho Chi Minh's communism became far more important in American eyes than his nationalism. By 1950 the United States was providing hundreds of millions of dollars in military assistance to France, hoping that they would be able to defeat the Communists and maintain control of their colony.

But France steadily lost ground in Vietnam, and Ho Chi Minh developed an army of more than 100,000 highly committed troops. In the spring of 1954, when French forces were about to undergo a humiliating defeat at the Battle of Dien Bien Phu,* France appealed for American air support and, if necessary, American ground troops to rescue the embattled French Expeditionary Corps from Ho Chi Minh's attacking army. President Dwight D. Eisenhower* ultimately decided not to intervene, and Dien Bien Phu fell to the Communists, all but destroying the French empire in Indochina.

With the French empire crumbling, Eisenhower worked to preserve a noncommunist base of some kind in Indochina. The domino theory* enjoyed increasing credibility among American policy makers, who believed that if Vietnam fell to communism, a chain reaction of falling dominos would begin that might eventually bring all of Southeastern Asia, and perhaps East Asia, under Communist control. In the Geneva Accords of 1954, the United States secured the division of Vietnam at the 17th parallel. North Vietnam would be Communist and South Vietnam would be non-Communist. In 1956 free elections would be held to reunite the country. Ho Chi Minh became the leader of the Democratic Republic of Vietnam (North Vietnam), and Ngo Dinh Diem, an anticommunist Vietnamese nationalist, became president of the Republic of Vietnam (South Vietnam).

When the Central Intelligence Agency determined that Ho Chi Minh would win handily in the north and the south, the elections were canceled. An angry Ho, feeling betrayed, began recruiting sympathetic Vietnamese into a southern army which became known as the Vietcong.* The Vietcong launched a guerrilla war against the American-backed regime of Ngo Dinh Diem, a corrupt, anti-Buddhist Roman Catholic whose self-serving policies soon alienated most South Vietnamese. The Vietcong kept gaining ground, and Eisenhower had to send in hundreds of U.S. military advisors to train the South Vietnamese army. By the time Eisenhower left the White House, more than 700 U.S. military advisors were in South Vietnam.

SUGGESTED READING: James S. Olson and Randy Roberts, *Where the Domino Fell: America and Vietnam, 1945–1995*, 2000.

VINSON, FREDERICK. Frederick Moore Vinson was born in Louisa, Kentucky, on January 22, 1890. His father was a local jailer. The younger Vinson took his undergraduate and law degrees from Centre College in Danville, Kentucky, and then he practiced law privately. A loyal Democrat, he was district attorney for Kentucky's 32nd judicial district until 1926, when he was elected to Congress. He was not reelected in 1928 but regained his seat in 1930 and served four terms. As a member of the House Ways and Means Committee, Vinson faithfully backed President Franklin D. Roosevelt and became close friends with Senator Harry Truman* of Missouri. In 1938 Roosevelt appointed him to the Court of Appeals for the District of Columbia.

During World War II, Vinson became director of the Office of Economic Stabilization and then the Federal Loan Administrator. Toward the end of the war, Roosevelt named Vinson to head the Office of War Mobilization and Reconversion. He became secretary of the treasury under President Truman, and in 1946, when Chief Justice Harlan Stone died, Truman named Vinson chief justice of the U.S. Supreme Court.

He had an undistinguished term. Never given to hard work, Vinson cut back drastically on the Court's docket and heard only half the usual number of cases. He also believed that the Supreme Court was the third branch of government in priority, and that the justices should generally defer to the executive and legislative branches. The leading lights of the court—Felix Frankfurter,* William O. Douglas,* and Hugo Black—considered Vinson an intellectual lightweight. Only on race relations could Vinson be considered progressive, and there he threw his weight behind the *Sweatt v. Painter** and *McLaurin v. Oklahoma State Regents** decisions. Vinson died suddenly of a heart attack on September 8, 1953.

SUGGESTED READINGS: *New York Times*, September 9–10, 1953; C. Herman Pritchett, *Civil Liberties and the Vinson Court*, 1954.

VON BRAUN, WERNHER. Wernher von Braun was born in Wirsitz, Prussia, Germany, on March 23, 1912, to a family whose roots stretched deep into the Prussian nobility. During the Weimar Republic of the 1920s and early 1930s, before Adolf Hitler came to power, von Braun's father served as minister of food and agriculture. Although he did poorly in school, the younger von Braun became fascinated with astronomy and rocketry, and he joined clubs devoted to both pursuits. As an amateur, he developed rockets that could be launched. Von Braun earned a bachelor's degree in engineering in 1932, and his skills had become well known among the German army brass. He accepted appointment as director of an army rocket-testing facility, and at the same time he worked on his Ph.D. in physics, which he received in 1934.

When Hitler came to power, von Braun was appointed director of a new rocket research center built near the Baltic Coast of Prussia. He was charged with developing the means of delivering warheads to battlefield locations far beyond the range of regular artillery. The research led to the development, deployment, and use of the V-1 and V-2 rockets, which struck Great Britain repeatedly during the end stages of World War II. By war's end, more than 3,600 rockets had been detonated in England and Belgium. At the end of the war, when von Braun defected to the American side, he was developing a rocket capable of delivering 20 tons of explosives over a 3,000-mile range, far enough to attack the United States.

In America, von Braun went to work for the U.S. Army developing short- and medium-range missiles, and in 1950 he became head of the Redstone Arsenal in Huntsville, Alabama. Von Braun became head of the development operations division of the Army Ballistic Missile Agency in 1957. After the Soviet Union launched *Sputnik** in 1957, von Braun's work assumed more urgency, and his Jupiter-C rocket, in January 1958, became the first U.S. rocket to lift an artificial satellite into orbit. Von Braun eventually became head of the National Aeronautic and Space Administration's (NASA) effort to put a man on the moon. To von Braun goes the primary credit for the development of the Saturn V rocket that put three American astronauts on the moon in July 1969. In 1972, after two years as deputy associate administrator of NASA, von Braun retired from government service and went to work for Fairchild Industries. Wernher von Braun was a prolific writer as well. Among his books are *Across the Space Frontier* (1952), *The Exploration of Mars* (1956), *First Men to the Moon* (1960), and *New Worlds: Discoveries from Our Solar System* (1979). Wernher von Braun died on June 17, 1977.

SUGGESTED READING: Erik Bergaust, *Wernher von Braun: The Authoritative and Definitive Biographical Profile of the Father of Modern Space Flight*, 1976.

W

WAGON TRAIN. *Wagon Train*, one of the most popular Western dramas in television* history, included in its cast Ward Bond as Major Seth Adams, Robert Horton as Flint McCullough, Terry Wilson as Bill Hawks, and Frank McGrath as Charlie Wooster. On September 18, 1957, *Wagon Train* premiered on NBC television. It soon became a top-rated Western, focusing on a wagon train heading from Saint Joseph, Missouri, to California during the years following the Civil War. Each week, the episode focused on the trials and triumphs of one member of the crew, or a historical figure who would be written into the script. As a result, *Wagon Train* had the characteristics of an anthology. All of these character studies took place against the backdrop of the great American West, with its huge landscapes, Indians, mountain men, cowboys, and desperadoes. When Ward Bond died of a heart attack in 1960, Robert Horton took over the lead as frontier scout Flint McCullough. The last episode of *Wagon Train* was broadcast on September 5, 1965.

SUGGESTED READING: Tim Brooks and Earle Marsh, *The Complete Directory to Prime Time Network and Cable TV Shows, 1946–Present*, 1995.

WARREN, EARL. Earl Warren was born in Los Angeles, California, on March 19, 1891. His father, a Norwegian immigrant, made his living as a railroad car repairman. The younger Warren worked his way through the University of California at Berkeley and then took a law degree there. He practiced law privately before and after World War I, and in 1920 he became assistant prosecutor of Alameda County, California. Active in the Republican party, he was elected as district attorney of Alameda County in 1925, where he earned a reputation as a tough but sensible law-and-order prosecutor. Fourteen years later, he was elected state attorney general, and in 1942 he won the California governorship, making him one of the country's most prominent Republican politicians.

As governor of California, Warren pushed for the relocation of Japanese

Americans into concentration camps, not only to control security risks but also to protect them from the hostility of other Americans. Warren later regretted his role in the affair for the rest of his life. In fact, some historians speculate that Warren's subsequent advocacy of civil rights and civil liberties was actually an act of atonement for what he had done to Japanese Americans. Among Californians, however, Warren remained the most popular governor in history, and in 1946 both the Democratic and Republican parties endorsed his reelection. In the election of 1948, Warren served as Thomas Dewey's vice-presidential running mate, but Dewey and Warren lost to President Harry Truman* and Alben W. Barkley.

In 1952 Warren became a favorite-son candidate for president of the United States, meaning that he had not formally declared his candidacy but enjoyed the support of California's delegation to the Republican National Convention. Warren hoped that Dwight D. Eisenhower* and Robert Taft,* the frontrunners for the nomination, might neutralize one another and the convention might look to him as a compromise candidate. At the last minute, however, Senator Richard M. Nixon* sabotaged Warren's hopes by throwing his support behind Eisenhower. Warren never forgot or forgave Nixon for the act of political disloyalty. Nixon, of course, parlayed his backing of Eisenhower into the vice presidency.

In September 1953, Chief Justice of the Supreme Court Frederick Vinson* died suddenly, and President Eisenhower selected Earl Warren to fill the vacancy, expecting him to preside with caution and pragmatic conservatism. At first, Warren found himself doing a balancing act between conservative justices like Robert Jackson and Felix Frankfurter* and liberals like William O. Douglas* and Hugo Black. But he soon sided more with the liberals than with the conservatives, and the Warren Court would come to be remembered as the most liberal in U.S. history. Eisenhower later confessed that appointing Warren chief justice was "the biggest damn mistake I ever made."

Warren had surprised everyone. The political philosophy of the Warren Court became abundantly clear in 1954 with the *Brown v. Board of Education of Topeka, Kansas** decision in which the segregation of public schools was declared unconstitutional. During the rest of Warren's tenure, the Court became known for its support of individual civil rights, civil liberties, voting rights, and personal privacy in such cases as *Baker v. Carr, Engel v. Vitale, Gideon v. Wainwright, Escobedo v. Illinois, Miranda v. Arizona, Loving v. Virginia*, and *Gaston County v. United States*. Warren became the judicial symbol of the 1960s.

In 1968 Warren decided to resign from the Court. He had become convinced that because of riots in the streets and opposition to the Vietnam War,* Democrats would not be able to keep control of the White House and that Republican Richard Nixon would probably become the next president of the United States. Warren loathed Nixon and did not want him to be able to nominate a new chief justice. Warren resigned from the court on June 11, 1968. Warren spent the rest of his life lecturing and writing. He died on July 9, 1974.

SUGGESTED READINGS: D. J. Herda, *Earl Warren: Chief Justice for Social Change*, 1995; Arnold Rice, *The Warren Court, 1953–1969*, 1987; Bernard Schwartz, *Super Chief: Earl Warren and His Supreme Court*, 1987; John Downing Weaver, *Warren: The Man, the Court, and the Era*, 1967; G. Edward White, *Earl Warren: A Public Life*, 1983.

WATKINS V. UNITED STATES (1957). On June 17, 1957, a day conservatives and anticommunists labeled "Red Monday,"* the U.S. Supreme Court handed down a number of important decisions concerning civil liberties, in particular the extent to which an individual could be punished for maintaining radical or revolutionary political views. One of those cases was *Watkins v. United States*, which concerned a union member who admitted to the House Un-American Activities Committee that he was a member of the American Communist party but who refused to identify any other party members. Because he would not "name names," Congress held him in contempt. He filed a lawsuit claiming that his constitutional rights had been violated.

The U.S. Supreme Court agreed with Watkins and overthrew the contempt of Congress citation. The Court's reason held that such a compromise of the Fifth Amendment was not justified, especially given the fact that Watkins had never advocated the overthrow of the U.S. government. J. Edgar Hoover,* director of the Federal Bureau of Investigation* (FBI), felt that the Supreme Court had helped promote the Communist cause with its decision in *Watkins v. United States*.

SUGGESTED READINGS: Richard Gird Powers, *Secrecy and Power: The Life of J. Edgar Hoover*, 1987; Athan Theoharis, *Spying on Americans: Political Surveillance from Hoover to the Huston Plan*, 1978.

WATSON, THOMAS, JR. Thomas Watson, Jr., was born in Dayton, Ohio, on January 8, 1914. That same year his father, Thomas Watson, Sr., had taken over the Computing Tabulating Recording Company and renamed it International Business Machines, or IBM. The senior Watson turned IBM into a prosperous concern specializing in manufacturing machinery for the punch-card tabulating business. Watson, Jr., who graduated from Brown University in 1937, spent World War II with the Army Air Corps, and when he was mustered out in 1946, he joined IBM, where he worked first as a salesman in the financial district of Manhattan. His rise through the ranks was based, of course, on his father's power, but it was also clear to everyone that Watson, Jr., was blessed with enormous business potential. Thomas Watson, Jr., was named president of IBM in 1952, and in 1956, he became chief executive officer.

Unlike his father, who was rather cautious and conservative about computer technology, Watson, Jr., regarded the computer as the building block of the postindustrial economy, and he aggressively pushed IBM into the electronic age, knowing that computers would make the electromechanical tabulating business obsolete. The future of the world would be determined by information, and computers would provide it. He was right. At the same time, he continued his father's insistence on sales and service, a strength that distinguished IBM from all of its competitors. IBM's large mainframe computers became industry standards. By the late 1950s, IBM had become the largest, most powerful company in the industry, surpassing Sperry-Rand, RCA, Honeywell, and General Electric. Thomas Watson, Jr., was recognized as one of the country's shrewdest businessmen.

He retired in 1971, and from 1979 to 1981, Watson served as U.S. ambassador to the Soviet Union, an appointment he received from fellow Democrat, President Jimmy Carter. He spent the rest of the 1970s and early 1980s assisting IBM in warding off a government antitrust suit. Thomas Watson, Jr., died on December 31, 1993.

SUGGESTED READINGS: *New York Times*, December 31, 1993; William Rodgers, *Think: A Biography of the Watsons and IBM*, 1969; Thomas Watson, Jr., *Father, Son & Company: My Life at IBM and Beyond*, 1990.

WATTS TOWERS. Beginning in 1931, Simon Rodilla, a resident of the Watts section of Los Angeles, began assembling urban trash—bottles, cans, cardboard, rocks, car parts, and glass—into three cathedral-like towers. Rodilla had never been trained in art or sculpture, but he was a man of vision in tune with the urban environment. For 33 years he worked on the towers, which became a perfect artistic expression of the grit, strength, and diversity of American urban life. In 1954 Rodilla put the last bottle cap in place and finished the towers, which today are recognized by art critics around the world as works of genius.

SUGGESTED READING: Bud Goldstone, *The Los Angeles Watts Towers*, 1997.

WAYNE, JOHN. John Wayne was born as Marion Mitchell Morrison on May 25, 1907, in Winterset, Iowa. When he was still a child, the family moved to California, and he was raised in Glendale, a suburb of Los Angeles. He graduated second in his class at Glendale High School and won a football scholarship to the University of Southern California. During the summer after his freshman year, he got a job working at the Fox Studio in Hollywood, where he met John Ford, the legendary director. Within a few months, he quit school and went to work full-time in the movie business.

He appeared in several bit roles in 1926 and 1927, but in 1928 director Raoul Walsh saw Wayne on the Fox Studio lot and hired him for the lead in his epic film *The Big Trail*. At that point in his career, Morrison took the stage name John Wayne. A box-office flop, *The Big Trail* put Wayne's career on hold. For the next ten years, Wayne made dozens of B Westerns and serials and became a familiar face to audiences in the small towns of the West, Midwest, and South. Wayne's big break came in 1939, when John Ford gave him a starring role as the Ringo Kid in *Stagecoach*.

During World War II and just after, Wayne made a number of films that projected him to superstardom in American popular culture. His war movies—

Flying Tigers (1942), *Reunion in France* (1942), *Pittsburgh* (1942), *The Fighting Seabees* (1944), *Back to Bataan* (1945), and *They Were Expendable* (1945)—made him Hollywood's most important male lead. By the end of the war, for millions of Americans, John Wayne truly *was* America. In the postwar years, he made films like *Red River* (1948), *Fort Apache* (1948), *The Sands of Iwo Jima* (1949), *Hondo* (1953), and *The Searchers* (1956). As cowboy or soldier, Wayne displayed a hardened implacability and a determined inflexibility that marked his best film roles and his actual life. Although his distinctive diction has been often imitated, he is better remembered for what he did on screen rather than what he said. He restored order. Sometimes his methods were harsh, occasionally his manner was gruff, but always the result was the same. He affirmed that there was a rough sense of justice at work and that if good was not always rewarded, evil was always punished.

During the 1950s and 1960s, Wayne also earned a reputation as a committed anticommunist and political conservative. He was an outspoken patriot who minced few words in his love for his country and in his disdain for those who criticized it. He made a series of films in the 1960s, including *North to Alaska* (1960), *The Comancheros* (1961), *The Man Who Shot Liberty Valance* (1962), *Hatari!* (1962), *How the West Was Won* (1962), *The Longest Day* (1963), *Donovan's Reef* (1963), *McLintock!* (1963), *Circus World* (1964), *The Greatest Story Ever Told* (1965), *In Harm's Way* (1965), *The Sons of Katie Elder* (1965), and *Cast a Giant Shadow* (1966). Wayne received a Best Actor Oscar for his performance as Rooster Cogburn in *True Grit* (1969).

During the 1970s, Wayne continued to act and to speak out on political issues. By that time, of course, he had become a certifiable popular culture icon and had perhaps the most recognizable face on the planet. His last film, *The Shootist*, was released in 1976. John Wayne died on June 11, 1979.

SUGGESTED READING: Randy Roberts and James S. Olson, *John Wayne, American*, 1995.

WEBB, JACK. Jack Webb was born April 2, 1920, in Santa Monica, California. As a child he became fascinated with radio, and he moonlighted at nights for several Los Angeles radio stations when he was in high school. He served in the Army Air Corps during World War II, and after the war he got a job with station KGO, an ABC affiliate in San Francisco. Webb's deep, baritone voice resonated well over the airwaves, and he did not remain a staff announcer and disc jockey for long. His program *The Coffee Club* was a moderately successful morning jazz show, and his 1946 *Jack Webb Show* was a zany comedy. But Webb's big break came with *Pat Novak*, in which for 26 weeks he played a hard-boiled waterfront detective.

Webb then left San Francisco for Hollywood, where he acted in such radio series as *Escape, The Whistler,** and *This Is Your FBI.** On the set of his 1948 film *He Walked by Night*, Webb became friends with Sergeant Marty Wynn of the Los Angeles Police Department (LAPD), who was working as a technical advisor for the movie. The two talked at length about the possibility of a radio series dealing with crime and police investigation, and the result was *Dragnet*,* which premiered on NBC radio on June 3, 1949. Wynn helped Webb gain access to LAPD records and personnel, as long as Webb promised to protect the confidentiality of officers and victims. The LAPD also required strict control of scripts, which Webb had no trouble granting, since he was a strong supporter of the police. For Jack Webb, the police were the good guys and the criminals were the bad guys, and there was no middle ground between the two.

In *Dragnet*, Webb starred as Sergeant Joe Friday, a hard-boiled detective committed to law and order. Friday gave criminals no quarter, but he also displayed a compassionate side. The series trafficked in realism—real dialogue and real crimes. Webb honed a deadpan delivery that soon became his trademark, and *Dragnet*, unlike other police dramas, was willing to deal with the underbelly of society—sexual crimes, murder, and other forms of abuse. By the early 1950s, *Dragnet* was one of NBC's most popular programs. It survived until 1957, when the network canceled it. Webb was not disappointed since he had already launched the television version of *Dragnet*, which was an even bigger hit than the radio version.

The radio and television versions of *Dragnet* propelled Jack Webb into the forefront of American popular culture, but as an actor, he could never transcend the role of Joe Friday. Jack Webb died of a heart attack on December 23, 1982. Out of respect for his portrayal of them, the LAPD flew all of its flags at half-staff for a day.

SUGGESTED READINGS: John Dunning, *On the Air: The Encyclopedia of Old-Time Radio*, 1998; *Los Angeles Times*, December 24–25, 1982; Jack Webb, *The Badge*, 1958.

WEST POINT SCANDAL. In 1951 Americans were startled to learn that 90 cadets at the U.S. Military Academy at West Point had been dismissed for violating the school's honor code. More particularly, they had been found guilty of cheating on classroom examinations. The cadets had secured copies of examinations in advance and then prepared the answers to the questions. Half of the guilty cadets were members of the football team. West Point trafficked in bravery, honor, and manhood, and the cheating scandal badly tarnished the academy's image. When news of the scandal broke, America was in the midst of the Korean War* and the Red Scare,* and pundits wondered what was happening to young people. Conservatives blamed the Communist infiltration of America, citing the cheating scandal as proof that no American institution was sacrosanct. Liberals claimed that college athletics had taken on a life of its own and that the West Point scandal, along with the college basketball scandals* of 1951, demonstrated a need for reform.

SUGGESTED READING: Randy Roberts and James Olson, *Winning Is the Only Thing: Sports in America Since 1945*, 1989.

WEST SIDE STORY. One of the most popular and enduring plays in American theater history, *West Side Story* opened on September 26, 1957, at the Winter Garden Theater in New York City. It was based on a book written by Arthur Laurents that was very loosely based on Shakespeare's play *Romeo and Juliet.* Leonard Bernstein* wrote the music and Stephen Sondheim the lyrics. Jerome Robbins* choreographed the dances. The play concerns the Sharks and the Jets, two rival New York City street gangs. Tony, played by Larry Kerr, is a Jet who falls in love with Maria (Carol Lawrence), the sister of the leader of the Sharks. The two gangs go to war, and in an effort to stop the violence, Tony accidentally kills Maria's brother. Tony is then killed in a counterattack, and Maria is left to mourn the passing of her lover and her brother. *West Side Story* produced three hit songs: "I Feel Pretty," "Maria," and "Tonight."

SUGGESTED READINGS: Gerald Bordman, *The Oxford Companion to American Theater*, 1992; *New York Times*, May 14, 1954.

THE WHISTLER. *The Whistler*, a crime melodrama, first appeared on CBS radio on May 16, 1942. For a number of years the broadcast was confined to West Coast audiences. The main character, "The Whistler," was a stereotypical man of mystery whom many listeners likened to the Shadow and the Green Hornet. The Whistler tracked down murderers, solved crimes, and protected the innocent, always managing to see what the police could not. He caught criminals in the logic of their own lies, tripping them up on the smallest of inconsistent details. The last episode of *The Whistler* was broadcast on September 8, 1955.

SUGGESTED READING: John Dunning, *On the Air: The Encyclopedia of Old-Time Radio*, 1998.

THE WILD ONE. During the early 1950s, Americans became deeply concerned about the problem of juvenile delinquency,* and the film *The Wild One* only reinforced that concern. Released in 1953, *The Wild One* starred Marlon Brando* as the leader of a motorcycle gang that terrorizes a small town somewhere in middle America. The town folk are innocent, hardworking, mind-their-own-business type people, while the cyclists are menacing and pathological. They have only contempt for the middle-class values of hard work, family, and citizenship. Along with other films like *Blackboard Jungle* and *Rebel Without a Cause,* *The Wild One* convinced millions of Americans that prevailing concerns about juvenile delinquency were not exaggerated.

SUGGESTED READING: *New York Times*, December 31, 1953.

WILKINS, ROY. Roy Wilkins, one of America leading civil rights figures, was born in St. Louis, Missouri, on August 30, 1901. His parents soon moved to Minneapolis, Minnesota, where he was raised. Wilkins graduated from the University of Minnesota in 1923 after working his way through school with odd jobs. He also edited the St. Paul *Appeal*, an African-American newspaper. In

1924 Wilkins moved to Kansas City, Missouri, and accepted a job as a journalist with the *City Call*, another African-American newspaper. As a Minnesotan, Wilkins had experienced some racial discrimination, but nothing prepared him for Missouri's Jim Crow system. Rigid segregation there raised his political consciousness, and he joined the National Association for the Advancement of Colored People (NAACP). "Kansas City ate my heart out," he later remarked. "It wasn't any one melodramatic thing. It was a slow accumulation of humiliations and grievances. I was constantly exposed to Jim Crow in the schools, movies, downtown hotels and restaurants." Wilkins was a patient, even-tempered man who despised discrimination, and he soon became a powerful influence in the national NAACP.

In 1931 he moved to New York City to work as assistant executive secretary to Walter White, head of the NAACP. Three years later, he was named editor of *Crisis*, the NAACP's official publication. At the time, the NAACP targeted lynching as a major evil requiring federal intervention. Wilkins in 1931 was arrested for leading a demonstration in Washington, D.C., against Attorney General Homer Cummings, who opposed a federal antilynching law. Throughout the 1930s, Wilkins kept up his crusade against the lynching of African Americans. In the 1940s, he turned his attention to desegregation* of the armed forces. He was the primary planner of the NAACP legal strategy that led to the famous *Brown v. Board of Education of Topeka, Kansas** decision in 1954. When Walter White died in 1955, Wilkins assumed the position of executive secretary of the NAACP. From that position, he was at the forefront of the NAACP's fight against segregation. Later in his life, some black militants accused Wilkins of being too conservative and too accomodationist, but he remained faithful to his convictions that the best chance for African Americans to secure equality was through legal and political action and education. Roy Wilkins retired from the NAACP in 1977. He died on September 8, 1981.

SUGGESTED READINGS: *New York Times*, September 9, 1981; Roy Wilkins, *Standing Fast: The Autobiography of Roy Wilkins*, 1994.

WILLIAMS, HANK. Hank Williams was born Hiram Williams in Mount Olive, Alabama, on September 17, 1923, to a poor sharecropping family. While working as a shoeshine boy at the age of six, he learned to play the guitar from a local street performer, and he had a talent for the instrument. By the time he was 12 years old, Williams was singing at local honky-tonks and earning a regional reputation. He possessed a fine singing voice and enough internal pain to give his music real power. A streak of profound sadness tinged everything he said, sang, and did. In the years after World War II, he earned a national reputation with such songs as "Your Cheatin' Heart," "I'm So Lonesome I Could Cry," "Lovesick Blues," and "I'll Never Get Out of This World Alive." Beginning in 1948, he became a regular performer on the two most important country music radio programs in the country: *Louisiana Hayride* out of Shreveport, Louisiana, and *Grand Ole Opry** out of Nashville, Tennessee. From 1950 to

1953, he consistently had a record in the top ten of the country music best-selling charts.

Williams had become the top country western vocalist in the country. Earning $175,000 a year, he did concerts five times a week and performed on the *Grand Ole Opry* and *Louisiana Hayride* on weekends. The schedule took its toll on him. He was a tortured man, given to violence, alcohol, and drugs. Williams became so unpredictable in 1953 that *Grand Ole Opry* banned him from its Nashville stage. His death fulfilled the expectations of his music, which had for so long trafficked in loneliness, misery, and heartache. Estranged from his family, he died of heart failure in a drug-induced stupor on January 1, 1953.

SUGGESTED READINGS: *New York Times*, January 2–3, 1953; "Sadly the Troubador," *Newsweek*, 41 (January 19, 1953), 55.

WOMEN. During the 1950s, American women faced a social, political, and economic establishment that limited their opportunities and enmeshed them in a powerful set of expectations and moral regulations. When the GIs returned from World War II, marriage rates boomed in the United States. In 1945 the country recorded 1.6 million marriages, but the number jumped to 2.3 million in 1946. In 1947 more than 3.8 million babies were born in the United States, and between 1948 and 1953, more babies were born in the United States than in the previous 30-year period. Predictably, the U.S. population boomed too, from 150 million people in 1950 to 179 million people in 1960.

During World War II, tens of millions of American women had worked outside the home or attended college, but those numbers dropped with the end of the war. Between 1945 and 1958, the percentage of women college students dropped from more than 54 percent to only 35 percent, and the number of women in the workforce experienced similar declines. Although 35 percent of adult women worked outside the home in 1956, they had few "career" opportunities and, except for those who worked as teachers and nurses, little chance of promotion and advancement.

Suddenly, tens of millions of American women found themselves tied to home with large, young families. They also faced a popular culture that expected them to enjoy and cultivate that situation. Television* bombarded them with advertisements to buy things—clothes, appliances, furniture, automobiles, TV dinners,* cosmetics, and a host of other consumer products. Situation comedies like *Leave It To Beaver** and *Father Knows Best** portrayed the ideal woman as a domestic goddess who prepared her family's meals, dispensed wisdom and common sense, and always kept herself well-dressed and appropriately coiffed. Magazines like *Life, Ladies Home Journal, Redbook, Look*, and *Good Housekeeping* urged women to build their lives around the home. One *Life* editorial even suggested that "truly feminine women, with truly feminine attitudes . . . will accept their wifely functions with good humor and pleasure. . . . They should use their talents in every conceivable way . . . so long as their primary focus of interest and activity is the home."

Even amidst the rigidly conformist expectations of the 1950s, a revolution was in the making. Bretty Friedan, a frustrated young mother living in a New York suburb, tried to write about her frustrations, but when she found no publication outlets for her ideas, she began to write a book. When it was published in 1963, *The Feminine Mystique* launched the modern women's movement.

SUGGESTED READINGS: Wini Breines, *Young, White, and Miserable: Growing Up Female in the 1950s*, 1992; Victoria Byerly, *Hard Times Cotton Mill Girls*, 1986; Stephanie Coontz, *The Way We Never Were: American Families and the Nostalgia Trap*, 1992.

X

X-MINUS ONE. *X-Minus One*, a popular science fiction program, premiered on NBC radio on April 24, 1955. It was a sequel to another NBC science fiction radio series, *Dimension X*. The most popular plots involved space travel or the arrival on Earth of aliens of one variety or another. As such, *X-Minus One* complemented the science fiction fascination of the film industry during the 1950s. The last episode of *X-Minus One* aired on January 9, 1958.

SUGGESTED READING: John Dunning, *On the Air: The Encyclopedia of Old-Time Radio*, 1998.

Y

YATES V. UNITED STATES (1957). On June 17, 1957, a day conservatives and anticommunists labeled "Red Monday,"* the U.S. Supreme Court handed down a number of important decisions concerning civil liberties, particularly the extent to which an individual could be punished for maintaining radical or revolutionary political views. One of those cases was *Yates v. United States*. Congress passed the Smith Act of 1950* making it a federal crime to advocate or to form an organization committed to the overthrow of the U.S. government. In the 1951 case of *Dennis v. United States*,* the U.S. Supreme Court upheld the constitutionality of convictions under the Smith Act.

Yates v. United States was a test of the same law. On this occasion, however, the Court distinguished between mere speech—discussing the merits of overthrowing the government—and a concerted attempt to do so. The Court held that discussion was different from behavior, and it was protected by the First Amendment. This decision placed a critical limit on the Smith Act.

SUGGESTED READING: 354 U.S. 298 (1957).

YOU ASKED FOR IT. *You Asked for It* was a popular audience participation show of the 1950s. Viewers wrote in requesting to see something on television* that they had heard about but had never seen, and the producers filmed whatever was requested: the Grand Canyon, the gold in Fort Knox, and oddball people with oddball skills. When it premiered on the DuMont network in September 1950, it was known as *The Art Baker Show*, which was hosted by Art Baker. In April 1950, the title was changed to *You Asked for It*. The show switched to ABC television in December 1951, and Jack Smith took over the emcee duties in 1958. The last episode of *You Asked for It* was broadcast on September 27, 1959.

SUGGESTED READING: Tim Brooks and Earle Marsh, *The Complete Directory to Prime Time Network and Cable TV Shows, 1946–Present*, 1995.

YOU BET YOUR LIFE. *You Bet Your Life* is widely considered by television and pop culture historians to be one of the most memorable shows in history. It was hosted by Groucho Marx, the quit-witted, sarcastic comedian who came to fame in the 1930s as one of the Marx brothers. It was ostensibly a quiz show, in which Marx would ask a team of two contestants to answer relatively easy questions, and in return for correct answers they received small cash awards. But it was really a vehicle for Marx to interview them about their lives, and he had a knack for getting people to reveal personal details that he could then turn into a comic routine. NBC televison premiered the show on October 5, 1950. The producers took an hour of film each week and then edited it down to a 30-minute program. In doing so, they could retain the best material and, if necessary, edit out Marx's more risque remarks. The highly popular show remained on the air in prime time throughout the decade. Its last broadcast was on September 21, 1961. It then survived for years as a popular syndicated rerun.

SUGGESTED READING: Tim Brooks and Earle Marsh, *The Complete Directory to Prime Time Network and Cable TV Shows, 1946–Present,* 1995.

YOUNGSTOWN SHEET & TUBE CO. V. SAWYER (1952). Because of the Korean War* and the need to maintain economic productivity, President Harry Truman* decided to avoid a steel strike at all costs, including ordering Secretary of Commerce Charles Sawyer to seize the nation's steel mills and operate under government edict. Truman took the action without notifying Congress. Youngstown Steel sued, arguing that the president had exceeded his authority under Article I of the Constitution. On June 2, 1952, the U.S. Supreme Court agreed, claiming that such an action by the federal government required congressional authorization, not simply executive edict. In so ordering, the court took a major step in preserving the separation of powers and checks and balances so important to the Constitution.

SUGGESTED READING: 343 U.S. 306 (1952).

YOUR SHOW OF SHOWS. *Your Show of Shows* is considered today to be one of the classic programs of early television. A weekly variety and comedy show, it premiered on NBC on February 25, 1950, and for the next four years was the anchor of the network's Saturday night program lineup. The show had one of the best writing teams in television history, at one time including Mel Brooks, Neil Simon, Woody Allen, and Mel Tolkin. In front of the camera, some of the best talent in the business performed weekly, including Sid Ceasar, Imogene Coca, and Carl Reiner. Some of the more memorable sketches included "The Hickenloopers" and "History As She Ain't." They regularly spoofed popular films but kept a relatively low political profile. The show ended at the peak of its popularity in June 1954 when Caesar and Coca decided to pursue other professional opportunities.

SUGGESTED READING: Tim Brooks and Earle Marsh, *The Complete Directory to Prime Time Network and Cable TV Shows, 1946–Present,* 1995.

Z

ZINJANTHROPUS. In 1959 British anthropologists Louis and Mary Leakey, working in the Olduvai Gorge in Tanzania in Africa, discovered several bones from a creature that had some human characteristics. The Leakeys had long been trying to determine when in the evolutionary cycle that human beings had broken away from chimpanzees, their closest primate relative, and the Olduvai discovery helped them enormously. Using the potassium-argon dating method, the Leakeys determined that the creature had lived approximately 1.75 million years ago. They named the creature "Zinjanthropus Boisei" and claimed it to be a human ancestor. The discovery was the first in a series of similar discoveries that allowed the Leakeys to proclaim, with the backing of scientific evidence, their conviction that human beings had originated in Africa.

SUGGESTED READING: Delta Willis, *The Leakey Family: Leaders in the Search for Human Origins*, 1992.

ZORRO. A product of the Walt Disney Studio, *Zorro* was first broadcast on ABC television on October 10, 1957. The show was set in Spanish California during the early nineteenth century. Guy Williams starred as Don Diego de la Vega, a wealthy Spanish landowner by day who by night was "Zorro," a dashing, masked Robin Hood–type figure who robbed from the rich to give to the poor, who protected the weak, especially fetching young women, and who eliminated criminals and desperadoes. His trademark was the letter "Z," which he frequently left as a calling card on the shirts of his enemies by cutting the letter with his sword. The last episode of *Zorro* was broadcast on September 14, 1959.

SUGGESTED READING: Tim Brooks and Earle Marsh, *The Complete Directory to Prime Time Network and Cable TV Shows, 1946–Present*, 1995.

Chronology of the 1950s

1950

The Brinks robbery takes place (January 17).

Alger Hiss is convicted (January 25) of perjury and receives a five-year prison sentence.

Senator Joseph McCarthy delivers (February 9) his famous speech in Wheeling, West Virginia, claiming to know the names of 205 Communists working in the State Department.

RCA releases (March 29) the first color television set.

The U.S. Supreme Court upholds (April 10) the contempt of Congress convictions of the Hollywood Ten screenwriters.

The U.S. Supreme Court overturns (April 24) a criminal conviction of a black defendant on the grounds that the grand jury that indicted him excluded blacks.

President Harry Truman formally initiates (May 8) a U.S. military mission to Vietnam.

Senator Estes Kefauver of Tennessee opens (May 26) his congressional investigation of organized crime.

The U.S. Supreme Court rules (June 5) in *Sweatt v. Painter* that a state university public law school may not deny admission to a black applicant just because a state "black" law school is available.

The U.S. Supreme Court rules (June 5) in *McLaurin v. Oklahoma State Regents* that segregated facilities in state higher education are unconstitutional.

Soviet-equipped North Korean troops launch (June 25) a surprise invasion of South Korea. The United Nations Security Council orders a cease-fire and calls for the withdrawal of North Korean troops from South Korea.

President Harry Truman orders (June 26) U.S. armed forces to come to the military defense of South Korea.

Seoul, South Korea, falls (June 28) to North Korean forces.

U.S. ground forces are deployed (June 30) to South Korea.

General Douglas MacArthur is designated (July 8) commander of United Nations forces in Korea.

The Battle of Pusan Beachhead begins (August 6) in South Korea.

President Harry Truman orders (August 25) U.S. troops to seize the nation's railroads in order to avert a railroad strike.

Althea Gibson becomes (August 29) the first African-American woman to compete in a national professional tennis tournament.

President Harry Truman announces (September 9) that he will increase the number of U.S. troops stationed in Europe by augmenting the existing two divisions with four more divisions.

The Battle of Pusan Beachhead ends (September 15) in South Korea.

UN forces launch (September 15) the amphibious invasion of Inchon and begin a sweep across the northern reaches of South Korea.

The Internal Security Act becomes law (September 23) when Congress overrides President Harry Truman's veto of the bill.

General Douglas MacArthur announces (September 26) that UN forces have liberated Seoul, South Korea.

U.S. forces cross (October 1) the 38th parallel and invade North Korea.

President Harry Truman and General Douglas MacArthur meet (October 15) at Wake Island to work out disagreements about Korean War strategy.

U.S. forces capture (October 20–21) Pyongyang, North Korea's capital city.

U.S. forces reach (October 26) Chosan on the Yalu River, the boundary between North Korea and Manchuria in the People's Republic of China.

Two Puerto Rican nationalists fail (November 1) in their attempt to assassinate President Harry Truman.

Guys and Dolls opens (November 24) at the 46th Street Theater on Broadway.

Chinese forces launch (November 26) a massive counteroffensive against U.S. forces in the Yalu Valley of North Korea. U.S. forces retreat back to the 38th parallel and abandon Pyongyang.

The Soviet Union vetoes (November 30) a United Nations Security Council resolution ordering Chinese troops to withdraw from Korea.

The Brussels Conference convenes (December 18), agrees to rearm all the nations of Western Europe, and names General Dwight D. Eisenhower as supreme commander of NATO forces.

Congress passes (December 29) the Celler-Kefauver Act.

1951

The Chinese counteroffensive succeeds (January 4) in driving U.S. forces out of Seoul and south to the Han River.

The U.S. launches (January 25) a counteroffensive against Chinese forces.

The Twenty-Second Amendment to the Constitution is ratified (February 26).

U.S. forces retake (March 14) Seoul.

France, West Germany, Italy, Belgium, Holland, and Luxembourg establish (March 19) the European Coal and Steel Community.

Julius and Ethyl Rosenberg are sentenced to death (April 5) for passing classified U.S. atomic bomb information to the Soviet Union.

President Harry Truman seizes (April 8) the steel mills to break the strike.

On grounds of insubordination, President Harry Truman removes (April 11) General Douglas MacArthur as commander of United Nations forces in Korea.

General Douglas MacArthur speaks (April 19) before a joint session of Congress.

The U.S. Supreme Court decides (June 20) the *Youngstown Sheet and Tube v. Sawyer* case.

At the United Nations, a Soviet delegate proposes (June 23) a cease-fire in Korea and an armistice.

CBS television broadcasts (June 25) the first television show in color.

Congress passes (June 30) the McCarran-Walter Act.

Truce talks begin (July 10) at Kaesong to end the Korean War.

The Japanese Peace Treaty is signed (September 8) in San Francisco by 49 nations. In the treaty, the Allied powers agree to restore full sovereignty to Japan and to gradually withdraw their troops, while Japan agrees to extend full independence to Korea and renounces all of its claims to Formosa, the Pescadores, the Kuriles, Sakhalin, and its former Pacific Islands.

I Love Lucy premieres (October 5) on CBS television.

The Korean War truce talks shift (October 25) to Panmunjom, but the fighting continues.

1952

The Today Show premieres (January 14) on NBC television.

Fulgencio Batista assumes (March 10) dictatorial authority in Cuba.

President Harry Truman orders (April 8) government seizure of the steel industry to avoid a strike.

France, Italy, West Germany, Belgium, and the Netherlands sign (May 27) an agreement to create the European Defense Community, with its own all-European army.

The U.S. Supreme Court overrules (June 2) President Harry Truman's seizure of the steel industry as an unconstitutional usurpation of authority.

The Democratic party nominates (July 23) Governor Adlai Stevenson of Illinois for president.

In South Africa, all non-whites formally lose (August 27) the right to vote.

Rocky Marciano wins (September 23) the heavyweight boxing championship from Jersey Joe Walcott.

Vice President candidate Richard M. Nixon delivers (September 23) his "Checkers" speech denying that he diverted campaign funds for personal use.

The Revised Standard Version of the Bible is published (September 30).

The United States detonates (November 1) a hydrogen bomb.

Former General Dwight D. Eisenhower is elected president of the United States (November 4).

President-elect Eisenhower visits (December 2–5) the front in South Korea.

1953

Senator John Bricker of Ohio proposes (January 7) the Bricker Amendment to limit presidential authority to enter into treaties.

American Bandstand premiers (January 12) on ABC television in Philadelphia.

The Taiwan Straits crisis begins (February 3) when President Dwight D. Eisenhower lifts the U.S. Naval blockade of Taiwan, ostensibly allowing Taiwan to consider a military invasion of the People's Republic of China.

King George VI of England dies (February 6) and Princess Elizabeth becomes Queen Elizabeth.

Soviet Premier Joseph Stalin dies (March 5).

The federal government removes (March 12) the last of the Korean War price controls.

The Boston Braves baseball team moves (March 17) to Milwaukee, Wisconsin.

Congress establishes (April 11) the Department of Health, Education, and Welfare.

The televised hearings of Senator Joseph McCarthy's investigation of the U.S. Army begin (April 22).

The U.S. Supreme Court rules (May 4) that so-called white primary elections that exclude black voters violate the Fifteenth Amendment.

The televised hearings of Senator Joseph McCarthy's investigation of the U.S. Army end (June 17).

Julius and Ethyl Rosenberg are executed (June 19).

The armistice ending hostilities in Korea is signed (July 26).

An armistice between the United Nations, North Korea, and the People's Republic of China ends (July 27) the Korean War.

Congress passes (August 1) a joint resolution to begin the termination of the trust status of American Indian tribes.

Congress passes (August 7) the Refugee Relief Act.

Shah Reza Pahlevi assumes (August 25) dictatorial power in Iran.

Ernest Hemingway's novel *The Old Man and the Sea* goes on sale (September 1).

Nikita Khrushchev becomes (September 13) first secretary of the Central Committee of the Communist party in the Soviet Union.

Earl Warren becomes (September 30) chief justice of the U.S. Supreme Court.

The first 3-D movie—*Bwana Devil*—is released (November 15).

AT&T announces (December 1) plans to lay the world's first transatlantic telephone cable.

The U.S. Senate condemns (December 2) Senator Joseph McCarthy.

President Dwight D. Eisenhower makes (December 8) his "Atoms for Peace" proposal.

1954

Secretary of State John Foster Dulles announces (January 12) his "massive retaliation" doctrine.

The United States and South Korea enter (January 19) into a mutual defense treaty.

The Army-McCarthy hearings begin (February 18).

Widespread clinical trials of the Salk polio vaccine begin (February 23).

The Senate rejects (February 24) the Bricker Amendment.

Vietminh forces begin (March 13) their attack on French forces at Dien Bien Phu.

The Geneva Conference on Indochina convenes (April 26).

Roger Bannister becomes (May 6) the first athlete to run a sub-four-minute mile, with a time of 3:59.4.

Vietminh forces defeat (May 7) the French at the Battle of Dien Bien Phu.

Congress passes (May 13) the Wiley-Donder Act authorizing construction of the Saint Lawrence Seaway.

The U.S. Supreme Court decides (May 17) the *Brown v. Board of Education of Topeka, Kansas* case.

Queen Elizabeth II is formally coronated (June 2).

A CIA-backed army invades (June 18) Guatemala from Honduras and overthrows the pro-Communist government of Jacobo Arbenz Guzman.

The first Newport Jazz Festival begins (July 6) in Newport, Rhode Island.

Sun Records releases (July 19) the first professional recording by Elvis Presley—"That's All Right, Mama" and "Blue Moon of Kentucky."

The Geneva Agreements on Indochina are signed (July 20).

The Geneva Accords go into effect (July 21) dividing Vietnam along the 17th parallel into North Vietnam (the Democratic Republic of Vietnam) and South Vietnam (the Republic of Vietnam).

Congress passes (August 2) the Housing Act of 1954.

Congress passes (August 24) the Communist Control Act.

Congress passes (August 30) the Atomic Energy Act of 1954.

Hurricane Carol kills 53 people along the Atlantic Coast (August 31).

Under U.S. sponsorship, the Southeast Asia Treaty Organization, or SEATO, is established with the signing (September 8) of the Manila pact. SEATO is formed as a mutual defense alliance between the United States, Great Britain, France, New Zealand, Pakistan, the Philippines, and Thailand.

The Tonight Show premiers (September 27) on NBC television.

Hurricane Hazel kills 249 people along the Atlantic Coast (October 15).

West Germany secures (October 22) official membership in the North Atlantic Treaty Organization, or NATO.

Ahmed ben Bella launches (November 1) the nationalist rebellion against French hegemony in Algeria.

1955

President Dwight D. Eisenhower holds (January 19) the first televised news conference.

Cat on a Hot Tin Roof by Tennessee Williams opens (March 24) at New York's Morosco Theater.

The United States helps establish (April 1), without formally joining, the Baghdad Pact, a mutual security pact between Turkey, Iran, Pakistan, Iraq, and Great Britain.

The success of the Salk polio vaccine is announced (April 12).

The United States, Great Britain, and France formally end (May 5) their military occupation of West Germany.

In response to the North Atlantic Treaty Organization, the Soviet Union joins (May 14) with Albania, Bulgaria, Czechoslovakia, East Germany, Hungary, Poland, and Romania to establish the Warsaw Pact.

Barbara Graham is executed (June 3).

Disneyland opens (July 17).

Chuck Berry's record "Maybellene" is released (August 20) and rockets to the top of the popular music charts.

President Dwight D. Eisenhower suffers (September 24) a heart attack.

Actor James Dean dies (September 30) in a car crash.

Beat poet Allen Ginsberg gives (October 13) his first public reading of his poem "Howl."

Ngo Dinh Diem becomes (October 26) premier of the Republic of Vietnam.

By refusing to step to the back of the bus, Rosa Parks launches (December 1) the Montgomery, Alabama, bus boycott.

The American Federation of Labor (AFL) and the Congress of Industrial Organizations merge (December 5) into the AFL-CIO.

1956

The FBI makes six arrests (January 12) in the Brinks robbery case.

Nikita Khrushchev denounces (February 25) deceased Premier Joseph Stalin as a murderous dictator.

Congress passes (June 29) the Federal Aid Highway Act appropriating $33.5 billion to build the federal interstate highway system.

The United States withdraws (July 19) its offer to assist Egypt in building the Aswan Dam.

President Gamal Abdel Nasser of Egypt announces (July 26) that he will nationalize the Suez Canal. With the tolls collected, he would build the Aswan Dam.

The *Andrea Doria* sinks (July 26).

Gamal Abdel Nasser proclaims (August 30) Egyptian sovereignty over the Suez Canal.

The U.S. Supreme Court rules (September 13) that Montgomery, Alabama's ordinance segregating city buses is unconstitutional.

AT&T's transatlantic telephone cable goes into operation (September 25).

New York Yankee pitcher Don Larson pitches (October 8) the first perfect game in a World Series.

The world's first commercial nuclear power plant begins operation (October 17) in Great Britain.

The Hungarian rebellion against the Soviet Union begins (October 23).

Israel's forces invade (October 29) the Gaza Strip and the Sinai Peninsula, driving to within ten miles of the Suez Canal.

Soviet tanks and infantry invade (November 4) Hungary and crush the anticommunist rebellion there.

French and British aircraft attack (November 5) Egypt, and French and British troops parachute into the region just north of the Suez Canal.

The United States and the Soviet Union jointly force (November 5) a cease-fire in the Middle East.

President Dwight D. Eisenhower is reelected (November 6).

Floyd Patterson wins (November 30) the heavyweight boxing championship.

1957

President Dwight D. Eisenhower announces (January 5) the so-called Eisenhower Doctrine, in which the United States pledged to assist any Middle East country threatened by armed aggression.

Congress passes (April 29) the Civil Rights Act of 1957.

"Red Monday" occurs (June 17) when the U.S. Supreme Court rules that criminal prosecutions of individuals advocating the violent overthrow of the government are unconstitutional.

The U.S. Supreme Court rules (June 24) that pornographic materials are not protected by the First Amendment.

Althea Gibson wins (July 6) the Wimbledon women's singles tennis championship.

The U.S. Supreme Court decides (August 30) the *Jencks v. United States* case.

President Dwight D. Eisenhower deploys (September 24) 1,000 U.S. troops to enforce school desegregation in Little Rock, Arkansas.

West Side Story premiers (September 26) at New York City's Winter Garden Theater.

The Soviet Union launches (October 4) *Sputnik*, an artificial satellite, into earth orbit.

The Soviet Union launches (November 4) *Sputnik II* into earth orbit.

America's first privately run nuclear power plant opens (December 2) in Shippingport, Pennsylvania.

1958

The United States launches (January 31) *Explorer I*, an artificial satellite, into earth orbit.

Egypt and Syria merge (February 1) into the United Arab Republic.

Nikita Khrushchev becomes (March 27) premier, as well as Communist party first secretary, of the Soviet Union.

Pianist Van Cliburn wins (April 13) the Tchaikovsky International Competition in Moscow.

President Dwight D. Eisenhower signs into law (April 16) the Federal Aid Highway Act.

Vice President Richard M. Nixon begins (April 27) his goodwill tour of South America, but he encounters (May 7–8, 13) violent protests in Peru and Venezuela.

Charles de Gaulle becomes premier of France (June 24).

Left-wing rebels overthrow (July 14) the pro-Western government of Lebanon.

Citing the Eisenhower Doctrine, President Dwight D. Eisenhower lands (July 15) U.S. Marines in Lebanon to protect the country's territorial integrity.

Congress establishes (July 29) the National Aeronautics and Space Administration.

The Taiwan Straits crisis is renewed (August 23) when the People's Republic of China begins bombardment of the islands of Quemoy and Matsu.

Congress passes (September 2) the National Defense Education Act.

Leonard Bernstein assumes (October 2) the directorship of the New York Philharmonic Orchestra.

1959

Fidel Castro assumes (January 1) power in Cuba.

Rock stars Buddy Holly, Richie Valens, and the Big Bopper die (February 3) in a plane crash.

Raisin in the Sun by Lorraine Hansberry opens (March 11) at the Ethyl Barrymore Theater in New York.

The Baghdad Pact changes (May 30) its name to the Central Treaty Organization.

Charles Starkweather is executed (June 25) for his murder spree in Nebraska.

Ingemar Johansson wins (June 26) the heavyweight boxing championship from Floyd Patterson.

The Saint Lawrence Seaway opens (June 26).

Congress passes (September 14) the Landrum-Griffin Act.

Soviet Premier Nikita Khrushchev begins (September 15) his tour of the United States.

The United States imposes (October 20) an economic embargo on Cuba.

Charles de Gaulle announces (November 3) France's intention to withdraw from NATO.

The press learns (November 3) that contestants on CBS's *The $64,000 Question* received questions and answers before broadcasts.

The Sound of Music by Richard Rodgers and Oscar Hammerstein II opens (November 16) at the Lunt-Fontanne Theater in New York.

After sustaining losses of more than $350 million, Ford Motor Company ends (November 19) production of the Edsel.

Selected Bibliography

CIVIL RIGHTS

Bartley, Norman V. *The New South, 1945–1980*. 1995.

———. *The Rise of Massive Resistance. Race and Politics in the South During the 1950s*. 1969.

Belknap, Michael R. *Federal Law and Southern Order*. 1987.

Berman, Harry C. *The Politics of Civil Rights in the Truman Administration*. 1970.

Bloom, Jack. *Class, Race, and the Civil Rights Movement*. 1987.

Branch, Taylor. *Parting the Waters: America in the King Years, 1954–1963*. 1988.

Burk, Robert J. *The Eisenhower Administration and Civil Rights*. 1985.

Burt, Larry. *Tribalism in Crisis: Federal Indian Policy, 1953–1961*. 1982.

Carter, Paul. *Another Part of the Fifties*. 1983.

Chafe, William. *Civilities and Civil Rights: Greensboro, North Carolina and the Black Struggle for Equality*. 1980.

Chappell, David. *Inside Agitators: White Southerners in the Civil Rights Movement*. 1994.

Dalfiume, Richard. *Desegregation of the U.S. Armed Forces*. 1969.

Donovan, Robert J., and Ray Scherer. *Silent Revolution*. 1992.

Duberman, Martin Bauml. *Paul Robeson*. 1988.

Duram, James. *Moderate Among Extremists: Dwight D. Eisenhower and the School Desegregation Crisis*. 1981.

Fairclough, Adam. *To Redeem the Soul of America*. 1987.

Farmer, James. *Lay Bare the Heart*. 1985.

Fixico, Donald. *Termination and Relocation: Federal Indian Policy, 1945–1960*. 1986.

Forman, James. *The Making of Black Revolutionaries*. 1985.

Frederickson, George. *Black Liberation*. 1995.

Garrow, David. *Bearing the Cross*. 1986.

———. *The FBI and Martin Luther King, Jr*. 1983.

Goldfield, David. *Black, White, and Southern: Race Relations and Southern Culture*. 1990.

Harding, Vincent. *There Is a River: The Black Struggle for Freedom in America*. 1981.

Huckaby, Elizabeth. *Crisis at Central High: Little Rock, 1957–1958*. 1980.

Kluger, Richard. *Simple Justice: The History of Brown v. Board of Education and Black America's Struggle for Equality.* 1977.

Lawson, Steven. *Black Ballots.* 1977.

Marquez, Benjamin. *LULAC.* 1993.

McCoy, Donald, and Richard Ruetten. *Quest and Response: Minority Rights and the Truman Admnistration.* 1973.

Miller, Douglas, and Marion Novak. *The Fifties: The Way We Really Were.* 1977.

Moody, Ann. *Coming of Age in Mississippi.* 1970.

Morris, Allen D. *The Origins of the Civil Rights Movement: Black Communities Organizing for Change.* 1984.

Muse, Benjamin. *Ten Years of Prelude.* 1968.

Oates, Stephen L. *Let the Trumpet Sound: The Life and Times of Martin Luther King, Jr.* 1982.

Potter, David. *People of Plenty.* 1954.

Raines, Howell. *My Soul Is Rested: Movement Days in the Deep South Remembered.* 1977.

Robinson, Jo Ann Gibson. *The Montgomery Bus Boycott and the Woman Who Started It.* 1987.

Schwartz, Bernard. *Inside the Warren Court.* 1983.

———. *The NAACP's Legal Strategy Against Segregated Education.* 1987.

Sellers, Cleveland, and Robert Terrell. *The River of No Return.* 1973.

Sitkoff, Harvard. *The Struggle for Black Equality, 1954–1992.* 1992.

Tushnet, Mark. *Making Civil Rights Law: Thurgood Marshall and the Supreme Court, 1936–1961.* 1994.

Tygiel, Jules. *Baseball's Great Experiment: Jackie Robinson and His Legacy.* 1983.

Weisbrot, Robert. *Freedom Bound: A History of America's Civil Rights Movement.* 1990.

Whitfield, Stephen J. *A Death in the Delta: The Story of Emmett Till.* 1989.

Williams, Juan. *Eyes on the Prize: America's Civil Rights Years, 1954–1965.* 1987.

Winkler, Allen M. *Life Under a Cloud.* 1993.

Woodward, C. Vann. *The Strange Career of Jim Crow.* 1974.

THE ECONOMY

Boyle, Kevin. *The UAW and the Heyday of American Liberalism, 1945–1968.* 1995.

Calleo, David. *The Imperious Economy.* 1982.

Clowse, Barbara B. *Brainpower for the Cold War: The Sputnik Crisis and the National Defense Education Act of 1958.* 1981.

Flash, Edward S. *Economic Advice and Presidential Leadership.* 1965.

Galbraith, John Kenneth. *The Affluent Society.* 1958.

———. *American Capitalism.* 1952.

McQuaid, Kim. *Uneasy Partners: Big Business in American Politics, 1945–1990.* 1994.

Morgan, Ivan W. *Eisenhower vs. "The Spenders."* 1990.

Saulnier, Raymond J. *Constructive Years.* 1992.

Sloan, John. *Eisenhower and the Management of Prosperity.* 1991.

Vatter, Harold. *The U.S. Economy in the 1950s.* 1990.

FOREIGN POLICY

Ambrose, Stephen. *Ike's Spies: Eisenhower and the Espionage Estabishment.* 1981.

Anderson, David L. *Trapped by Success: The Eisenhower Administration and Vietnam, 1953–1961.* 1991.

Blum, Robert. *Drawing the Line: The Origin of the American Containment Policy in East Asia.* 1982.

Boyer, Paul. *By the Bomb's Early Light: American Thought and Culture at the Dawn of the Atomic Age.* 1985.

Brands, H. W., Jr. *The Devil We Knew: Americans and the Cold War.* 1993.

Brinkley, Douglas, ed. *Dean Acheson and the Making of American Foreign Policy.* 1983.

Callahan, David. *Dangerous Capabilities: Paul Nitze and the Cold War.* 1990.

Cohen, Warren I. *America in the Age of Soviet Power, 1945–1991.* 1993.

Cook, Blanche. *The Declassified Eisenhower.* 1981.

Divine, Robert A. *Blowin' in the Wind: The Nuclear Test Ban Debate, 1954–1960.* 1978.

———. *Eisenhower and the Cold War.* 1981.

———. *The Sputnik Challenge.* 1993.

Freeland, Richard. *The Truman Doctrine and the Origins of McCarthyism.* 1970.

Gaddis, John L. *The Long Peace: Inquiries into the History of the Cold War.* 1987.

———. *Strategies of Containment.* 1982.

Gardner, Lloyd. *Architects of Illusion.* 1970.

Head, William. *America's China Sojourn.* 1983.

Hess, Gary. *The United States' Emergence As a Southeast Asian Power, 1940–1950.* 1987.

Hogan, Michael. *The Marshall Plan: America, Britain, and the Reconstruction of Europe, 1947–1952.* 1987.

Hoopes, Townsend. *The Devil and John Foster Dulles.* 1973.

Immerman, Richard. *The CIA in Guatemala.* 1982.

Iriye, Akira. *The Cold War in Asia.* 1974.

Isaacson, Walter, and Evan Thomas. *The Wise Men: Six Friends and the World They Made,* 1986.

Kalb, Madeline. *The Congo Cables: The Cold War in Africa from Eisenhower to Kennedy.* 1982.

Kaplan, Fred. *The Wizards of Armageddon.* 1983.

Kaplan, Laurence. *The United States and NATO.* 1984.

Kolko, Joyce, and Gabriel Kolko. *The Limits of Power: The World and United States Foreign Policy, 1945–1954.* 1972.

Koppes, Clayton. *JPL and the American Space Program.* 1982.

Kuniholm, Bruce. *The Origins of the Cold War in the Near East.* 1980.

LaFeber, Walter. *America, Russia, and the Cold War, 1945–1980.* 1993.

Leffler, Melvyn P. *A Preponderance of Power: National Security, the Truman Administration, and the Cold War.* 1992.

Lipton, Lawrence. *The Holy Barbarians.* 1959.

MacDougall, Walter A. *The Heavens and the Earth.* 1985.

Marks, Frederick, III. *Power and Peace: The Diplomacy of John Foster Dulles.* 1993.

McCoy, Donald R., and Richard T. Ruetten. *Quest and Response*. 1973.

Melanson, Richard, and David Mayers, eds. *Reevaluating Eisenhower: American Foreign Policy in the 1950s*. 1987.

Miscamble, Wilson D. *George F. Kennan and the Making of American Foreign Policy, 1947–1950*. 1992.

Oakes, Guy. *The Imaginary War*. 1994.

Oakley, J. Ronald. *God's Country*. 1986.

O'Neill, William. *American High*. 1986.

Paterson, Thomas. *Contesting Castro: The United States and the Triumph of the Cuban Revolution*. 1994.

Rhodes, Richard. *Dark Sun: The Making of the Hydrogen Bomb*. 1995.

Schaller, Michael. *American Occupation of Japan: The Origins of the Cold War in Asia*. 1985.

———. *The United States and China in the Twentieth Century*. 1979.

Stueck, William, Jr. *The Road to Confrontation*. 1981.

Swenson, Lloyd, et al. *This New Ocean*. 1966.

Tucker, Nancy. *Patterns in the Dust: Chinese-American Relations and the Recognition Controversy, 1949–1950*. 1983.

Walker, Martin. *The Cold War: A History*. 1994.

Welch, Richard E. *Response to Revolution: The United States and Cuba, 1959–1961*. 1985.

Whitfield, Stephen H. *The Culture of the Cold War*. 1990.

Winkler, Allen M. *Life Under a Cloud*. 1993.

Woods, Randall B., and Howard Jones. *Dawning of the Cold War*. 1991.

Yergin, Daniel. *Shattered Peace: The Origins of the Cold War and the National Security State*. 1977.

GENERAL

Bremer, Robert H., and Gary Reichard, eds. *Reshaping America*. 1982.

Carter, Paul. *Another Part of the Fifties*. 1983.

Coontz, Stephanie. *The Way We Never Were: American Families and the Nostalgia Trap*. 1992.

Diggins, John P. *The Proud Decades: America in War and Peace, 1941–1960*. 1988.

Donovan, Robert J., and Ray Scherer. *Silent Revolution*. 1992.

Gilbert, James. *A Cycle of Outrage*. 1986.

Goldman, Eric. *The Crucial Decade and After 1945–1960*. 1960.

Halberstam, David. *The Fifties*. 1993.

Hodgson, Godfrey. *America in Our Time*. 1976.

Jexer, Martin. *The Dark Ages: Life in the United States, 1945–1960*. 1982.

Leuchtenburg, William. *A Troubled Feast*. 1983.

Miller, Douglas T., and Marion Novak. *The Fifties: The Way We Really Were*. 1977.

Oakley, Ronald. *God's Country: America in the 1950s*. 1986.

Patterson, James T. *Grand Expectations: Postwar America, 1945–1974*. 1996.

Potter, David. *People of Plenty*. 1954.

Ravitch, Diane. *The Troubled Decade*. 1983.

Whitfield, Stephen J. *The Culture of the Cold War*. 1991.

KOREAN WAR

Cowdery, Albert. *The Medics' War*. 1987.
Cumings, Bruce. *The Origins of the Korean War*. 1981.
Foot, Rosemary. *The Wrong War*. 1985.
Halliday, Jan, and Bruce Cumings. *Korea*. 1988.
James, D. Clayton. *Refighting the Last War: Command and Crisis in Korea, 1950–1953*. 1992.
Kaufman, Burton. *The Korean War*. 1986.
Schaller, Michael. *Douglas MacArthur*. 1989.
Spanier, John W. *The Truman-MacArthur Controversy and the Korean War*. 1959.
Stueck, William, Jr. *The Korean War: An International History*. 1981.
Toland, John. *In Mortal Combat: Korea, 1950–1953*. 1992.

LITERATURE AND INTELLECTUAL LIFE

Baughman, James L. *The Republic of Mass Culture*. 1992.
Bell, Daniel. *The End of Ideology*. 1960.
Cook, Bruce. *The Beat Generation*. 1970.
Gilbaut, Serge. *How New York Stole the Idea of Modern Art*. 1983.
Horowitz, Daniel. *Vance Packard and American Social Criticism*. 1994.
Horowitz, Irving. *C. Wright Mills: American Utopian*. 1983.
Lipsitz, George. *Class and Culture in Cold War America*. 1981.
Miles, Barry. *Ginsberg: A Biography*. 1989.
Nash, George. *The Conservative Intellectual Movement in the United States*. 1976.
Nicosia, Gerald. *Memory Babe: A Critical Biography of Jack Kerouac*. 1983.
O'Neill, William. *A Better World: Stalinism and the American Intellectuals*. 1983.
Pells, Richard. *The Liberal Mind in a Conservative Age*. 1984.
Whitfield, Stephen J. *The Culture of the Cold War*. 1991.

POLITICS

Ambrose, Stephen E. *Eisenhower: The President*. 1984.
Ballard, Jack. *Shock of Peace*. 1983.
Brendon, Piers. *Ike: His Life and Times*. 1986.
Broadwater, Jeff. *Adlai Stevenson and American Politics*. 1994.
———. *Eisenhower and the Anti-Communist Crusade*. 1992.
Brownell, Herbert. *Advising Ike*. 1993.
Burk, Robert F. *Dwight D. Eisenhower*. 1986.
Clowse, Barbara. *Brainpower for the Cold War: The Sputnik Crisis and the National Defense Education Act of 1958*. 1981.
Dunar, Andrew J. *The Truman Scandals and the Politics of Morality*. 1984.
Farrell, Robert. *Harry S. Truman and the Modern American Presidency*. 1983.
Fite, Gilbert. *Richard B. Russell, Jr.: Senator from Georgia*. 1991.
Greenstein, Fred. *The Hidden Hand Presidency: Eisenhower as Leader*. 1982.
Lee, R. Alton. *Eisenhower and Landrum-Griffin*. 1989.
———. *Truman and Taft-Hartley*. 1966.

Martin, John Martlow. *Adlai Stevenson and the World.* 1977.

Matusow, Allen. *Farm Politics and Policies in the Truman Years.* 1967.

McCoy, Donald R. *The Presidency of Harry S. Truman.* 1984.

McCullough, David G. *Truman.* 1992.

Miller, Richard. *Truman: The Rise to Power.* 1986.

Morgan, Ivan W. *Eisenhower vs. "The Spenders."* 1990.

Pach, Chester J., Jr., and Elmo Richardson. *The Presidency of Dwight D. Eisenhower.* 1991.

Parmet, Herbert. *Eisenhower and the American Crusades.* 1973.

Reichard, Gary W. *Politics as Usual.* 1988.

———. *The Reaffirmation of Republicanism: Eisenhower and the 83rd Congress.* 1975.

Rose, Mark. *Interstate Express Highway Politics, 1939–1989.* 1991.

Sloan, John. *Eisenhower and the Management of Prosperity.* 1991.

Sundquist, James L. *Politics and Policy: The Eisenhower, Kennedy, and Johnson Years.* 1968.

Wallace, Patricia Ward. *Politics of Conscience.* 1996.

Wills, Garry. *Nixon Agonistes.* 1971.

Yarnell, Allen. *Democrats and Progressives: The 1948 Presidential Election As a Test of Postwar Liberalism.* 1974.

RED SCARE

Barson, Michael. *"Better Red Than Dead!" A Nostalgic Look at the Golden Years of Russophobia, Red-Baiting, and Other Commie Madness.* 1992.

Belknap, Michael R. *Cold War Political Justice: The Smith Act, the Communist Party, and American Civil Liberties.* 1977.

Caute, David. *The Great Fear.* 1978.

Ceplair, Larry, and Steven Englund. *The Inquisition in Hollywood: Politics in the Film Community, 1930–1960.* 1980.

Diamond, Sigmund. *Comprised Campus: The Collaboration of Universities with the Intelligence Communities, 1945–1995.* 1992.

Dick, Bernard. *Radical Innocence: A Critical Study of the Hollywood Ten.* 1988.

Freeland, Richard M. *The Truman Doctrine and the Origins of McCarthyism.* 1985.

Fried, Richard. *Nightmare in Red.* 1990.

Gentry, Curt J. *Edgar Hoover: The Man and His Secrets.* 1991.

Griffith, Richard. *The Politics of Fear: Joseph McCarthy and the Senate.* 1987.

Kutler, Stanley I. *The American Inquisition: Justice and Injustice in the Cold War.* 1982.

Lamphere, Robert, and Tom Schachtman. *The FBI-KGB War.* 1986.

Leffler, Melvyn P. *A Preponderance of Power: National Security, the Truman Administration, and the Cold War.* 1992.

MacDonald, J. Fred. *Television and the Red Menace.* 1985.

Navasky, Victor. *Naming Names.* 1980.

Newman, Robert P. *Owen Lattimore and the "Loss" of China.* 1992.

Nielson, Mike, and Gene Mailes. *Hollywood's Other Blacklist: Union Struggles in the Studio System.* 1996.

O'Neill, William. *A Better World: Stalinism and the American Intellectuals.* 1983.

O'Reilly, Kenneth. *Hoover and the Un-Americans: The FBI, HUAC, and the Red Menace.* 1983.

Oshinsky, David M. *A Conspiracy So Immense: The World of Joe McCarthy.* 1983.
Powers, Richard G. *G-Men: Hoover's FBI in American Popular Culture.* 1983.
Radosh, Ronald, and Joyce Radosh. *The Rosenberg File.* 1983.
Ross, Andrews. *No Respect: Intellectuals and Popular Culture.* 1989.
Schneir, Walter, and Miriam Schneir. *Invitation to an Inquest: A New Look at the Rosenberg-Sobell Case.* 1983.
Schrecker, Ellen W. *No Ivory Tower: McCarthyism in the Universities.* 1988.
Theoharis, Athan. *Seeds of Repression: Harry S. Truman and the Origins of McCarthyism.* 1971.
Theoharis, Athan G., and John Stuart Cox. *The Boss: J. Edgar Hoover and the Great American Inquisition.* 1988.
Weinstein, Allen. *Perjury: The Hiss-Chambers Case.* 1978.
Williams, Robert. *Klaus Fuchs: Atom Spy.* 1987.

ROCK AND ROLL

Belz, Carl. *The Story of Rock.* 1972.
Berry, Chuck. *The Autobiography.* 1987.
Escott, Colin. *Good Rockin' Tonight: Sun Records and the Birth of Rock and Roll.* 1991.
Gillett, Charlie. *The Sound of the City: The Rise of Rock and Roll.* 1983.
Guralnick, Peter. *Last Train to Memphis: The Rise of Elvis Presley.* 1994.
Jackson, John A. *Big Beat Heat: Alan Freed and the Early Years of Rock 'n' Roll.* 1991.
Nelson, George. *The Death of Rhythm and Blues.* 1988.
Szatmary, David P. *Rockin' in Time: A Social History of Rock and Roll.* 1991.
Ward, Ed. *Rock of Ages: The Rolling Stone History of Rock and Roll.* 1987.

SOCIAL LIFE

Donaldson, Scott. *The Suburban Myth.* 1969.
Donovan, Robert J., and Ray Scherer. *Silent Revolution.* 1992.
Eisler, Benita. *Private Lives: Men and Women of the Fifties.* 1986.
Gans, Herbert J. *The Levittowners.* 1967.
Hayden, Delores. *Redesigning the American Dream.* 1984.
Herberg, Will. *Protestant, Catholic, Jew.* 1955.
Hudnut-Beumler, James. *Looking for God in the Suburbs.* 1994.
Inglis, Fred. *The Cruel Peace: Everyday Life in the Cold War.* 1991.
Jackson, Kenneth T. *Crabgrass Frontier: The Suburbanization of America.* 1985.
Kaledin, Eugenia. *Mothers and More.* 1984.
May, Elaine Tyler. *Homeward Bound: American Families in the Cold War Era.* 1988.
Meyerowitz, Joanne, ed. *Not June Cleaver: Women and Gender in Postwar America, 1945–1960.* 1994.
Miller, Douglas T., and Marion Novak. *The Fifties: The Way We Really Were.* 1977.
Oakley, J. Ronald. *God's Country.* 1986.
Olson, Kenneth W. *The GI Bill, the Veterans, and the Colleges.* 1974.
O'Neill, William. *American High.* 1986.
Potter, David. *People of Plenty.* 1954.

Rupp, Leila, and Verta Taylor. *Survival in the Doldrums: The American Women's Rights Movement, 1945 to the 1960s.* 1987.

Silk, Mark. *Spiritual Politics.* 1988.

Skolnick, Arlene. *Embattled Paradise: The American Family in an Age of Uncertainty.* 1991.

Whitfield, Stephen H. *The Culture of the Cold War.* 1990.

Winkler, Allen M. *Life Under a Cloud.* 1993.

TELEVISION AND FILM

Anderson, Kent. *Television Fraud.* 1978.

Barnouw, Erik. *The Image Empire.* 1970.

——. *Tube of Plenty: The Evolution of American Television.* 1990.

Baughman, James L. *The Republic of Mass Culture: Journalism, Filmmaking, and Broadcasting in America Since 1941.* 1992.

Biskind, Peter. *Seeing Is Believing: How Hollywood Taught Us to Stop Worrying and Love the Fifties.* 1983.

Boddy, William. *Fifties Television: The Industry and Its Critics.* 1990.

Lipsitz, George. *Time Passages.* 1990.

MacDonald, J. Fred. *Television and the Red Menace.* 1985.

Marc, David. *Demographic Vistas: Television in American Culture.* 1984.

Marling, Karal Ann. *As Seen on TV.* 1994.

Rosenberg, Bernard, and D. M. White, eds. *Mass Culture.* 1957.

Sayre, Nora. *Running Time: Films of the Cold War.* 1982.

Spiegel, Lynn. *Make Room for TV: Television and the Family Ideal in Postwar America.* 1992.

Taylor, Ella. *Prime Time Families.* 1989.

WOMEN

Breines, Wini. *Young, White, and Miserable: Growing Up Female in the 1950s.* 1992.

Byerly, Victoria. *Hard Times Cotton Mill Girls.* 1986.

Coontz, Stephanie. *The Way We Never Were: American Families and the Nostalgia Trap.* 1992.

D'Emilio, John, and Estelle Freedman. *Intimate Matters: A History of Sexuality in America.* 1988.

Eisler, Benita. *Private Lives: Men and Women of the Fifties.* 1986.

Escott, Colin. *Good Rockin' Tonight: Sun Records and the Birth of Rock 'n' Roll.* 1992.

Jones, Landon V. *Great Expectations: America and the Baby Boom Generation,* 1980.

Kaledin, Eugenia. *Mothers and More.* 1984.

May, Elaine Tyler. *Homeward Bound: American Families in the Cold War Era.* 1988.

Meyerowitz, Joanne, ed. *Not June Cleaver: Women and Gender in Postwar America, 1945–1960.* 1994.

Rupp, Leila, and Verta Taylor. *Survival in the Doldrums: The American Women's Rights Movement, 1945 to the 1960s.* 1987.

Skolnick, Arlene. *Embattled Paradise: The American Family in an Age of Uncertainty.* 1991.

Spiegel, Lynn. *Make Room for TV: Television and the Family Ideal in Postwar America.* 1992.

Taylor, Ella. *Prime Time Families.* 1989.

Tuchman, Gaye et al., eds. *Hearth and Home: Images of Women in the Mass Media.* 1978.

Warren, Carl. *Madwives: Schizophrenic Women in the 1950s.* 1987.

YOUTH CULTURE

Breines, Wini. *Young, White, and Miserable: Growing Up Female in the Fifties.* 1992.

Doherty, Thomas. *Teen Pics.* 1994.

Gilbert, James. *A Cycle of Outrage: America's Reaction to Juvenile Delinquency in the 1950s.* 1986.

Graebner, William. *Coming of Age in Buffalo.* 1990.

Index

Boldface page numbers indicate location of main entries.

About the Author and Contributor

JAMES S. OLSON is Distinguished Professor of History at Sam Houston State University, where he had taught since 1972. He is the author of more than 20 books on U.S. and world history, including *Historical Dictionary of the 1970s* (Greenwood, 1999) and *Historical Dictionary of the 1960s* (Greenwood, 1999).

TRACY STEELE earned her undergraduate degree from Georgetown University and her Ph.D. from the London School of Economics. She is an Associate Professor of History at Sam Houston State University.